RIDING THE NEW WAVE

RICHARD IVAN JOBS

Riding the New Wave

*Youth and the Rejuvenation of France
after the Second World War*

STANFORD UNIVERSITY PRESS

STANFORD, CALIFORNIA 2007

Stanford University Press
Stanford, California

Printed in the United States of America on acid-free, archival-quality paper

Library of Congress Cataloging-in-Publication Data

Jobs, Richard Ivan.
 Riding the new wave : youth and the rejuvenation of France after the Second World War / Richard Ivan Jobs.
    p. cm.
 Includes bibliographical references and index.
    ISBN: 978-0-8047-5452-1 (cloth)
    ISBN: 978-0-8047-5453-8 (pbk)
1. Youth--France--History--20th century. 2. Popular culture--France--History--20th century. 3. National characteristics, French. I. Title.

HQ799.F8J57 2007
305.2350944'09045--dc22
2006033703

Typeset by Bruce Lundquist in 10/14 Janson

For Kim

Table of Contents

List of Figures

Acknowledgments

At last. One would think that acknowledging others with thanks at the conclusion of such a long project would be a great pleasure. While that is true, it is also terribly difficult. To adequately thank all those who have influenced my book and life (which have been inextricably entwined for nearly a decade) is a formidable task and one I have delayed. First, I must thank Rutgers University, the French government, and Pacific University for the funds that have enabled me to complete my archival research with repeated trips to France. While there, I benefited from the support and diligence of archival staff who made documents and collections, many of which required special permission, available to me. I thank the staff of the Archives Nationales, the Bibliothèque Nationale, the Bibliothèque de l'Histoire de la Ville de Paris, the Bibliothèque du Film, the Centre des Archives Contemporaine, the Archives de l'Armée de Terre, Mahmoud Ghander at the Archives d'UNESCO, and Christine Sibille at the Centre Nationale de la Bande Dessinée et de l'Image. I also want to thank the participants of various conferences and panels who have commented on my work as it has progressed, especially the Rutgers Center for Historical Analysis, where I participated as a fellow.

I want to commend the Department of History at Rutgers University, which I found to be a remarkably collegial place where faculty and graduate students alike were intellectually invigorated. Among the many faculty who directly influenced me there I want to thank Belinda Davis, Don Kelley, Matt Matsuda, Nicole Pellegrin, and Steve Reinert. Moreover, the community of graduate students was immensely helpful in their willingness to read papers, pass on citations, discuss ideas, and, perhaps most importantly, share a beer or two. Rebecca Boone, Jennie Brier, Rene Burmeister, Noah Elkin, Matt Guterl, Richard Keller, Max Likin, Hilary Mason, Tamara Matheson, Jennifer Milligan, and Todd Shepard greatly improved my life as a graduate student. Most importantly, Roxanne Panchasi and Patrick McDevitt have given me the most as scholars and friends. They have read the most chapters and consumed the most beer, both stateside and abroad. Roxanne is the better cook, Pat more ready to debate and willing to put our lives on hold to watch and discuss the NCAA basketball tournament.

My committee at Rutgers was a remarkable group of scholars who offered their ideas, feedback, and criticisms generously. The impact of their work on my own is evident throughout. I thank Jim Gilbert for agreeing to come aboard and offer an outsider's perspective on my work, which has helped me to place it within a context outside postwar France. Joan Scott has challenged me with her unrelenting intellect always to think more complexly and never to settle for an easy explanation. She has expanded the way I see the world and my own scholarship. I thank John Gillis for the example he sets through his astute questions and comments, his eagerness to engage equally the ideas of famous scholars and those of graduate students, his prompt, detailed, and helpful feedback on my work, his passion and excitement for the life of the mind, and his raucous laughter, which echoed through the basement of Van Dyck. Finally, I must thank Bonnie Smith, whose stare, odd sense of humor, and work ethic can terrorize young graduate students—to her delight, I believe. She has urged me to push further, dig deeper, face up to obstacles rather than go around them, all the while insisting that I find the answers, that I solve the problem, that I approach scholarship as hard work, and that I conduct myself as a professional. She has fed me, entertained me, and stored my belongings in her leaky basement. She continues to advise and counsel me as a professional and as a friend, and I thank her with great affection.

I was fortunate to land at Pacific University in Oregon, where my colleagues have created a wonderfully rewarding and supportive place to work as I have completed this book. I thank Larry Lipin, Martha Rampton, Jeffrey Barlow, John Hayes, Betty Horn, Alex Toth, Virginia Adams, and Wanda Laukkanen for their particular efforts in enabling me to finish this book. Elsewhere in the profession, I thank Herrick Chapman, Sarah Fishman, William Irvine, Jim Miller, David Pomfret, and Whitney Walton for lending me their expertise, as well as the editors of *Young* and *French Historical Studies* for publishing earlier versions of the third and sixth chapters. I owe Norris Pope at Stanford University Press my thanks for being so engaged, enthusiastic, and responsive throughout the publication process, as well as Anna Eberhard Friedlander and Ruth Steinberg for shepherding this book through editing and production.

I cannot exaggerate the value of the friendships I have collected across time and place. The phone calls, emails, and visits of my friends, though spread far and wide, keep me grounded in a world outside academia. They enrich my life in ways they cannot imagine, and, in ways unknown to them, they even help inspire my work. In particular, I thank Tom Dlugos, Eric Easley, Mark Etherton, Mark Henderson, Paul Hieb, Natalie Hodge, Yahn Jeannot, Ari Kellner, Bill Maddox, Julie Perko, Tony Russell, Sue Spann, Terry Strieter, Mitch Thomas, and Larissa Wardeiner. There are some friends that are really more like family. Like aunts and uncles they have opened their hearts and homes, given me love and guidance, and yes, kept me well fed. Thank you very much to Joe and Suzanne Keeslar, John and Joyce McDevitt, and Debbie McConnachie.

And then there is family. Though I'm not as talkative, animated, or spirited as they (nor as neat and tidy), Dennis, Judi, and Sara Brodkin (now Zietz) have welcomed me into their lives and conversations. Always interested, always engaged, the Brodkin clan is curious and interested to learn what is going on and to be active participants in each other's lives. They have a great enthusiasm for life and embrace it with a dynamic sensibility, eager to be active and to offer advice, love, and support for one another. I am very lucky to be a part of their lives, and I have learned to intermingle colorful Yiddish expressions with my own southern colloquialisms—*oy vey*, y'all.

As for my own family, I must commend them for their patience. They had no idea what they were in for when I decided to go to graduate school and become a historian. Just why does it take so long to research and write a book? My mom and dad have indulged and encouraged my interests in a way that only loving parents can. Sid and Loretta were always willing to give me space, always available if I needed them, always eager for me to come home, always full of love, and always ready to take pride in my accomplishments, no matter how meager or grand. I thank them for everything, and especially for who I am. My brother Andy and his wife Barbara have demonstrated a generosity above and beyond familial bonds. Andy invited Kim and me to live with him while we finished our dissertations (little did he know that this would take three years). Once Barbara was on board and living with us as well, we had the makings of a hit television sitcom: two poor graduate students live in the same apartment with two corporate executives—think of the hilarity that would ensue! This kind of love and support can never be repaid. They enriched the dissertation process, and first draft of this book, through their companionship and love, which is what home is all about.

If nothing else good had come out of graduate school, there would still be Kim. She is my companion, colleague, friend, and partner. She reads every word I write, helping me to clarify my ideas and strengthen my prose. My relationship to this project and to her both began at the same moment; at the time I thought nothing of it, but after a decade, it seems more serendipity than mere coincidence. The two have been the constants of my life for a decade, and I cannot imagine the past ten years without one or the other. So, while my name may appear on the cover, hers is on the dedication page. I love her sharp mind, always ready with an opinion, her bright smile that breaks into giggly laughter, and her engaged attitude and interest toward the world around her. In short, she improves me, she improves my life, and I love her.

RIDING THE NEW WAVE

From Liberation to Rejuvenation

In October 1957, *L'Express*, a weekly newsmagazine founded in 1953, set out to address the issue of what characterized the rising generation that would soon come to dominate France and its institutions. As individuals, perhaps, they represented no great thing. However, together, "they are going to build or destroy the future, give rise to or refuse dignified or disgraceful leaders, they will transform or perpetuate society. Nothing will be done without them, nothing will be done against them, because, together, they make up youth."[1] *L'Express* and Françoise Giroud, the project's director, named this postwar generation the *nouvelle vague*, or "new wave," a term that evoked a sense of momentum, of volume, of a mounting undercurrent carrying forward an inevitable and unstoppable progression that appropriates and transforms all in its path. According to *L'Express*, this group of young people carried with it France's aspirations and opportunities for change, renewal, and rejuvenation, and therefore merited extensive study.

The *nouvelle vague* became an inescapable topic in the public discourse of

1

the late 1950s. A proliferation of commentaries and articles flooded news-papers and magazines, seeking to confirm, deny, or interpret the study's conclusions. The postulation of this generation as being markedly differ-ent permeated French society, and, accordingly, the concept of the *nouvelle vague* was adopted by the public. "New Wave" became a term of common usage and was indiscriminately applied to anything having to do with the idea of youth or involving young people. This fixation with the postwar generation had not begun with Giroud's study, however; rather, her study had picked up on an existing preoccupation with young people, carrying it further, while also providing the postwar generation with an appellation that contributed to the public enchantment with all things "new."

Both coincidentally and intentionally, the postwar fixation with newness became identified with the young, indirectly and directly. As educator Jean-Marie Despinette argued, it was necessary to integrate the young into French society for the very newness they offered, because "in an old society, in a pre-constituted society, the new elements, the bearers of new ideas, of new possibilities, of new enthusiasms, represent in each instance the germ of re-generation, of reform, even of revolution for this society."[2] The postwar cul-tural phenomena of the New Novel, New Look, New Cuisine, New Europe, New Wave, and New Generation were conceptualized as different, innova-tive, novel, and youthful. This enormous yearning for newness was also a yearning for change, a yearning to break with the past and to seek a new legitimacy in the future.[3] At times, "new" and "youth" became synonymous, interchangeable terms, as French society worked to reinvent itself in the wake of the Second World War. It would be wrong, however, to credit this moment with the invention of "the new"; other eras have utilized semantics similarly to denote a sense of creation or momentous transformation or opportunity. Yet the sheer proliferation of *new*-ness in postwar France was indicative of a particular frame of mind, one that broadly emphasized innovation and change over tradition and convention. In fact, even before and after the First World War there had been calls for a rejuvenation of France through its young, but it was only after the Second World War and during the Fourth Republic that this sort of rhetorical articulation reached its apogee and pervaded the social discourse underpinning the country's postwar cultural reconstruction.[4] As a semiotic device, this conceptual blurring of "the new" with youth offered a discursive climate conducive to cultural reconstruction and renewal, the implication of which posited the adult generation as outdated, outmoded, and in decline—a sign of the past as opposed to a sign of the future.

This book is about the idea of youth in postwar France, and about how the concept of youth operated as a mechanism of cultural reconstruction in the postwar period. It investigates the adult preoccupation with youth as a cultural concept and with young people as social actors, and considers what this preoccupation reveals about the way French society reimagined itself in the wake of occupation and collaboration. The postwar cultural category of youth was a point of convergence that provides insight, not only into the young but also into the adult, and, taken together, into the meaning of age in postwar French society. This book traces the political, social, and cultural emergence of the category of youth, and suggests how age categories can be analytic tools comparable to race, class, or gender for exploring social and cultural meanings. The concept of the "new wave," then, was a product of the profound project of rejuvenation that dominated France's cultural reconstruction as it dealt with the aftermath and terrible consequences of the Second World War.

Early on August 25, 1944, what would be Paris's day of Liberation, crowds began to assemble on the city's periphery, anxiously awaiting the arrival of the Allies.[5] A carnival atmosphere filled the streets as tanks rolled into the city from various points of entry. Clusters of young people gathered around the vehicles, forcing them to halt, as young women climbed aboard to kiss their liberators, French and American alike (Figure 1). Bottles of wine were thrust into the hands of the soldiers, who were toasted and cheered. By nightfall, the revelry had filled the streets. People hugged, danced, and kissed, sat down to celebratory feasts, toasted the victory, and feted their liberators. The merriment was widespread, continuing throughout the night and extending into many bedrooms. In fact, one Catholic group hastily distributed tracts bearing a caveat for the young women of Paris: "In the gaiety of the liberation do not throw away your innocence. Think of your future family!"[6] Despite such counsel, a sense of euphoria and unbridled optimism accompanied the Allied troops as they swept through France. By the end of September 1944, nearly all of France was free of the Germans. Although the war itself would not be over for many more months, in France the heady days of exultant jubilation continued, with gala balls, grand banquets, and late-night parties with dancing in the streets.

Figure 1. Liberation of Paris, 1944. Agence Keystone.

As exuberant as the revelry was, however, it could not simply erase recent history—the cold hard facts of defeat, collapse, occupation, and collaboration. In a matter of weeks in 1940 the Germans had captured Paris and forced the French government to flee. The terms of the 1940 armistice had left the entire Atlantic coast as well as the north of France in German hands. The new French government at Vichy maintained sovereignty over the remaining south and west of France, albeit only through the sanction of the Nazis. At the time, the Occupation was viewed as merely a brief and temporary wartime arrangement. The French fully expected the British to soon submit to Hitler's onslaught, just as most of Europe already had. Thus, the Occupation was a relief to many, since it promised to spare France the hardship of battle and the terrible destruction of war that it had experienced for the entirety of the First World War.[7]

But the reality of occupation and the complexity of collaboration were not nearly as transitory or innocuous as many imagined them to be. Marshal Philippe Pétain, with the full approval of the French parliament, dissolved the Third Republic and established his new French government in the empty hotels of the spa town of Vichy. France became complicit in its own subjugation through its new government, which was eager to please its Fascist master. The Germans, as a result, were in the enviable position of having a conquered nation govern and police itself in the Nazi interest. France even financed the cost of its own occupation, through an imposed system of reparation payments.[8]

There were those who disagreed with France's easy capitulation, who denied Vichy's authority and who continued the struggle against the Nazis—most famously, the junior general Charles de Gaulle, who had fled France for London and eventually formed a rival government in exile. Resistance efforts inside France soon formed, in small, isolated pockets around the country, though not, at first, in significant numbers or with coordinated activity. As with collaboration, the resistance varied in its degree of commitment and took many forms. As the war progressed, however, both collaborators and resistors became more strident and pursued their goals more vigorously. Toward the end, a civil war was being fought, under cover and in darkness, between the collaborators' brutal police gangs, the Milice, and the resistors' roving bands of armed young men, the Maquis. A terrible experience for France, the war years were characterized as much by betrayal and treachery as they were by heroism and sacrifice.[9]

Consequently, the Liberation had a darker, vengeful side to its jubilant celebrations, as many sought to impose a severe justice. Collaborating shopkeepers were beaten and their stores looted and vandalized. Civil servants were abused and humiliated. Women who had engaged in sexual liaisons, or *collaboration horizontale*, with the Germans were stripped naked, their shaved heads marked with tar swastikas, and paraded around to suffer jeers and beatings. In some areas, mostly in the south and west, a near reign of terror ensued, as the Resistance executed its absolute justice by shooting known collaborators on sight.[10]

Four years of occupation had ended. The defeat had been overcome. The collapse had been reversed. While some sought vengeful satisfaction, most sought merry gratification. It was not merely the expulsion of the Germans that was being celebrated, nor the foreseeable end to wartime hardships, but the open possibilities that the reconstruction period would offer. It was time to remake France, to renew and rebuild. The clear failure of Old France, and of the Old Guard, would provide the context for fundamental change, a chance to create a more equitable and just society, a New France. The elation and determination that accompanied the Liberation was not only a celebration marking the end of past troubles, but also an embrace of the future and the prospects it offered. As the masthead of the Resistance paper *Combat* declared, the end of the war was a chance to move "From Resistance to Revolution."

Reconstruction represented much more than merely the repair of buildings or the construction of roads, bridges, and railways. True, the physical destruction of the war had been devastating, more than twice as severe as that of the First World War—and true, factories would have to be rebuilt, flooded coal mines drained, roads resurfaced, railways mended, collapsed bridges raised, harbors opened, minefields cleared, munitions disposed, telephone lines connected, housing erected, medicine distributed, and people fed. It was an awesome task. But the material destruction of battle had lasted less than a year in France. Much more damaging to the French psyche were the four years of occupation and collaboration that had followed the political collapse of 1940.

In 1944 France was faced not only with rebuilding its infrastructure, reestablishing its economy, and redesigning its government, but with rejuvenating its society. During the war, people from a variety of social and political backgrounds had begun to make wish lists of what should characterize the new France. They established goals, outlined ideals, issued programmatic statements, contrived a social revolution. But the reality of cultural reconstruction could not be planned or organized in the same way that a rail network could be diagrammed or an economy could be state-managed. The mechanisms of cultural reconstruction were more diffuse and defied simple centralization within a government ministry. Societal change tends to happen slowly and emerges from scattered, unforeseen sources. The passage of time and the advantage of hindsight allow the historian to identify patterns and find connections that perhaps went unrecognized by a society as it generated them. Looking back to postwar France, it becomes clear that the concept of youth became an organizing principle for the new society.

At the end of the Second World War, following the collapse of 1940, the crushing Nazi Occupation, and the need for Allied intervention, France faced the daunting task of rehabilitating itself. As all of Europe rebuilt, young people as a group became the object of countless debates and innumerable government policies, as they represented the hope of a future unburdened by the devastation of the recent past. Youth, as a cultural category and a social group, became a pivotal point around which elements of the new society would be built. Young people were at the forefront of social and political discussions; they became the object of cultural reconstruction and the means through which the French state approached renewal. After the war, France reconsidered itself in terms of youthfulness; it socially reconstructed itself through the categories of age.

This is not, however, a history of the new wave or baby-boomer generations—yes, France too had a postwar baby boom and a very significant one at that. In the modern period, the term "generation" has become a part of the standard vocabulary when speaking of youth, and often the two concepts are conflated since a generation usually finds its definition or character while young.[11] Yet a generation is not always young, and the social category of youth itself carries meaning distinct from that of generation and merits exploration. Even as successive generations move through the social categories of age—such as childhood, youth, adulthood, and old age—the meanings of age categories are culturally defined within any particular moment's historical context. This book is a history of the cultural category and social body of youth in the context of postwar France rather than a history of a particular postwar generation.

The idea of generation is an abstraction categorizing social groups by age; it is a means of breaking down society temporally into age cohorts of common historical experience. Like social groups based upon class,[12] the boundaries between generations are soft and blurred rather than hard and fast, and allow for the possibility that a particular individual may be a member of different generations, depending on the given set of parameters. Usually, a generation is defined by its core, with its peripheries left inexact and its boundaries unclear. The ongoing flow of births does not readily provide clear demarcations of generation—between which two births does the line get drawn?—so the strict distinctions between generations tend to be arbitrary.[13] A generation may be defined by an act of self-appraisal distinguishing a common identity in opposition to other generations, or it may be defined by an imposed definition from outside the social grouping, or, more likely, by some kind of combination of these two circumstances.

Yet age cohorts do not necessarily gel into generations of common characteristics at all. They may lack a collective experience of sociohistorical significance, or may simply never achieve a sense of collective identity or self-definition. "Moreover, the variety of individual experiences among the members of a generation, as with other social groups, renders broad conclusions about that generation or its members reductive by glossing over diversity or eliding difference. Nonetheless, historians have made extensive use of generation as an explanatory paradigm because the concept of generation is a convenient one.[14] Some historians have seen the rhythm of successive generations as a key element in the historical process of change, as one generation supplants its predecessor in a teleological progression.[15] For example, the French baby-boomers have recently been described as the "palimpsest generation," erasing all that came before and redefining what generation is and can be as the quintessential generation.[16] But this assumes a cohesion of identity, like-mindedness, and purpose that is lacking among age cohorts from different classes, genders, races, and regions.[17] Therefore, generational histories tend to rely on the biography of articulate elites who are chosen for study as representative ideal-types.[18]

During the Fourth Republic, the French did at times refer to a postwar generation—a precisely identified social group with specific boundaries of age and characteristics, such as *la nouvelle vague* or *les baby-boomers*—but they much more frequently spoke of the young generally, as simply *la jeunesse*, as "youth," or literally, "the youth." As such, they were indeed using the term more broadly and more ordinarily to describe the young in a more general sense, invoking youth as a category of age and, significantly, in opposition to "adult" as a category of age. The word "generation" was usually used in its plural form—"adult generations" and "young generations"—implying that "adult" and "young" as age categories were large concepts capable of holding a multiplicity of generations. And when employing the term "young generation," it was used more as a contrast to "adult generation" than to identify a specific group of age cohorts whose membership exhibited a common identity. So the specificity of generational thinking, such as that of the new wave or the baby-boomers, needs to be considered a part or even a product of this more general fixation on youth and the young.

Indeed, as will be shown, "youth" as a term was used willy-nilly, flexibly applied to a broad range of ages, though sometimes to a narrow range. The parameters and definitions of who made up the postwar social group of "youth" varied according to the institutions or individuals making the determination. A 1951 study used the boundaries of seventeen and twenty-five, and estimated age twenty as the epitome of youth. The 1957 *nouvelle vague* investigation used the experience of the war to identify postwar youth as all those aged eighteen to thirty. Another study, in 1964, defined youth as those aged sixteen to twenty-four. The Youth and Culture Houses (MJC) used ages fourteen to twenty-five as a guideline, but in practice the age range of participants was even greater. The moral outcry that surrounded the "existentialists" of Saint-Germain-des-Prés, Françoise Sagan, and Brigitte Bardot was in part about their youth, yet many of them were well into their twenties. Likewise, the ages of those who identified themselves as "young," or as a part of "youth," reached all the way up to thirty and sometimes beyond.

Meanwhile, the state's definitions of the young after the war increasingly identified age eighteen as the threshold differentiating legal minority and majority. The 1945 establishment of the new juvenile justice system and the *rééducation* program set eighteen as the age limit for juvenile offenders. The 1949 law on juvenile publications set eighteen as the age minimum to purchase "adult" periodicals. Like the new 1961 film regulations, the 1953 and 1959 ordinances for the protection of the young from the immoral influence of bars, dance-halls, casinos, and cabarets, which initially excluded all those under sixteen, raised the minimum age to eighteen as well. Thus, the protection of the young from the pernicious amusements of adult entertainment and recreation, as well as the age for criminal prosecution, defined the legal boundary between youth and adult as the age of eighteen. Ironically, voting was still denied to anyone under age twenty-one. Notably, this would be one complaint of young protesters in 1968. Depending on the context, then, "youth" was alternately defined as children, adolescents, or everyone under thirty. Though the term, category, or idea of youth was applied flexibly, it was always understood as a definitive contrast to "adult."

The relativity and reflexivity of this relationship is important in understanding not only the meaning of youth in the context of the postwar era, but also what the meaning of youth says about the adult in postwar France, and what they both reveal about French society. Like gender, age categories are predicated upon a relationship to one another. The social category of youth is established only by a comparative juxtaposition to the adult or the infantile. As a stage of life, it is relative, defined by what sets it off from other life stages, and this relativity is significant because it is only vis-à-vis the adult that youth became so meaningful in 1945. Likewise, most of what French society thought of the young and about the young, how society considered and interpreted the young, was shaped by adults. Journalists, politicians, bureaucrats, social scientists, educators, writers, community leaders, priests, judges, editors, businessmen, administrators, scholars, filmmakers, and, of course, historians, were adult. Undoubtedly there were exceptions, but the people participating most in the organization, production, and distribution of information and ideas or in the management of society were, as a rule, adult. Like most marginal groups, the young were more imagined than understood, more represented than self-actualized. Consequently, adult France's interpretations reflected their concerns with the activity, attitude, morality, and character of the young and with the culturally produced category of youth and, to their mind, the future of France.

This discourse of youth was riddled with paradox, however. There was a tension between the ideas of "good youth" and "bad youth," between youth as hope and youth as threat, inspiring either praise or fear. On one hand, postwar adult France worshipped its young, and on the other, it condemned them. Various programs and initiatives in France sought to protect the young from the influence of adults, while others sought to protect adults from the influence of the young. The postwar obsession with youth was as much about potential disaster as it was about a messianic future. Thus, youth as an idea was employed inconsistently and characterized by instability. Indeed, as I show, invoking youth as a concept worked as a handy justification for all kinds of purposes. Since the turn of the century, the young had been increasingly conceptualized as a social group capable of provoking society's degeneration or regeneration, and even as far back as the French Revolution, the idea of youth had carried great symbolic weight. Perhaps most notoriously, the Fascists of the interwar period and the Vichy collaborators had made significant uses of youth as a social group and symbolic concept, and it is striking that the category of youth emerged from the Second World War largely untainted by this association. Because the concept was utilized by nearly everyone, it belonged to no one.

Still, the advantage to mobilizing around the idea of youth was its sheer convenience. Everyone, from all social groups, geographic regions, political ideologies, or religious backgrounds, had youth in common. Everyone was once young, and most adults had a vested interest in young people—their own children, grandchildren, or others in the community who would eventually grow to responsible adulthood. Youth served as the lowest common denominator that crossed other social categories and invited speculation about the future, particularly in the wake of the war and the long-awaited baby boom. Moreover, the category of youth was capable of incorporating other issues such as class, gender, ethnicity, nationality, criminality, sexuality, or morality. With the destructive antagonism of recent class and nationalist struggles still so fresh, the concept of youth was an agreeable matrix through which adult France could deliberate on its past, present, and future.

That is not to say that the young did not participate in this process. On the contrary, part of this story is about how the young increasingly participated in public life. In these postwar years, young people became a commercial, cultural, political, and social force, a postwar phenomenon that exploded in the sixties and has remained viable ever since. Particularly in the realm of popular culture, young people became a presence both as producers and consumers influencing the style and content of literature, music, and film. Politically, some protested against France's war in Algeria and participated in the premiership of Pierre Mendès-France. Socially, others experienced a newfound sense of independence and worried many by their love of jazz, all-night parties, and the bohemian lifestyle of the young "existentialists" in Saint-Germain-des-Prés. This book, then, is also a history of how the role of young people and their visibility in French society changed between the end of the Second World War and the 1960s.

This is also not a history of youth subcultures in France, such as the *zazous*, *blouson noirs*, or *yéyé*.[19] Studies of the young in Europe since 1945 have tended to focus on the sociological development of subcultures where the cultural practices of the young are interpreted as a defiant subset of society at large.[20] These studies richly detail and interpret the practices, behaviors, and belief systems of specific groups of young people. Where these studies tend to focus by necessity on the micro, this book seeks to consider youth in a more pervasive, macro approach. Though there are profound thematic parallels, postwar youth culture in France was distinct from that in other

Western societies. For example, rock 'n' roll and television did not really infiltrate France until after 1960. There was no 1950s French equivalent to the English teddy boy or rocker, nor to the American teenager or greaser. Likewise, there was no English or American equivalent to Brigitte Bardot or Jean Genet. Yet some similarities are striking, such as the English Angry Young Men, the American Beats, and the French "existentialists," though notably in France the most famous of these young, disaffected intellectuals tended to be women. In many ways, this work shows that the mid-twentieth century was a transitional period for a conceptual crystallization of youth, from the nineteenth-century emphasis on an individual's life-stage between childhood and adult to the late-twentieth-century distinction of youth as a culturally produced mass social group operating prominently within society.

Young people, then, lived within this sociocultural category of youth. I hope to show how youth, for the young, was a social experience of a cultural construction. One did not necessarily need to be young, nor did one who was young necessarily experience "youth." That is, the concept of youth was often deployed and enacted quite independently of actual young people; though, of course, they themselves articulated, inhabited, and utilized the idea and identity of youth for their own purposes. Thus, throughout this book I have tried to differentiate for the reader the distinction between "youth" and "young people." The first term refers to the concept or construct of youth as a cultural category, and the second to the actual social participants or actors who were young. I have chosen this shorthand as an imperfect solution to this semantic problem. In some ways, this is articulated in French as the difference between the terms *la jeunesse* and *les jeunes*. One way to think about it is that the first term is singularly (*la*) conceptual, articulating both a mass social group and a discursive concept, while the second implies a collective plurality (*les*) of individuals. Thus, youth and those who are young are not necessarily the same, despite significant overlap.

Youth—as an idea, as a concept, as an age category, and as a social group participating in society—has a history larger than the experiences of individuals or groups of young people, or even of a generation, although those experiences each play an important part in defining youth as a cultural concept and social group. To find the meanings of youth in society one must go beyond the investigation of cultural practices or idiosyncratic behavior that often fails to consider young people within the context of historical specificity. Although some of the conclusions of the social histories of Philippe Ariès and John Gillis have been successfully challenged, their assertion that the meaning of childhood and youth is historically determined remains certain.[21] The changing societal role played by the social group of youth from 1945 to 1960, then, is grounded within the historical situation of the postwar period, and is therefore not simply about the young, but about France as well.

Because the time frame for this work roughly corresponds to France's Fourth Republic (1945–58), it is also a history of how the Fourth Republic dealt with the war's legacy and prepared France to be a more modern nation. Recent scholarship has suggested that government policies directed toward the young were absent during the Fourth Republic or, at best, typified by a "benign neglect," and that young people generally were socially "invisible" in this period.[22] Yet, as this study shows, young people and the category of youth were essential to the conceptualization of France's postwar cultural reconstruction in formal, official ways as well as in a more ephemeral, cultural manner. Jean-Pierre Rioux, historian of the Fourth Republic, has pointed to this period as a moment when new "mythologies which promoted a social model of youthfulness now underpinned the efforts of the people to come to terms with modernity," while "signs of French society's infatuation with the young were everywhere."[23] This modernity had a specific context that structured itself around the idea of youth: new issues of collaboration/resistance, wars of decolonization, Cold War power struggles, an expanding welfare state, a technocratic economy, and mass pop-culture consumerism. Thus, another element of this study is a reevaluation of the much maligned and often ignored Fourth Republic, and an acknowledgment of the programs, trends, and policies that formed the framework for the significant role youth and the young played in the decade that followed, the 1960s.

The Fourth Republic has been studied much less than the regimes preceding and succeeding it. Yet because it sits at the crucial juncture in French history between Vichy and the Fifth Republic, reconsidering the Fourth Republic helps us to understand better the significant continuities and ruptures in this remarkable period of transition. Because of the Vichy programs and ideologies of the 1940s targeting the young, and the ubiquitous youth culture of the Fifth Republic in the 1960s, focusing on youth offers a unique opportunity to evaluate how the Fourth Republic bridges these two distinct eras. This moment has its own unfolding developments, yet with significant historical continuities that reach back to the Third Republic and forward to 1968. Looking at youth offers a valuable means to study the relationship of the Fourth Republic to the larger history of France.

This book explores the Fourth Republic's shifting concept of youth, through the combination of government policy, popular culture, and social discourse, in two parts. Part I, The Promise of Youth, topically explores the reconstruction's frameworks of rejuvenation, modernization, and citizenship, while Part II, The Problem of Youth, examines delinquency, sexuality, and censorship. Thus, the book is organized thematically and topically across the period, rather than by a narrative chronology. It has elements of an intellectual history that traces the idea of youth and its use as a discursive category, a social history that follows the lives of young people and their role in postwar French society, a cultural history of France's rejuvenation and reconstruction following the Second World War, and a political history of the programs and policies of the Fourth Republic welfare state.

The end of the war's tumult and the beginning of new political and social structures in France repositioned young people as a mass social group and reoriented their rank and place in French society. Set within the wake of the war and the Fourth Republic's efforts of reconstruction, this case study of popular conceptions of youth in tandem with government initiatives reveals how social and political institutions interacted with the production of social groups to redefine national identity in times of crisis. This history reveals youth, both as a concept and as a social group, to be a primary mechanism in France's postwar rejuvenation and its cultural reconstruction because the young, through their buoyant energy and dynamism, symbolically pointed the way to the future.

Although many of my conclusions arise out of the particularities of France, the West more generally was dealing with similar trends and issues: the meaning of democracy and government in the wake of Fascism, the role of the state in the welfare of its citizens, the material reconstruction and modernization of infrastructures, the extension of compulsory education, the expanding influence of the young in the marketplace as consumers and producers, a booming popular culture dominated by the young, the moral panic of juvenile delinquency, the worry over young libertines, the gap of understanding between generations, and the political and social mobilization of young people. Because the young have become such a visible and viable presence, and because the adult preoccupation with the social group of youth has permeated society and politics since 1945, this analysis of the meaning of age is vital to understanding the postwar period in the West more broadly. Using France as a specific case study, this work should resonate with anyone interested in understanding the developing role and meaning of youth in the postwar West.

PART I

The Promise of Youth

CHAPTER I

Youth of Today, France of Tomorrow

In 1944 the exhilarating moment of the Liberation infused France with the hopeful enthusiasm born from difficult accomplishment and inspired a belief that fundamental change was not only desirable but possible. The crucible of war and occupation had melded together people of markedly different social and political backgrounds to fight a common enemy for a common goal. Groups that before the war had been strident adversaries were able to set aside their differences and past grievances to work toward the expulsion of the Nazis from France and the overthrow of the Vichy regime. The success of their endeavor in 1944 inspired many to hope for an extension of this cooperative spirit into the postwar period, to rid France not only of Fascism but of injustice and inequality as well. In fact, this attitude led to the famous Resistance charter, issued in 1944, which outlined socialist goals for the postwar period. [1] Because those involved with the Vichy government were besmirched with ignominy, the political stage was open to those who had been active in the internal Resistance or in Charles de Gaulle's Free

France government. The unity of the moment and the euphoria of Liberation encouraged a hopefulness in France that the dark days were over and a bright, open future awaited, a future that must be made better than the recent past. As Albert Camus wrote in the resistance newspaper *Combat*, "The Allies have made our liberation possible. But our freedom is our own; it is we who must shape it."[2] Jean-Paul Sartre, meanwhile, wrote in the first issue of *Les Temps Modernes* that the "distant goal we set for ourselves is that of a liberation," and proposed further change beyond the immediate Liberation from wartime occupation.[3]

As terrible a tragedy as the war had been, it offered France an opportunity. The physical destruction, political collapse, military defeat, economic depression, and moral compromise of the war years meant that France, by necessity, had to be remade. The ruin of war demanded that the nation start over. A new France had to be planned, fashioned, and achieved as an exceptional alternative to the preceding one. As Simone de Beauvoir wrote in her memoirs, "We believed that the country had been shaken deeply enough to permit a radical remodeling of its structure without new convulsions."[4] As she implied, this "radical remodeling" was not conceived as a violent revolution in the tradition of 1789 or 1917. Substantial violence to society had already been done; the task at Liberation was to put a new society in place. The idealistic spirit of the Liberation placed its optimism in an imaginable future that could be achieved through the manipulation of the present. What this new France should be like was debatable; whether it entailed a socialist program, as advocated by the Resistance movement, or a powerful state returned to national grandeur, as promised by Charles de Gaulle, the Liberation was a moment filled with utopian visions of a future France.[5]

The conceptual underpinnings of France's postwar reconstruction implied a desire to break with the recent past and usher in an era of renewal based upon a transcendent future. "No one spoke of putting back the clock," wrote Beauvoir, "we all sang in chorus our hymn of the future."[6] In fact, this passion for renewal, for rethinking France, characterized the nation throughout the 1940s and underlay the efforts of the Popular Front, the Vichy regime, and the nascent Fourth Republic to comprehensively reform France.[7] In spite of the contrast in ideological underpinnings of each endeavor, there was a great deal of continuity between their reformist approaches: each stressed welfare policies and programs for families and youth;

each promoted technocratic and entrepreneurial cadres; each sought a new civic spirit of community and cooperation; and each attempted to organize economic and social interests in harmony with state planning. Underlying the work of policymakers in the 1940s was a vision of an ideal future France that contrasted with the image of a prewar France in steady decline. In the 1930s, many believed the French Third Republic to be a flagging democracy, stumbling from one governmental crisis to another.[8] In fact, 1940s reformers often used the Third Republic as a "negative model," making its antithesis fundamental to the debates over the future.[9]

One such reformist polemic, written and published clandestinely in the last months of the German Occupation by Michel Debré and Emmanuel Monick, under the pseudonym Jacquier-Bruère, was *Remaking France: The Effort of a Generation*. The book called for sweeping changes to French institutions and offered proposed reforms that advocated a socialist liberalism. Acknowledging that "everyone speaks of the future of France, yet if they agree on the goals, they are divided on the means," Debré and Monick identified the urgency of increasing the birthrate, modernizing the economy, reorganizing the empire, and restructuring the government. Underlying all of these reforms, however, was the crucial need in France for the "rejuvenation of its civilization," a rejuvenation that required the vigorous participation of the young. "The rising generation in France is marked for this great destiny. It cannot escape it," they exclaimed.[10]

The historian Marc Bloch, in his 1940 book *Strange Defeat*, sought to explain the sudden conquest and collapse of France. Although he blasted the military high command for gross incompetence, he was in agreement with Pétain that the root of the problem lay within Third Republic society generally. France was mired in old ways of doing things, old ways of thinking, old ways of fighting wars, old ways of governing. By no means a Pétainist (Bloch was executed in 1944 as a member of the Resistance), Bloch considered Third Republic France to be backward, old-fashioned, out of date, and undynamic. His essay is a striking indictment of the military, educational system, political parties, government administration, and big business capitalists. Bloch believed that French society had placed too great an emphasis on the veneration of age and thus, as a nation, suffered from the inflexibility and stagnation intrinsic to custom and tradition. "France in defeat will be seen to have had a government of old men. France of the new springtime must be the creation of the young," he wrote.[11] Bloch proposed that in order for France to renew, rebuild, and re-create itself, in order to become a modern nation, it must not return to the old ways that had failed France; the postwar period would, by necessity, be a time for rejuvenation.

As Bloch predicted, following the Third Republic's decline and the Vichy regime's notorious collaboration with Nazi Germany, the national consensus at Liberation was a profound desire for something new.[12] And it was a consensus that optimistically identified the young as the key element for the reform of France. At Liberation, Simone de Beauvoir thought it "the most fantastic piece of luck" to be young, because for them, "all roads lay open . . . as if their future depended on no one but themselves."[13] For nearly fifty years, young people had been increasingly credited as being the harbingers of a better time, becoming the object of state initiatives designed to develop their potential. The Popular Front had created a new department to mold and shape the young in addition to its educational reforms, and Vichy had placed young people at the center of its National Revolution, privileging them with extensive state-directed programs. This culminated in 1944, as all of France looked to and talked about its future. Youth and youthfulness now became the image, the goal, and the means of cultural reconstruction. Catholic intellectual Emmanuel Mounier warned, however, that this youthful energy sweeping France, while a good thing, must be harnessed, controlled, and directed. He said that the "myth of youth," on which "we have decided to model France," implies that "virtue is no longer in the accomplishment, but in the design, nor in the creative force, but in the unleashed energy, nor in responsible intelligence, but in unreflective enthusiasm." Mounier, in fact, had been among a group of right-wing, nonconformist intellectuals who, in the interwar period, had championed the young and youth to be the "new men" to lead Europe. In 1944 Mounier urged the new government of France to consider carefully its programs and initiatives for the young, for through those planned policies it also planned France's future.[14]

Similarly Jean Planchais, a journalist whose specialty was military affairs, wanted France "to understand the importance, for the present and future of the country, . . . of a consistent policy for youth that should be one of the principal preoccupations for those who have our destiny in their hand."[15] Another journalist, Raymond Millet, thought that "the state should know that it cannot rebuild France without having aroused youth, nor can it arouse youth without having already initiated the renovation of France."[16] Even General Douglas MacArthur noted that "there had arisen a new element, the youth inside France which would be her salvation. . . . From this youth would come a new patriotic and progressive French leadership."[17]

In one sense the postwar baby boom obliged the state to reconsider the young: observe the ubiquitous prams in the Luxembourg gardens in 1947 (Figure 2). France experienced a jump in fertility rates, with more than 11 million new births between 1944 and 1958. Before the war, the French birth rate had been 14.9 births per 1,000 people, between 1946 and 1950 it rose to 20.9 per 1,000, and throughout the 1950s it remained at over 18 per 1,000.[18] Though in the 1950s the birthrate declined slightly, the infant mortality rate was cut in half, so the population of France continued to swell. In 1946, the population of France was roughly what it had been fifty years earlier at the end of the nineteenth century. After nearly a century of very low birth

Figure 2. Afternoon in the Luxembourg Gardens, 1947. AFP.

rates and failed state pronatalism, this demographic shift to a much younger population helped to reposition the focus of French society by creating a demand for products, resources, programs, projects, and activities designed for the young. For decades France had had a disproportionately elderly population, but by 1958 nearly a third of France was under twenty years of age. This willingness to reproduce was hailed as an affirmation of France's newfound national vitality and general faith in a promising future—that through repopulation, France would be able "to remake and rejuvenate itself."[19]

At the mid-century turning point of the Second World War's end, the French self-consciously deliberated on their future, looking beyond the present triumph of the Liberation and the failures of the past to plan a better society. The postwar reconstruction became not just an opportunity to modernize a dated infrastructure, but a chance to rejuvenate an infirm cultural identity as well. Youth and youthfulness became a key site around which France imagined and planned this future. As a social group, the young became a visibly active part of the physical reconstruction of the nation, laboring for the national recovery; they emerged as an object of state planning and government programs; and they became the subject of scrutiny, as the French public sought to understand its future through the study of the young. As an icon of rejuvenation, the creative energy of youth became the reconstruction's motivating spirit. As the supreme representative of the future in the present, youth and youthfulness became a mechanism for cultural reconstruction as France sought to remake itself after the calamities of the Second World War.

The Promise of Youth

The breadth of destruction and the scope of hardship in the Second World War seemed to have made many in France ready to accept a kind of cultural revolution that was characterized by a refusal to return to the status quo.[20] In contrast, after the First World War, there had been a stress on continuity with its prewar era, when society resisted rather than welcomed dramatic changes to the social, cultural, and political order.[21] At that time, "Yesterday's France Tomorrow" became a rallying cry for postwar reconstruction, and it was during the 1920s that the pre–World War I years became known as the Belle Epoque, as a time when life was good, replete with satisfaction, harmony, and plenty.[22] Looking back across the upheaval and devastation of the First World War, the prewar world seemed a better place in retrospect.[23] This situation was exacerbated by the Great War's incredible loss of life and the cult of memory that developed around the mourning for the 1,350,000 French dead. A commemorative culture emerged across France, marked by pageantry, ceremony, and more than thirty-five thousand monuments dedicated to remembering the dead and acknowledging their sacrifice.[24] The mourning throughout 1920s Europe was typified by a "backward gaze" that faced the past, not the future, which helps to explain why 1945, not 1918, represents the real rupture in twentieth-century European cultural life.[25]

If the material destruction of the Second World War was much worse for France than that of the First, the loss of life was considerably less so. Official figures estimate war-related deaths between 550,000 and 600,000—less than half of the First World War total. Furthermore, the diversity of wartime experience in France meant that there was no "war generation" after the Second World War in the same way that there was after the First.[26] The young population of 1940s France did not share a unique historical experience in common, as the millions of mobilized soldiers in the First World War had. During the Second World War, some lived in the Occupied North, others in the Vichy-controlled South. Some collaborated, others resisted; some did neither. Some joined the Milice, others the Maquis. Roughly 840,000 young workers were deported to German factories; another 950,000 soldiers were prisoners of war; Jews and Communists were singled out for persecution. Rural peasants hoarded food, city-dwellers suffered strict rationing; collaborators and black-marketeers were enriched while others were left in penury. The war experience could not be broken down along strict generational lines as it had been in the First World War, where young soldiers were seen to be the victims of old generals and politicians. The divergent circumstances, varied loyalties, and incompatible conditions of the war did not lend themselves to a sense of collective experience among generational age groups.[27] Hence, the war was not understood as precisely generational, yet the cultural reconstruction that came afterward was permeated with references to categories of age, with youth invoked as the redemptive elixir for an older, failed France.

Throughout Europe, debates about the meaning of generation predominated during the early twentieth century and the years around the

First World War. Generational theories during this era were formulated in several countries and from a variety of national, intellectual, and social perspectives.[28] The concept of generation was used to divide national bodies into social groups based upon a common historical experience determined by age. In France, for example, Charles Péguy's famous *Notre jeunesse* reflected on the Dreyfus Affair's impact on his generation.[29] The generational concept became an explanation of progress and national destiny set within a biological rhythm that determined cultural and social change—a *regener*-ation that occurred as each new generation inevitably came to power. The experience of the Great War and the divide it created between the young soldiers who fought and died on the battlefront and the elder statesmen who commanded and supervised from the safety of the home front led to the postwar conceptualization of a generational conflict and to the notion of a "lost generation." The collective nature of the experience of the First World War contributed to a sense of cohesion that organized itself around the concept of generation. This is understandable when one considers that at that time there existed a predisposition to the theoretical framework of generation, so that the development of generational theory before and after the First World War exactly coincided with the perceived existence of a "generation of 1914."

In France just before the Great War, there was an extensive discussion of the Agathon (a pseudonym for Henri Massis and Alfred de Tarde) survey of 1912, conducted for the Parisian daily *L'Opinion* and published a year later as the book *The Young People of Today*. The survey studied only the young educated elite, yet they were made to stand for all of the young in France, not an uncommon phenomenon, as whole generations are often defined by the small number of its political, intellectual, and literary elite. One of the conclusions to come out of the Agathon discussion was the readiness of the young to go to war with Germany to reclaim French hegemony and prove the virility of French grandeur. The young men of the Agathon survey were considered the standard-bearers of a revitalized and mighty nation, who, some hoped, would soon have the chance to prove themselves on the battle-field.[30] That these young men were credited with being the great hope of France, the vital force of the nation-state, and the harbingers of glory days coincided with the historical meaning of youth as it had developed over the previous century.

Throughout the modern period, youth has been imbued with the ability to foster change. The French Revolution was saturated with the rhetoric of regeneration, with the killing off of the old so that the young might flourish.[31] The insolence and impudence of Rousseau's *Emile* stood as an appropriate forerunner to the headstrong revolutionaries bent on nothing less than the complete transformation of their world, as demonstrated by the youthful passion and ardor of Saint-Just or the precocity and talent of the young Bonaparte. The concept of regeneration, of the young supplanting the old, resonates throughout the founding texts of the first French Republic.[32] The Revolution at times articulated that the young represented change, dynamism, and opportunity, as opposed to the old, who represented privilege, stagnation, and obstacle. In short, the young were identified as revolutionary and the old as reactionary.[33]

This conceptualization extended throughout the nineteenth century and is visible throughout most of Western Europe as youth was identified with the task of social and political transformation.[34] In literature, the bildungsroman, or coming-of-age novel, was manifested as symbolic of the potential and dynamism of modernity itself, of great expectations and sentimental educations.[35] In the late nineteenth century, as an effort to harness and direct this energy among its citizenry, nations sponsored universal education and social welfare reforms to develop the young.[36] Additionally, various private youth movements flourished at this time, seeking to instill specific values among the young, such as patriotism, discipline, religiosity, or political awareness. As the twentieth century began, the young were increasingly organized by adults to foster change according to an adult ideological paradigm.[37]

European nation-states took advantage of these growing youth movements to mobilize for the excesses of the First World War. The outcome of the war tremendously contributed to the notion of a rupture between young and old. After the war, political extremists of the left and right capitalized on this disenfranchisement and the interwar period became the zenith of the ideological youth movement, as political groups sought to marshal the support of young people and inculcate them within a particular political vision.[38] It seemed that every political and religious group, no matter how marginal, maintained an affiliated youth organization and articulated its ideology through programs for the young.[39] In France, the strongest youth movements belonged to the Communist Party, the Catholic Church, and the Scouts, who vied, along with the Socialists, Action Française, and other right-wing groups, for influence among the young.[40] Since the Revolution, then, youth had moved from being the symbolic embodiment of a spontaneous revolutionary energy to a malleable social group to be wooed and manipulated for the purposes of adults who offered a vision of tomorrow, whether it be a socialist utopia, a thousand-year Reich, or even the triumph of God's Kingdom on Earth.

The Newness of Youth

Although there was significant continuity between the prewar and the postwar periods, and even though by the late forties France had settled into some of the patterns of the past, there was a state of mind in French society that embraced the transformative power of invention. The rupture of 1945 was in many ways more one of mentality than actuality; French society willed itself to believe change was possible, desirable, and imminent. As will become evident over the course of this volume, the continuities with Vichy and the Third Republic were often considerable in terms of programs and agendas, political and economic institutions, administrators and personnel; even the very ideas of reform and youth-as-the-future were grounded in what had come before. Yet the desire for change was acute and profoundly evident as well, and this often manifested itself in the condemnation of the past and celebration of the future, or by venerating the new and disparaging the old. It was the French revolutionaries, after all, who invented the concept of the ancien régime; similarly, the rupture of 1945 was a strategic one.[41] During the reconstruction, this willed rupture enabled France to plan its society, organize its future, and modernize its economy, infrastructure, and institutions. This embrace of change permeated the cultural trends of the postwar era as they developed over the decade and a half following the Liberation. Indicative of this fixation was the association of novelty and "newness" with change, with progress, and with the young—a recurrent and wholly pervasive theme in French culture of the 1940s and 1950s.

    For example, the "New Novel" was associated with the work of Alain Robbe-Grillet, Nathalie Sarraute, and Claude Simon among others; they believed that the postwar world was demonstrably different from the past and required a new kind of literature for a new kind of era, one devoid of traditional character, plot, or narrative. The New Novel sought to break definitively with the forms and traditions of the literary past.[42] Coincidentally, the "New Novelists" were first identified as such in a 1954 issue of Georges Bataille's journal, *Critique*.[43] Founded in 1946, *Critique* was associated with what became known as the "new criticism," and featured the early work of Roland Barthes, Michel Foucault, and Jacques Derrida, among others.[44] What is significant here is the supposition that this criticism represented something "new," something markedly different from the "old" or the "traditional." One critic commented: "New Novel. New Cinema. New Wave. For ten years, we are in the new. Never, perhaps, in the history of letters has there been such willful deliberation to free oneself of tradition, to break with the past, to create a form and spirit absolutely original."[45] Although this commentary primarily reflected upon literary movements that emerged in the 1950s, the remark reminds us that the "New Novel" was part of the larger trend of *new*-ness that predominated across postwar French culture.

One of the first of the "new" in the postwar era was Christian Dior's exceptionally successful "New Look" of 1947. Dior had opened his own fashion house only one year earlier, and this first line guaranteed his success and became a symbolic marker dramatizing France's desire to leave the austerity of the war behind. Dior's "New Look" was characterized by long, voluminous skirts, pinched waists, narrow, sloping shoulders, and round, padded hips. There was an emphasis on the "feminine" silhouette that required corsets and petticoats to restrict, contort, and shape women's bodies beneath the generous folds of luxurious cloth. Indeed, for a "New Look," Dior's designs harkened back to the past, to the feminine shape of the Belle Epoque. Nonetheless, it was not considered a re-creation of styles, and there was a conscious consensus that regarded the New Look as welcome innovation and as notably progressive—hence its *new*ness. This can be explained by the years of wartime restrictions, when cloth had been strictly rationed during the shortages of the Occupation and remained severely limited until as late as 1949. Dior's designs, which included an afternoon dress that required an astonishing fifty yards of material, flaunted extravagance, opulence, and plenty in a time profoundly marked by scarcity. This contrast was particularly evident in a street skirmish at the Rue Lepic market in Montmartre, where a mob of disgruntled housewives attacked a group of Dior models who had come for an outdoor photo shoot. Confronted with the abundant amounts of fabric clothing the models, several women set upon the young beauties, ripping and tearing at the dresses, effectively stripping the models of material that could afterward be used as valuable scrap. In the context of scarcity, the profuse abundance of Dior's fashion designs became associated with an expectation of prosperity that many hoped would characterize the recovery and allow France to turn its back on the deprivations of the past. Christian Dior himself claimed that, for France generally, his hugely successful New Look of 1947 became symbolic of youth and hope and the future—this despite the fact that his fashions targeted the tradition and old wealth of the middle-aged bourgeoisie.[46]

French gastronomy as well was perceived to be undergoing change. In the late fifties and early sixties, food critics Henri Gault and Christian Millau coined the term *nouvelle cuisine* in their restaurant guide and magazine to describe a new cooking style characterized by lightness, purity, and simple, distinct flavors that stressed the use of local, fresh products. A rebellion against Escoffier orthodoxy spearheaded by innovative chefs such as Fernand Point, who died in 1955, *nouvelle cuisine* was later popularized by the young chefs that followed, such as Paul Bocuse and Michel Guérard. Interestingly, also *à table*, the popularity of fresh, fruity Beaujolais wine dates from this period as well. Initiated in Lyon in 1951, a remarkably successful marketing scheme coined the phrase "Beaujolais Nouveau" and definitively established a festive ritual each fall, as gourmets and gourmands alike await the third Thursday of November for the latest vintage of a wine best drunk young.[47]

Perhaps the most well-known cultural phenomenon to emerge from the late fifties as part of this *new*ness was the New Wave Cinema. Associated with the work of directors François Truffaut, Jean-Luc Godard, Eric Rohmer, and Claude Chabrol among others, the *nouvelle vague* cinema was credited with invigorating a moribund French film industry dominated by predictable costume dramas high on literary pretension but low on substance. With energetic dynamism, a few young directors—several were former film critics from *Cahiers du Cinéma*—made their first feature films with tiny budgets, skeleton crews, and amateur actors. Subsequently, these directors dramatically transformed the content and cinematic style of French film. Innovative filming technique, fresh subject matter, original ideas, and directorial vision (the *auteur* theory of film) garnered some immediate successes, most famously Truffaut's *The 400 Blows* (1959) and Godard's *Breathless* (1960), and resulted in a spirited discussion of an emerging *jeune cinéma*. By 1962, over sixty young directors had debuted films in France. While some garnered critical awards and financial prosperity, others, of course, faded into obscurity, but this does not diminish the profound impact these young innovators had on French cinema.

What is significant, however, is that the term "New Wave" was imposed upon these varied directors by the press; there was no movement per se, no central organizing theme nor programmatic declaration grouping these filmmakers together, other than, perhaps, a general iconoclasm for the established film industry. The 1959 Cannes Film Festival even sponsored a special roundtable discussion of approximately thirty young directors, in a session that the festival, not the participants, entitled "La Nouvelle Vague." The roundtable was charged with determining the characteristic traits of this emerging young cinema. Recognizing the trend in French film of movies about, for, and by young people, Cannes the next year sponsored a special showcase, *Le Jeune cinéma*. This late-fifties phenomenon of an emerging youthfulness in film production, subject matter, and audience, to which Cannes was attuned, was sometimes referred to as *le jeune-nouveau cinéma*—explicitly linking "young" with "new." In the end, *nouvelle vague*, or New Wave, was the moniker that held, and would be impulsively applied to a broad range of films continuing through the following decade, and some films would even be considered New Wave retroactively, such as Roger Vadim's *And God Created Woman* (1956). Importantly, the use of the term *nouvelle vague* explicitly linked the cinematic phenomenon to postwar youth by appropriating a catch phrase that had been specifically applied to the generation that culturally and politically matured after the Liberation, one that was originally conceptualized and articulated in a weekly newsmagazine.[48]

In 1957 *L'Express* founding co-editor Françoise Giroud, in association with the Institut Français d'Opinion Publique (IFOP), set out to investigate young people sociologically through a widely disseminated questionnaire that was simultaneously published, on October 3, in *L'Express*, *France-Soir*, *Paris-Presse*, and *La Terre Nouvelle*, as well as distributed at factories, stores, and universities. The goal was to get feedback from a variety of milieux across the nation rather than just the urban middle classes or the readers of *L'Express*.[49] That way, through a core sampling of the eight million young people between eighteen and thirty, the magazine might be able to "discern the particular features of contemporary French youth and discover their common denominators."[50] The age range was determined by the war; the *nouvelle vague* was defined as those who had matured after the Liberation and thus did not carry the "shadow of the past." Thus, for the parameters of this study, it was the socio-historical experience of the Second World War that differentiated youth from age.

The survey was comprised of twenty-four questions designed to determine the young's ideals, influences, beliefs, opinions, and perceptions regarding both their personal lives and the life of the nation as a whole. The Institut Français d'Opinion Publique specialized in opinion surveys designed to provide a statistical sampling representative of the population under study. The Nouvelle Vague study was therefore considered a scientific enterprise, supervised by a legitimate institution that employed the most modern methods of statistical analysis—Giroud even referred to it as an "exact X-ray" of the young's state of mind.[51] Hence, the study was granted much more credibility than it would have had as a simple magazine reader's poll.[52] As a result, the report was credited with for the first time giving voice to the young people of France across economic class lines and geographic regions. Beginning October 10 and each week thereafter for the next couple of months, *L'Express* published a selection of individual responses as they arrived, including those of young celebrities like Françoise Sagan—letters that the magazine felt were notably prescient and provided a range of personal experiences and opinions. By December, IFOP had received over fifteen thousand responses, the tallied results of which were published in a full report with extended commentary by Giroud in the December 5th and 12th issues of *L'Express* (Figure 3).

The survey was designed to bring out the ideas that the young held in common across boundaries of class, gender, education, or region, and was thus used to define a social group by intentionally homogenizing and generalizing the young. It revealed that young people were nominally happy yet harbored a significant skepticism that revealed very little confidence in the ability of the individual to foster change. Other conclusions included

Figure 3. Cover of *L'Express* (1957): Rapport national sur la jeunesse.

that they held "contempt for ideology" and maintained a strict desire to not be deceived by their elders. They felt a profound sense of rupture with the preceding generation and attached importance to an individual's conduct during the war, yet conversely, three-quarters of them believed their generation would be no different from that of their parents, and only half considered themselves fortunate to be living in the postwar era at all. They were less dogmatic, and "less convinced that France [was] the center of the world." The Algerian crisis and the need for a stable government were the two most important issues facing France as a nation, and while they desired material comfort and success, they did not believe either could guarantee personal fulfillment.[53]

Subsequent to the media blitz generated by *L'Express*, the *nouvelle vague* provoked a flood of public commentary, as a variety of figures sought to interpret the significance of the study and the young. Marxist scholar Henri Lefebvre was struck by the political disenchantment that the survey revealed. He acknowledged that young people "suffer from a history not of their making, in which they see no way to intervene," and he used their

seeming political cynicism as a way to critique the floundering Fourth Republic: "Incontestably, young people are convinced that political decisions
are made beyond and without them, beyond the citizenry and without it,
beyond the masses and without them."[54] Demographer Alfred Sauvy noted
that the *nouvelle vague*'s primary material desires—vacation, personal transportation, entertainment—all reflected a tendency for evasion, which he
interpreted as a legitimate "flight before social servitude." This evasion,
he believed, reflected a passion for independence from the difficulties of
France's political-economic system, an independence he described as "the
most elementary form of power." The survey revealed that "the young" recognized the problematic complexities of France's economic infrastructure,
which indicated that they already held, in Sauvy's eyes, a "strange kind of
power" that their elders seemed to lack.[55] Indeed, the Nouvelle Vague study
and the commentaries of Lefebvre and Sauvy preceded the collapse of the
Fourth Republic by only a few months.

Georges Hourdin, a Catholic activist and religious reformer, was en-
thralled and inspired by the Nouvelle Vague study. "We speak a lot of
French youth," he wrote. "They are at the center of our preoccupations."
Yet Hourdin was most intrigued by the survey's lack of concern for matters
of faith. Consequently, he initiated a new study, in conjunction with IFOP,
to make up for this oversight. His study concluded that a third of young
France practiced religion regularly, while three-quarters considered themselves Catholic. Hourdin found these results promising because it meant
that the current generation had not slipped away from God any more than
the preceding one and that the "dechristianization" of France had, perhaps,
slowed.[56]

Due to the remarkable public interest generated, Françoise Giroud decided to publish a book in 1958, *The New Wave: Portraits of Youth*, comprised
of the statistical results supplemented by a collection of 200 responses culled
from the 15,000, and a lengthy commentary by Giroud herself. The published letters were chosen to emphasize the differences and varieties among
the young, as a complement to the statistical analysis that was designed to
reveal the patterns of commonality. Interestingly, the book's structure di-
vides the responses according to gender: part 1 is comprised only of men,
while part 2 is of women. The men are then further subdivided by economic
category: bourgeois, worker, or farmer; whereas the women are subdivided

according to marital status: single or married. It seems that despite the novelty, innovation, or newness that Giroud credited to this generation, she nevertheless decided to organize them according to the most traditional of gender roles: men work and women marry.[57]

Nevertheless, the New Wave became a profound phenomenon, as the public not only embraced the premise but appropriated the term as well. Exploiting this success, *L'Express* even added a subtitle to its masthead, naming itself the "Journal de la nouvelle vague," as well as creating a literary prize, Le Prix Nouvelle Vague, both in the hope, no doubt, of capturing the market share of the New Wave generation's magazine consumption. Though *L'Express* had solidified the association of youth with the "new," this scrutiny of the young and youth had not begun with Giroud's investigation; instead, it was a part of an ongoing examination by adult France of young France.

In the midst of the *nouvelle vague* phenomenon, *Arts* magazine featured its own exposé of the postwar generation in the spring of 1958. André Parinaud's review focused on the glitz and glamour of young celebrities as exemplars of the rising generation and its "conquest of Paris."[58] In contrast to Giroud's broad sociological study, Parinaud provided a weekly glimpse into the lives of notable luminaries under thirty years of age, such as the artist Bernard Buffet, film director Roger Vadim, actress Brigitte Bardot, author Françoise Sagan, and fashion designer Yves Saint-Laurent. Parinaud maintained that these "hundred men and women constitute the phalanx of a new elite," and that the influential position and celebrity acquired by these young people were not merely coincidence, but a harbinger of change, an indication of the collective effect this generation would have on France.[59] Parinaud's concentration on the symbolic status of young stars as the embodiment of a generation was indicative of the iconic status awarded these individuals in a media increasingly dominated by youthful patterns of consumption within a cultural market itself more and more predicated on youth and youthfulness. Undoubtedly, this media obsession for the postwar generation in part sought to commodify the young as a product. Yet even if the media were simply supplying marketable merchandise, it would be wrong to assume that they had invented the demand for phenomena that had, in fact, been building for years.[60]

In May 1949, François Mauriac published an editorial in which he proposed a study, similar to the 1912 Agathon survey, that would take stock of the young French intelligentsia.[61] Throughout the summer of 1949, *Le Figaro Littéraire* ran a seven-part series of articles that investigated young France.[62] The study resulted in the 1951 publication of Robert Kanters and Gilbert Sigaux's *Twenty Years Old in 1951: An Investigation of French Youth*, which set out to provide a rough portrait of postwar French youth by analyzing the results of a questionnaire.[63] The thirty-five questions in the survey were much more concerned with the drama of Cold War politics and France's role on the world stage than was Giroud's later study. Young people aged 17–25 were asked about the USA, the USSR, democracy, Communism, the atomic bomb, and the struggles for independence in colonial empires, in addition to the requisite questions about personal relationships and leisurely pastimes. Though not the phenomenon that Giroud's *nouvelle vague* study would be, Kanters and Sigaux's book did spark public interest by providing a collection of extracts culled from the total responses, though by no means from as broad a base as Giroud's.

There were countless other investigations. *Le Monde* published an eight-part series in 1948 called "Visit to Today's Youth." *La Nef* ran a special issue in 1954 titled "Youth, Who Are You?" And IFOP launched yet another extensive study in 1961.[64] A different inquiry, entitled "Youth of Today, France of Tomorrow," appeared in the literary review *Les Nouvelles Littéraires* in thirteen installments between January and September 1957, and was later published as a book, *France and Her Youth*.[65] In these articles, Henri Perruchot presented a social group that recognized it could no longer depend upon its elders and, while not a generation of rebels, it was independent-minded and aspired to create its own rules, values, and hierarchies.

Interest in French youth even extended outside France. In 1955, *Time* magazine published a cover story profiling young France written by correspondent Stanley Karnow. His portrayal was not a glamorous one: "French youth dares not dream. It must face a reality partly restricted by tradition, partly by history, partly by the failure of its nation's leaders to govern wisely and fairly."[66] His impression was of a disoriented and disenchanted generation full of bilious contempt and longing for change. His depiction of the postwar generation enraged many in France, who denounced Karnow for maligning French honor. *Paris-Presse* printed a translated copy of the article on its back page, encouraging its readers to respond. One wrote that "Monsieur Karnow deserves a slap in the face," while others demanded he be expelled from France altogether.[67] His article and the passionate response it provoked indicate not only the concern for and significance of the young in France, but the recognition that youth was a contested site of struggle for the representation of France generally. Moreover, as an outsider, Karnow seemed to be uncommitted to the French project of rejuvenation. This was the animated forum that Giroud's New Wave study entered into, effectively pinning down France's preoccupation with both the new and youth.

Despite the variety of dispositions among the young that all these surveys revealed, youth was still treated as a homogenous whole distinct from the adult. The very logic of these studies was predicated upon such an assumption. Yet the studies had in fact shown that there was great continuity across categories of age, that young people had very similar opinions and expectations as adults of similar backgrounds. The circumstances of region, gender, education, and class influenced individuals as much as age or generation. Nonetheless, the rhetoric of rejuvenation and the perception of French youth as markedly different remained because it had become such an essential part of the social narrative and because these studies, in fact, reified "youth" as a visible social category. Henri Lefebvre said as much in his commentary on the Nouvelle Vague study. He pointed out that adult France complained that the young were either not at all or at least badly integrated into French society. Yet how, he asked, "can the young integrate themselves into a society that specifically makes them a group apart?" According to Lefebvre, it was not the mass of young people, but French society itself, that created the social group of youth through the articulation of its existence. Through study and objectification, through the conceptualization of the young as youth, adult France brought this social group into being. Likewise, it was not the young who "affirmed themselves as new," but French society who insisted on such a proposition, one that was based on an implicit moral dichotomy between the past and the future, between old and young.[68]

The Temporal Agent of Destiny

René Clément's classic film *Forbidden Games* (1952) is a meaningful allegory that contrasts the purity and tender lyricism of children against the harsh brutishness of empty-headed adults. Set during the Second World War, the film opens in the midst of a German air attack as planes strafe the crowded roads and as city refugees scramble by foot, wagon, and automobile, desperate to escape the advancing Nazis yet clinging to valued possessions. During the attack, the bourgeois parents of five-year-old Paulette are killed. She is orphaned, and remains bewildered and unaware of this significant turn of events. Soon, she is found by an eleven-year-old peasant boy, Michel, who brings her back to his family's farm for protection. There is an immediate bond between the two, a companionship based on mutual understanding and committed trust. The adults in the film, however, are suspicious, quarrelsome, and combative, even fighting among themselves at a solemn cemetery burial. These peasants are stuck in the empty gestures of ritual and the ignorance born of a traditional past. They are coarse and seem to lack an appreciation for the significance of the war around them; they remain more concerned with maintaining age-old quarrels and bitter grudges than with sorting through the confusion of the war. The children, meanwhile, take care of each other and deal with the chaos of war by creating a secret cemetery for the animals inadvertently killed, including Paulette's dog. The cemetery is discovered, the children get in trouble, and Paulette is taken away to an orphanage amid the crowds of refugees who continue along the road.

The film was a huge hit worldwide and won awards at many festivals, including Cannes, Venice, and the Academy Awards. Only the rituals with which the children buried the animals stirred any protest, by some who considered it blasphemous of Catholicism. The interpretation of the film was clear, since it is structured based on the opposition of the adult world and that of children. The adults represent the vulgar reality of humanity as it rails against itself—hateful, petty, contemptuous, and dishonest. The children, however, stand for the purity of the human spirit before its corruption in adulthood—generous, caring, indulgent, and loyal. Paulette and Michel walk together through the adult world, oblivious to its pitfalls; they are the force of life in the midst of death. The young and the old in this film emphasize the Janus-faced inversion of humanity's goodness and badness.

It is important to remember that age categories are predicated upon a relationship of relativity to one another, and that the conceptualization of one affects the conceptualization of the other—if not explicitly, at least implicitly. In postwar France, the words and concepts that looked to the future embracing the limitless possibilities of posterity carried with them an unspoken condemnation of the past, what has been identified as the "rhetoric of renewal."[69] The war itself stood as a profound marker of historical experience, dividing those old enough to have experienced it as responsible adults and those too young to be accountable. It appears that a dividing line formed based upon life experience or, rather, a lack of it; the old were equated with the aggravation of a recent past, while the young were conflated with building an expectant future. Furthermore, as this instance shows, age categories themselves became associated with the temporal conceptualization of past, present, and future. In any given moment, the past, the present, and the future may be represented by the old, the middle-aged, and the young living in that moment.

French society's fixation on the young partly reflected a desire to repress issues of adult responsibility for the past. This new concern for youth manifested itself as a desire to focus on the future and worked as a device to avoid reconciliation with the issues of recent history—defeat, Vichy, collaboration, and occupation. It could be considered as an outgrowth of what Henry Rousso has termed the "Vichy Syndrome," or France's inability to deal directly with its role in the harsh realities of the Second World War.[70] The "Vichy Syndrome" was not a phenomenon of collective guilt for the war, but rather an act of collective denial, an unwillingness to consider or deliberate on the unsavory aspects of the French war experience. The postwar obsession with youth and the future allowed France to avoid scrutinizing the past and delay examining issues of collaboration, issues that remain problematic for France today, several decades later. Questions of culpability for the young were moot, and their undeniable innocence in the context of the war's dirty legacy promised a new beginning for France. Focusing on the future was a convenient way to insist on a distinct rupture with the recent past, while the concept of youth served as the ideal mechanism to facilitate and emphasize this rupture and ignore, almost deny, the strong continuities with Vichy, or the Third Republic for that matter. Meanwhile, the concern for the young implicitly corresponded to an anxiety about the reproduction and reinvention of the social order in the wake of the Second World War, an anxiety about a new France that could be better than the old.

As the euphoric moment of the Liberation dwindled away and the solidarity and consensus of 1944 steadily eroded year by year, the political realities of the postwar period became increasingly irreconcilable. The National

Resistance Council's (CNR) charter for a socially progressive France quickly became a dead letter, and the cooperative spirit of the Resistance dissolved into ideological factionalism; the Cold War superpowers demanded conflicting loyalties from the political left and right; the 1946 Constitution increasingly revealed itself to be unworkable—from 1944 to 1958 the Fourth Republic had twenty-five governments, each lasting an average of seven months—and no single party was ever capable of consolidating power; the political leaders of France quibbled and bickered as coalition governments were assembled like pieces from diverse puzzles that, predictably, never quite fit, despite the endless variations. For many, the political turnover of the Fourth Republic confirmed that the leaders of France had squandered an opportunity. Within just a few short years, the optimistic glow of renewal had dimmed, and the dilemma of reconciling the intransigent visions of the postwar rendered the anticipated renaissance impossible. Simone de Beauvoir revealed these difficulties and disappointments compellingly in her novel *The Mandarins*, winner of the 1954 Prix Goncourt.

In 1945, the future belonged to all of France. As Beauvoir noted, "This victory was to efface our old defeats, it was ours, and the future it opened up was ours, too."[71] But the disappointments of the following decade, the failure to achieve political stability or to fulfill the utopian ambitions, broke this optimistic anticipation, despite the fact that France had regained its economic stability, emerged from the wartime hardships, and managed to modernize much of the nation. As the years passed, the future increasingly became the exclusive domain of the young. By 1958, Beauvoir recognized and envied the young's takeover. They were "so much ahead of us at their age" that "it's hard to keep the future as a dimension in one's life when one already feels one's been buried by those who are coming after."[72]

By the mid-fifties, the solutions to France's problems were increasingly identified as connected to the concept of youth. André Monteil, a former minister and MRP member, wrote that "the particular problems of youth, and the condition of their solution, are the more general problems of the rejuvenation of [France's] political, economic, and social institutions." For, "it is on youth that rests the hope of our country's recovery," and it is up to them "to build a more durable and more just regime."[73] Alfred Sauvy likened the young to a social class, stating that "the rise of the young classes to which the old generation refuses their place is our great chance. We rely on this renaissance of youth to be a party to progress and hope."[74] In yet another correlation between the new, youth, and the future, technocratic physicist Francis Perrin wrote that for "the grandeur of our country, we should take the essential lesson: *faire du nouveau*. It is necessary to work for the future . . . but we should think for the future and not dream it. The best people for this work are the young who have at the same time imagination and vitality and for whom the future of the country is their future."[75] Louis Armand, the director of France's railways, classified the problems of the young as the most important issue for France's recovery, because "resolving one will resolve the other" by making "the child the man that our future needs."[76] Kanters and Sigaux said their study of youth was to "reassure ourselves against the uncertainties of the present and to find for the future a comfort in hope"; that due to the "tormented history of these last years, we should make a history of tomorrow," and that, therefore, youth "interests us as the temporal agent of destiny."[77] In 1957, as a sharp contrast to the adult generations, Françoise Giroud identified the *nouvelle vague* as "the part of the French engaging in the present the future of the nation."[78] Catholic reformer Georges Hourdin justified the studies and discussions, considering it "a legitimate exercise" that "we should seek to know how [the young] envision their present and our future."[79] Jacques Laurent, commenting on the older French literati's obsession with the work of Françoise Sagan, noted: "Today it is the old who listen to the young with the hope of learning by example. I do not point out this particularity to mock it." He continued, "It proves the uncertainty of a nation, the panic of a civilization."[80]

That the age category of youth became bound with the temporal category of the future makes sense, of course. Individually, the young advance to old age through the passage of time, so that imagining their lifespan is, necessarily, to imagine the future, whereas to imagine the lifespan of an adult or senior is often to reflect on the past. In postwar France, interestingly, part of the advancing public consciousness of youth as the future was also about the adult past. At the same time that youth was being heralded as France's last hope for the future, there was a related surge of concern that youth was suffering from the vestiges of an adult past; that the sum of traumatic upheaval in the twentieth century was adversely affecting the young; that there was a congenital ailment not of their making, inherently related to the fundamental sicknesses of the century and designated as *mal du siècle*.

In the 1950s there was a broad consensus that young people suffered from disaffection, a torpor that threatened to sap the young of their inherent vitality and enthusiasm. *Arts* magazine published a four-part analysis of French youth between February 27 and March 20, 1957 (Giroud's Nouvelle Vague study appeared later that year). Directed by the young writers Jean-René Huguenin and Renaud Matignon, these commentaries were characterized by a tone of pessimism and melancholy that acknowledged France's growing obsession with the young but denied the hopeful exuberance it often associated with them. Rather, the Huguenin and Matignon portrayal presented a cynical and alienated youth that was disconsolate and disinterested in public affairs.

This "crisis" was alternately referred to as *mal de jeunesse* or *mal du siècle*. Although neither of these were new terms—in fact, *mal du siècle* permeates the modern period—they both took on new significance after the Second World War.[81] This ailment, this *mal du siècle*, was repeatedly blamed on the adult generation—a version of the "sins of the fathers visited upon the sons." Addressing this issue, one professor proposed, "The events of this century have too clearly shown the failure of values on which the preceding generations have lived." He continued by asking if, "in the midst of such chaos, is it not a healthy reaction to want to break with a past whose ruins are still visible for all to see?"[82] Another commentator believed that "our twentieth century is too tragic for this youth to content itself in the same way as those who preceded them."[83] And still another said that "it is society that is guilty," because adults themselves "have created a posterity of despondency."[84] The religious scholar and activist Mireille Baumgartner, like the others, attributed the crisis to "the distress of our epoch, after the ravages of two wars and faced with the menace of a third. . . . [The young] are suffering from an ambient dread of war and an uncertain future." Standing in the way of the future, she continued, were the "older generations, prisoners of their interests and their prejudices, . . . [who] are ill-equipped for the needs of the time." Hence, the *mal du siècle* is, rather, "a symptom of a larger crisis of civilization . . . which corresponds to the man of the past who no longer accommodates the present."[85] Still another observer noted that "in losing the war, in botching the Liberation, we have disqualified ourselves in their eyes. The young conclude that we have not only failed in the war, but also the entire twentieth century as well."[86] Clearly, there was a worry that the past, bleeding through to the present, would jeopardize and infect the future, that the snare of adult failings would entangle and threaten the young. The very concept of *mal du siècle* carries with it, in effect, the condemnation of the past and, likewise, a reproach for those identified with it.

The young were caught between their own unknowable future and the adult generations' problematic past, as if the past and future were crushing in on the present like two opposed forces creating a tremendous amount of pressure. The young themselves recognized this. In 1954, *L'Express* sponsored a debate, called "Youth Before the Future," attended by more than two thousand students. One commented, "We have in the present day the intense and agonizing feeling of gambling our future, or more exactly and even more worrying, that our future is being gambled for us."[87] The leaders of a host of youth organizations wrote, in an open letter to Pierre Mendès-France, the premier of France who made youth a conceptual priority of his administration, that the young had "seen its future compromised each time a policy postpones until tomorrow solutions to the problems facing the nation [today]." For "renewal, and for all policies that engage the future of the country, youth should be associated," they argued, demanding not simply to be "an instrument" but a "partner in full" with "the means to make itself heard on all aspects of the nation's problems that particularly concern [the young]."[88] In fact, one legacy of Pierre Mendès-France's premiership was the creation of a High Commission for Youth Affairs, which eventually evolved into the Ministry for Youth.

Uprising Youth

If the future was increasingly conceptualized as the rightful territory of the young, it seems evident that the young would become more socially and politically viable as an age-based constituency seeking to influence and direct government policy. This was a phenomenon that crystallized in the 1950s and would continue to expand exponentially through the course of the 1960s as the young became more politically visible and vocal. In the mid-1950s, this idea was articulated most lucidly by the organization Soulèvement de la Jeunesse, or "Uprising Youth." This consciousness-raising group published a monthly periodical, a party organ of sorts, from

June 1952 until the summer of 1955, promoting youth, both as an idea and social group, as the source of modern revolution.[89]

The centerpiece of the Uprising Youth movement and the most explicit proclamation for the revolutionary potential of youth was that of avant-garde *lettriste* Isidore Isou's "Manifesto of Uprising Youth," first published in 1950, though the initial version dated from 1947.[90] In the midst of the Fourth Republic, Isou defined Uprising Youth as a rallying point for all young people dissatisfied with their present circumstances to come together as a revolutionary social body. In his manifesto, Isou pointed out that political parties dismissed youth as a temporary condition of life and thus did not truly defend the interests of the young. Moreover, the struggle between classes had resolved nothing; what was needed was a struggle based on age. Revolutions, Isou said, were made by youth and beyond any consideration of class. Hence, youth as a mass social body needed to organize and fight for its own liberation from the adult superstructure.

Isou declared youth to be a slave to social hierarchies based on age, which themselves were premised upon familial patriarchy. "[Young people] are slaves, tools, splendid objects, the property of others, regardless of class, and because they do not have free choice, the family decides for them." Adults, he claimed, "want to stay in their place, do not desire to change things, they want it all to continue. It is the masses of young people who struggle for dramatic change. Young people, who have nothing to lose, will constitute the Attack [and] the Adventure."[91] Likewise, the real economic conflict was between youth and age rather than between classes, because age controlled capital, resources, and government and thus profited by its exploitation of young people.

Isou demanded that social, institutional, and economic structures should be placed in the hands of the young, the only truly creative and innovative members of society and the only ones capable of radical change. How society could be reorganized in this way remained unclear, and the details of such a revolution remained unexplored in Isou's eight-page manifesto. He desired to reduce the number of schooling years in order to free the young for more productive tasks; he sought a reduction in tariffs and taxes; and he was against any nationalization of industry or bureaucratization of the economy. In truth, "Isouian economics" were rather bizarre, naive, and easily dismissed. In fact, Isou's influence was extremely limited and the

"Manifesto of Uprising Youth" did not generate a mass following by any stretch, but remained utterly marginal. However, Isou's ideas were credited for inspiring thousands of young people in Stockholm to destroy goods, buildings, and cars, and to insult passing adults in the winter of 1957. Apparently, by the late fifties and into the sixties, Isou had acquired a following in the major cities of the world: New York, Budapest, Sydney, London, and, of course, Paris.[92]

Yet Isou, an artist out to provoke, was not all that involved in the movement itself. Though his manifesto was the centerpiece of the first issue of the newspaper *Soulèvement de la Jeunesse* (1952), he remained absent as the director or voice of the group. Instead, a twenty-two-year-old woman, Yolande du Luart, was the founder, director, and editor-in-chief. In her first editorial, "I Hate Youth," du Luart proclaimed, "All that represents youth today disgusts me." This was so, she continued, because everything "youth"—Catholic youth, Communist youth, Scouting youth—was produced within a paradigm established by, and for the benefit of, age.[93] The newspaper's first issue chronicled a series of excerpts, culled from Parisian dailies, demonstrating how the representation of young people and youth penetrated modern consciousness for symbolic explanatory purposes. Whether to show the brutality or the generosity of adults, the young, in all of the examples, were the device that reflected meaning and value back to the adult.[94] Likewise, there was a photo spread of interwar youth movements—Fascist, Nazi, Communist—showing how adults manipulated and mobilized youth for their own political purposes. The paper lamented that these young people "were never conscious of their strength," yet were "the driving force of the world."[95]

Amid advertisements for furriers, cars, and Cinzano, the paper maintained in repeated articles that youth was the only viable revolutionary force. While the paper also maintained an arts and culture page, as well as reporting on world news, its repeated emphasis was on the bankruptcies of political and national ideologies and their inability to deliver social justice and revolution, which meant that youth should be the new ideological group that cut across geopolitical borders. Right- and left-wing young people needed to deny the traditional sociopolitical philosophies and join together, thereby constituting, through their political consciousness, an age-based ideology of youth. Uprising Youth proposed a "state of permanent destruction, that is to say, renewal." Du Luart persisted, "We will destroy their old worlds, for the accession of a new world, a new life, born of permanent revolution."[96] She placed both a rhetorical and ideological emphasis on youth as progress, as renewal, as the ideal agent of change: "Once in power, youth will impose its TASTE FOR THE NEW to lead to PROGRESS." This was, according to her, an apparent benefit of constant renewal and permanent revolution;[97] hence, "youth is the only guarantee of a new world."[98]

Yet, Uprising Youth recognized a fundamental problem. Youth, as such, did not yet exist. Youth as a mass revolutionary force, it maintained, can only come about through mass consciousness. A photograph of a group of young people, each sitting alone, lost in thought while reading near the Medici fountain in the Luxembourg gardens, made the point well. The caption read: "Youth does not exist. Only young people exist."[99] Youth as a social group, as a concept, did not exist among young people until they themselves became conscious of inhabiting such an idea. Young people, in this sense, were not a revolutionary force; only the collectivity of youth was. Thus, the paper and the organization saw its primary duty as one of consciousness-raising. They urged young people to think of themselves as a social class of youth, cognizant of its rights and duties, and to make social and political demands based upon this collectivity. Youth needed to become aware of its possibilities, they said. And "these possibilities cannot be found in the past, in history. Youth is totally in the present and future. Its role is to seek the new, in all domains and all moments, because only the new informs the future." But sadly, youth itself "is currently only a possibility, it does not yet exist."[100]

Significantly, being a part of youth did not correspond to a strict categorization "relative to age but to new thought compared to old thought." Thus, youth was "all individuals without distinction of age who walk in step with the revolutionist idea." Becoming a part of youth was a state of mind. Youth corresponded to an idea, a worldview, not an age. Youth was the "dynamic mass of *becoming*," whereas the elders made up "the static mass who impose *being*." Becoming youth was an intellectual embrace of radical change as opposed to the maintenance of the status quo. According to Uprising Youth, being a part of youth did not necessarily require one to be young, but it helped. The young were predisposed to becoming youth in a way that the old were not, simply because the young were more open to the possibility of such consciousness.[101]

The influence of Uprising Youth is difficult to measure.[102] They distributed their papers at universities and factories and held weekly meetings that peaked with a couple thousand members. They sought to implement a plan of action for organizing syndicates around a central board, with action committees for young workers, university students, *lycée* students, and so on, but that never amounted to much of anything. They attracted the attention and support of Jean Cocteau, who wrote an op-ed piece for *Soulèvement de la Jeunesse* in 1952. Interestingly, Yolande du Luart was even profiled in *Elle* magazine as a young, up-and-coming, career-oriented woman seeking political change.[103] Thus, Uprising Youth's activities did garner attention from some in France, and even inspired a scathing feature editorial in *Arts*.

Jacques Perret's "Le Syndicat des enfants terribles," a 1952 cover feature of *Arts*, was a biting condemnation of Uprising Youth, full of derisory sarcasm. Perret, a Resistance hero and successful writer, was flatly sick of all the youth worship, of the "pagan cult of youth" that predominated in postwar France, trumpeting that "Youth is sacred." What more could the young want, Perret mused, as they already have everything. He wondered "if the young in question were rising themselves against the insouciant privilege" that comes with the advantage of being young. Perret continued by arguing that if youth were to rise up and take power, then they themselves would become old in the process. By organizing as a movement and seeking power, didn't that imply that these young people abandoned youth and became adult?[104] Still, despite Perret's objections, and his clever evaluation of Uprising Youth's inherent contradictions, the premise of the organization's ideas echoed throughout France. Uprising Youth's manifesto and movement reveal the larger conceptualization of youth as a revolutionary rallying point prevalent during the Fourth Republic, and these ideas would reappear in the writings of the Situationists in the years leading to 1968.[105]

In 1954, Pierre Voldemar lamented that adult France, in fact, needed young France to become *more* radical and revolutionary, but, instead, they seemed to be too much like their elders. As he said, "To reassure ourselves we proclaim youth revolutionary, adventurous, and anti-conformist. If it were so, as it should be, it would be a healthy sign. But youth is, like us, quiet, well-behaved, and conformist, and that is a bad sign."[106] In some measure, Voldemar and adult France had been demanding for years that youth foster change and bring forth a new France. The programs and initiatives of the Fourth Republic were premised on shaping the identity of youth for just such a task, encouraging youth to think of itself as the redeemer of an older, failed France. Yet by the late 1950s the promises of radical change and reform in France that had predominated after the war remained unrealized. In the 1960s, young people began to question how much things had really changed, and what, in fact, was their future and France's.

In 1957 Roger Vadim predicted that the young were "preparing a surprise" for France. He believed that at some point in the future, youth, as a social group, would exert its inchoate power. "Either directly or inadvertently, young people have moved away from their elders," he said. "It is not a passing sullen mood, but a long voyage. It is not anger, it is not revolt, it is a sentiment of detachment, of distance, of solitude and, sometimes, of disgust—disgust against no one in particular, but against society. And this society for the moment still belongs to the elders. When the new generation comes to its social maturity, it will contain a great surprise."[107] In 1961, Senator André Maroselli stated in *Combat* that French youth would "inevitably" bring about "the revolution of the sixties."[108]

Similarly, Alfred Sauvy warned France that if it did not make way for the rising tide of youth, if it did not open economic, social, and political structures to them, the result would be youthful "political disturbances." He said, in short, that "they will explode."[109] In 1959, Sauvy, the social economist and founder of the National Institute of Demographic Studies, published the polemic *The Rise of the Young*, a synthesis of work he had been publishing since the mid-1950s, in which he investigated the socioeconomic promise of the young entering positions of political and economic power as the *jeune cadres* of the new technocracy. Issuing forth examples of France's outdated approaches to social, political, and economic problems while acknowledging the demographic realities of the postwar *bébé-boom*, Sauvy urged France to prepare the way for a rejuvenation of its institutions, and demanded that the old graciously step aside to make way for the rising tide of the young that would renew and revitalize an otherwise infirm France.[110] "If France succeeds in accommodating the young, in preparing them for life, it will benefit from the powerful effects of rejuvenation," he wrote. "The sick man of Europe will become full of health and life." Sauvy continued by saying that, "as much as the weight of the past morally burdens France and suggests countermeasures liable to aggravate the situation, the promise of the future provides a salutary response liable to alleviate it." Focusing on the future meant rejuvenating France with a youthful energy, which took government initiative: "To be young, what is it? For a person, it is chance; for a nation, it is a program. The Belle Epoque is not behind us, it lies ahead."[111]

On the heels of Sauvy, Edgar Morin, a sociologist researcher at the Centre National de la Recherche Scientifique (CNRS), wrote *The Spirit of the Time*, in which he predicted that the energy and vitality of the emerging youth culture would recast France's stodgy cultural identity, themes he had already been exploring in *Arguments*, a journal he had helped to found a few years earlier, and in his book *The Stars*, in which he wrote of young cultural heroes "bearing the new message of adolescence."[112] Youth, Morin believed, had been the force behind the expansion of postwar mass culture and would be the vanguard of an imminent cultural revolution. Throughout the 1950s there had been a "promotion of juvenility," and French society was "in the process of a *dégérontocratisation*," both of which combined to form a "broad movement." As a consequence, "this universal rising of the young" corresponded to "the universal devaluation of the old," which, he believed, would result in "the rejuvenation of society."[113] Sauvy and Morin are just the more well-known and influential of a flood of scholars whose works postulating about the coming influence of the young saturated France in the late fifties and early sixties.[114] Not all of the studies focused entirely on the future, however. For example, in 1960 the conservative historian Philippe Ariès published his landmark *Centuries of Childhood: A Social History of Family Life*, a pioneering study that made the young a focus of serious historical inquiry and provided a historical context to bolster the flourishing interest in youth and the young.[115] Whether as part of the past or as part of the future, youth became a privileged site of inquiry for France to reflect upon itself.

The conflation of youth with the future is a part of the much larger process that Pierre Nora identified as the "legitimation by the future," which replaced "legitimation by the past." Nora argues that in the mid-twentieth century, beginning with the deficiencies of the Third Republic in the 1930s, *society* began to supplant the *nation* as the conceptual framework for France. Unlike a nation, a society had to be planned and organized—hence, the mid-century rise of urban planning, social policy, and welfare systems, plus the expansion of education, health care, and employment programs. Nora proposed that the continuity and stability formerly associated with the transition from the past to the present and future was forever altered by the "acceleration of history," by the rapidity of change in the mid-twentieth century, and that this change needed to be predicted, monitored, controlled, and manipulated. French society became "fundamentally absorbed by its own transformation and renewal. By its very nature that society values the new over the old, youth over old age, the future over the past."[116] The widespread emphasis on youth as the future corresponded to the leftist humanism of the Liberation.

A utopian project reimagines and reorganizes society, socially, politically, and morally, into an idealized form. Often this is overtly expressed with a detailed proposal outlining the systems and structures of such a perfect place, but more often, perhaps, it is merely a state of mind, maybe even a habit of mind. Utopianism, then, can equally be an expression of transcendence—a hopeful conviction that things will get better, that the world must improve for its own sake; utopianism can be an optimistic attitude in addition to an itemized program. Emphasizing this conceit of utopia as a frame of mind, Albert Camus urged France at the Liberation to "choose today between either antiquated political thought or utopian thought," because "antiquated thought is killing us." In his *Combat* editorials, Camus addressed the issue of this vague and intangible optimism in France as a "relative utopia" that advocated a limited and peaceful social revolution. Because "absolute utopias in reality destroy themselves through their enormous costs . . . it will be necessary to choose a new kind of utopia—one that is more modest and less destructive."[117]

The premodern utopias of Plato and Thomas More were located spatially, some*where* else, in an ideal place; but following modern notions of time and progress, utopias were increasingly located temporally, some*time* else, in an ideal past or an ideal future. The context and experience of postwar France conceptualized the social group of youth as a revitalizing agent, as an idealized catalyst of rejuvenation, and as a conceptual representative of the future in the present. The opacity of the future meant that it represented everything unknown—both opportunity and pitfall—while the past was already determined, certain and known. Because of its possibilities, the future offered a haven, a refuge from an uncertain present and problematic past; but it was also a future that must be organized, worked for, and planned. If youth represented the hope of the future, it stood for the threat as well—hence the anxiety and concern for the young in the public consciousness. But by shaping and molding the young, many hoped France could manipulate its future through the social group of youth.

As an age category, youth is often invested with meaning by the aged. In many ways, the old envy the young—their physical strength, energetic vitality, buoyant health, sexual virility, active lifestyle, carefree indulgences: as some have put it, youth is wasted on the young. To many, a young person's life is defined more by potential than by accomplishment or failure, and, therefore, in the eyes of those older, it glows with possibility and opportunity. Likewise, the young are imagined as not entangled in society's circumstances or predicaments; they are thought to lack financial obligations, familial duties, political responsibility, and even moral accountability, all of which makes them ideally suited for risk. Therefore, being young can be imagined as the age when risk is worthwhile, the ideal moment to foster change. Youth becomes a kind of utopia for the old, who can imagine a better world but fear a loss of privilege or material plenty that might result from any attempt at it. Youth, then, as a concept, becomes more than a designation of a particular period of life, but a *value* that transcends any concrete age or individual person. Yet, also, it is a hollow value that must be filled with symbolic meaning. This was precisely what made youth such a powerful point of convergence in this period.

The impressive array of voices that articulated this project of rejuvenation emerged out of a cultural and political scene that was, in other ways, extraordinarily contentious, as the stability problems of the Fourth Republic reflect. It is astonishing to see people as different as Michel Debré, Simone de Beauvoir, Alfred Sauvy, Henri Lefebvre, Georges Hourdin, Françoise Giroud, François Mauriac, and even Douglas MacArthur, among others, speaking in similar terms about youth and its role for France. Amid these immense differences in spirit and politics, from the right wing to the left wing, from strict secularists to religious advocates, from intellectuals to technocratic public officials, some common notions of youth were nevertheless shared. Thus, this commonality is all the more remarkable if one appreciates how much these people disagreed with one another in other respects. The symbolic concept of youth condensed and unified a rich diversity of meanings because it could be used by different people in different ways. The ambiguous value of youth, that it had no single precise meaning, allowed it to be used by a broad diversity of people. As a cultural and political symbol, it allowed postwar France to build solidarity without requiring consensus.[118] Invoking the concept of youth masked the complexities and discordances of the Liberation and postwar period, and thus helped enable the reconstruction and modernization of France.

The physical destruction, political collapse, military defeat, economic depression, and moral compromise of the war meant that France had to be remade. The Liberation provided the opportunity for France to start anew. Although the desired political reforms remained unfulfilled by the Fourth Republic's coalition gridlock, the larger project of material reconstruction was a success. The Monnet plan modernized the infrastructure and economy as the Ministry of Reconstruction and Town Planning built a new France. More than a million youth made substantial contributions to these tasks as laborers rebuilding the nation through the national and international networks of youth groups and service organizations. But more importantly, as the postwar period progressed, a consensus built that identified the young as France's future, and that served as the philosophical underpinning of the reconstruction's motivating spirit. By thinking in terms of youthfulness, France gave itself a cognitive framework within which to renew and rebuild, to imagine a future of promise, a transcendent vision of a better France that would surpass its past and present. French society's postwar preoccupation with the idea of youth anticipates and prepares the way for the demographic dominance of the young as a social group in the 1960s. This revitalizationist discourse was itself futuristic, not only because it posited youth as the future but because it planned youth to be the future. Thus, the discursive process itself was both preparatory and anticipatory in nature. The rhetoric of rejuvenation emerged as a fundamental social narrative of the postwar years that reified the category of youth in the public consciousness and undergirded the cultural reconstruction of France.

CHAPTER 2

Managing a Modernized France

In the early 1960s Harvard economist Charles P. Kindleberger sought to explain the booming postwar economy of France. He came to the "frustrating" conclusion that "the basic change in the French economy is one of people and attitudes." He attributed the fundamental change in the growth of the economy to personnel and perspective, to "new men and new attitudes," and thus to the underlying social and cultural conditions that had embraced the future and the possibility for change that were the preconditions of substantive growth. Certainly, capital investment and the modernization of infrastructure were essential components undergirding this success, but for Kindleberger, the magnitude of growth was due to a fundamental attitude of rejuvenation.[1] The transformation of France was not merely due to the advancement or adoption of technologies, but to a profound effort to reshape and update the social and cultural dynamics inherent to France's economic system while attending to an urgent desire to maintain or restore a particular sense of "Frenchness."

Amidst the Fourth Republic's founding and the emergence of the Tripartite coalition between the Communists, Socialists, and MRP Christian Democrats, the colossal task of reconstruction was typified by an uncharacteristic cooperation between the traditional economic adversaries of labor and management.[2] In the fall of 1944, upon his return to France from Moscow, where he had awaited the war's end, Maurice Thorez, head of the French Communist Party, announced that his party and the labor unions they controlled would cooperate fully in the reconstruction of France. Thorez famously proclaimed that it was time to "roll up our sleeves," because the "reconstruction is the battle of the future." The Communist Party managed to prevent strikes in those first years, despite worsening conditions for labor and continued economic hardship. In 1947, however, Communist support for a series of massive labor strikes broke the uneasy political coalition of Tripartism and resulted in the expulsion of Communist Party members from cabinet positions. In three short years the noble spirit of political cooperation was beginning to unravel, though the strikes of 1947 did not stop the ongoing economic recovery and reconstruction of France, nor did they impede a general consensus across party lines that regarded increasing productivity as essential to France's economic well-being. At Liberation, there was a widespread embrace across the political spectrum of the notion that increasing material prosperity could and must simultaneously transform and sustain France in the postwar world. The challenge was to undertake such an endeavor without sacrificing Frenchness by becoming too overtly consumerist (American) or productivist (Soviet).

Even before France was liberated, the need for a systematic plan of economic recovery was foreseen. Planning and managing economic modernization coincided with and was a part of the "planning consensus" that typified France's proactive approach toward organizing its future.[3] The 1930s had been marked by a penchant for technocratic proposals for coordinating and directing economic activity that were offered as countermeasures to the ongoing economic depression. One advocate of prewar *planisme*, Jean Monnet, had spent most of the war in the United States, where he observed the American wartime economic mobilization firsthand. Approved as the head of the Commisariat Général du Plan in January 1946, Monnet set out not only to revitalize the French economy but to modernize it as well. He wanted to utilize the latest technologies, machinery, materials, and managerial techniques. The Monnet Plan was one of the great successes of the post-war period and set in motion the French economic miracle that has become known as *les trente glorieuses*, the thirty glorious years that lasted until the oil crisis of the 1970s.[4]

To avoid political squabbles, Monnet steered clear of ministerial super-vision and hierarchy, relying instead on his charm and ability for personal persuasion to garner cooperation from government agencies, business lead-ers, and labor unions. Although a number of industries had been nation-alized at the time of the Liberation—insurance, banking, gas, electricity, coal—Monnet did not seek to impose a command economy in which the state dictated economic production. Rather, he sought a close partnership between the state and industry to establish and implement goals, and he stressed voluntary cooperation of business and labor to avoid bottlenecks and coordinate sustained growth. His approach, in other words, was more managerial than commanding. The first plan (1947–53) emphasized heavy industry, energy production, and infrastructure. The second plan (1954–57) focused on housing and regional development. Monnet's team served as ideal intermediaries or technocrats whose expertise and personal rapport managed the bureaucracy of reconstruction. With Monnet's plan already in place outlining the necessities of economic recovery, France was able to take full advantage of American financial assistance as announced by U.S. secre-tary of state George Marshall in June of 1947.[5] As a result of the postwar transformation during the first half of the "thirty glorious years," the Fourth Republic was thrust into the top tier of world economies.

Following the class conflicts of the Depression and the war, postwar mod-ernization in France emphasized an embrace of capitalist social practices of consumption and a broadening of the middle class to incorporate the two politically dangerous classes, the militant working class and the reaction-ary lower middle class.[6] The interests of capitalist modernization worked together with the bourgeoisification of France in order to provide both the personnel and customers for this new economy. The young played a key role in this transformation. First, they labored for the reconstruction itself, in the fields, factories, and households of France. Significantly, this labor was mobilized and conceptualized within the terms of civil service and duty to the national community rather than to a class or social group. Second, the young were the target of a series of measures, however unsuccessful, to update education along lines of specialized knowledge combined with technical and managerial expertise. These two factors laid the groundwork for the emergence of a new social type, the *jeune cadre*, a manager who stood at the intersection of the ideals of capitalist consolidation and class leveling and the discourse of youth and rejuvenation. In a significant way, the young were conceived as the cohorts of French attempts at modernization, with each intended to mature in tandem.

The Service of Reconstruction Work

The physical task of rebuilding was given to the new Ministry of Reconstruction and Town Planning. Although the war had only been fought in France for a few weeks in May–June 1940 and the last half of 1944, with aerial bombardments in between, the material destruction wrought by Second World War combat was double that of the First World War, which had been fought on French territory for four years. The ruin of the First World War had been confined to fourteen departments along the Belgian and German borders, whereas in World War II nearly all of France became a battlefield, with massive Allied invasions sweeping across France from the north and south in the summer and fall of 1944, affecting seventy-two departments. Undoubtedly, the stalemate of the Great War had utterly devastated the landscape of northeastern France; the inability for either side to force a substantial breakthrough meant that the same villages, the same roads, bridges, and railways, the same forests and farms, were repeatedly pounded with artillery, carved with trenches, and littered with mines. World War II, however, was a war of movement, where destruction followed in the wake of battling armies. In 1918 there were 927,000 destroyed buildings in France, in 1945, 1,804,000; in 1918, there were 5,000 kilometers of ruined railways, in 1945, 18,000.[7]

The foundation for the postwar reconstruction, to rebuild and restore French cities damaged by the German invasion and Allied bombardments, was laid by the Vichy regime. It has even been argued that the reconstruction period actually began in 1940 and that the success of Fourth Republic endeavors owed much to the groundwork put in place by Vichy, though this continuity was strictly denied at the time. Essential laws were codified and promulgated during Vichy, central-planning bureaucracies were established, and key administrative personnel were trained and put in place, ready to take on the awesome task of the Monnet Plan's modernization of the material infrastructure, as well as the institutional enterprises of state and economy.[8]

This postwar renewal and capitalist modernization operated within the discourse and mentality of rejuvenation. Raoul Dautry, the Minister of Reconstruction, wrote in a 1946 brochure titled "The French Reconstruction" that the nation preferred "the construction of a new France to the repair of an old France."[9] The war's material destruction, following on the economic difficulties of the Depression, presented postwar France with an opportunity: since infrastructure, industry, and housing must be rebuilt, why not utilize the most modern materials and techniques to develop a new and improved France? However, the reconstruction of the workplace also entailed a reconstruction of work itself, as the old habits of labor had to give way to the new, modern ones.

During the reconstruction, even before the war was over, various youth movements took advantage of their national networks and existing organizational structures to mobilize the young, both rhetorically and tangibly, morally and materially, to participate in the immense task of reconstruction. The young would not only participate in the physical labor of reconstruction, but their vital, buoyant energy and unwavering idealism would also serve as the motivating impetus for French renewal. As those who would reap the benefits of an improved France, the young provided a lucid meaning, through their discernible presence, to the reconstruction. Their participation was conceived as beneficial not only to France but also to themselves, as the chore of reconstruction taught lessons of sacrifice, commitment, responsibility, diligence, cooperation, and patriotism, which, in turn, would doubly benefit France with a reinvigorated citizenry cognizant of its civic duties.

In its first issue after the Liberation, *Coeurs Vaillants*—a popular comic book that featured "Tintin" among its serials[10]—portrayed a boy with a broken arm nobly refusing treatment in order to direct rescue workers through his ruined quarter.[11] Throughout 1946, this serial encouraged its young readers, many of them members of the Coeurs Vaillants (boys) and Ames Vaillantes (girls) clubs, to carry forward into all the homes of France "the great lesson of courage For the Reconstruction of Our Dear Country," a bold imprimatur that appeared on the cover of each issue. On the afternoon of Thursday, May 2, 1946, *Coeurs Vaillants* sponsored massive assemblies across France to rally the young for the country's reconstruction. This publication and its associated clubs had strong ties to the Catholic Church, and all of these rallies bore a prominent Christian overtone.[12] In Paris, at the Parc des Princes stadium, sixty thousand young people gathered to cheer and participate in the spectacle: choral groups, dance troupes, cyclists, gymnasts, athletes, and others paraded and performed before flags and banners declaring that the new France would be built on the solid rock of Christian charity and sacrifice. As an immense tricolor waved in the wind and the "Marseillaise" anthem resounded off the stadium walls, the main program portrayed the triumphant liberation of France, the boundaries of which had been traced in a white hexagon on the playing field. Boys and girls then built a foundation of stone in the field's center, where a giant cross was erected as the guiding icon for the construction of the "New City." Before this cross, sixty thousand young people "affirmed their will to follow Christ in order to reconstruct the country solidly on the rock of Christianity." As a concluding note, and echoing the regeneration rhetoric of the previous fifty years, Cardinal Suhard delivered a rousing speech and declared that the young, through their fierce faith, would not only rebuild France but "resuscitate the hearts of their elders," and "united, make a more wonderful France."[13]

The inspirational character of this rally, if not the sacred pageantry, was typical of the language that was used to encourage the participation of the young. A new France was not only to be built *for* the young, but *by* the young as well. As Raymond Millet said of youth's responsibility for this *plan de l'esprit*: "Their mission amidst the ruin is to remake the world, establish a new scale of values, and regain harmony. This formidable task is also the most appealing that they can choose because the very function of youth is to create."[14] As youth programs sprang up to work for the reconstruction of France, the rhetoric of renewal permeated their programmatic statements and declarations. Some groups were local, others national; some were associated with larger organizations, others remained independent.[15] In public proclamations, founding statutes, and recruiting propaganda, these groups avowed their dedication to remake France, not only through reconstruction efforts but also through the commitment to create better citizens in service to their society. These groups claimed that they were formed to "help build a better future,"[16] to "coordinate and organize the social tasks demanded of the young,"[17] and to "promote a new youthful politics based on social justice" by "instructing and molding the young for civil life."[18] Participating in the reconstruction would educate the young "in the strict civil sense of the rights and duties of the citizen," give them "a sense of responsibility, a notion of freely consented discipline," and make them "more capable of understanding the laws that govern and more apt to participate in this government."[19] Thus, the process of reconstruction should "accomplish a human education for young workers that prepared them for all their civil tasks," a kind of technical humanism.[20] Another group claimed that, "It is not enough to build a new country, it is necessary to make new men for this transformation to be real. . . . The young should be these new men who will tomorrow put themselves in the service of the country—physically strong, fully developed, conscious of their rights and duties as citizens and workers, ready to assume the responsibilities of daily public life. . . . We will be united to build the France of tomorrow."[21]

Despite the vast number of groups and the political or religious nature of some of them, there was a lack of the competition or rivalry one might expect to emerge from groups of such conflicting political dispositions. Indeed, this effort to play down ideological or ecumenical differences typified the major political parties of Tripartism as well; the Communists refrained from talk of revolution and the MRP Catholic party avoided outward signs of religiosity. Likewise, the various youth service groups professed a common desire for a benevolent cooperative spirit. In their charters and statutes, many expressly stated that all faiths and political dispositions would be welcome, even though the groups themselves were sponsored by larger organizations of very definite political and/or religious beliefs. For example, the Catholic group Equipes d'Entr'Aide Ouvrière actually forbade "all discussion of a political or religious character" as a measure to maintain cooperative harmony.[22] Most groups encouraged their members to participate in as many reconstruction programs as they were able. This uncommon spirit of cooperation was produced partly by the euphoria of liberation, partly by the necessity of a national crisis, and partly by the prevalence of former Resistance groups among these youth organizations and the participation of young resistors themselves. Thus, the young were expected to put aside their social, political, or class interests, and to labor for the reconstruction through a variety of groups and organizations.[23]

The largest and most effective of these groups, and one within which the others participated, was Service Civique de la Jeunesse, which was "born of the common will of the young to maintain a dedication to the moral and material recovery of the country," and thus was "a direct emanation of the Resistance and the spirit of unity that characterized it."[24] But this organization also had a direct connection to Vichy because it had benefited from the liquidation of the Equipes Nationales, a Vichy program, first voluntary but then compulsory, set up for those from age fourteen to twenty-five to assist in rescue operations following Allied bombardments, as well as to help coordinate efforts to feed and house refugees or to serve as messengers and guides for essential services. Rather than entirely dissolve the valuable Equipes Nationales at Liberation, the provisional government integrated it into the new Service Civique de la Jeunesse, which benefited from the administrative structure, equipment, and vast membership already in place.[25] This underlying association with Vichy no doubt contributed to the movement's grand statements of dedication to de Gaulle, the provisional government, and the Resistance, and to the assertion that Marshal Pétain was "national traitor no. 1."[26]

Vichy had a number of service organizations intended to mobilize male youth, such as the Chantiers de la Jeunesse, which established training and work camps for young conscripts; the Compagnons de France, intended to be a service and cultural activity movement; and the Equipes Nationales, the emergency response group mentioned above. Yet these organizations had very limited appeal and success, in part because the German occupiers frowned upon any effort to organize and train young men into units capable of responsive action.[27] Still, there were some successes. The most famous effort followed the bombardment of Boulogne-Billancourt, an industrial area near Paris, on April 4, 1943. In the immediate aftermath, several hundred members from the Equipes Nationales reported for duty, organized, and put themselves at the disposition of the local government, serving a critical purpose. Over the next few days, thousands more responded to help clear debris, run canteens and reception centers, deliver messages, safeguard material goods, and aid the wounded.[28] Thus, these groups helped provide an experienced organizational infrastructure for the postwar coordination of the young, though there was more owed in this regard to the Resistance than Vichy.

In the fall of 1944, the Forces Unies de la Jeunesse Patriotique (FUJP), a national umbrella organization made up of the varied youth movements that worked in the Resistance, established Service Civique de la Jeunesse as its service group to work for the task of reconstruction. Thus, not only did Service Civique benefit from having the ex-members and administrative apparatus of the Equipes Nationales, but it also had a vast national network of Resistance activists from which to recruit.[29] By the fall of 1945, Service Civique had a membership of roughly 100,000, a number that reached 250,000 during the campaign to assist returning prisoners and deportees. According to government reports, an estimated 1,000,000 young French participated in the reception and support services for "DPs," or displaced persons.[30] Service Civique worked on numerous projects in the summer of 1945: in Ain participants collected merchandise and foodstuffs to prepare meals for displaced persons; in Melun and Saint-Nazaire they repaired buildings destined to become community centers for the young; in Carcassone they built a footbridge; in the Ardennes forest they cleared fire-damaged woodland; in Bouches-du-Rhône they repaired a bombarded school for girls; in Isigny they built new sidewalks; in Outreau they laid new water pipe; in Saint-Etienne they distributed coal to the elderly; in Bordeaux they set up a day care center for children; and in Paris alone they tallied 36,000 hours of labor each month.[31] Within the general tasks of the reconstruction, the particular work of the young was typified by service to community welfare.

In addition to Service Civique, two other large and effective groups, both affiliated with the Catholic Church, organized young people for reconstruction and recovery projects. The first was Equipes d'Entr'Aide Sociale (EES), created by the members of Mouvements de Jeunesse Catholiques, an umbrella organization for the various Catholic student groups across France. This group primarily attracted bourgeois students, some of whom had participated in a related Vichy program called Jeunesse Secours, which was created for those who had refused to participate in the Equipes Nationales. The second group was Equipes d'Entr'Aide Ouvrière (EEO), created at Liberation as the civil-service wing of the Jeunesse Ouvrière Chrétienne (JOC), a very large and influential Catholic youth movement for workers.[32]

Government reports indicate that the Equipes d'Entr'Aide Ouvrière was considered, "in all objectivity the most effective civil service organization" for the young. For example, in the winter of 1944–45 participants raised fifteen million francs in cash and forty-eight tons of supplies in Normandy alone.[33] Although it was organized by a Catholic group, the EEO was open to all young workers, male and female, between fourteen and twenty-five years of age, regardless of political, religious, or philosophical persuasion. In just over a year after its founding, the EEO had a task force of 150,000. Each team (*équipe*) consisted of either ten boys or ten girls, headed by a team leader, who was in turn coordinated by an adult "general" for various work projects.[34] In Maison Blanche, EEO teams removed seventy mines without incident from roads and railways during the last weeks of the war; in Arnouville they repaired a fallen bridge for the passage of American troops; during the siege of Marseilles they supplied the city with bread and potable water; in Lille they cleared away rubble and debris, set up an information center, and looked after displaced children; in Ales they collected coal, foodstuffs, and clothing for the elderly; in the region of Paris they collected six hundred tons of material for redistribution to the needy; and in Arras, they organized a Christmas celebration for prisoners, deportees, and refugees, in which they distributed five hundred packages.[35]

All three of these main groups—Service Civique, EES, and EEO—had a mixed membership of both boys and girls. The participation of young women and girls was categorized as "social service," as opposed to "civil service." Significantly, their work was characterized by help for the families of casualties or deportees, childcare, voluntary hospital work, visits to wounded soldiers, preparation of meals, and administrative assistance. It is difficult, however, to distinguish the extent of female participation because the categories of "youth" and "young" always seem to have assumed a universal male. Usually the participation of young women is specifically noted only for particular "female" activities, such as baking cakes for refugees each Sunday in Bourg, or taking care of children in Bordeaux.[36] Moreover, girls collected foodstuffs and supplies, sent packages and letters to soldiers and prisoners, and made visits to hospitals—fourteen thousand young women from Equipes d'Entr'Aide Sociale visited eighteen thousand patients in 1944. The government encouraged young women's activities to be of a "familial and domestic order."[37] It believed that it was not "desirable" to encourage young women to participate in the "work" of reconstruction, and that young women should instead "respond to one of the very great needs of the country, that of the family." This work would have the double benefit of not only aiding those in need, but it would also prepare girls for future motherhood and familial duties.[38] Still, since the bulk of services provided by the young, both male and female, was characterized as satisfying immediate social needs—such as collections, receptions, visitations, and supply distribution—the distinction between the activities of boys and girls seems to have been more of an imposed interpretation of gender roles than a stark contrast in actual achievement. In 1945, for example, the Union des Jeunes Filles Patriotes (the female division of the FUJP) had eighty thousand members working within the Service Civique reconstruction network. The young women, like the young men, were responding to the very real needs, regardless of their "social" or "civic" nature, of a country suffering from the hardships of war.

Despite the official nature of these efforts, the widespread participation of the young in private programs and the thousands of hours dedicated to reconstruction projects troubled some authorities, who voiced concerns about the possible deleterious effect these activities might have on the young. Only a few days after the announcement of the new coordinating committee in March 1945, de Gaulle issued a memorandum to his ministerial cabinet outlining his concerns: "It is indispensable not to lose sight that at their age, young boys and young girls should devote themselves first to their education. Useful service to the country is only one element of this education and it should not have a harmful effect on the aggregate harmony of the whole."[39] The expectation was that the reconstruction activity itself should have an educational value that supplemented the work. The predominant activity of these groups had been amassing supplies, clearing away rubble and debris, and running errands or delivering messages, and it was unreasonable to expect the young to contribute substantially to vast construction projects that required skilled labor. Although the young had had tremendous success collecting foodstuffs, coal, potable water, clothing, wood, medicine, milk, grain, money, and the like, the only obvious lesson garnered through these activities was that of sacrifice and community service, which, while viewed as valuable, was considered insufficient for the full development of future French citizens. The Ministry of Education was charged with the task of developing a government program that would utilize the young in the reconstruction of the nation as well as teach fundamental technical skills, promote physical fitness, and build moral character.[40]

In May 1946 the Director of Youth Movements and Popular Education announced a voluntary work program for the young in conjunction with the Ministries of Work, National Education, and Reconstruction and Town Planning, as well as with the cooperation of the General Confederation of Labor, the largest labor union, and the national organization of youth movements.[41] Aide des Jeunes à la Reconstruction (AJAR) was designed as a summer program, aimed at male students and unemployed workers between the ages of seventeen and twenty-five, who would work on projects that would benefit the reconstruction of the nation as well as the physical and moral well-being and technical abilities of the organization's young volunteers. Fourteen projects were set up for the summer of 1946 in the wooded hills of eastern France, where the young would have ample opportunity to engage in organized leisure activities such as hiking or mountaineering outside the work of building simple chalet retreats and other prefabricated housing five days a week, eight hours a day. In addition to having a project director, initial plans called for a director for physical education and one for cultural activities, as well as technical advisors to direct the construction projects. It was hoped that through these coordinated activities the AJAR would build not only housing but the intellect, body, character, and vocation of modern young men.[42]

The project quickly ran into difficulties that first summer, however. The design of the program was top-heavy in administrative positions as well as the number of adult leaders required for each work site. AJAR had difficulty filling the initial staff positions and was forced to eliminate or merge the tasks assigned to each.[43] Furthermore, the response of student volunteers, as opposed to conscripts in the case of Vichy's Chantiers de la Jeunesse, was rather meager, and the departures of those who did register were often delayed, which consequently resulted in many cancellations because of the time limits inherent to a student's summer break.[44] As a result of these start-up difficulties, AJAR was quickly modified from being a summer program designed for students to a year-round trade program for the young unemployed from working-class backgrounds.[45] Thus, initially intended to give bourgeois students—the future managers—hands-on experience with manual labor, AJAR essentially evolved into an apprenticeship program for working-class youth.

By March 1948 the program's results remained unimpressive. A report concluded that the contribution to the physical task of reconstruction was "negligible." Though simple in design, most of the projects were poorly executed and came in grossly over budget compared to the costs required to hire qualified professionals for the same tasks. The return for the 300 million francs invested was considered "disastrous." Furthermore, the project did not have the desired results of professional technical training for either bourgeois youth to become better managers or for working-class youth to become better tradesmen; most of those doing the work were either the staff members themselves or young workers who arrived already skilled. The number of young who participated did not total more than a few thousand. The mismanagement, high cost, and failures of the project led an investigating committee to conclude that AJAR had become "more of a burden than a help." The large amounts of money siphoned away from other projects to fund AJAR led others to quip that the "Aide des Jeunes à la Reconstruction is less the help of the young to the reconstruction, than it is the help of the reconstruction to the young!"[46] The report recommended the cancellation of the AJAR project, and the Minister of Finance seconded the idea. Over the course of 1948, the AJAR program was dissolved.[47] This failure was in fact typical of efforts by the Fourth Republic to provide a comprehensive technical education to the young.

Regardless of AJAR's failure, the contrived social revolution that it and the other, more successful programs typified was a distinct element of the postwar reconstruction, in which the young would revive France through their committed and diligent service work to the nation and society. This, of course, smacks of a distinct continuity, both rhetorically and institutionally, with Vichy's rhetoric of national renewal and its short-lived programs, such as the Chantiers de la Jeunesse. This sort of right-wing, even anti-democratic, revitalizationist rhetoric extended back into the interwar period among, in particular, the Catholic intellectuals of the journals *Plans*, *Esprit*, and *Ordre Nouveau*, who championed a "third way," to be led by "new men" and "young Europe" for a "spiritual" and political revitalization of a "New France," as a counterpoint to socialist or liberal democracy.[48] Notably, the stress by postwar state planners, politicians, and interest groups on patriotic civic service and moral duty articulated a nostalgic traditionalism in rapport with a technocratic modernity that itself emphasized advanced techniques of management and industry. At the intersection of these socioeconomic discourses was the social group and cultural category of youth.

This work of reconstruction amid the heady optimism of the Liberation defined the work of youth as service to the nation. Youth service developed in the context of a larger cooperation between government, industry, and labor that typified the years immediately after the war. That dynamic changed dramatically over the course of 1947 and 1948, a turning point in the history of the Fourth Republic. Internationally, the advent of the Cold War was well outside French control, but it exerted a tremendous pressure on the Tripartist government nevertheless. Domestically, though workers in France had been laboring under poor social conditions of scarcity, rationing, a thriving black market, a freeze on wages, and spiraling inflation, they did so without disruption or protest. But that changed in the spring of 1947, when the Paris press went on strike, as did workers at Renault. May Day saw huge demonstrations and housewives instigated bread riots. The strikes spread swiftly and industrial unrest affected the metallurgy and transport industries and the public sector throughout the year. A strike by miners in the fall of 1948 turned severely violent. This worker unrest was more massive and pervasive than any during the Depression, and would be the largest ever in France until 1968. The end result was the collapse of Tripartism when Communists were, to their surprise, expelled from the ministerial cabinet in May. After a year of struggles, exhausted and demoralized, the trade union movement splintered because the strikes had achieved so little.

The cooperative ethos of the Liberation dissipated as conflict emerged among parties motivated by self-interest or self-preservation, however interpreted. Yet the notion of youth as a social group in service to their society rather than their class remained, and was even heightened precisely because of these renewed tensions. A wide diversity of folks in France wanted to see the young in this manner and used the idea of youth itself as the intermediary concept to manage this process. In this way, the young, particularly, became conceptualized as the agents of socioeconomic transformation, working for the welfare of France, ensuring its future prosperity, and, hopefully, simultaneously assuaging class conflict. Subsequently, a conceptualization of work as service typified the role of the young in France's economic transformation and structured the debates about educational reform, which were themselves intended to produce a technocratic and modernized pedagogy.

Modernizing the Education of Work

In 1946 Jean-Pierre Guinot published a history of work training and education in modern France to urge the Fourth Republic to get more involved in
the training of its workforce. Guinot wanted the state, in conjunction with
management and labor, to determine the needs and direction of technical
and worker education for the social and economic benefit of France. Guinot
proposed that technical education, in which a series of exercises introduced
children to skilled manual labor, should be a significant part of the curriculum of the primary schools. After age thirteen, those not going on to *lycée*
would pass through a series of workshops before settling on a particular
technical education for three to four more years.[49]

There were others, notably Georges Friedmann, who simultaneously insisted on the importance of adopting Taylorist and Fordist ideas, yet warned
against becoming too technical. In a series of books, Friedmann argued for
a humanistic approach to technological and industrial education, pointing
out that because technology developed so rapidly, it was important to have
a labor force that could adapt appropriately through a "plasticity" of skills.
He advocated against a slippery slope toward technocracy, while simultaneously embracing modernization. Friedmann wanted a particularly French-
styled, holistic "technical humanism" to dominate the creation of modern
producers and consumers, because "the technological, the physiological, the
psychological, and the social are inseparable." Emphasizing the larger societal repercussions, Friedmann wrote that "such a training implies a new,
complete conception of education in which, in addition to the old 'humanities,' a humanism will be expressed that reconciles culture and work." That
is, France should use education and the young to modernize economically
and industrially, but within a distinctly French cultural paradigm.[50]

Within the Liberation's consensus and centralized planning between labor, industry, and government, the need for a vital skilled-labor pool was essential to France's reconstruction and modernization. In 1946, 67 percent of
the male workforce had had no training whatsoever.[51] The Monnet Plan itself emphasized the need for an up-to-date and well-trained workforce. Better initial training and retraining of labor, as well as technical and scientific
research, was an essential element to the transformation and specialization
of industrial firms. The enterprises of the state and the economy were to be

transformed as well, through the use of specialized experts, technocrats who relied on rationality to optimize efficiency. Thus, the structural bureaucracy of institutions was to be reconstructed as well.[52] All of this required a more technically trained workforce, both managers and laborers. Despite these imperatives to reconfigure an outdated, or as some would say "backward," educational system, the Fourth Republic was unable to take significant steps in this direction. By 1944, the long conflict between proponents of clerical and lay education had largely subsided. The new tension concerned the demands of putting the educational system at the service of a modern industrial economy while also expanding adequately to incorporate the massive influx of new students without jeopardizing the construction of a distinctly French sociocultural identity.

Technical and vocational education in France did, in fact, fit oddly into the hierarchical educational system. During the Third Republic, parallel systems of technical schools, one developed by the Ministry of Education, the other by the Ministry of Industry and Commerce, typified vocational education. Yet this rivalry between government functionaries in commerce and education left a large majority of young French workers without any training at all. There were significant reform efforts in the interwar period, particularly by Jean Zay, but both the technical division, under the tutelage of the Ministry of Commerce, and the teachers of the national educational system resisted Zay's reforms.[53] The need to update education was clear to many, but the problem was what form that should take.

Even before the war had ended, the provisional government established a new ministerial commission to reform and modernize the entire educational system, not merely its technical aspects. The desired new system was intended to be holistic in its pedagogy and inclusive in its student body. The state empowered the commission to conduct a broad, long-term investigation by setting up subcommittees, seeking depositions, and accumulating data and documentation. With the leftist physicist Paul Langevin as the appointed chairman, the commission was comprised of twenty members from various branches and levels of the educational system, as well as from a variety of social classes and political dispositions. The Langevin Commission worked for three years, issuing its final report and recommendations in June 1947.

As early as 1944, Paul Langevin testified for the need to create a more egalitarian and democratically structured system that would emphasize scientific and technical expertise while building fundamental civic virtues for the state.[54] Langevin had been active in promoting interwar educational reform and was quite taken with the Soviet model, a posture that became problematic once the Cold War began. The Langevin Commission rejected the traditional rigid hierarchy of French education, with its bourgeois exclusivity and emphasis on an arcane curriculum based on classical humanism. It wanted to make education democratic, scientific, and appropriate to the needs of a modernizing society. The goal was "educational equality for all children, regardless of their social or ethnic origin, in order to permit each child, in the interest of all, fully to develop his personality with no other limitation than that of his aptitudes."[55] Philosophically, the Langevin Commission sought a social leveling through national education; it viewed the current system, where wealth and position accorded different opportunities, as unjust. In this way, the commission's work resonated with the principles of the National Resistance Charter and the welfare aspirations of the Tripartist government.[56]

With an emphasis on social justice, democracy, and national modernization, the language of the report resonated with the humanistic optimism of the Liberation. However, the Langevin Commission's final report, known as the Langevin-Wallon Plan, suffered from poor timing. The report was issued in June 1947 with the tacit support of the Communist Party, just as the Ramadier administration had succeeded in pushing the Communists out of the government. With Tripartism in the midst of collapse, the Fourth Republic coalition splintering, the Cold War emerging, and a series of massive strikes undermining the recovery, governmental support for such egalitarian measures simply evaporated and the educational system continued to flounder, unreformed. The Langevin-Wallon Plan was not so much defeated as ignored.

Meanwhile, the ongoing economic modernization of France, along with the demographic push of new births, stimulated demand for education, as the collective needs of society intersected with the ambitions of individuals and families. In the 1950s, the growth in the school-age population would crush the unreformed educational system. In fact, the number of students in secondary education doubled between 1948 and 1958, with no significant change in facilities or curriculum.[57] A secondary system, with a classical humanities curriculum designed for the elite, was woefully inadequate to manage the influx of the masses. The technical schools and apprenticeship centers limped along, neglected, despite pressure from industry and families to improve. The force of mass demand began to democratize education in the face of governmental inability to respond.

A series of bills in the 1950s, more or less based on various aspects of the Langevin-Wallon recommendations, failed to pass. Jean Berthouin, who served as the Education Minister under Pierre Mendès-France, produced a bill in 1955 that repackaged the Langevin-Wallon recommendation for a meritocratic educational hierarchy of a "streaming" middle school. Berthouin's approach was much milder and more palatable than the overt aspirations of social engineering proposed by Langevin-Wallon. Yet Berthouin's plan was unable to navigate through the gridlocked parliamentary government and would not be implemented until Charles de Gaulle decreed it as law at the emergence of the Fifth Republic. Thus, it was not until 1960 that the French educational system was at last overhauled, though by standards established during the Fourth Republic, which had been unable to push through significant reform despite dire need. The political will was simply not there, a fact that stands as one of the more glaring failures of Fourth Republic intransigence.[58]

With the 1960 "Berthouin" reforms, technical education was at last fully integrated into the general educational system. During the Fourth Republic, progress in technical education had been slow and insufficient, but significant nevertheless. Degree exams were standardized, vocational advisory boards were established, and teacher training was improved.[59] In 1946 three technical *baccalauréat* degrees were created to meet the demand for technicians. Yet out of 40,000 *baccalauréats* awarded in 1955, only 1,600 were in technical fields. Thus, there remained a lack of *baccalauréat* diplomas among technicians and skilled labor, as well as insufficient numbers of both groups overall. Still, the number of students in technical and vocational education in 1956 was four times what it had been in 1939. Technical education expanded considerably in the 1950s, when 1,000,000 young people earned degrees from apprenticeship centers, compared to only 168,000 in the 1930s. In the 1950s, about a third of technical students were girls, studying 56 specialties, most in clothing and textiles, but also secretarial, home economics, and medico-social work. Boys, meanwhile, studied 133 specialties, the majority of which were industrial.[60]

Notably, some pedagogues thought young women should be trained and given a métier as well. It was not enough simply for young men to work for the future of France; young women ought to be appropriately educated in technical expertise as well.[61] After all, in the postwar period, approximately 2.5 million women had already joined the workforce. But other observers feared that educating young women would lead to the disappearance of the *jeune fille*.[62] By educating young women and raising their expectations, they might become sophisticated and ambitious, or "*jeune filles arrivistes*."[63] In the midst of the education reform debates, Paul Crouzet, an inspector general of education, weighed in with a polemic arguing that by educating young women, France risked losing its *jeune filles*. "It is a mistake," he wrote, "to provide a general masculine education for women." Crouzet wanted to prevent the masculinization of girls by emphasizing sexual difference in education. Women were naturally different, he said. If France educated young women like young men, it would result in a "new slavery." For Crouzet, offering technical degrees in domestic science was a way to offer progress to young women and to France while also confirming the societal role of women in terms of gender differences.[64] This sort of attitude characterized the evolution of *travailleuse familiale* (family worker) programs, which typified gendered notions of work, service, and education for young women.

Family Workers and Fairy Homemakers

A new program emerged immediately after World War II that hoped to manage the difficulties of domestic life for housewives, at the same time that it trained young women in modern domestic science. It sought, somewhat contradictorily, to modernize French households within a very traditional familial framework. Yet this example shows one of the central tensions in France's postwar "modernization," specifically that of a nostalgic traditionalism in concert with a technocratic modernity.

Conceived in the context of the postwar reconstruction, and conceptualized as a form of civil service for young women to contribute to the nation's rejuvenation, the *travailleuse familiale* programs prepared young women to serve temporarily as household domestics for families in need. In 1946, Monsieur Reverdy, the Director of Social Affairs for the Prefecture of the

Seine, issued a call to arms to the mothers of France: "Ladies, you have given your sons for the country's liberation! Give your daughters for its recovery!" Though there were already 2,500 young family workers in the Paris region, Reverdy went further in his suggestion that this work constituted an equivalent to young men's military service by proposing the conscription of young women to meet the national demand for this unique form of civil service.[65] Similarly, in 1945, Alfred Sauvy and Michel Debré advocated an obligatory national service of one year for all girls between the ages of eighteen and twenty—an initiative that was troublingly reminiscent of Nazi programs. This tour of duty for young women would parallel military service for young men, with at least three months of instruction preceding the young women's placement in positions of maternal and familial assistance. After completing their year of service, all young women would then remain "reservists," ready to respond to national or regional calamities or to disasters such as war. In this way, Sauvy and Debré imagined young women working toward the recovery of France by augmenting and utilizing their unique and specific role as women trained in modern techniques of domesticity.[66]

Though this proposed mandatory conscription was never fully considered by the Fourth Republic, the Family Worker program was conceived as a kind of national service for young women to work toward France's recovery and modernization. The vice-president of the group Assistance to Mothers described this work as essential to the "familial renewal" of France in all "moral and social" aspects of the "familial community."[67] Recruiting information declared that to be a family worker was to "fulfill your work as a woman. . . . It is to take part, as much as possible, in the grand life of the Nation."[68] Interestingly, young women were to work toward France's reconstruction through their spousal and maternal duties in the domestic household, yet, ironically, they would do so without actually being wives or mothers.

Addressing the housewives of France, in 1946 the women's magazine *Marie France* described the program as part of the mutual aid social services of the Ministry of Public Health "to shape and direct these young women who put themselves at your disposition to facilitate your noble and difficult task." The article's intent was to inform French women of the viability of the family worker program, as well as to direct needy families on how to take advantage of this opportunity. Mothers applied for aid through private assistance organizations, which compiled data on "the family, its morality, [and] its sanitary state," and assigned a young worker for a variable duration according to each case. This aid was temporary and renewable, but rarely permanent. Of undeniable utility, this assistance was intended as a "reprieve, following which the family should have a new self-sufficiency."[69]

A 1946 recruitment campaign indicated that the potential family worker must be at least eighteen years of age and in perfect health. Though certain elementary knowledge of home economics was indispensable, each family worker was trained in cooking, cleaning, laundering, childcare, first aid, domestic economy, and hygiene, which was followed by a supervised internship of three months. Most importantly, the qualified auxiliary would present certain moral qualities, such as honesty, discretion, common sense, and devotion. It was necessary that she be neat and exacting. Paid by the organization, she earned an hourly wage of eighteen francs and worked forty hours a week. In addition, she received travel and housing costs and all the advantages reserved to workers: social insurance, family allocations, paid leave.[70] The young auxiliaries were expected to work eight-hour days, with Sundays and holidays off. The task of the family worker was to ensure the health of the family and the salubrity of the household while the mother was incapacitated due to pregnancy, childbirth, illness, accident, hospitalization, or the like. The young women's presence was a temporary measure designed to help mothers and families get through the difficulties, hardships, and scarcities of the postwar period.

The family worker program had its origins in a private philanthropic organization, Aide aux Mères (Assistance to Mothers), which had been founded in Paris in 1920 for young women to help take care of the children of mothers in need. That program soon spread to other cities, and in 1927 a national federation was established. In the pronatalist context of the interwar period, a key element of this assistance program was to encourage large families and a high overall birthrate. Later, in 1942, Le Service Familial de Jeunes Filles was created in Lyon. The purpose of this private organization was to assist mothers who found themselves alone due to the circumstances of the Occupation. Furthermore, Le Service Familial was created with the added aim of allowing young women to avoid forced work in Germany; Vichy considered their familial work as comparable to such service in Germany, while at the same time valuing the program's instructive component as integral to its own domestic National Revolution. There were numerous similar programs across France, sponsored by various private philanthropic groups of ecumenical, social, and political origin. By 1947 there were seven family assistance groups, by 1950 the number had increased to two hundred, and by 1965 there were thirteen hundred groups operating within various networks.[71]

The Second World War marked a real shift in the rationale for such programs, however. No longer simply intended as maternal assistance, they now stressed the educative development of young women as a valuable and desirable component. "In helping the mother of the family in her heavy task," one recruitment article noted, "you pursue your own apprenticeship."[72] Indeed, the *travailleuse familiale* program was promoted not only as an ideal way to train young women to be better mothers in the future, by learning to sew baby bibs (see Figure 4), for example, but as an experience that would generate a desire to become mothers within the girls who participated.[73]

Figure 4. Center for Maternal Auxiliaries, 1945. Agence Roger-Viollet.

"What luck" one worker declared, "that our trade permits us to live fully as women," all the while developing a specialized knowledge and managerial expertise.[74]

The Fourth Republic took an official interest in these various private initiatives, and by the end of 1947 began the process of making it a national program.[75] Initially, the young women were considered volunteers, but when the state social security system began to finance their services, in late 1947, it became possible to remunerate them as professional agents of the state. Since the war, they had been known as family volunteers, family auxiliaries, family assistants, or rural family assistants, but in 1949 the state formally classified them as "family workers," *travailleuses familiales*. By 1947, approximately 1.5 million families had already been assisted through the various private organizations that sponsored family workers throughout France. Government coordination and financial support were seen as a means of expanding the program. Young women would now be trained in the most modern methods of housekeeping and child-rearing, and they would, in turn, carry their expertise and efficiency into the more unrefined households of France.[76]

After 1949, the government oversaw and regulated the standards for certification of the women involved. The Ministry of Public Health and Population approved and monitored training facilities, established standards, created certification exams, and otherwise administered the professionalization of the family workers. It instituted a Certificat de Travailleuse Familiale, which required a minimum of seven months of technical training (which soon thereafter was raised to twelve months), and included coursework at an accredited center, a series of short internships, and the successful completion of a professional aptitude test that had written, oral, and practical components.[77] In 1950, examinations were administered in fourteen locations around France, as well as in Tunis. Of the 423 women who sat for the exam, 372 passed. In 1951, the examinations were administered in thirty locations to 1,174 applicants, of whom 1,094 passed.[78]

While the young family worker brought to the mother a precious and valuable assistance in meeting the material needs of the household, she was also there to manage and instruct the inexperienced mother, to whom "she dispense[d] enlightened counsel."[79] Many mothers and housewives, it was claimed, had a rather "limited knowledge in household matters" and did "not see the need to acquire new ones. These mothers learn by the example of the *jeune fille* in seeing the facility and rapidity with which she executes her work."[80] Thus, the public discourse of industrial productivism entered the private sphere. These young family workers were conceived as agents of modernization bringing domestic science and home-economic ingenuity into coarse households, thereby elevating the overall national standard of household technique, in terms of hygiene, efficiency, and expertise. Rather than mere apprentices, the family workers were auxiliary consultants advising on the benefits of modern household management. In fact, "the judicious coordination of various daily tasks" was considered "the art of family assistance." The lessons of Taylorism were not only applied to the household, they were also introduced into those households with the least amount of access to such advances of technique. The program as a whole intentionally targeted specific social groups, mainly lower-middle-class, working-class, and rural households.

Importantly, the family worker program was not available to women who already had domestic help, nor was it meant to relieve the difficulties of women engaged in wage work.[81] Specifically, the family worker program was designed to assist women who could not afford help yet remained committed to the ideal of being full-time mothers and housewives. Thus, the program was meant to encourage lower-middle-class and working-class households, as well as rural households, to seek the bourgeois ideal of patriarchal domesticity not only materially and practically, but morally and culturally as well. The family worker played "an important moral role inside the home where her unpretentiousness, good humor, and method should develop an ambiance of order and calm favorable to the harmony of the couple and education of the children."[82] While it was acknowledged that the family worker must above all establish and maintain the assigned family's trust, the worker also bore a responsibility to report problems to social services, thereby, in a small capacity, aiding the state's surveillance of its citizens.[83]

Furthermore, there is strong evidence that controlling and shaping domestic consumption was a critical component of managing this transformation while also preserving French distinctiveness. In the Moselle, for example, one of the primary tasks of the family worker was to inculcate among rural working-class and immigrant women an awareness of the proper, or "French," utilization of the domestic skills and products of the emerging consumer society. While one of the critical tasks of the home worker was to mediate the construction of a new, classless society by stressing uniform standards of cleanliness, hygiene, and so on, she was also charged with instilling a sense of thrift and compromise among rural and working-class populations during a moment of shortages and hardship. Just as important was her role in reproducing Frenchness, through such seemingly banal practices as choosing suitable color schemes and dinner menus, directing the proper decoration and utilization of domestic space, and overseeing the cultural education of children by influencing reading habits and the like. Thus, the family workers were intended to transform these households through the techniques of modern domestic science, but in a manner that reflected and bolstered French taste, custom, and national identity in a specifically bourgeois fashion.[84]

Notably, the government took an active interest in the family worker program immediately following the widespread strikes initiated across France by the General Confederation of Labor and other leftist unions in 1947. Working-class women participated in these strikes in large numbers, protesting low wages, food shortages, and high prices; most conspicuously, a September demonstration of women in Le Mans turned into a riot.[85] Immediately following the ouster of the Communists from Tripartism, the Fourth Republic embarked on its sponsorship of the family worker program, one goal of which seemed to be to make working-class and rural households more middle-class and thus less prone to political extremism. The postwar period in general was marked by an elevation of the middle-class domestic ideal and a fear of the adverse impact working women might have on the French family. In 1946, the government began paying allowances through the Caisses d'Allocation Familiale (CAF), the primary institution of the French welfare state, to families with more than one child, with additional allowances for each additional child. Moreover, there were special allowances designed for non-working mothers, grant programs for the costs of school and transportation, even tax reductions proportionate to the number of children.[86] This is in part a lasting remnant of state pronatalism, yet in the midst of what was the postwar baby boom, it also stands out as an intentional program of bourgeoisification. Much of the focus of this energy fell particularly on young women who were being trained to be technocratic domestic engineers within an emerging consumer culture.[87]

In a 1948 keynote address entitled "Domestic Science Education as Social Service," a Madame Morin recounted the terrible state of French households, one result of the disruption and privation of war, the breakup of families, and the growing problem of working women. She advocated the promotion of housework as a *métier*, as a profession requiring education, training, and competency. Neither the school nor the family was doing enough to develop the domestic potential of young women, and France as a whole suffered because of this. Teaching domestic science was a social service of the first degree, Morin proclaimed, and should be a priority of the state and society. She asserted that perhaps in the case of the thirty-five-year-old woman, the moment was lost. Thus, it was upon the *jeune fille*, the eighteen-year-old woman, that France should focus its energies, to elevate the quality of familial life and, in turn, France generally.[88] This sort of attitude had been typical throughout the Third Republic as well, when domestic science education was seen as a way to instill republican ideals of bourgeois thrift and orderliness as a measure to draw women away from their attachment to the church. Furthermore, standardizing domestic education had been a way to bring the far reaches of France into the fold—a sort of housewives-into-Frenchwomen effort to consolidate national identity.[89] In the postwar period, young women, as students and as family workers, became the agents of this consolidation across France.

During the Liberation period, domestic science education expanded rapidly. Textbooks went through multiple editions, emphasizing that housework should be based on observation and analysis, on the rational organization of work with an emphasis on order: order in things, order in time, order in tasks, order in budgets. Effort, time, and space were to be managed with the utmost efficiency. This embrace of technocratic Taylorism dated to the interwar period, when the appearance of Paulette Bernège's *De la méthode ménagère* (1928) influenced millions of French housewives to apply these techniques to their households.[90] In the postwar years, the number of schools and students grew remarkably, as domestic science education was increasingly viewed as a necessity for the ongoing national rejuvenation, a priority for society as a whole rather than simply for individual households.[91] An official diploma for domestic science, the Certificat d'Aptitudes Ménagères, was introduced, and schools were founded in the provinces for the specific purpose of bringing modern household management to the rural outreaches. In particular, CAF administrators hoped that the lessons learned by the peasant daughters would influence the household practices of the peasant mothers and thus modernize the French countryside from the inside out.[92] Notably, this "modernization" of the provinces implied a bourgeois homogenization that standardized the domestic cultures of households, in terms of practice and consumption, that were deemed both "modern" and particularly "French."

A national competition for outstanding domestic science students was initiated as a joint project by CAF and the Ministries of Education and Public Health. These ministries sought to promote domestic science education as an integral element of postwar social welfare because the "material and moral life of the home" is essential to progress, as is the "good apprenticeship of the *jeune fille* to her future role as mistress of the house." It was clear that the housewife was viewed as a critical agent in the process of national modernization. Schools nominated their best students over sixteen years of age for eighteen regional competitions held across France in December 1948. In all, 1,557 students participated, with 125 finalists converging on Paris in March 1949, almost all of whom were between the ages of seventeen and twenty. The competition included four practical tests in cooking, sewing, ironing, and darning, and oral examinations that covered topics of domestic economy, nutrition, familial hygiene, morality, and child rearing. The juries were comprised equally of domestic science professors and CAF representatives. The final competition, in Paris, was a featured attraction of the annual Salon des Arts Ménagers, with gleaming appliances as the coveted top prizes. The national winner had a choice of a shiny new gas or electric range.[93]

The Salon des Arts Ménagers began in 1923 as a competition among companies producing household equipment to promote new industrial products. Each year, well over a hundred thousand visitors flocked to the Grand Palais to see the latest household gadgets. Over time, the salon evolved into more of an exposition of consumer durables, as the technological prizes grew less and less significant, though prizes for housekeeping began to appear. Although the salon was interrupted for nearly a decade by the war, when it reemerged in the late 1940s it initiated this new contest as a competition among the young technicians rather than the technologies.[94] This significant shift in emphasis reflects the postwar preoccupation with technocracy as well as youth, and the expansion of domestic science education for young women particularly.

The press baptized the inaugural 1949 winner, seventeen-year-old Denise Chicault from Dijon, as *la fée du logis*, "the fairy homemaker," a phrase that continues as slang for the perfect housewife, though *Le Figaro* initially pushed for the sobriquet "queen of the mayonnaise." The press coverage was extensive, with many newspapers proclaiming the contest to be the high point of the exposition overall. In fact, the *fée du logis* competition became the centerpiece of the reinvigorated salon, which had one and a half million visitors by 1955. Denise Chicault became an overnight celebrity of sorts: her photograph graced the front pages of several newspapers as she knelt before her grand prize range with a baby doll in hand (see Figure 5). The articles speculated on her prospects for marriage by championing her ability to prepare a perfect roast, iron creaseless shirts, and nurture a healthy baby in a spotless apartment.[95]

In 1952, a magazine article caught up with the top three finishers from the inaugural 1949 competition. Denise Chicault was, ironically, still single, but pursuing a career as a professor of domestic science in Dijon. Louise Debains, the runner-up, had become a *travailleuse familiale* in Paris and

Figure 5. Denise Chicault, the inaugural Fairy Homemaker, 1949.
L'Aube, March 15, 1949.

gushed about bringing her expertise into the homes of the less fortunate. Finally, the third-place winner, Odile Gueguen, was now Madame Bernard and living in Nantes. She was a mother and housewife, with an eight-month-old boy and a husband who extolled the benefits of being married to one so skilled in modern household technique.[96] These three trajectories—home economics teacher, social worker, and housewife—exemplified the varied social roles for young women sanctioned by the postwar project of technocratic domesticity in the context of national rejuvenation.[97]

For the professional family workers, the process of specialization was ongoing. During the 1950s they were trained in new techniques and kept up-to-date through a trimesterial journal that informed them of the latest advances and technologies in household management that they could then pass on to their assigned families. Covering everything from the useful advances in plastics to new theories of developmental psychology, synthetic textiles to technologically savvy sewing machines, this trade journal focused on and promoted the modernization of the working-class household. Significantly, its offerings were intended for an audience that had few resources. While the journal did feature new consumer durables, its emphasis on practicality and creative thriftiness was a sharp contrast to the gleaming modern kitchens advertised in the mainstream women's magazines targeting the middle class.[98]

Overall, the family worker program was increasingly professionalized over the course of the 1950s, until it was no longer dominated by, nor specifically designed for, young women. Not only did those who were initially recruited continue to work as they aged, but even those applying for licenses were no longer necessarily young.[99] In fact, in 1955 the minimum age requirement itself was raised from eighteen to twenty-one, the voting age, and consequently there was a steep applicant drop-off in 1956. Over the next couple of years, there was an ongoing debate over the utility of the minimum age requirement, but in 1958 the Ministry officially refused to lower the requirement and it remained at twenty-one. By the end of the Fourth Republic, the family worker program was considered a success, with local and national organizations seeking more funding to expand their operations.[100] However, the program, as initially conceived, was a victim of this success. As the war, Liberation, and the reconstruction period receded, so did the conceptualization of the family worker program as national civil service. It was no longer meant as a temporary apprenticeship for young women, both to serve their country and learn the skills of motherhood, but was undergoing a broad professionalization as a social service that would lead, in 1974, to the recognition of *travailleuses familiales* as career social workers, though the importance of their work as "modernizers" did not necessarily diminish as a result.[101]

Moreover, in the 1960s, young girls were brought from the colonies to work as family workers in France. They were trained and credentialed and allowed to immigrate to France for work. This not only reflects the shift of population flows in the postcolonial metropole, but also indicates that the family worker was no longer meant to serve as an example of the ideal young French woman edifying the underclasses.[102] In fact, the program had earlier been extended into Algeria, with the express intent of facilitating colonization in the midst of the escalating war there. André Dulac, of the military government in power, repeatedly wrote to France seeking to develop the family worker program in Algeria as a "very effective" means of establishing solidarity across cultures, ideally by introducing family workers of "European origin" into Muslim households. However, this civil service was not meant exclusively for white Europeans; young Algerian women were also to be trained in the practicalities of domestic science, which corresponded to attempts in the metropole to train Algerian women in how to be French. There was already a private system in place in Algeria, set up in 1955 according to the Fourth Republic's 1949 criteria, through which family workers had served in hundreds of homes, mostly those of the working-class *colons* but also in the occasional Muslim household. Dulac sought official government confirmation and endorsement of the program to fund the expansion of this policy of household colonization. He believed that the program would not only "favor the evolution and improvement of the condition of young Muslim women," but also help "to penetrate the closed family milieu" of Algeria, which would "adroitly contribute to the success of the social policy pursued by the government." Government approval was finally secured in the spring of 1959, but the program collapsed soon after, along with French authority there.[103]

The young family workers and fairy homemakers of the Fourth Republic show that the emphasis on domesticity was not only a new concentration on the political economy of the household or the colonization of the household and housewife in the midst of decolonization.[104] Indeed, in the postwar period, hygiene and cleanliness were metaphors of the need to come clean, the need for moral clarity after the dirty war. The emphasis on youth and the young was yet another mechanism in this desire for a recaptured inno- cence and moral purity. Thus, youth, by the fact of being young, lacked the stains of the past war and served as the ideal intermediary of this phenom- enon. Moreover, the cultural emphasis on consumption and cleanliness op- erated in tandem with the domestic ideal of womanhood, but there was also a significant effort to extend middle-class norms as prototypically French by using young women particularly as catalysts of a managerial and tech- nocratic modernization. Indeed, the family workers were at times referred to as *cadres* or as trained domestic technicians serving the larger national project of rejuvenation that characterized the cultural reconstruction. In some ways, the *travailleuses familiales* were the female equivalent of the *jeunes cadres*, the vanguard of the new young managerial technocracy championed as the harbingers of a modernized France, who would administer its future. Yet, unlike the male *jeunes cadres*, there was no upward mobility for these young women, no opportunity to access power in the technocratic state; instead, though they were efficiency experts, they remained relegated to the household, even if it was not their own.[105]

The Emergence of the Jeune Cadre

The rise of the *jeune cadre*, the managerial technician midway between owner and worker, as a socioeconomic figure has been proposed as an al- legory for postwar French modernization overall.[106] Others referred to the pioneering technocrat modernizing France in the postwar period as simply the "new man," the "engineer-economist," or the "philosopher of the new."[107] With a Fordist worldview that emphasized technological inno- vation, long-term planning, mass production, and mass consumption, the *jeunes cadres* stood at the center of the predominant discourse of youth and the future converging with a new economy based on consumption and ac- cumulation. The *jeune cadre* represented the young male managerial class emerging during the "technopolitical regimes" of the Fourth and Fifth Re- publics (Figure 6).[108]

Figure 6. The savvy and confident student as *jeune cadre*. Agence Rapho-Top, Boubat.

The term *cadre* emerged in the 1930s to describe managerial positions that could not otherwise be precisely defined within the industrial hierarchy because those who held these positions were neither workers nor owners. It was not until the postwar period, however, that this new social group consolidated and, moreover, that *jeune* became integral to the conceptualization of this new social type. The *jeune cadre* emerged as a social force just as education became standardized and democratized to make way for a new educated public that some hoped would be dominated by technocratic humanism. The *jeune cadre* came to predominance in the late fifties and early sixties, as the successful transformation of a modernized (some would say Americanized) postwar France was confirmed.[109]

The authority of the *jeune cadre*, or technocrat, was based on knowledge and expertise as opposed to ownership. The problem facing France was not improving its technology, but managing it. Thus, education and training took on significant import. It was the human relationships and the coordination of labor within a modernized, technical economy that needed invigoration. The *jeunes cadres* were the budding careerists of the postwar corporate economy. By 1960, roughly 150 institutions specialized in the training of cadres, with tens of thousands participating annually in seminars, night classes, and on-the-job training.[110] Even adults underwent apprenticeship to become retrained in new methods, to update their expertise, and to become "new men."

Young technocrats began to be championed as the means to achieve the social justice and utopian future that the era of Liberation had failed to produce. A 1957 brochure from Electricité de France's Chinon nuclear facility concluded that "it is up to the young generations, to the future engineers, technicians and scientists, to build a new civilization: it is their luminary value, their desire for peace and social progress, on which the future of the world depends."[111] Later, in *A Plea for the Future*, Louis Armand and Michel Drancourt wrote that France needed to place its hopes on youth to reign in a new era of technocracy. France, they wrote, was changing regardless, but it was important to manage and control that change through a technocratic youth. Thus, preparing for the future meant preparing for technocracy, which meant preparing the young to be future technocrats.[112]

The discursive tone promoting the *jeunes cadres* varied from sacred morality to militaristic triumph to epistemological metaphysics, a language that no doubt derived from interwar prescriptions for national rejuvenation among Catholic intellectuals and the nonconformists.[113] A 1957 feature on a school for electricians at Gurcy-Le-Chatal in northern France described the technocratic education there as one that developed moral value and gave the young a sense of their larger responsibilities, of their duty to serve the public, and even of their contribution "to the well-being and development of their country." More than that, their education and future work were sacred; their school was "a temple of faith in youth and the future of the country," with "its faithful, its priests, its initiates," as well as "its visitors and converts."[114] This religious rhetoric contrasts with the militaristic language used immediately after the war in pushing for technical education for the future economic prosperity as well as the political independence of France. In 1946, the journal *Technique, Arts, Science* wrote that these new cadres would be the "soldiers, lieutenants, and officers in the Grand Army of Work" fighting for France's future.[115]

Intellectual advocates emphasized that France could no longer stumble blindly into the future; it came too quickly, and time was accelerating. France must do more than the planning of Monnet and must adopt a "prospective attitude," a systemic approach to managing the long-term future. A journal was founded to promote "prospective" thinking and action. The men of action necessary for this work, according to the prospective thinkers, must be young, if not in age, at least in spirit. An essential element of a "prospective attitude" was youthful thinking. To imagine and plumb the depths of the future, and thus plan for it, one must think through the prism of youth, because "we do not live in an old fatigued world that has already produced its most precious fruits, but rather in a world that never ceases to rejuvenate because its own renewal . . . offers more and more possibilities and its shape is each day more surprising."[116] Thus, for the prospective thinkers, "the future is already available in the present [and] this present is the future in formation."[117] This type of thinking was meant to incorporate all of social, political, and cultural life, not simply that related to industry and the economy. The technologist must be trained to think holistically. The best place to begin, the prospective thinkers argued, was with the young.[118]

The state itself had founded the Ecole Nationale d'Administration (ENA) in 1945 as a *grande école* training facility designed to provide France with a youthful civil corps to manage the new government with dynamism and competence.[119] Although its first graduates would not reach significant positions until the mid-1950s, this effort of the state to create its own system of *jeunes cadres* to administer a rejuvenated France is indicative of its overall pattern of molding young people and using them as a source of renewal. Michel Debré, one of de Gaulle's chief advisors and the author of *Remaking France: The Effort of a Generation*, spearheaded the effort to establish the new school, which would give the state and the French people a sense of "assurance for the future" by training the young as effective bureaucrats to administer not only the government but private corporations and companies as well.[120]

Students began study, on average, at twenty-six years of age. They spent their first year as administrative interns either in the empire, the provinces, or embassies abroad; their second year in coursework in Paris (later moved to Strasbourg); and their third year in another internship that gave them specific expertise in a designated field.[121] This system of class work and internships offered both educational study and practical experience according to each student's identified strengths and weaknesses, so that "through [the student's] multiple experiences, he is a better man today and will be a better servant to the state tomorrow. Admittedly, we are demanding of our students an ideal servant of the state and an ideal spirit of public service."[122] Above all, the ENA sought to build civil servants of high character to "reform," "remake," and "rejuvenate" France.[123] The Third Republic and Vichy, which incidentally had initiated a similar but unsuccessful school at Uriage, were both seen as having been run by old men who had failed their country. Because the students of the ENA were in their mid-twenties, the state viewed them as young innovators capable of reconstructing the administration of France.[124]

In December 1945, the first ENA entrance competition was reserved for young veterans, resistance fighters, prisoners, deported persons, and even widows of the war. One original purpose of the ENA was to democratize access to government positions across regional, class, and gender barriers. The first few classes admitted to the new school were, in fact, rather diverse in terms of region and class, although with an extremely small percentage of women.[125] Despite the democratic and egalitarian intentions, within a decade the ENA had fallen into a pattern dominated by an inner circle of upper-middle-class Parisian males, a homogenized clique of self-interest for which it is still criticized because nearly all high-ranking public officials in France are now ENA alumni, or *énarques*.[126] These men began their careers in low-level appointments in the late 1950s and early 1960s, but by the mid-1970s they had come to dominate French politics and industry.[127]

Pierre Mendès-France criticized this growing dependence on the *énarque* elites who began to dominate the lower administrative echelons of the nascent Fifth Republic. Referring to them as *les jeunes messieurs*, Mendès-France was wary of the emerging elitism and asked for a democratization of ENA, which did not happen. Mendès-France had himself been one of the early supporters of ENA, had taught there, and was the first to make some *énarque* appointments to his administration in the mid-1950s. Renowned for his managerial style, he nonetheless believed that the ENA functionaries and technocratic bureaucracy of the Fifth Republic stifled France's democracy.[128] Indeed, situated as the middle gatekeepers, the *jeune cadres* began to shape the channels of power and influence in the public life of government and industry.

By the late 1950s, interestingly, even the large unions called for additional young technicians and an expansion in the education of these middle-management functionaries. *Le Peuple*, the organ of the General Confederation of Labor (CGT), maintained that the health of the economy and the nation required an increase in the value and number of technical cadres. The CGT wanted education as a whole expanded in these measures, calling for schools and institutes to be established, and, most importantly, asking that admission to these advanced schools be broadened to lower-class families of limited means.[129] Force Ouvrière, the CGT's rival union, which formed in 1947, also championed the cause of producing more engineers and technicians, and opening up this education to the lower orders so that broadening scientific education would work toward class leveling as well. Putting education "in harmony with industrial and economic realities" would "prove that France remains a young country."[130] It seems likely that the unions recognized the emerging power of technologists and technocrats and sought access to the emerging group of cadres in order to strengthen their position against the state and industrialists.[131] In the context of the broadening middle social stratum, the unions wanted to tap into the growing influence of this emergent social group.

Instead, though a syndicalist confederation for cadres had been founded in 1944, in 1961 some *jeunes cadres* took it upon themselves to found two new unions to work in their particular interests as young managerial technicians.[132] Perhaps this was due to the fact that generational conflicts were on the rise within this new class of workers, as documented by a 1957 sociological study.[133] Now, a consciousness based on age emerged, both among the new cadres themselves as they organized for their own self-interest, as well as in the larger public discourse of the late 1950s and early 1960s that emphasized the technocratic management of France's economic future.

Throughout the 1960s, the *jeunes cadres* became the subject of remarkable sociological inquiry and the focus of theoretical explanations of change.[134] Notably capitalizing on this, the weekly newsmagazine *L'Express*, which had proclaimed itself the "Magazine for the New Wave" in the late 1950s, rechristened itself the "Magazine for Cadres" in the early 1960s, maintaining the implied connection to the young and youth but with a shift in emphasis from sociology to economy. By the end of the Fourth Republic, the concepts of youth and cadre and technocracy had become somewhat conflated in the public mind.

Managing Youth

The emphasis on the young, the future, and rejuvenation after World War II implied an embrace not only of values associated with the concept of youth but also a profound modernization to make old France new. This project entailed a socioeconomic dimension meant to overcome the conflict of labor and industry, the rivalry of social classes, and the material rift of urban and rural life. In this way, modernization was not merely material reconstruction of a dilapidated infrastructure, but a cultural transformation of the social landscape meant to manage this transition from old and outdated to new and improved.

In the postwar period, right-wing chauvinism and revitalizationist rhetoric intersected with left-wing social engineering and central planning that together sought to "modernize" France through increasing material prosperity and economic competitiveness. Though economic productivity and material prosperity were championed for their ability to transform France, this particular "modernization" was also necessarily defined against something else, whether a lumbering, "backward" French past or a threatening, "modern" American future.[135] The concept of rejuvenation itself has the dual senses of giving new vigor as well as restoring to an original state that suggests some of these tensions. These imagined past and future Frances were invoked and used as contradistinctions. Though rejuvenation certainly suggested a break from the past, it also reflected a desire among political elites to preserve French particularism through movements, education, and work programs designed for the young and articulated within the cultural framework of youth. In this way, state planners defined a course against or between those being steered to the west and east, by embracing both consumerism and productivism in ways that emphasized a particular sense of French cultural identity that played upon nostalgic traditionalism and technocratic modernity.

As a social group, youth had been mobilized to work for the reconstruction and transformation of the greater national community of France while also serving as its underlying spirit and motivation. Like the reconstruction itself, the work of the young was idealized broadly as service to the national community rather than narrowly as the interest of an individual's career, family, class, region, or other social identity.[136] Through various service organizations, well over a million young people labored together for the reconstruction effort, cooperating effectively with one another despite the possible ecumenical, political, or social tensions that could have arisen. Together in a united effort, the work of youth was meant to stabilize antagonistic social classes.

The Liberation's emphasis on social justice and social equality had championed a democratic social leveling. Various measures to reform work and education for young people had emphasized just these sorts of values and prioritized the young as the starting point for a more just future and a modern economy by creating a scientifically trained and technologically minded youth. In some cases, such as the Langevin-Wallon Plan, political support for reforming education simply evaporated as the cooperative climate of the Liberation passed. In other cases, such as the administrative *grande école* ENA, the emphasis on education, training, and expertise actually empowered a new elite rather than rendering access to power more democratic. This was a fundamental problem for the embrace of technocracy to resolve class tensions, because technocracy is, by definition, inegalitarian and undemocratic. An elite is trained and selected through a bureaucratic process on the basis of specialized knowledge, merited or not, to create a new level or stratum of authority situated in a vertical hierarchy. Rather than youth inspiring and generating a democratic social equality, the *jeune cadre* represented the inegalitarian ambitions of new elites to situate themselves favorably within a hierarchy meant to manage those below in order to render the labor strife and class tensions less threatening.

Economically, postwar reconstruction and modernization had caused production to soar, reaching the pre-Depression levels of 1929 by 1949. From 1950 to 1958, gross national product and national income grew by 41 percent, hourly wages by 40 percent, consumption by 47 percent, exports by 44 percent, and productivity by 33 percent. Industrial production grew by 6 percent annually. French industry and economy had never experienced such rapid or sustained growth.[137] A modern industrial capitalism had returned in force, and a booming France had prospered. An ongoing cultural process drew in the petite bourgeoisie through the expansion and broadening of the middle classes as a consumer capitalist economy took hold in a modernized France poised to compete in a global economy. The modernization commissions of the Monnet Plan reconstruction underlay these significant gains, but as economist Charles Kindleberger has indicated, there was simply more to it than that.

By the 1960s the modernized socioeconomic situation in France was neither more egalitarian nor more democratic. Instead, the class conflicts of before the war had seemingly been neutralized by a bourgeoisification of France within an affirmed capitalist order and a hierarchy of prosperity. As *travailleuses familiales*, young women modernized coarse domestic households using Taylorist lessons of efficiency; as *jeunes cadres*, young men managed the Fordist technocracy of modern economic life. From the working-class household to the administrative office, the young of postwar France were conceptualized as the agents, representatives, and managers of this social modernization. Youth, like the *jeune cadre*, was the intermediary, managing social groups and diffusing the self-interest of class conflict while working and planning for a modernized France. Rather than meet the Liberation's aspirations for social leveling, the Fourth Republic accomplished a social managing that enabled the capitalist modernization. Youth, as concept and social group, functioned as a primary medium through which this modernization was articulated, implemented, and managed.

CHAPTER 3

Making the Future French Citizen

After the war, the French government in tandem with various private organizations and associations sought to educate, shape, and mold the young of France into an idealized citizenry. The thrust of this national project aimed beyond the household and the classroom and utilized popular education programs that organized and structured leisure activities. The diverse programs used art, music, sport, travel, film, outdoor excursions, recreation, physical fitness, and professional training to create firm moral character, cultural fluency, and strong bodies. Significantly, this was not simply a government policy emanating from Paris, but a broad-based grassroots initiative that flourished in the provinces as well, albeit with tacit governmental approval and support. Integrating the young into the life of the nation was a cultural project designed to unify the French polity after the divisive years of the late Third Republic and Vichy. The civic, moral, and physical development of the young was considered a means to enfranchise France's future citizens into the political, cultural, and even military life of the nascent Fourth

Republic. In essence, improving the young would in the end improve France by creating an ideal citizenry capable of active participation in a modern republic based on democratic and egalitarian ideals. Such work would figure in "the foundations of a new France."[1]

One significant result of these various programs was the differentiation of youth within the French polity as a distinct social body harboring specific needs as well as particular rights and duties. To some degree, the efforts mentioned above created an emerging consciousness among some young people that youth could be an organizing principle for political action. Cognizant of their status as a social group, many young people claimed the idea of youth as a point of mobilization to express political opinions, particularly concerning the ongoing war in Algeria. Ironically, as the Fourth Republic came to a close, thousands of young people did indeed recognize and exercise their rights and duties as young members of a democratic French society in order to protest government policy. At the Fourth Republic's outset, the young had been the object of numerous programs to ensure the postwar rejuvenation of France.

The solutions to material and physiological needs, though grave, were obvious: France needed to house, feed, and care for the young as well as the rest of its population. Given the lack of resources, precarious conditions, and grand scale, these were difficult and important matters, but ones that could be managed through organized assistance programs and material aid. More difficult and less tangible than the programs for reconstruction or the institutional reform of education was contending with the great psychological impact of the war, that is, on what impact the war and occupation had on the character and moral state of the young. There is, of course, a relationship between the technocratic management and moral citizenship of the young. As with the *jeune cadre*, the moral citizenship of postwar French youth had a class and gender dimension that, while including the lower classes and young women, prioritized middle-class males. Though modernization emphasized a technocratic, managerial youth that would advance France economically, the logic of the rejuvenation project also insisted on the particularity of a republican French citizenship.

The psychologist Jean Blanzat prepared a detailed report for the government deliberating on youth's moral state and civic spirit at the war's end. Though he simultaneously celebrated and condemned the young, his opinion was typical of the rhetorical platitudes bandied about regarding French youth. Quick to concede the variety of experiences, backgrounds, and character of the young, Blanzat nevertheless described French youth in total as "bold, generous, [and] selfless," but with "a profound egoism, great violence, [and] serious lack of discipline." The war, by its suspension of normal laws and mores, had exacerbated both sets of characteristics, resulting in the "triumph of the worst and best" in young people. On one hand, Blanzat held up the broad participation in the Maquis and the Resistance as exemplary of the "the best kinds of young people," those who could serve as "a resource of civic spirit" for other youths as well as for France more generally. Yet conversely, young people had also experienced the "failures of public morality," the dispersion of households, the absence of parental (particularly paternal) authority, the selfish profit-mongering of the black market, and the disruption of daily routines of school, work, and leisure. More problematic, the young had been the target of extensive Fascist propaganda as Vichy sought to indoctrinate them within its short-lived National Revolution. Worse still was the noxious presence and immoral influence of the German soldiers and administrators, who undermined the very Frenchness of the young (a similar though less vituperative charge would also be made against the liberating American armies). Saddest of all was the failure of adults in their moral duties, "the horror of which was spread before the eyes" of French youth. Blanzat concluded that by saving the generation that had matured during and after the war, France would save itself. The young were "pure resources," "reserves of our civic spirit," and "seeds of our union."[2]

A second government report on the problems of youth advocated increased state intervention into the lives of the young to ensure the appropriate formation of "our future citizens." The young must be adapted to the life of the nation, it said. Both the school and the family had proven insufficient in this matter, and the opportunity to acclimate the young to the national community lay within the effective use of leisure. The strident youth movements of the 1930s needed to be controlled, the political, social, and cultural divisions mended, and a democratic constituency firmly grounded within a common French culture created. "It is instructive to note that it is youth," the report proclaimed, "of all means and in all societies and most particularly in a democratic one, that can have the most fruitful effect on the future, and it is by the formation of this youth that we can have an effect perhaps more revolutionary than all political or social legislation."[3]

Past republican governments had also engaged in similar programs to expand the base of popular support, democratic participation, and patriotic citizenship. One need only recall some of the impetus behind the vast expansion of primary education in the late nineteenth century, or the use of the French military as the great "school of the nation."[4] Even the city-states of ancient Greece had an educational practice known as *paideia* that sought to mold the young man into the functional citizen.[5] The challenge to democracy by Fascism and Communism, and the hardship of the Depression followed by that of the war, guided Western Europe toward the interventionist welfare state after World War II. Though the welfare state was not a uniform institution from country to country, and not a concept unique to the postwar period, after 1945 the state in Western Europe envisioned an expanded role for itself to provide services and benefits for its citizens, notably in employment, housing, health care, education, and social work. State intervention in social welfare policy was accepted as a means to secure the well-being of citizens, foment democracy, and weaken challenges by ideologies of the far right or far left. In France, this translated into an expanded government with new ministries and departments administering the welfare and well-being of French citizens. Not surprisingly, a main thrust of many of these programs was to make a healthy, educated, moral, patriotic, and public-spirited youth that took part in the political, cultural, and social life of the nation.

Political Citizenship and Pierre Mendès-France

The Fourth Republic's constitution established a parliamentary system that made each governing administration subject to the tacit support of a powerful assembly. Due to the waxing and waning of political fortunes among the various parties, governments were cobbled together out of assembly coalitions that resulted in remarkable ministerial instability. On average, a government lasted only seven months before the premiership changed hands and the ministerial appointments were reshuffled. These inconsistencies at the top levels of government made actual policy reform difficult, and many projects would go through a series of false starts before being realized or abandoned. This was the case for a project designed to establish a Ministry for Youth after the war.

In 1945 the provisional government proposed an interministerial committee for youth to shepherd appropriate legislation through the National Assembly, as well as to coordinate policy among the varied ministries relevant to the young, such as the Ministries of Education, Public Health, Work, Agriculture, and Defense.[6] This committee was designed to serve as an "indispensable instrument for a coherent and effective policy for youth" that crossed the numerous and diverse ministerial departments. However, the proposal was quick to point out that this would not be a "super-ministry," but merely an instrument among ministries to forge cooperation and coordinate policy administration.[7] But others wanted to go further and create a new Ministry for Youth in order to give priority to the young in the renewal of France, and "to assure the physical and moral health of the young and to prepare them to take over from their elders. The only sure guarantee of the future." However, there were still others who opposed a new ministry because it smacked too much of Vichy's Secretariat, under Georges Lamirand, which sought to create a uniform Fascist youth.[8] Nevertheless, in January 1947, under Paul Ramadier's government, an autonomous ministry was created to coordinate youth affairs, sport, and the arts, under the young and energetic leadership of Pierre Bourdan. Bourdan died unexpectedly in late 1947, however, and with him died the new ministry, when Ramadier's government fell in mid-November and responsibility for youth affairs returned to the Ministry of Education under the Henri Queuille government.[9] As with the educational reforms of the Langevin-Wallon Plan, the project for a youth ministry fell to the side in the politically difficult years following 1947 and did not substantially resurface until the dynamic premiership of Pierre Mendès-France seven years later.

Pierre Mendès-France made his reputation as a politician in the early 1930s, as part of the "Young Turks," a group of youthful, left-leaning members of the Radical Party who wanted to modernize the party and reform the political procedures of the Third Republic. As he said, "All we really had in common was our youth and our more or less critical attitude to the authority of the leaders."[10] In 1938, at age twenty-five, Mendès-France became an undersecretary for the Finance Ministry, in Léon Blum's second government. At age twenty-seven, as an Assembly deputy from the Eure, Mendès-France voted against giving power to Pétain, and later became a courageous member of the Resistance. After the war, he was an instructor at the newly founded Ecole Nationale d'Administration, teaching France's future administrators about the fiscal and budgetary problems posed by the reconstruction. Mendès-France's brief tenure as premier, from June 1954 to February 1955, is today considered the most dynamic and most effective of the Fourth Republic. *Mendésisme* was an optimistic political outlook that believed the Fourth Republic was suited for renewal, capable of finding new solutions to old problems, and willing to make difficult decisions about fiscal reform, economic modernization, and the troubled empire. To govern, Mendès-France believed, was to choose. Problems must be addressed, not neglected; decisions must be made, not avoided or put off. His leadership style was managerial rather than demagogic and he embraced progressive technocratic reform in the face of an entrenched opposition, such as the forces of colonialism and the powerful wine and alcohol lobby. An integral element to this spirit of reform, as Mendès-France saw it, was the young of France, who embodied the dynamism and enthusiasm he valued.[11]

Mendès-France first attempted to establish a government in June 1953, based on his proposals to extricate France from a costly war in Indochina, to expand economic modernization, and to invest in industry and education rather than the military. He received only 301 of the 314 votes he needed, however, and he was forced to wait another year before he was able to come to power. Between his first attempt to form a government in June 1953 and his successful bid for the government in June 1954, two things had happened to swing support to Mendès-France and his policies: the first was the growing influence and circulation of *L'Express*, a weekly newsmagazine; the second was the infamous battle at Dien Bien Phu in Indochina, where the French suffered a devastating loss to the Viet Minh in May 1954.

In May 1953, two young editors, Jean-Jacques Servan-Schreiber and Françoise Giroud, founded the new weekly magazine *L'Express* for the primary purpose of promoting the ideas of Pierre Mendès-France.[12] It was *L'Express* that dubbed him PMF and referred to his government program as "Le New Deal," evoking the will to reform, bold decision making, and staying power of FDR. Mendès-France was able to use *L'Express* as a forum for his ideas, to build popular support among the young (this is the magazine that later dubbed itself the "Magazine of the New Wave"). Incorporating youth into his political constituency was one of Mendès-France's primary goals, and giving the young a voice in government was an essential priority. In fact, the general outline of his coherent short- and long-term policies for France, which would guide his administration, was published first as "A Call to Youth" in *L'Express* on May 14, 1954. He emphasized progress and modernization, creating cadres of responsible technocrats to manage a strong and dynamic France and ridding France of old problems, most notably that of Indochina. "Policy," he said, "should be made for the young. It should also, as much as possible, be made by the young, with their cooperation, their support, their demands, and their will." He spoke of "a great crusade of renewal," and of France's destiny as linked steadfastly to France's young. He urged youth to take a role in public life, because nothing "can resist the will of youth once it manifests itself."[13]

Moreover, like FDR, PMF gave a weekly radio broadcast each Saturday during his tenure in office, often with a special message addressed to the young of France. He identified the war in Indochina as especially troubling for the young, and talked about "their plans, their ambitions, their hopes," of which he "never stopped thinking." As he set off for Geneva to negotiate the terms of France's withdrawal from Indochina, he urged the young to "be ready to harness yourselves for the immense work of reconstruction awaiting us all."[14] In a treatise written a few years after his fall from power, PMF still maintained that it would be the young who would lift France because they had a civic spirit and sense of citizenship different from their elders. It was a civic spirit based on action and achievement rather than abstract patriotism. He insisted that France needed to adapt its local and national institutions to suit the young, not the old, and that this should be accomplished through technocratic planning. "In the last resort, this is what it is all about: the citizen is a man who does not leave it to others to decide his fate or that of the community as a whole." To be modern, France must embrace youth, not simply as a social group but as a state of mind.[15] To think of, for, and through the idea of youth was, for PMF, a methodology for governing. To him, democracies were at their weakest when they only considered the immediate present; by thinking in the terms of youth, one structured the present in the function of the future. Thus, the stability of the new republic, he believed, was intimately tied to the interests of youth. Pierre Mendès-France promoted youth as an ideological concept.[16]

Young activists in France responded to these appeals and demanded a greater voice in government, though PMF's larger interest among the young remains unclear.[17] Seven young leaders of national movements and organizations, representing hundreds of thousands of young people, wrote an open letter to Mendès-France and the French government in October 1954. In it, the youth leadership demanded that government consult the young of France on policy issues, and that, at last, a permanent high commission for youth affairs be established that not only coordinated programs among the relevant government ministries and departments but also incorporated representatives from the youth associations as well.[18] Fundamentally, these young leaders and representatives of youth were demanding direct access to the government and a consultative role on the policies that affected them directly: housing, education, military service, popular education, professional training, and physical education. The leaders of Uprising Youth chimed in as well; in response to the proposed Ministry of Youth, their newspaper declared that "the creation of such an institution is AN HISTORICAL NECESSITY," and a crucial step in the goal of "YOUNG PEOPLE TAKING POSSESSION OF THEIR POWERS AND THEIR RIGHTS."[19]

This expression of an invigorated civic responsibility was well received by the Mendès-France administration, which in mid-November appointed André Moynet, age thirty-three, as Minister of Youth; Moynet proclaimed, "Youth is not the age of a man, but his quality." He sought to create within each ministry a "youth commission" to function as a representative and advocate of the young. Each youth commissioner would, in turn, report to the new Ministry of Youth. In this way, the young would have a direct hand in policy and could rejuvenate a stagnant bureaucracy by spreading youthful vim and verve. "The word 'youth,'" Moynet said, "is above all, in my view, a spiritual state and a moral engagement."[20] As was typical of the Fourth Republic, however, Mendès-France fell from power just as the new ministry was being organized.

In a matter of only seven months in office, Mendès-France attacked lingering problems of France's colonial and foreign policy. He freed France from the quagmire in Indochina within thirty days, dividing the colony into the independent states of North and South Vietnam; he settled the conflict in Tunisia by granting the nationalists self-government; and he began talks for a similar future for Morocco. He did not, however, make any significant moves on Algeria, which erupted in open revolt in November 1954. Closer to home, he killed the stagnant European Defense Community measure and coordinated the rearmament of Germany under NATO's authority. Domestically, his progressive modernization to update the French economy, as well as his attack on French alcoholism, met with considerable resistance, particularly from small businessmen, artisans, peasant farmers, and the wine industry, all of which helped to give rise to Pierre Poujade, an outspoken peasant agitator critical of the state and the technocratic leadership of Mendès-France. Thus, PMF's maneuvers had alienated a significant number of powerful interest groups. Moreover, the cult of Mendès-France promoted by *L'Express* irritated other career politicians. By February 1955 there was enough opposition to vote out his government during Assembly debates on the future of North Africa because many deputies were not pleased with his rapid dissolution of imperial holdings.

Despite the fall of PMF, nonpolitical specialists such as Jean-Marie Despinette, writing in *Educateurs*, urged the government forward in its endeavor to "integrate the young and youth into the political, social, and civic realities" of France, a necessary move for the "rejuvenation of the country."[21] Some even interpreted the fall of Mendès-France as a confirmation of the rigid corps of old men unwilling to embrace rejuvenation and choosing instead to limp along in cranky agedness.[22] A poll conducted by the IFOP in 1955 showed that 54 percent of the French were in favor of creating a Ministry of Youth and 18 percent were against it.[23] It was this popular support that extended the measure beyond the government of PMF. The new government formed under Edgar Faure, did, at last, establish a permanent High Commission for Youth Affairs, though not a new ministry. The commission lasted for the duration of the Fourth Republic. In 1958, the Fifth Republic expanded the administrative and policy duties of the commission into an autonomous department under the leadership of Maurice Herzog. In 1966, the High Commission for Youth and Sports was expanded further and became the Ministry for Youth, under the leadership of François Missoffe. Thus, the Ministry for Youth was not realized until two decades after it was first proposed. Mendès-France, though he never regained office, continued to emphasize the young and the idea of youth in his political writings throughout the 1960s and 1970s.[24]

Popular Education and Democracy

Efforts to incorporate the young into the artistic and cultural life of the nation were far more successful than those designed to incorporate them within overtly political or civic institutions. For example, in 1950, the annual Salon des Jeunes Peintres, which continues today, was founded at the Galerie des Beaux-Arts for painters under thirty years of age (later pushed to thirty-five) to exhibit, reward, and encourage young artists.[25] In 1960, the Fifth Republic even sponsored an exhibit, "Paintings: Witnesses of Their Time," that celebrated youth as the very inspiration and guiding principle for the artistic enterprise: "Our young people know very well that they are the object of a cult." The catalog was dominated by figurative portraits of young women as the incarnation of spring, symbolizing the postwar rebirth of France.[26] Far more significant than these "high" artistic endeavors or representations, however, was the extensive popular education movement designed to mold and shape the young through appreciation of and participation in French culture. This postwar popular education movement, largely a private initiative, incidentally, was premised on the notion that by fashioning the young culturally, the youth of France would participate more fully and more effectively in the national community as adult citizens.

In 1944 the provisional government had created the Direction for Youth Movements and Popular Education, under the guidance of Jean Guéhenno within the Ministry of National Education (in 1948 it changed to the Direction for Youth and Sports). The mission of the office was "to sustain, encourage, coordinate, and control" the varied private youth movements and popular education programs in France. By promoting "thought, culture, and knowledge" throughout France, these movements could "at last establish an indispensable unity across the diversity of inclinations."[27] The department had six bureaus for extra- and post-curricular education, leadership training, organized leisure, cultural programs, youth movements, and personnel and equipment.[28] It promoted legislation and statutes, the expansion of municipal facilities and resources, and the approval and distribution of state subsidies for the young.

The new department had been founded immediately after the Liberation in the midst of the reconstruction. Thus, another of its tasks was to coordinate the reconstruction activities of the various youth civic service and mutual aid groups, as well as to oversee the liquidation and dissolution of collaborationist youth programs, the resources of which were turned over to programs and groups deemed favorable to the new republic.[29] Moreover, the department set up a national network of inspectors in 1946 to reinforce state control over private organizations and to ensure the appropriate moral and ideological tone of each. These inspectors reviewed account books, appraised program effectiveness, recommended financial support, evaluated receptiveness to the new republic, ensured that the vitriolic propaganda of Fascism was eliminated, and favored those programs deemed "strictly neutral."[30] Thus, the new department was not simply there to support the good work of private organizations, but also to monitor and maintain control over these organizations. This was a significant departure from the prewar era when the government did not adequately intervene to curb the activities of extremist youth movements.

There had been widespread movement in popular education since the late nineteenth century, but the French government did not become actively involved until the 1930s. This was the short-lived era of the Popular Front, which was characterized partly by a great effort at "popularization" or "democratization" of culture. The Popular Front government attempted to widen access to the arts across class barriers, endorsed and sponsored leisure activities, as well as championed the cultural practices of workers, the folk traditions of rural France, and the need to develop the young appropriately. Indeed, the Popular Front established France's first governmental department for youth, sport, popular education, and leisure, in 1936, under the guidance of the Socialist Léo Lagrange. Lagrange was interested in developing both the mind and body, and his promotion of physical fitness dominates his legacy. In fact, his department was eventually moved from the Ministry of Education to the Ministry of Public Health.[31]

After the war, popular education was imagined as an ideal mechanism of social leveling and social harmony by virtue of its ability to expose the popular classes to the fine arts, cultural traditions, and historical heritage of

France. For some, this education was a way to instill greater solidarity and understanding between classes. For others, it was a way to bring the rural outreaches into the national community. Still others saw popular education as a way to incorporate those whom the school system had failed. But above all, popular education was seen as the surest means of safeguarding democracy: by including everyone in the richness of French culture, a national community would develop that transcended class or regional differences. What was shared was seen as more important than what was different. In the wake of Fascism, popular education was perceived as a vital measure of national reconstruction.[32] In fact, the preamble to the Fourth Republic's Constitution even held a guarantee of equal access to culture for all French citizens.

It follows, then, that during the Fourth Republic, the popular education movement expanded exponentially. Among the most famous programs were Jean Vilar's Théâtre National Populaire, a professional touring company that performed classic and modern theatrical productions on farms, in factories, on sidewalks and streets, and just about anywhere they could reach a new audience, which was, often, the young, though not exclusively so.[33] In 1944 a former resistance group, the Vercors Maquis, founded Peuple et Culture in Grenoble. This group wanted to raise cultural literacy while engendering a sense of community and cultural/moral standards among ordinary people. Its most lasting success came from training *animateurs culturels* (community arts workers) who were dispersed throughout France to guide and direct local cultural activities among the popular classes.[34] Other large groups included Travail et Culture, and Travail et Tourisme, but the most successful and most widespread popular education program was the Maisons des Jeunes et de la Culture, the Youth and Culture Houses that would over time number in the thousands and touch the lives of millions of young people in France.

Cultural Citizenship and the Maisons des Jeunes et de la Culture

The culture house as a means of popular education was not a new concept. The Bolsheviks had established cultural houses in the Soviet Union soon after the revolution, and, correspondingly, the first cultural houses in France were set up by French Communists in the 1930s. At first, the newly created French Communist Party (PCF) had renounced "high" culture as bourgeois and corrupt, but the prevalent participation of artists and intellectuals in the PCF, combined with the rising challenge of a coarse and vulgar Fascism, reversed this policy and Communists began to champion the rich tradition of France's artistic past. A number of left-leaning cultural groups sprang up in the mid-1930s, including the Association des Ecrivains et Artistes Révolutionnaires (AEAR), established in 1932 to rally leftist intellectuals to the anti-Fascist cause. Notable among its members were the novelist André Gide; Jean Guéhenno, the writer and future director of the Fourth Republic's Department for Youth Movements and Popular Education; and André Malraux, the future Minister of Cultural Affairs for the Fifth Republic. In 1934 this association called for the establishment of cultural groups that would bring together workers, teachers, and intellectuals into a forum that celebrated France's rich artistic and cultural heritage. The result was the first Maisons de la Culture. The AEAR evolved into the Association des Maisons de la Culture et des Cercles Culturels (AMC), and by 1937 it claimed seventy thousand members nationwide.[35]

Following the Popular Front's demise and the subsequent defeat by the Nazis, the Vichy government of Philippe Pétain immediately closed the Communist culture houses and opened its own, with a significant shift away from workers and toward the young. Vichy's "National Revolution" placed great emphasis on the development of French youth into a unified social body that was fluent in the traditions of an agrarian, decidedly *un*-cosmopolitan and *non*-Parisian France. Vichy followed up on many of the policies of the Popular Front, but with a markedly different ideological thrust that stressed a haughty superiority of the French tradition, nation, and race. The General Secretariat for Youth was set up, under Georges Lamirand, within the Ministry of Education in September 1940. Moreover, Vichy promoted the semi-official organization Jeune France, which, under the leadership of Pierre Schaeffer and the influence of Emmanuel Mounier's Catholic *Esprit* group, was dedicated to promoting cultural activities among regional youth. Thus, the idea of culture houses was adapted to the Vichy project and specifically targeted youth, though it emphasized folk traditions as opposed to high artistic endeavor. Meanwhile, some of the country's intellectuals recognized the importance of cultural hegemony and significantly supported high culture as well.[36] A handful of cultural centers, known as Maisons Jeune France, were sponsored sporadically across the country to foster creativity, strengthen folk traditions, and provide a social and civic education that would shape the young into an idealized social group in service to the French nation. However, the leaders of Jeune France were not strictly Fascists, and as the war progressed they were troubled by the harsh policies of Pierre Laval and the mounting influence of the Nazis in France. In March 1942 Jeune France was officially dissolved by the Vichy government after a year and a half of activity. Interestingly, many of its disillusioned adult leaders and youth members would eventually find their way into the Resistance.[37]

Nevertheless, the Vichy cultural houses continued under a new national association more firmly under the thumb of Laval's government. Les Amis des Maisons des Jeunes was established in Lyon in September 1942 and dedicated to getting the young to "take root in the solid ground" of the new French state. The Vichy youth houses sought to create a "rural elite" ready to act in service to the nation. The stated goal was "to replenish the duties of man and citizen . . . to work in common, to think in common, to achieve in common, [and] to take joy in common." Notably, the Vichy youth houses were established only for boys, because the inclusion of girls would create what Vichy believed to be obvious "pedagogical" problems.[38] Girls would be a bothersome distraction for the important work of shaping boys who were conceptualized as the future civic actors. The Maisons des Jeunes sought to teach these young men that they were "of the same race" and "of the same soil," and to "respect the authority of the state," without which France would devolve into "anarchy." The individualist egoism of the Third Republic would be a part of the past. Vichy's youth houses sought to develop strong personalities "in the service of the same national ideal" within the auspices of "traditional" communities and local organizations.[39] As the war progressed, the government suggested that the houses should serve as the "local center of mobilization for all civic and social tasks," particularly in conjunction with the network of youth relief and rescue groups, the Equipes Nationales.[40] Like so much of the Vichy project, however, the culture houses, of which there were few, never really got off the ground before the exigencies of war pushed the Nazis to tighten their grip on France, undermining and diminishing Vichy's influence.

In October 1944, as the Allies were liberating France, André Philip, a former Socialist deputy and associate of the Catholic intellectual Emmanuel

Mounier, established a Maison des Jeunes et de la Culture (MJC) in Lyon. This was the first of what would become a vast network of youth clubs and cultural leisure centers throughout France that offered a range of activities such as amateur theater, fine arts classes, choral singing, and folk dancing, as well as game rooms filled with billiard, chess, and ping-pong tables. Philip transformed the skeletal remains of the Vichy association into a new organization, the République des Jeunes, founded in the fall of 1944 to spread youth culture houses across the nation. The name itself emphasized a secular and civic independence from Vichy and the desire to involve the varied totality of French youth on a democratic, egalitarian basis. By October 31, 1945, a mere year after its founding, the République des Jeunes had sixty-five youth and culture houses established or in development and eighteen others proposed across France, with the largest concentrations in the rural areas around Lyon and Toulouse and only one in Paris, on the rue Mouffetard, in the heart of the Latin Quarter.[41]

In 1947 the République des Jeunes reorganized itself and evolved into the Fédération Française des Maisons des Jeunes et de la Culture (FFMJC), with ninety houses in operation providing a "veritable public domain at the disposition of the young."[42] The federation's goals were to propagate the idea of the youth and culture houses and facilitate their activities, recruit and train the directors while aiding their work through material and technical support, prepare and secure funds for a national budget, act as a liaison with the government and other popular education organizations, and rapidly expand the number of houses nationwide.[43]

The new Maisons des Jeunes et de la Culture were open to all youth aged 14 to 25, regardless of their social or professional milieu, political or religious affiliation, or gender. It recruited its directors, who were at least twenty-five years of age and had completed military service, from those who had been active in other youth organizations and popular education. A committee made up of local community leaders managed each house and oversaw the fiscal, administrative, and maintenance needs. Each house was then represented in a general assembly of the national association and was subject to inspection by the government.[44]

Although they varied in available facilities, each MJC sought to provide space and equipment for outdoor recreation (basketball, volleyball, tennis, soccer, boules), indoor recreation (ping-pong, chess, checkers, billiards), and organized physical education (fencing, gymnastics, judo, track and field). Yet the emphasis and perceived value of the MJC program, as indicated by an editorial cartoon that appeared in *Les Nouvelles Littéraires* (Figure 7), were the spaces available for cultural pursuits, such as artistic studios (painting, woodworking, photography, drawing, pottery, reading), performance space (choral, theatrical, musical, puppetry, rhythmic and folk dance), and meeting rooms (conferences, lectures, study groups, kitchens for gastronomy). Some houses even had a restaurant, bar, lounge, library, or cinema. Hiking, cycling, camping, and skiing clubs organized outdoor excursions. Art, theater, and travel clubs would visit museums, attend performances, and tour regions.[45] Importantly, as the caption states, the houses were open to all.

At the rue Mouffetard in Paris, for example, by 1955 there were fifty-two activity groups that met on the house's five levels and provided a variety of pastimes such as language instruction, theater, puppetry, judo,

Figure 7. "A young and pleasant club: the House is open to all."
Les Nouvelles Littéraires, September 1, 1955.

photography, guitar lessons, and painting. Additionally, well-known luminaries, such as Jean-Paul Sartre, Simone de Beauvoir, and film director
Henri-Georges Clouzot, gave lectures and led thematic discussions. There
was even space provided for temporary artistic and historical exhibitions
that circulated within the nationwide network. In 1955, among the eight
exhibits traveling between some of the 153 youth and culture houses, were
programs on the frescoes of Raphael, the mosaics of Ravenne, and the life
and work of Leonardo da Vinci.[46]

The house in Vincennes provided activities for approximately 10,000
young people in its first decade of operation. By 1956, the house was drawing approximately 450 regular participants: 307 young men with an average
age of twenty-three, and 133 young women with an average age of twenty-
one. To the local community, the success of the endeavor was unquestioned,
but the facilities remained meager and the equipment modest. At the community's insistence, a large expansion project was sponsored by the City of
Vincennes and the Ministry of National Education. They built a vast new
modern youth and culture house that not only had space for cultural and leisure activities, but also athletic fields, a medical clinic, restaurant, bar, professional training center, and dormitory with one hundred beds for young,
transitory workers.[47]

By the end of 1958, the program of Maisons des Jeunes et de la Culture was an astounding success. There were 200 houses established across
France, with 100 others in development (an aggressive expansion policy
would lead to a total of nearly 1,500 by the end of the 1960s). The culture
houses had even extended into the sub-Saharan West African empire.[48]
The Belgians and Swiss were both developing their own networks based
on the French model, and UNESCO had spotlighted the program as an
outstanding example of effective cultural education for the young. In 1958
alone, the national association estimated that there were 30,377 members
(those who registered and paid nominal dues) and 23,350 regular non-
member participants, and that a grand total of 307,456 young people had
had some kind of involvement with an MJC during the previous year.[49]
On average, participating boys outnumbered girls by a ratio of 3 to 2. The
average age for both was in the early twenties. Significantly, a quarter of
all participants were over twenty-five years of age. This attests to the lack
of comparable cultural and popular education programs for adults that the

Fifth Republic's newly created Ministry of Cultural Affairs would seek to remedy in the 1960s.[50]

The MJC program also suffered from this success and rapid expansion. As a private organization, the entire enterprise was dependent financially upon community goodwill plus municipal or national subsidy. The Fourth Republic's revolving door of administrations made consistent financial support from the government a difficulty, and many of the local communities, particularly in rural areas, were themselves poor. It was very rare that equipment and facilities actually kept pace with the growing demand of users. In general, MJC directors were underpaid, undertrained, and overworked. The houses were staffed with volunteers who were too few in number and too inconsistent in skill and reliability. And yet despite these struggles, what a success it was! There was a broad consensus in France of the indisputable value and public service of the MJCs; their rapid expansion attests to this support because the initiative to establish each new house had to come from the local, grassroots level.[51]

From the outset, the new French government was quite keen on the organization. Despite the unsavory link to Vichy, the Fourth Republic was satisfied that the new organization had expunged the Vichy "goal of Fascist and totalitarian propaganda" and was instead a salutary environment for the cultural development of the young. The new youth and culture houses were not a government program, yet the Fourth Republic favorably subsidized their budgets and provided equipment and property through the liquidation of various Vichy youth groups, particularly the Chantiers de Jeunesse, which effectively turned former youth work centers into leisure and culture houses.[52] The Fourth Republic deemed these efforts to acclimate the young to French culture to be such a worthwhile cause that, beginning in 1945, the government promised to supply 75 percent of the start-up costs for each new house and 50 percent of the functional costs for the first year of a new house. This budgetary promise was reiterated throughout the Fourth Republic but rarely secured in full.

Reconstruction groups as well saw the new organization as an excellent mechanism to build rapport among French youth in a nation that had suffered from vitriolic divisiveness. The committee for the coordination of the reconstruction enthusiastically recommended that the reconstruction effort do all that it could to facilitate the expansion of the République des Jeunes

(FFMJC) and to remain in constant liaison with it as it developed and directed the young.[53] In fact, the MJCs became such a success that the Monnet Plan's second phase (1954–57) which focused on housing, included the construction of youth and culture houses within the new designs for neighborhood development. In Caen, for example, local municipalities included youth and culture centers alongside family housing in their urban planning, because the "social and cultural facilities of the country are as important for the future as are economic facilities; they are the conditions of success" and stand as "a guarantee of hope."[54]

One of the primary thrusts of the new MJCs was their nonsectarian, nonpartisan nature. Repeatedly, there was an emphasis placed on the unifying nature of the youth and culture houses. The decades preceding the war and the war itself had been characterized by strident ideological competition in France. The political divisions of the left, right, and center, and the religious divisions of lay, Catholic, and Protestant held sway over the various youth movements of the late Third Republic. Each group competed with the others to inculcate its political, religious, or social program among the young.[55] And, of course, Vichy had its own very particular vision of a nationalist and Catholic youth. But the Liberation was heralded as an era of cooperation infused with the self-sacrificing spirit of the resistance. De Gaulle himself emphasized the unity and singularity of France's resistance and recovery and, while this was not a completely valid claim, his rhetorical strategy was accepted and echoed throughout France, accentuating the cooperative tone of postwar France.

From the outset, the MJCs declared that they were "open to all youth" regardless of their "social or professional background, political or religious affiliation, and movement or group membership." However, "it is understood that young people come there as individuals and rigorously refrain from any proselytism or propaganda in favor of their movement or group." Moreover, the MJC "is not a new movement, nor a movement of movements, and it does not aspire to become one."[56] Importantly, the MJCs were a reaction against the divisiveness of recent years, and they intended for their inclusiveness to create a neutral forum for the young French of varied social, political, and religious backgrounds to interact. The MJCs identified themselves as a "public service" providing an "environment of freedom and tolerance" that allowed the personalities of the young "to flower" and "develop a consciousness of their role in the community."[57] Raymond Millet of *Le Monde* celebrated the MJCs as "a great innovation" that "breaks the barriers of prejudice and class, accepts variety, and bases this diversity of inclinations in its unity of aspirations."[58] The MJCs envisioned themselves as the sole public space outside of school where the young of France could congregate and interact as a distinct social group beyond the machinations of political or religious ideologies. And hence the young would develop a sense of community, belonging, and well-being, which in the future would translate into a more unified, tolerant, and cohesive France. Lucien Trichaud, the head of the national association of MJCs, told *Les Nouvelles Littéraires* that "little by little, the participants gain the sense of life in a community. They realize that the point of living in society is not the immediate goal of owning property or the accumulation of savings, but is, above all, the common good."[59]

Although Vichy had also envisioned its culture houses as a means of creating a unified social group, the pluralist tolerance of the MJCs was a striking contrast to Vichy's Fascist intolerance. No one was to be excluded because of his or her political association, religious belief, or class background, and no one was to be pressured to embrace a particular political, religious, or class consciousness. Rather, these varieties of milieux were included under the broad rubric of a shared French cultural heritage. Moreover, the intentional inclusion of girls, as opposed to their exclusion under Vichy, parallels the Fourth Republic's 1944 enfranchisement of women into the body politic. Even if the young of France emerged from different backgrounds and life experiences, the common denominator among them all was, and should be, a cultural Frenchness more broadly defined than under Vichy. The FFMJC believed that by reforming youth "through collective action" they would, in turn, "reform communities at their base."[60] More than simply providing distraction for the young or organizing pastimes, the MJCs envisioned their task as developing the cultural citizenship of French youth—male and female, rich and poor, urban and rural—that would surpass any differences and create, in the end, a national life that was "more happy, more noble, and more humane."[61]

In the wake of the destructive forces of Fascism and the powerful opposition of internationalist Communism, the MJCs considered themselves to be safeguarding French civilization through the preservation and popular expansion of French culture, while at the same time speeding France's recovery from World War II, because "a civilization cannot put itself together without culture." Moreover, "culture gives guidance and also inspiration; its spread assures the beauty and nobility of the civilization it engenders."[62] As a part of cultural reconstruction, the MJCs would "be the center of a new life" at a time when "our civilization trembles on its base." They sought to create "valuable men, conscious citizens, and active elites" who would constitute a "national renewal."[63] The MJCs, like France generally, held the young of the postwar baby boom responsible for not only the demographic but also the cultural rejuvenation of a moribund French populace.

Importantly, the MJCs were spaces designed for participatory activities that not only linked young people of varied milieux, but developed skills that created "a taste for expression and a sense of beauty," as well as recognized "mediocrity and inspire[d] a sense of quality" that would allow the young as adults to participate more fully and effectively in France's cultural life.[64] These skills made the young into more "valuable men and better citizens," who would "build the future" and "safeguard the civilization" while stewarding France through its "necessary evolution." The MJCs sought to provide youth with the "indispensable means of achieving their mission," which was nothing less than the renewal of France.[65] In essence, the MJCs wanted to build character that made a well-rounded individual capable of fulfilling the duties of citizenship: "Our ambition is to make complete men who can simultaneously adapt themselves on a social level, economic level, and civic level."[66] As FFMJC director Lucien Trichaud proclaimed, "An MJC is not a ciné-club, photo-lab, or theatrical performance where young and old go to consume culture, but rather a testing-ground for citizens."[67]

Indeed, France's citizenship is based upon the notion of a shared cultural heritage that emerges within the territorial boundaries of France. Civic inclusion is achieved by cultural assimilation; what makes someone French is not blood descent, but cultural fluency in language, taste, customs, history, and institutions.[68] In the late nineteenth century, the Third Republic undertook to assimilate the nether regions of France and the lower social classes through its vast expansion and reform of both public primary education and the military. Both of these, obviously, targeted young people. Likewise, the MJCs were conceived as a necessary supplement to public education. In fact, the program compared its role in popular education during the Fourth Republic to the spread of primary education in the Third: "Our task is to create a Maison des Jeunes in each village, each medium-sized city, and each quarter of a large city just as the Third Republic built its schools there."[69] In truth, most of the first MJCs were located in rural areas deep in the French provinces (many were known as Foyer Ruraux, but were still a part of the MJC network). Urban areas were targeted for MJCs a little later, and they began mostly in working-class neighborhoods. From the outset, then, the MJCs sought to bring cultural education to the poor and the isolated, rather than to the well-off and cosmopolitan, who presumably would already have access to such "cultural capital," to use Pierre Bourdieu's term. In fact, after Bourdieu's pioneering 1964 study linking cultural fluency with educational success and class distinction in French society,[70] the MJC was championed as an ideal mechanism to combat these disparities, bringing culture to the popular classes and thus broadening the stratum of the bourgeois middle classes.[71]

Cultural education renders "men more complete" by building character. The popular education movement and the MJCs were seen to be completing the deficiencies of the school and family. While schools and families provided intellectually and materially for the young, both often lacked a civic, cultural, or spiritual component, and thus "the school and the family [were] insufficient to satisfy the needs of the child or adolescent."[72] Mandatory education ended at the age of fourteen, the very age targeted by the MJC, so cultural education was envisioned as a supplement to the school, although it strove not to be seen as simply an "annex." Additionally, the young often learned bad traits and behaviors from their parents, such as "impatience, aggravation, contradiction, [or] an absence of sensibility," instead of good traits. Popular education was designed to compensate not only for the cultural insufficiencies of the French household, but the civic and moral ones as well. At an MJC, young people would learn a "scale of values" and would make "appropriate judgments" through a moral, cultural, and civic education.[73] Notably, these private popular education movements, with the support of the state, were advocating a secular, cultural morality that continued the republican project of reducing the role of the church in French life, a significant continuity with Third Republic *laïcité*. Furthermore, the households deemed to be insufficient were, of course, those of the working class and the rural peasantry, households in the very neighborhoods and provincial areas targeted by the MJC network. For these people, "culture is in a certain sense a liberating diversion, a compensation to work." By including them in the fold, popular education would create a "homogenous experience and knowledge that sustains a common spirit that characterizes a people's civilization."[74] Thus, a central element of the popular education movement was to homogenize the national community, to produce a standard of cultural normalcy that would create a common bond of Frenchness. In the postwar period, then, cultural appreciation and cultural practice were viewed as a means to stabilize France as it reinvigorated its national identity in the wake of the Nazi Occupation. Even though the MJCs were local institutions, they participated within a top-down initiative to consolidate the nation via local endeavor. By assimilating the young culturally, the MJCs were conforming the young civically to create a national constituency fluent in the grandeur of French culture and ready to participate in the national community.

Despite this desire to create a standardized sense of culture across class and geographic boundaries, there was also an acceptance of regional variety in the MJC and popular education movement. Jeune Alsace, for example, sought to participate "in all sorts of useful operations for the rapid reintegration of our youth into the French cultural movement," while simultaneously celebrating and maintaining unique Alsatian cultural customs.[75] Alsace, of course, is an exceptional example, as it was a region eager to demonstrate its Frenchness after its annexation by the Germans during the war. But Alsace was not the only region where the MJC project of a national culture worked in tandem with regional cultural varieties. The pluralist tone of the MJCs extended to an acceptance of local custom in folk traditions, cuisine, and heritage. Nonetheless, these regional varieties were always viewed as subsets of a larger, singular, and unitary French culture. Popular education programs used two primary tools to familiarize the young with the cultural landscape of France: film screenings at youth *ciné-clubs* and travel in the expanding youth hostel network.

Touring France

Cinema was celebrated by some as the "most perfect" means of cultural education because of its ability "to transport man instantaneously to the most varied sites, milieux, and periods, to give not only verbal but visual understanding, and to express the reality of life without resorting to any analytic conjecture." Using cinema correctly for this task was delicate, however, because cinema was also capable of flattering the basest instincts through immoral, vulgar, or unnatural artifice. Therefore, a structured environment for the screening of films was desirable and, if utilized correctly, could be educational, inspirational, and enriching. The committee on reconstruction recommended the expansion of *ciné-clubs* across France, particularly for the young, to help them develop taste, appreciation, and understanding of the world and France.[76]

By 1952 the French Cinémathèque, founded immediately before the war, had established fifteen film banks around the country to distribute films to the rapidly expanding network of youth *ciné-clubs*, many of which were associated with local MJCs. Each film bank contained the same thirty documentaries on varied cultural or historical subjects, plus those in Paris and Lyon had thirty additional films that circulated among the other banks.[77] The French federation of *ciné-clubs* established guidelines for "acceptable" and "recommendable" films that would help youth develop their sensibility, imagination, and character. Although the "recommendable" films were usually educational documentaries that portrayed either the variety of landscapes and cultural traditions of France or historical and biographical subjects, "acceptable" films included fictional movies that were deemed "anodyne," or those without "gunshots or kisses."[78] Of course, another goal of the *ciné-clubs* was to develop the young's taste and appreciation for film as an artistic form and to value French cinema in particular. The end of the war had brought a backlog of American films into the French market, and the French film industry, naturally, wanted to create a market demand for French films. Hence, with the exception of Charlie Chaplin movies, almost every film shown at youth *ciné-clubs* was of French origin. Whether the *ciné-clubs* managed to create a market specifically for French films is debatable, but it does seem clear that the postwar explosion of the clubs did encourage an affinity for film among the young. By 1954, at the same time that the French film industry began to orient its production toward a younger demographic, the young made up 43 percent of film audiences, and by the end of the decade they outnumbered adults.[79] In fact, one historian has referred to the *ciné-clubs* as the "iron lance" spearheading the late-fifties renewal of French cinema.[80]

A more palpable, physically invigorating, and experiential way to familiarize the young with the regions and cultural heritage of France was through
the tangible adventure of travel (see Figure 8). After the war, both the private sector and the government championed travel within the French youth
hostel system as an ideal means to acquaint the young with the diversities of
France, where "they come to know in depth the sites, monuments, history,
folklore, and customs of each region." From the rugged coast of Brittany
to the Alpine slopes of Savoy, from the chateaux of the Loire to the caves
of Lascaux, the new government wanted French youth to explore the natural and cultural landscape of France. Hostelling was thought to serve as a
means of geographic and cultural education and appreciation of the French
hexagon.

More than this, however, *ajisme* (the practice of travel in the Auberges
de la Jeunesse) was a "call to universal fraternity." In their "moving and
interchangeable communities," the traveling youth of France encountered

Figure 8. Two young men spend their Easter vacation traveling near Melun, 1951.
Agence Keystone.

one another outside the normal milieux of class, workplace, school, city, or province.[81] *Ajisme* assured "salubrious, agreeable, and inexpensive" vacations for the young, who yearned for some "open air, change, locomotion, and communion with others their age amidst the beautiful sights of nature or historic monuments so plentiful in France." Thus, hostelling garnered the support of the department for youth, sports, and popular education.[82] In fact, after the war the government took a very active role in what had been an area dominated by competing private organizations.

The first youth hostel was opened in 1907 by Richard Shirmann in Althena, Germany, as a function of the thriving *Wandervogel* movement there. The first youth hostel in France was opened in 1930 by Catholic humanist Marc Sangnier, on his own property, in the rural Belleville southwest of Paris. In 1936 Léo Lagrange planned to develop the youth hostel network in France as an essential link in the social policy of the time. However, like so many other Popular Front initiatives, this project was never adequately undertaken. By 1939, various hostelling factions had emerged, but hostelling was dominated by two adversarial youth hostel organizations—one Catholic, the other lay.[83] During World War II, their activities were largely suspended and most hostels were used to quarter occupying German soldiers. At Liberation, French youth hostels were left in disrepair and stripped of valuable equipment. However, the two main organizations quickly reestablished themselves and began a vehement competition for both facilities and participants. These two main groups even splintered into militant and moderate wings, each exalting a particular Catholic, lay, or political worldview. The rapid expansionist policies generated by this competition left many hostels lacking accommodations adequate in terms of sanitary hygiene, competent management, physical and moral security, and material stability.[84] Soon, the Fourth Republic intervened.[85]

In 1949 the government created the National Federation of Youth Hostels, to ensure both the quality of facilities as well as the ideological tone of hostels. The private associations were compelled to participate in the new umbrella organization and to meet standards established by the government if they were to receive any state subsidies. In fact, throughout the 1950s roughly one-third of the new national hostel association's annual budget came from government coffers, and over the next decade the government tightened its grip on the youth hostel network, which by the 1960s it basically controlled.[86] The state viewed hostels as "a public service at the disposition of young men and women," and demanded an end to the "anarchy" created by divisive and vitriolic private groups. As Albert Jenger, the president of the new state-sponsored organization, said: "The hostel is not simply a roof. It is also and above all a crossroads of friendship and culture, a school of human development." The new organization was "a home for all *ajistes*, a home for all the young." In other words, French youth should feel "at home" anywhere in France, no matter how far from their family or household. The government trumpeted that the new national system of youth hostels was "secular," "democratic," "technical," "educative," and "independent," the very characteristics it championed for the new and improved France it sought to build and the cohesive citizenry it sought to shape generally, not only for, but primarily through, the young.[87] Americans say colloquially that "travel broadens the mind," yet notably, the equivalent French adage is "Les voyages forment la jeunesse." Thus, travel is conceived as having a particularly educative and developmental value for the young; namely, it shapes youth.

After 1949, youth hostels were subject to inspection by the Ministry of Health and the Ministry of Education, each of which had the power of sanction and closure. Each hostel was required to have a commons area, kitchen, and separate dormitories for boys and girls. For every fifteen beds, there must be a toilet, shower, and bath. The hostels must be well lit and well ventilated. The hostels welcomed girls as well as boys and charged a minimal fee for each overnight stay. They were intended for both group and independent travelers aged 16 to 30, as well as for groups of young people under age sixteen if accompanied by adults. In 1946 there were 130 youth hostels in France, recording 95,755 nights of use.[88] A decade later, in 1956, there were 338 hostels with over 300,000 nights of use, but the long-term expansion policy hoped to have an eventual total of 1,800 hostels. Approximately 69 percent of the hostel users were male and 31 percent female. Interestingly, the numbers of students and workers were roughly equivalent and together they made up over half of all users. The convenience, affordability, availability, and quality of the hostels seem to have attracted youth from across class, educational, and regional barriers.

Perhaps most importantly, the new government regulations for youth hostels required a *père aubergiste* or *mère aubergiste* to be present at all times, not only to manage the hostel but to "guarantee the morality" of the young. Surveillance by these parental figures was designed not only to thwart mischief or chaperone frisky adolescents, but also to ensure the neutrality of the space so that no group could create a politically or religiously hostile environment for others.[89] At the same time that the government championed hostel travel as a way for the young to experience the variety of France, the state simultaneously standardized and normalized this experience, in full awareness of, and in response to, the belligerent climate of the prewar and war years, thus emphasizing the need for inclusion rather than exclusion.

This project, of a national culture bounded within a geographic territory, was able to incorporate regional cultural varieties. The pluralist tone of the youth hostels extended to an acceptance of, even an emphasis on, local custom and regional distinction. Thus, the hostel network was an attempt to extend the concept of what France included, while undercutting regional differences by making them familiar. The distinct and varied parts were acknowledged and appreciated while simultaneously incorporated into the sum that was France.

The hostel system became part of a modern democratic (as opposed to the premodern aristocratic) Grand Tour that was as much about familiarizing oneself with other people as with other places. More specifically, *ajisme* was a way for the young French to get to know each other in the wake of foreign intrusions. In the recent past, France had been overrun by outsiders. First the Germans invaded and occupied France, then came the Allied armies' own invasion, followed by the postwar stationing of American soldiers and the arrival of refugees and displaced persons, not to mention the tourist boom of the 1950s. Travel in the youth hostel system was a way for the young French to get know to one another as a response to the presence of so many outsiders in France. Thus, the hostels to some degree did function as congregating spaces, where transitory French youth independently converged, intermingled, and dispersed again as part of France's ongoing project of building a national community. Although most hostel users at this time were French, the percentage of foreign youth using the system grew slightly each year in the 1950s, adding an international element to this fluctuating convocation of young travelers. Nevertheless, *ajistes* throughout this period were overwhelmingly French, and the discursive rhetoric supporting the system emphasized its importance for France's youth.[90]

Another important element of the youth hostel system was its ability to combine vacationing with sport and athleticism. Hostels were often located in areas replete with outdoor activities, where young people could rent equipment cheaply for cycling, skiing, hiking, canoeing, or mountaineering. The very act of traveling from hostel to hostel could be a physical challenge that made muscles sore. But it was the activity itself, the getting-out-to-the-great-outdoors sense of adventure, the fresh air, sunshine, and bold enterprise of independent travel that so pleased hostelling advocates. *Ajisme* not only built character, encouraged self-reliance, and ennobled spirits, but it built strong bodies and encouraged healthy habits as well, another priority in fashioning young French men and women.

In fact, at the war's end there was a great push to get the children of France to spend part of their summer vacation at camps in the countryside, or *colonies de vacances*. The youth mutual aid society L'Entr'Aide Française, which was so active in the task of reconstruction more generally, set out on a vast campaign to encourage families to send their children away for the summer of 1945. They called their campaign the "Crusade for Pure Air."[91] The government and children's advocacy groups viewed a prolonged stay in the open, clean air of the French countryside as vital for a child's physical recovery from the deprivations of the war. Moreover, this vacation was viewed as a necessary respite for the maternal duties of women who were exhausted from the scramble to provide for their families during the war.

Colonies de vacances had existed for several decades. Various groups and movements of a religious or political nature had developed their own summer camps by the late 1930s, and these were much better organized and functioned far more effectively than did the hostels. Designed to combat problems of public health and hygiene among the urban poor in the late nineteenth century, *colonies de vacances*, as a common experience of both working-class and middle-class children, became a familiar rite of social life in mid-century France. Initially, private charity and public primary schools sent small groups of children to the countryside for a few weeks of play in the fresh air. In the interwar period these programs expanded exponentially and evolved into municipal, collective summer camps with a more pedagogical orientation that sought to shape the child into an idealized adult (an idealization that varied according to political or religious persuasion). In 1945 the Fourth Republic did not seek to supplant these camps, but, like so much else dealing with the young, intended to expand their availability and monitor their activities and management so that the benefit of the *colonies de vacances* "trickled up" to the middle classes as well.[92]

The exercise, activity, and vibrant sunshine offered by the summer camps was only one element that appealed to the government in its desire to exert a more thorough control over the young population (a desire that explains why rural youth, who one would think had access to fresh air, were also encouraged to attend). Several ministries contributed to the project of making *colonies de vacances* available and efficacious for France's children: the Ministry of Education established four national centers to train directors and camp counselors; the Ministry of Reconstruction repaired and updated facilities; the Ministry of Transportation provided reduced fares and special trains for transport to and from remote regions; the Ministry of Health administered physicals and provided medicines; the Ministry of Industrial Production provided appropriate footwear and equipment; and the Ministry of Supplies provided foodstuffs to ensure a proper and healthy diet regimen.[93] In the wake of war, the *colonies de vacances* were a prime opportunity to house, clothe, feed, and medicate, as well as exercise, French children, albeit for a short duration. In 1945, 350,000 children went to these summer camps; in 1946, 500,000; in 1947, 800,000. By 1948, the figure had reached over 1,100,000.[94] As baby-boom children became old enough, they further expanded this truly national program. By 1949, the summer camps required over twenty thousand camp counselors.[95] This was a national effort so "remarkable" that other European countries came to study it.[96] Yet the *colonies de vacances* are only one example of the corporeal aspects of reconstruction and popular education.

Physical Citizenship and Formation Prémilitaire

France wanted to develop not only the intellect and character of its future citizens, but also their physical fitness, which had suffered during the privations and hardships of the war.[97] At Liberation, the provisional government "assigned sport a mission of public service in transforming [young] athletes into 'ambassadors' of renewal."[98] The promotion of sport and athleticism was predicated upon the national benefit of physical fitness in terms of health, morality, education, character, work, prestige, and, of course, military strength.[99] Young bodies were to be made useful to the national task of rejuvenation. The hunger, malnutrition, and physical hardship of war were to be exorcised from the national body through the exercise of the national body. Sport was fundamental to the modernization of France, "because tomorrow, to be victorious, the soldiers of the reconstruction must be strong."[100] France lacked a mass sporting tradition comparable to Germany or Britain, however. Sporting in France had been promoted more in private athletic clubs and youth movements than in state institutions. After the war, and in continuity with both Popular Front and Vichy policies, the Fourth Republic attempted to prioritize physical fitness among the young, though with very mixed results.

The National Resistance Council (CNR), an influential body made up of former resistors seeking to remake France at the time of the reconstruction, sponsored a massive rally in 1946 to suggest that sport and athleticism should be a part of the national agenda for renewal. On May 15, CNR sponsored sporting activities and athletic competitions involving thousands of young people across France to promote an upcoming conference in Paris. Basketball, gymnastics, and cycling were all a part of the promotion, but the most illustrative activities were the relay races emphasizing speed, determination, cooperation, momentum, and forward progression that were held in Dunkirk, Saint Lô, and Oradour-sur-Glane. These places, epitomizing the war's worst episodes, in terms of retreat, destruction, and massacre, resonated with a symbolic vibrancy.[101] The CNR saw the "physical and moral renovation of youth as one of the most urgent of all structural reforms" in France's reconstruction, and in June held a national congress on this issue, comprised of twenty-seven commissions and attended by 730 delegates plus political, military, and intellectual notables.[102]

The congress produced a report of several hundred pages outlining the issues relevant to the physical and corporeal renewal of the national citizenry. "Sport," it said, "spontaneously, unconsciously, and automatically shapes, in every way possible, desirable character traits. Without knowing it, without wanting it, through the exhilaration of joyous competition, young athletes forge a more virile, more serene, more ardent, more determined character; they make ready a team spirit that is the embryonic form of a national spirit; they prepare themselves for useful public life." Report subjects ranged from the physical status of the nation to the medical control of athletes, from sport in the workplace to sport in the schoolyard, from the countryside to the empire at large, from amateurism to professionalism, from athletic equipment to cultural representations.[103]

Notably, the congress also emphasized the need to develop sport among girls. As the role of women expanded in public life after the war, so too did the perceived need to shape girls for this public life. "Her important place in intellectual, social, and political domains, the role that she played against the invader, and the place that she now holds in peacetime production and the reconstruction of France, as well as her pivotal role in family life, militates in favor" of such an expansive program. More to the point, and in more traditional terms, "the health of the woman conditions the health of the child, and that is to say, the health of the nation." The CNR report advocated expanded programs for women's sports, even gender-mixed sports, but it clearly excepted violent sports such as boxing, soccer, and rugby.[104] Moreover, the most significant and expansive physical education program begun by the Fourth Republic, Formation Prémilitaire, excluded girls entirely.

The CNR congress helped to pressure the Fourth Republic to expand its programs and facilities for physical education. During the Popular Front, Léo Lagrange had begun efforts in this area by establishing the Brevet Sportif, a certificate designed to reward youngsters who demonstrated basic skills in running, jumping, throwing, climbing, and swimming. In 1937, 420,000 boys and girls received a certificate, out of 600,000 who attempted it.[105] The Fourth Republic revived this standard of athletic ability, and by 1950 there were over 1,000,000 male and female recipients of the Brevet Sportif.[106] Sports were placed in the new Department for Youth Movements and Popular Education, yet despite wordy validations to the contrary, the Fourth Republic did not generate an adequate expansion of municipal athletic facilities or school gymnasiums. By 1958 there were still fifty-two French *départements* that did not have an indoor pool, and eight had no pool at all; forty-three *départements* had no indoor sports arena, and eleven had no stadium. By the end of the 1950s, France ranked last among European nations in per capita sporting facilities.[107] Moreover, the state continued to rely predominantly on sporting clubs, rather than on a comprehensive physical education program in schools, to foster athleticism among the young. There was, however, a new physical education program, jointly sponsored by the

Ministry of Education and the Ministry of Defense, designed to coordinate general physical fitness with military preparedness, known as Formation Prémilitaire.

The Formation Prémilitaire program was created at Liberation to foster physical fitness among male youth who might be called into immediate military service before the war's close to facilitate France's participation as an equal partner in the Allied victory.[108] In December, following the war's end, the Ministry of Education held a conference in Paris for all interested parties to plot out the exact parameters of Formation Prémilitaire's continuation and to get program input from the various private and public youth organizations and associations, including, of course, the military.[109] While some sporting groups and youth movements expressed concern about a possible militarism reminiscent of Fascism, on the whole they were enthusiastic supporters of the new program and were ready to participate actively in order to ensure the fitness, military preparedness, and "civic education" of French youth.[110]

An ordinance of April 22, 1945, established the Formation Prémilitaire program, jointly administered by the Ministry of Education and the Ministry of Defense. Participation in the program was obligatory for all male youth beginning at age seventeen, for three years of physical, technical, and moral training before their mandatory entrance into the military at age twenty. In 1946 the program included 750,000 students (those who continued schooling after age fourteen) and 2,000,000 workers and farmers.[111] These young men reported to a Formation Prémilitaire center for at least 3.5 hours a week for forty-three weeks, totaling a minimum of 150 hours a year. Thousands of centers were set up all over the country, with ideally no more than 200 young men per center, who were divided into four sections of 50 men each, each section composed of three activity groups of 15 to 20 boys. Young men were not assigned to a particular center or group, but were encouraged to enroll with their friends, fellow students, or workers, or jointly as members of a club or association, in order to facilitate a positive attitude among peers.[112]

The Ministry of Education was responsible for the first two years of Formation Prémilitaire, which was essentially physical education that entailed 3.5 hours of exercise a week designed to produce "physical qualities" (endurance, strength, coordination, speed), "virile qualities" (determination, confidence, courage, daring), and "social virtues" (camaraderie, team spirit, discipline, cooperation). Or, in other words, the program would ensure, "by definition, the formation of men and character." Each center director determined the weekly program, but he was expected to vary the activities between individual sports (cycling, swimming, track and field), team sports (rugby, soccer, basketball), and combative sports (boxing, judo, wrestling). The young men were subject to frequent medical examinations and physical challenges and thereafter categorized according to fitness and ability, which would, in some part, determine their future place in the military.[113]

The final year of the three-year program was known as *service prémilitaire* and run by the Army. Physical conditioning continued, but the program was augmented to orient the young men of France with military procedure before they entered their eighteen months of military service. That is, there were activities designed to train young men in basic military drill, command structure, and technical skills, and to familiarize them with the various opportunities offered by the armed services. This resulted in a twofold selection process: first, it helped a young man to determine in what aspect of military service he was interested; and second, it gave the military an opportunity to evaluate the physical, mental, and leadership ability of each conscript before his class entered military service.[114]

Importantly, Formation Prémilitaire was not conceived as simply providing young men as improved resources to the military, but it was also intended to "complete their character and civic development without which a man cannot become a soldier or complete citizen."[115] In fact, Formation Prémilitaire was imagined as a military public service to youth and France, as opposed to social welfare for future warfare. Some even considered military service as the final component of popular education. It completed the work of the youth and culture houses by providing a collective civic and social experience "essential to the development of young men." This character development was so valuable that France even proposed a similar, mandatory, noncombat civil service for girls, an idea considered but never implemented.[116]

Military service removed young men from their familial and neighborhood milieu and placed them in contact with others from a range of social classes and provincial regions. It thus served as the ultimate institution for cementing a bond of national community across regional and class diversities. Military service was imagined as furthering the "pursuit of popular education policy," by permitting the gathering together of and co-operation among youth of all backgrounds, providing a civic and cultural education for those who had left school at age fourteen, making the young physically fit, and, finally, training them with technical skills and mechanical expertise that would benefit them, and France, in the workplace.[117] The completion of military service was often regarded as a male rite of passage to adulthood. Thus, military experience was conceived as the culmination of the development and training of young men. More than France giving fit young soldiers to the military, the military was expected to give well-rounded citizens back to France.[118] A common military experience, like a common education, was seen as forging a common national identity in the wake of wartime ruptures.

The French Revolution had introduced universal conscription at a time when soldiering was for men in the prime of life. Over the course of the nineteenth century, the military had slowly evolved into an institution dominated almost exclusively by young, malleable conscripts, as opposed to fully developed, mature men. The responsibility of society to produce a good soldier for use by the Army shifted to one of the Army providing a good citizen for use by society. Moreover, as each military class entered mandatory service, young men became part of a national collective experience based on age. Among male youth, a more restricted age group formed that based its solidarity on a given year's class of conscripts. Thus, modern conscription contributed to an age-cohort collective identity that lasted a lifetime and, along with the extension of public education, helped to establish youth as a definitive social group in modern Europe.[119]

After the Second World War, Charles de Gaulle had wanted France to abandon universal conscription and adopt a military of professionals, but politicians viewed the tradition of the citizen-soldier as too fundamental to the Republic. The left feared a professional Army dominated by militarists, and the right believed in the patriotic values the military instilled in French youth. Until the reforms of 1966, military service in France was indeed universal, compared to Britain or the United States, where deferments were easily obtained and widely granted.[120] Thus, through the comprehensive inclusion of male youth in Formation Prémilitaire and national service, the French military sought to make its own contribution to the betterment of youth.

A 1947 report made by and for the Army identified the social problems facing young men aged 14 to 22, and speculated on the Army's role in
resolving these difficulties. In addition to the young being physically under-
weight and undersized, their character "appears as very unique: they are at
the same time ultra-conformist in their apathy, lack of originality, and ease
with which they can be swayed, and yet non-conformist in their loathing of
all rules and structure." At root psychologically was a "grave demoralization," wrought by the war that rendered youth incapable of "distinguishing
good from bad," and one that left them with a "civic indifference" to society. And yet, the report concluded, paradoxically, that youth could still be a
"permanent force of renewal" and "serve as the basis of a new society."[121]

The report stated plainly that the Army's "objective is to achieve the education of the citizen." There needed to be "character, independence, a sense
of reality and responsibility, a spirit of mutual aid, and a civic conscience"
developed among the young. The restoration of a democratic state and
"France's future for dozens of years to come rely on the civic preparation
of these new generations." The Army advocated involvement in programs
that would structure the young's physical education and leisure activities,
renew fundamental values of character development, provide professional
training, and emphasize collective life. "It is through the long practical experience of common activity, common ownership, and common benefit that
a community constitutes its citizens."[122] But the French military also had
something of a public relations problem with the young of France, which it
sought to remedy.

In November 1953 the military established the Army Youth (Armées-
Jeunesse) Commission, "to facilitate a quasi-permanent conversation between representatives of the national defense and representatives of youth to
study the principal problems between one and the other." The commission
was composed of ten to fifteen military officers and ten to fifteen representatives of youth movements, associations, and organizations. In November
1955 the commission was made an official legal body by government decree
and held a prominent seat on the new High Commission for Youth Affairs
established by Pierre Mendès-France a year earlier. The dialogue generated
was intended to facilitate a deep understanding by each side of the needs and
societal role of the other. The military hoped to gain access to the youth of
France through the young leaders of various national organizations and, by

using the Army Youth Commission as a vehicle, to promote the military as a modern, viable, and essential public service to youth and France.[123]

The commission was established in the midst of an unpopular colonial war in Indochina, however. The Communist leader Ho Chi Minh led a nationalist independence movement after World War II that by 1947 had escalated into war with the French empire in Indochina (modern-day Vietnam, Laos, and Cambodia). Professional French troops, not conscripts, became locked in a frustrating struggle against the Viet Minh guerrillas there. The French military was determined to quell the movement, both to demonstrate its renewed vigor as well as to discourage independence movements in other parts of the empire. With the military unable to deliver a knockout blow, the war dragged on and grew unpopular in France, where Indochina was increasingly seen as too far away and not vital to national interests. In May 1954 the Dien Bien Phu debacle humiliated the military and led to the quick withdrawal of France from Indochina by Mendès-France. After the bungling of the Ruhr Occupation in 1923, the quick defeat by Nazi blitzkrieg in 1940, the embarrassing loss to a rag-tag guerrilla army in 1954, and the perplexing faux pas of the Suez Crisis in 1956, the French military was more determined than ever that the new conflict in Algeria was its last stand, since public opinion of its abilities was at an all-time low.

The Algerian war began on November 1, 1954, when small groups of Algerian partisans from the National Liberation Front (FLN) carried out coordinated bomb attacks killing eight people.[124] The FLN was a militant rebel group, inspired by the Viet Minh victory, that sought Algerian independence from France. Initially, police forces were sent to maintain order and protect French *colons*, but by late 1955 the power of the FLN had grown and the violence had escalated, leading to the occupation of Algeria by the French military. Just a few hundred miles across the Mediterranean Sea, Algeria was very different from Indochina in the French national imagination; it was considered an integral part of metropolitan France and its three departments even had representation in the French National Assembly. There were over one million French citizens, known as *colons*, or *pieds noirs*, living in Algeria (mostly of French and Italian descent), out of a total population of ten million. Moreover, de Gaulle's provisional government had operated from Algeria during the war, and many politicians and civil servants had begun their careers there as administrators. Many people in France had relatives living there, or had worked or visited Algeria themselves. Thus, Algeria, unlike Indochina, was seen as vital to the national interest and an essential part of the nation.

By 1956, France was engaged in a full-scale military occupation that would require a permanent force of 500,000 young conscripts until the war's end in 1962. In total, almost three million young Frenchmen would cross the Mediterranean Sea to serve in Algeria, and 35,000 of them would die there. Importantly, the Vietnam conflict had been fought by volunteers and, while unpopular, it did not directly engage with the daily lives of young people as a social group or even France more generally, as the Algerian war did. As a consequence of the massive military mobilization of French young men to serve in Algeria, the influential National Union of French Students (UNEF) publicly criticized the war in Algeria and announced that it would leave the Army Youth Commission, as a protest, in late December 1956.[125] Other groups followed, but the commission doggedly persisted with its mission. To continue the work of public relations between the military and youth, it began publishing, in April 1957, a quarterly review, *Fascicules Armée-Jeunesse*, promoting itself to young people. The first issues discussed the general demographic, educational, and professional difficulties that youth faced, as well as the current problems of the French Army. Later issues outlining what youth should expect from the Army and what the Army should expect from youth trod over the familiar terrain of character, morality, training, and discipline. Filled with optimism, and avoiding any direct discussion of the continuing conflict in Algeria, the campaign enjoyed minimal effectiveness as, in private, the military itself recognized.[126]

The Citizenship of Youth and the Algerian War

The war in Algeria grew increasing bloody and unpopular, and the government of the Fourth Republic seemed incapable of managing it. The *colons* (Algerian French) were determined to maintain their positions of powerful privilege in Algeria, the military wanted to crush the FLN nationalists unmercifully to prove its might, and both expected unwavering support from the government. But at home in France, the war's continuation became a heated struggle between those who saw Algeria as the linchpin to national prestige and imperial grandeur and those who saw the ongoing conflict as anathema to republican virtues. Violent protests erupted between those who supported the war and those who wanted it to end. The growing opposition movement in France did not have the support of any major political party, not even those of the far left.

Confidence in the government's ability to deal with the crisis plummeted. Rumors of torture and inhumane treatment of the Algerians by the military and *colons* incensed a public informed by its own suffering under the Nazis.[127] These rumors were confirmed by the journalist Henri Alleg, in his book *The Question*, an account of the torture undertaken by the French military in Algeria, and, closer to home on the mainland, by another volume, entitled *The Gangrene*, a collection of testimonials from Algerian students in Paris who had been tortured by French police.[128] Both books were immediately banned and copies confiscated, though each had a tremendous impact on public opinion, which began to recognize torture as not simply an unfortunate incident of the war but as a fundamental element of it. The government announced, in May 1958, that it would seek a negotiated peace with the FLN. With the support of Army generals, who plotted an invasion of France to instigate a coup against the civil government, French colonists revolted. This challenge led to the fall of the Fourth Republic. Charles de Gaulle was invited to form a new government, but he insisted on a restructured Constitution that would empower the executive branch of government. Thus, the Fifth Republic was established in 1958.

During the course of the war, the whole of the conscript army was sent to Algeria for the full term of military service, which was raised from eighteen months to twenty-four months, and later to twenty-seven. As early as the fall of 1955, angry crowds gathered at embarkation points and railway stations to protest the use of young conscripts in Algeria.[129] These protests expanded in the spring of 1956: on May 3 in Lézignan, demonstrators blocked a train of young soldiers as it departed for Marseilles; on May 10, hundreds gathered at the train station of Saint-Aignan-des-Noyers and threw stones at the gendarmes, who threw tear gas in turn; on May 17 at the Mans train station, there was rioting and fighting with the CRS riot police; on May 18 in Grenoble, an organized protest escalated into a street battle with local police; and on May 23 twenty people were wounded in a riot at Antibes. Significantly, these protests were often organized and populated by the young, such as the Committee of Young People for the

Peaceful Solution of the Problems of North Africa. The young protestors and potential draftees demonstrated a solidarity with the young conscripts being sent off to war, invoking their cohesion as a social group with
particular interests. Still, these initial protests across France were largely
quieted by an effective presidential speech at Verdun, invoking *la patrie*,
discipline, and order.[130] Despite this early controversy, the draftees continued on to Algeria.

Young conscripts came from all sections, all classes, and all regions of
French society. Unlike career officers, most of these student, worker, and
peasant conscripts were not as committed to the military or the Algerian war, and many were appalled by what they witnessed there. A young
scholar, Pierre Vidal-Naquet, documented their experiences in Algeria by
conducting interviews and collecting data, particularly in regard to torture.
Vidal-Naquet claimed that the problem of torture was so widespread and so
general that "it constituted a problem for the whole mass of young Frenchmen called up for service in Algeria." He made this connection more explicit, writing that the "simultaneous use both of torture and the mass of
young conscripts" were intimately linked, and that these two conditions,
torture and youth, provided the war with its unique character. The young
conscripts were not fighting an army nor a conventional war, but attempting to occupy and control an indigenous Muslim population of ten million,
often through forced resettlement and concentration camps. Many soldiers
returned home disillusioned, recounting brutal tales of the torture, murder,
and massacre of Algerian men, women, and children. Vidal-Naquet even
claimed that the practice of torture in Algeria bore a large responsibility in
domestic France for "the problem of youth today."[131] This idea was echoed
in the published results of a 1960 survey of young veterans, organized by
La Vie Catholique Illustrée, which proclaimed that there was a new voice for
contemporary youth, a new generational experience that defined the young
of France, one that had eclipsed the *nouvelle vague*. This was "the generation
of the *djebel*," the two million soldiers who had served in Algeria, 1.2 million of whom were young conscripts, who were shaped by the brutality of
occupation in northern Algeria, and who were, upon their return, reshaping
the character of French youth, or so it was feared.[132] Before, the young of
France had been identified as the *nouvelle vague*, or New Wave, generation,
carrying France forward on its rising tide; but now this social group, this

youth, was threatened by a dangerous undercurrent originating along the coastal *djebel* region of Algeria.

If service in the military was the final component in the popular education of male citizens, the irony of Algeria as the final testing ground is clear. As soldiers in Algeria, conscripts were not championing democracy nor promoting the republican virtues of *fraternité*, *égalité*, and *liberté*. Leaving Algeria, these soldiers returned to a charged and volatile environment in France, where disagreement over the war caused furious conflict. Increasingly, the war was seen as adversely affecting young people as a social group. An editorialist in *L'Express* lamented that "these boys are going to finish their civic instruction in Algeria," where they are "apprenticed in brutality" through a "violence without limit or goal."[133]

In the summer of 1958, fifty-one national youth organizations, representing millions of young people, formed GEROJEP (Groupe d'Etude et de Rencontre des Organisations de Jeunesse et d'Education Populaire), which united youth groups across the religious and political spectrum to protest the Algerian war and demand its end.[134] On August 8, the young leaders of GEROJEP issued a manifesto that confirmed their fidelity to "form freely conscious citizens of united and fraternal youth," while simultaneously condemning the bloody and ignoble war in Algeria. The manifesto emphasized that the "moral consequences of the conflict" burdened most heavily the young expected to fight the war. They interpreted the war as violence done against the young of France by the adults of France. Young men were the ones required to fight the "dirty war" of adults, at their demand and under their orders. GEROJEP worked as a youth-based interest group, pressuring de Gaulle and the Fifth Republic to end the war in Algeria. On June 2, 1960, GEROJEP reiterated its demands and sponsored a protest that attracted thousands of young people. It claimed that the war created an "extremely unfavorable climate for [youth's] commencement of responsibilities" as French citizens. The front-page headline of *Le Monde* declared that youth was "Taking a Common Position for the First Time," assuming their rightful place as a viable social group with specific interests in the French polity.[135]

One part of this emerging consciousness in response to the war was the rise of an autonomous and aggressive student radicalism that sought to influence French public opinion through mass confrontation. Over the course of the Algerian conflict, the National Union of French Students (UNEF) became increasingly politicized. For example, as a demonstration of solidarity, in 1960 UNEF announced its support for the outlawed General Union of Algerian Muslim Students (UGEMA)—a move that cost UNEF its government funding. In fact, this politicization split UNEF along ideological lines. In 1961 the National Federation of French Students (FNEF) formed a splinter group that it said represented the interests of students who supported the government's war and disagreed with the leftist principles of UNEF.[136] These rightist students dominated the political scene at the University of Montpellier, where FNEF was founded, and they devoted themselves to the patriotic promotion of French sovereignty. Their activities, however, were not limited to Montpellier; like the leftist students, they sought to influence public opinion throughout France. These university student groups, basing their political and social legitimacy on the principle of being young, on the idea of youth, seized the role of national political leadership in the domestic conflict over the war in Algeria.[137]

This definition of a young French citizenry was a gendered and classed one. While young women were included in the projects of cultural citizenship—the youth and culture houses, hostelling, the *colonies de vacances*, even sporting events—they were excluded from the more overtly political ones. For example, GEROJEP was male-dominated, and the youth leaders who in 1954 demanded and received from Pierre Mendès-France a High Commission for Youth Affairs were all male and predominantly bourgeois, as were the appointees to the new High Commission. Young women were also excluded from the conceptualization of the citizen as soldier. The Formation Prémilitaire program, national service, and the Army-Youth Commission all considered youth as a social body of potential soldiers and, thus, as male. Despite the enfranchisement of women generally, young men were still defined as future civic actors in a way that young women were not.[138] On the whole, the social body of youth was conceptualized as male.

An interesting exception is the voice of Françoise Sagan, who frequently expressed opposition to the war in Algeria. In 1960 she published an editorial in *L'Express* entitled "La Jeune fille et la grandeur." In it, Sagan blasted the French torture of Djamila Boupacha, a twenty-two-year-old Algerian *jeune fille*. Sagan utilized the conceit of the *jeune fille*, or young lady, to emphasize "the impaling of a virgin girl on a bottle." She lamented the loss of virginal innocence and implied the sadistic rape of Boupacha by the brutal French state. Underscoring Sagan's article was her sense of connection with this young Algerian woman, a solidarity based on gender and age. She concluded, "I don't imagine that the fanfare of grandeur can cover the screams of a *jeune fille.*" Here, Sagan used the idea of youth and the spoliation of its innocence as a political device to condemn the criminal activities of the French military in the pursuit of de Gaulle's trumpeted desire to reestablish French grandeur.[139]

Still, though youth was not a social group of young people with a monolithic point of view, as a mass social group of both young men and women it was developing a political consciousness in the crucible of an unpopular war of colonial oppression. Many young people, such as the right-wing extremists who made up Jeune Nation or the FNEF university students at Montpellier, supported the war.[140] However, one of the ways opposition to and support for the war organized itself was around the cultural category of youth. Youth as an idea was a point of political mobilization for the young of both the left and the right. Traditional political parties offered no leadership in this area. Only intellectuals in France offered a comparable engagement to that offered by the young.[141] New radical groups opposed to the war, such as Jeune Résistance, used their status as youth to mobilize opposition in France. Jeune Résistance was a small but militant underground desertion movement that, by seeking to organize a generational opposition to the war in Algeria, foreshadowed the leftist *groupuscules* of 1968. Founded in 1959 by the army deserter Jean-Louis Hurst, this group was quite small, though it did help to protect draft dodgers while fomenting popular opposition to the war through its clandestine press campaign of broadsides and pamphleteering.[142] In a sixteen-page brochure, Jeune Résistance claimed that if the young could organize themselves, they "can persuade their elders" and "provoke the awakening of the French people."[143] Increasingly, it was recognized that a dividing line existed between young France and adult France.

Notably, a confidential military report, entitled "Patriotism '57," recognized the growing gulf between the young, the military, and public life. It outlined the failures and shortcomings of the military in the eyes of the young and the growing skepticism and disdain young people held for both the military and the government. This contempt extended beyond the military, however, and targeted society more generally. Interestingly, the report seems sympathetic to these attitudes, suggesting that given the state of affairs and recent history, young people had good reason to be disillusioned.[144] Most troublesome, however, and most significant, was that "the young are themselves more and more numerous. Pushed to unite and organize themselves by the difficulties of life, they have become conscious of their strength, conscious more and more of their duty toward one another, toward all youth, toward the country—it is a very new situation."[145] Thus, the military was concerned that the young of France were developing a mass consciousness, as "youth" and not simply as "French."

The young had been treated as an age-based social group, as youth, by the military and government alike, and so these institutions had contributed to this emergent mass consciousness. After the Second World War, the category of youth increasingly became institutionalized and standardized, through both public and private programs seeking to make an effective use of the young in French society. Some, such as the High Commission for Youth Affairs and the Army Youth Commission, even recognized the growing significance of youth as a social group by granting them small amounts of influence and access to government institutions. Whether these gestures were largely symbolic or simple pandering, it is significant that adult France recognized and even negotiated with young France as a collective social body with particular needs, desires, and interests. In the postwar period, a vast movement in France had sought to shape and mold the young into a democratic citizenry capable of participating in the national community on political, social, and cultural levels. This movement stressed the need to mend the divisions created by the vitriolic political groups of the 1930s and the Fascist intolerance of the war. Many young people in France had become adapted to the public life of the nation and did begin to participate in it, not merely as French citizens, but as youth. A savvy number of the young recognized the viability of using the idea of youth for political mobilization. Justifying themselves as representatives of the relevant social body "youth," young activists began to demand representation in government institutions relevant to them, as well as an end of an imperial policy they saw as threatening to them. The concept of youth was invoked in anti-imperialist literature, much as it had been for the rejuvenation of France during the period of reconstruction. That is, the literature expressed that youth represented the future and that it was up to youth to foster change, end imperialism, and usher in a more just and humane world society.

The Algerian war provided the young of France with a political issue around which to organize, either in support of the war, as was the case with Jeune Nation, or against it, as with Jeune Résistance. The war was an issue that affected them directly, a matter even, for some, of life and death. Thus, many young French became politically engaged as a social group of youth expressing a collective self-interest on a mass level. Though this was not universally true for all young French people, it is significant that tens of thousands of them did begin to mobilize as a constituency organized around the age category of youth. Yet they did so in the streets, outside of the institutional framework of politics. Despite the efforts to integrate them into the nation and the republic, they continued to be excluded from civil society in the most fundamental way: the voting age remained at twenty-one. To some degree, the community building and citizenship training of France's postwar popular education programs can be deemed a success in the context of this protest movement. The young participated in the public life of the nation in ways unanticipated only a decade earlier. No longer simply acted upon, the

Figure 9. "We, the young, want something more." *L'Express,* June 16, 1960.

social group of youth seized its citizenship status and acted out in ways that anticipated the decade to come. Conscious of both their rights and duties as future citizens and members of French society, a great number of the young in France demonstrated solidarity and began to participate in public life as a self-interested mass social group organized around age, claiming youth as its point of legitimacy, as opposed to region, class, or economic circumstance. A 1960 issue of *L'Express* featured on its cover the face of a young man with a black block over his eyes (see Figure 9). His blocked-out eyes make him, ostensibly, anonymous and universal, though, significantly, he is identified as a *lycéen*, which classes this "universal youth" as bourgeois, in addition to gendering him male and rendering him a possible future technocrat as well. The caption below the photo, ostensibly his own words as a spokesperson, reads: "We, the young, want something more." What we see at this moment and in this image is the crystallization of the young as a mass social group, based on age, with specific interests and demands subject to the age category of youth. The full impact of this development would not be felt, however, until the end of the decade, in the events of May 1968.

PART II

The Problem of Youth

CHAPTER 4

Rehabilitating Delinquent France

On the night of April 9, 1949, Vincent Scheld and his father, both tailors in Valence, returned to their home around midnight. As Vincent's father opened the garage door for the car, two burglars pounced upon him and struck him twice in the head with a baton. At the loud shouts of the old man, the burglars lost their resolve and fled, but Vincent quickly pursued. As he caught up to the fleeing robbers, one of the prowlers turned and fired three pistol shots. Gravely wounded, Vincent Scheld, age twenty-seven, died hours later. A simple robbery had gone terribly wrong, ending in the victim's death from gunshot wounds. Within forty-eight hours, the two brigands were in police custody.

The murderer was a young woman, Josette Orfaure, a twenty-year-old hatmaker from nearby Bourg-les-Valence, and her accomplice was Jacques Mayent, twenty-seven, an agricultural worker from Valence. The investigation revealed that two others had actually planned the botched job: Jacques Greve, twenty, the brother-in-law of the victim, Vincent Scheld, and a sixteen-year-old boy, the lover of Josette Orfaure. Evidently, Jacques had mentioned that his brother-in-law would be carrying a substantial sum of money that night on his return home. With this information, the young group laid plans to ambush the Schelds and make off with the loot. Prompted by her young lover, Josette bought a .22 caliber revolver for the holdup, while the boy acquired a baton and convinced Mayent to wield it. The crime, it seemed, had been instigated and planned by a sixteen-year-old.[1]

For France, the notorious "Gang des J-3," or "Les J-3 de Valence,"[2] as they became known in the media, served as a cautionary example of the world gone awry. *Le Monde* scolded, "This painful story shows one more time with unique insight the problem of the juvenile delinquent: idle, lazy, reckless, and cruel, eager for easy money and impassioned by the adventures of fringe society, he takes the worst criminal as a role model, admiring the dangerous life and risky exploits."[3] The paper added later that "the crime, like a true juvenile crime, was stupid, clumsy, odious, and inexcusable." Much of the news coverage focused on the sixteen-year-old mastermind of the affair, noting how cool and collected he was, how "businesslike." When asked in court why he wanted the money, he responded, "Why, to play! What a question!"[4] In his coverage of the trial, Jean Couvreur of *Le Monde* pondered, "Are these the century's children? This century has, thank God, other examples of youth . . . but these young people are of their time. We could not place them in any other epoch." He recalled the ravaging effect of war on the collective psyche of youth. He lamented that these were young people, "without fathers, bread, or milk," that they had matured amidst "the crash of bombs and the cries of cut throats," and that "we, their elders, do not always understand them."[5]

The case from Valence was merely one link in a long chain of juvenile crimes that captured the public eye in the postwar period. The Guyader Affair of 1948, the Dupriez Affair of 1953, Alain Montevardi, Les Trois d'Angers, and Yvan Shaaf, among other scandals, helped maintain an ongoing debate about problem youth. This fixation found expression in political debates, policy initiatives, academic journals, and popular novels and films, as well as editorial journalism. As Couvreur's comments indicate, postwar France cultivated a complex preoccupation with the juvenile delinquent, as society sought to come to terms with the ill-effects of war and occupation. Yet there was another parallel and paradoxical narrative circulating about delinquent youth, one characterized more by a guilty sympathy than an outraged condemnation.

That sympathetic reaction emerged in response to other sensational incidents. For example, one year before Valence, in early January 1948, Serge Tonelli, age eleven, was placed by his parents, who were following a recommendation by social services, in the Petites Ailes institution of Montmorency. Private correctional institutions often accepted charges from private families in addition to those appointed by the court. On February 21, the infirmary notified Serge's father that the boy had an abnormally low temperature. Monsieur Tonelli removed the boy from Petites Ailes and rushed him to the local hospital, where doctors discovered that his feet were so frozen that they nearly required amputation. Evidently, Serge had been forced to march four kilometers through snow without shoes. An investigation revealed that Jules and Violette Monnier, the directors of Petites Ailes, had inflicted severe punishments on their wards, such as plunging fully clothed boys and girls into frigid baths or beating them for pilfering food from the dog's dish, whom the Monniers apparently fed better than the children. While the Monniers pocketed state funds and hoarded supplies, their charges slept without blankets or heat in dormitories that had broken windows. The abusive exploits of the Monniers at Petites Ailes incited public outrage and brought sympathy to delinquent minors. During their trial, in July 1948, *Le Monde* compared the actions of the Monniers to those of the Gestapo and Nazi war criminals and regretted that the penal code allowed a maximum sentence of only three years imprisonment. The paper concluded that "the Napoleonic Code did not anticipate monsters." On July 24, 1948, the court sentenced the Monniers to three years imprisonment and each was required to pay a 50,000-franc fine, while other members of the Petites Ailes staff complicit in the crimes received lesser sentences and the home itself was closed. The trial lasted only three days.[6]

The publicity surrounding the Petites Ailes scandal added fuel to France's growing preoccupation with troubled youth, and spurred the government to introduce legislation to augment its ability to monitor and control those private institutions that operated within the state juvenile justice system. On November 4, 1949, the Commission of Family, Population, and Public Health, in a report and proposed law introduced in the National Assembly, recommend the regulation of all private establishments who received minors. The legislation represented the combined work of the Ministries of Justice,

Public Health and Population, and National Education and sought "precise regulation and effective control" of private institutions. It established strict standards and criteria for directors and staff, including degrees of certification, medical exams, and extensive background checks, so that "the morality of personnel is rigorously controlled." Major appointments would be subject to review by the appropriate mayor, prefect, executive, inspector, and/or departmental director. The state also gave these administrators the power to inspect private institutions at any time, day or night, and to take any immediate action deemed necessary, such as closure or arrest of the proprietors. "The state should control and demand guarantees of morality, competence and employment," the report stated. "It should oversee the management of institutions and . . . it should be armed with effective sanctions."[7]

It would take a few years for the legislation to be enacted as law, due to the labyrinth of committees and subcommittees that characterized the parliamentary system of the Fourth Republic. For Monsieur Gallet, a deputy from the Commission of Family, Population, and Public Health, the infamy of the Petites Ailes case had shown that the state had an "obligation to protect the weak against exploiters," and that above all the essential problem of young people "engages with the future" due to the oncoming maturity of the baby boom. Louis Rollin, a deputy from the Commission of Justice and Legislation, noted that the "tragedy" of Petites Ailes was "necessary" and "salutary," in that it revealed the government's failure to protect its young people.[8] Repeatedly, the reproachful circumstances of Petites Ailes were made to stand for the failure of France to safeguard its progeny. Legislators reiterated that it was the duty of the state to shelter the young from those who would exploit and damage them. The rhetoric surrounding this case affirmed the concept of youth as victim, as blameless innocents at the mercy of negligent adults, despite the fact that many of these juveniles were guilty of criminal offenses. Parallel to and constitutive of the scandal of postwar delinquency, there was an emerging consensus confirming that young people were "no longer considered as responsible or culpable in the sense of an adult, but as threatened and in need of special assistance."[9]

For France, the problems of young people had a specific currency in the wake of the war, namely, how to rehabilitate wayward youths into exemplary French citizens. On one hand, as the public recoiled from sensationalized juvenile crime, delinquency was considered a vital threat to France's well-being, undermining and threatening the cultural reconstruction in process. On the other hand, delinquency was seen as a social problem that stemmed from French society itself, symptomatic of larger societal failings. Thus, delinquents were paradoxically threats, like the Gang des J-3, and victims, like the wards from Petites Ailes. The implications of this tension, moreover, pointed to larger concerns of how to reform France generally. As France wrestled with the difficulties of reconstituting society and building a new future, postwar concern for the juvenile delinquent functioned as a metaphor for larger discussions of cultural rehabilitation, of innocence and guilt, of accountability and victimization. This, in turn, shaped the conceptualization of youth as a social group, particularly in terms of how "youth" was or was not a classed category and how it operated as such within French society.

Delinquency and the War Experience

Juvenile crime rates had risen dramatically during the turmoil of war, as daily routines were ruptured and traditional authority was fractured by the Nazi Occupation.[10] Following a brief decline immediately after the Liberation, by 1946 delinquency rates again were on the rise and remained well above prewar levels for years afterward (see Table 1).[11]

TABLE I

Juvenile Delinquency in France, 1939–1958

Year	No. of Cases	Year	No. of Cases
1939	12,165	1949	22,761
1940	16,937	1950	19,239
1941	32,327	1951	16,261
1942	34,748	1952	15,823
1943	34,127	1953	15,352
1944	23,384	1954	13,504
1945	17,578	1955	13,775
1946	28,568	1956	16,468
1947	26,841	1957	17,863
1948	27,638	1958	18,900

Specialists expected the stability of the Liberation to counterbalance the lingering effects of war, yet in the search for an explanation it became clear to them that the experience of the war years was profoundly embedded in the disposition of young people and was exacerbated by the continuing challenge of material shortages into the late 1940s. Jean Chazal, chief judge of the Parisian Juvenile Court, remarked that "the black market, the spectacle of death, destruction, and misery caused grave emotional trauma for children and devalued their most essential human values."[12] Doctor Georges Heuyer, the leading pediatric neuropsychiatrist, agreed: "The war is over, but its memory remains with the silent anguish of a new threat to people and, above all, to youth. The German Occupation left profound traces in their minds and hearts. It created implacable hostility. The hatred and vengeance that can seem legitimate at certain times has persisted in the heart. . . . The Occupation has instilled habits that have left their mark on the behavior of young people."[13] And Jean Sarrailh, a student, despondently wrote: "The lesson of the last conflict weighs cruelly on our souls, and if, forgetting the past, we turn toward the future, what do we see there if not more peril?"[14]

The newspaper headlines of "Gang des J-3" or "Les J-3 de Valence" were, in fact, references to both the ordeal of the Occupation (J-3 refers to an age category introduced by the rationing system) as well as to a popular Roger Ferdinand play that was a runaway success of the Liberation period. The play *Les J3 ou la nouvelle école* (The J3 or the New School) premiered in 1943 and ran for 1,300 consecutive performances; it was also made into a film in 1945. It is set in a provincial school in Normandy that is filled with incorrigible adolescents who are trafficking in the black market and in various immoral pursuits. The play implies that they have been led astray by the vagaries of the Occupation and that, at base, their moral equilibrium needs to be rebalanced. A dedicated young female professor arrives at the *lycée*, determined to reform the five young men who are the protagonists and turn them into model scholars and citizens. A struggle of wills ensues. Roger Ferdinand, a prolific playwright, followed up on this success with the 1948 play *Ils ont vingt ans* (They Are Twenty). This play, also a hit and also made into a film (1950), gathers the same five young men in a Parisian dorm eighteen months later. They have matured and become, on the whole, fairly decent fellows. Together, the two plays reflect an emerging conventional wisdom that blamed the war and the Occupation for juvenile delinquency and suggested that the solution lay in a form of reeducation for the young ne'er-do-wells—a "new school." Ultimately, these young men were not truly bad, but the product of an unfortunate situation.[15]

In an effort to outline the deleterious effects of the war on young people, Doctor Simone Marcus-Jeisler organized a survey of professional psychiatrists, psychologists, justices, educators, counselors, and social workers. She published the survey results in the March 1947 issue of *Sauvegarde*, a journal dedicated to the exchange of information among specialists concerned with the moral protection of young people and the problem of juvenile delinquency. Marcus-Jeisler's conclusions were not surprising: "In general, promiscuity, moral obscurity, and insecurity created an unhealthy atmosphere. The war, like all cataclysms, caused a great human turmoil that swept up vulnerable dispositions." The antagonism of instability, the influence of immoral example, and the hardship of deprivation created an environment that diminished young people's "ability to discern between right and wrong."[16]

According to the survey responses, the most immediate effect of the war on young people was the rupture of daily routine and the breakup of family units. Marcus-Jeisler noted that, at the outset of the war, fathers were mobilized while mothers worked in factories and children were evacuated away from the rapidly advancing Germans. This is something of a canard, however, because by 1945 French men had been restored to their households, yet delinquency numbers remained high.[17] Still, Marcus-Jeisler blamed the German Occupation, which followed the collapse of the military and the defeat of France, for the relocation of "workers to Germany, the deportation or imprisonment of parents and resistors, and the departure of hundreds of men for North Africa or England." Due to these circumstances, "one understands that few children had effective supervision or education." The regulatory power of the school, the church, and the household were all undermined by the chaos of war and the Occupation, which had interrupted the usual mechanisms that provided discipline and order to the lives of the young and thus encouraged some to run wild. "During this troubled period," Marcus-Jeisler explained, they "inevitably had free time and, lacking helpful supervision, this created an atmosphere favorable to unlawful acts."[18] Moreover, the example of these unlawful acts originated with adults themselves.

The ultimate source of authority in such instability was the occupying military force, and subsequently "the presence in France of German garrisons brought about the corruption of many minors." The nefarious presence of the Nazis helped to create a harmful environment that "from the outset of the war had led to a slackening of morals." According to Marcus-Jeisler, this moral laxity was most evident in the fact of "certain women . . . practicing prostitution, at times with Germans." It is significant that Marcus-Jeisler never mentions collaboration as an act of dubious behavior or an example of amoral complicity, yet the fraternization of women with German soldiers showed that "often the bad example is given directly by the family."[19] It seems that, for Marcus-Jeisler and the specialists she surveyed, war profiteers and traitorous informants left far less of an indelible stain upon the fabric of youth than did the sexual practices of women.

The German presence further produced unhealthy circumstances through the requisitioning of foodstuffs and the rationing of supplies. These policies, coupled with the privation inherent to wartime, created a black market that actively exchanged goods and provided "easy money" for young thieves and swindlers. The very real need for sustenance was augmented by a "fevered thirst for money and the pleasures it could procure." Furthermore, "young people, particularly intoxicated by the power of their earnings, found at the same time a great adventure, a sense of danger and risk."[20]

Yet, even here, the report revealed that specialists did not blame the juvenile delinquent for his criminal actions, but instead celebrated him as a hero of France, as a great resistor doing his "patriotic duty by diverting goods requisitioned by the Germans." Moreover, Marcus-Jeisler went on to proclaim, "In a word, the Occupation created an *obligation* of disobedience to the law and an exaltation of private initiative," which, in the end, caused an "inversion of moral values" for young people—the unforeseen aftereffect of the supposed nation of resistors. The problem, then, was that in the postwar world the ability of young people to determine right from wrong had been obscured, because "lying and thieving [had been] virtues during the Occupation," but that these bad habits were now anathema to Liberated France.[21] Juvenile delinquents needed to be reconditioned to fit into a new postwar France. Toward these ends, the French government promulgated a new ordinance in February 1945 with the intention of significantly revamping the juvenile justice system from one of punishment to one of treatment.

Reeducation: Juvenile Justice Transformed

When the Ministry of Justice presented the new ordinance to the provisional government, it noted that "France is not so wealthy in children that it can neglect anything that might make them healthy," and that "the question of problem children [*l'enfance coupable*] is one of the most urgent of our time."[22] Indeed, there were grounds for concern. The number of juvenile cases before the court in 1944 had been 24,484, down from the wartime peak of 34,127 in 1943, but still twice the prewar number of 12,165 cases in 1939.[23] According to legislators, the "rigid" principles of the thirty-year-old law needed to be "softened," gaps needed to be "filled," and obsolete arrangements "abolished."[24]

Building on decades of debate and discussion, the government decided that the problems facing young delinquents called for solutions radically different from those applied to adult criminals. Because young people were malleable, they were also salvageable. The ordinance of February 2, 1945, established a new system that favored education and socialization over strict penal sanction. This new system considered minors thirteen and under to be completely outside the jurisdiction of the penal law, while the crimes of those from thirteen to eighteen would be reviewed case by case. This, in effect, ended the principle of discretion, or *discernement*, that had guided juvenile justice for a century and a half. The court was given the power to determine the "social reinsertion" of the delinquent following an elaborate investigation that included medical, psychiatric, and psychological examinations, as well as an extensive inquiry into the social milieu of the delinquent's family, school, and, if applicable, work. The new system was based on the desire to have a broad knowledge of the minor's character and the social conditions in which he or she lived, with a particular emphasis placed upon the family, to determine the appropriate action by the state.[25]

During the period of observation, the delinquent might remain with his family or might be placed with an appropriate institution, such as an observation center (*centre d'observation*) or a youth reception center (*centre d'accueil*). Following the inquiry, the judge would determine suitable treatment from a series of options: supervised probation within the home environment (*liberté surveillée*), counseling within a structured institution (*éducation surveillée*), long-term placement within a rehabilitation center (*rééducation*), and, in

exceptional cases, penitential incarceration. These "treatments," as opposed
to punishments, operated along a continuum of intervention dependent
upon the assessed severity of the minor's situation. These reforms marked
a significant alteration in the legal and social interpretation of delinquency
from one of criminality to one of conditioning, and of the delinquent from
villain to victim. The focus, then, was not on the crime, but on the criminal;
the hearing concentrated not on the act, but on the personality.

In terms of criminal punishment, the Penal Code of 1810 considered the
convicted child as an adult in miniature, with the age of majority set at sixteen. Articles 66 and 67 of the code based conviction of juvenile offenders
on the concept of discretion (*discernement*); that is, those committing crimes
who acted with discretion were aware of the consequences and should be
punished accordingly, as responsible adults. There was no separate tribunal
or penitentiary system for minors, although an 1814 ordinance did create
special quarters within customary prisons. By the mid-nineteenth century,
however, there was a social movement to reassess the problem of convicted
delinquents. Private institutions were established to remedy the lack of public
reformatories for juveniles; they were designed to teach wayward youth the
value of honest hard work in the wholesome agrarian environment of a farm.
This was the era of the repressive agricultural colonies of Oullins, Neunhoff,
Mettray, and, for girls, La Solitude de Nazareth. Under the influence of this
"philanthropic" movement, the Second Republic passed the law of August 5,
1850, which established public *colonies pénitentiaires* and advocated severe discipline at these penal colonies to promote a moral, religious, and professional
education for convicted minors. Importantly, this new system was intended
for both those who acted with discretion and those who did not.[26]

It would be another half-century before any real change or reform was
made to this system. The law of April 12, 1906, raised the age of majority
from sixteen to eighteen, but it was the law of July 22, 1912, that significantly altered the juvenile justice system. First, a juvenile court system was
established separate from that of adults; second, minors under the age of
thirteen were now considered to be outside the jurisdiction of penal law;
third, a probation system was established that introduced the concept of
liberté surveillée into the penal system. In the end, the fate of the thirteen- to
eighteen-year-olds again rested on the court's interpretation of his or her
discretion during the criminal act.[27]

With the growing influence of psychology and psychiatry, in the 1920s and 1930s, a major critique developed about the assumptions of this juvenile justice system. Experts argued that the court should not base its decision on a minor's discretion, but instead should focus on the underlying causes that led to crime. They believed the juvenile justice system should rely on the testimony of specialists to determine proper treatment. There was an emerging consensus among some experts that delinquent behavior was largely the result of poor socialization. Specialists agreed that though children might be born with certain innate characteristics influenced by heredity, their environment, salubrious or nefarious, exerted an influence just as significant, if not more so. Thus, because bad conditions were believed to be the determining factor in the criminal behavior of minors, emphasis should be placed on diagnosis and treatment rather than stern punishment. It became more important to investigate a delinquent's character than the crime itself.[28] The rupture of war and the concomitant rise in delinquency rates enabled advocates of reform (psychologists, psychiatrists, lawyers, judges, social workers) to bring about massive legal and institutional changes to the juvenile justice system.

Despite Fourth Republic claims of being the inspired progenitors of the new law, its passage was in fact the culmination of decades of reform efforts that actually came together most effectively during the Second World War as the Vichy government took measures to overhaul the juvenile penal system.[29] By 1941, as the rapid increase in juvenile crime became evident, the Vichy government sought new solutions to empower the state to regulate social tensions and maintain public order.[30] Considering the central role that the family and the young occupied in Vichy's ideological vision, it should not be surprising that efforts were made to improve the stock of young people particularly through the improvement of their familial and social milieu, something professional experts had been advocating for more than a decade. Thus, there was a common interest between the reactionary chauvinism of Vichy and the professional therapeutic critique. Interestingly, it seems that the top-down authoritarianism of Vichy helped authorize sweeping systemic reforms that had been resisted by institutional intransigence throughout the 1930s, while the shock of defeat, collapse, and the Occupation convinced others of the need for such sweeping changes. The July 27, 1942, law replaced that of 1912 with a new "code of delinquent youth." The new law, however, never went into effect, as Pétain's National Revolution was extinguished under the boot of the Nazi Occupation, and later the post-liberation government rejected most Vichy legislation as a matter of policy. Yet the new code of 1942 would be reproduced with a few key modifications in 1945 by the provisional government of Charles de Gaulle.[31] Though the committee responsible for the 1945 law deliberately obfuscated and denied the influence of Vichy initiatives, the text of 1945 reflected in broad contours that of 1942, demonstrating, as with so much else, that the details of social policy could be maintained despite radical shifts in ideological underpinnings.[32]

The 1945 law sanctioned new concepts of culpability and new methods of rehabilitation, radically altering France's juvenile justice system from one of punishment to one of treatment. Rather than punish the wayward youth, the new system sought to convert him (the implied assumption that he was a boy was implicit) from social deviant to productive citizen and (also implicitly) from lower class to middle class. The Ordinance of 1945 was not merely an attempt to reduce juvenile crime, but also an effort to apply a standard of homogeneity to the daily lives of young people operating within their family and, most importantly, within society as a whole. In 1945 the government charged the juvenile court to regulate relations within families and neighborhoods, with the ultimate goal of integrating "endangered" young people as responsible adult members of French society. By refashioning the flawed parts of society, the French state hoped to improve the constituent whole. In this way, reeducation would not only better the individual, or even a generation, but upon their maturity these former delinquents would contribute to a new, improved, and homogenized France as well.

It is important to recognize the distinction between concern for the well-being of a young individual and anxiety for the deleterious effect this individual could have on the well-being of the group. Although these worries were not mutually exclusive, the language and rhetoric of postwar reform in France seemed to emphasize the latter over the former. Alfred Potier, in a 1953 report on juvenile delinquency, warned that "a child or adolescent offense that is of little worry at present, can constitute a social reality much more worthy of attention [later]."[33] This attitude reveals an assumption of a causal connection between the dalliance of unruly kids and the debauched malevolence of adult criminals. If the origins of adult criminality lay within the confines of childhood experience, then the state could intervene to prevent future criminality, and as the nature of reeducation makes clear, these interventions assumed a particular social class. A later meeting of juvenile court judges and directors of juvenile corrections institutions confirmed that while the paternal power of the state was not absolute, "society does have a word to say because the child is a future citizen. In sum, paternal power belongs to parents under a double condition: the right of the child to develop his potential and the right of society to exercise control."[34]

The law of 1945 presumed minors under the age of eighteen were not criminally responsible. A delinquent was "no longer considered as culpable, but as a victim, a victim of his family, of his heredity and of his milieu," or, in other words, of his social position, familial conditions, neighborhood, or class.[35] Thus, he should be protected, reeducated, and readapted to life in a society dominated by bourgeois norms of morality. The state believed that the true solution to the problem was prevention. The remedy to delinquency lay in improving the social conditions surrounding young people in their homes, neighborhoods, and schools. It abandoned the repressive penal code that had sanctioned the use of penitential colonies such as the infamous Mettray, where boys worked as agricultural laborers under harsh living conditions and severe punishments. That system had failed; it hardened the problem child into the criminal adult, creating graver problems than it resolved.

Auguste Le Breton's popular 1956 novel *Les Hauts murs* (The High Walls) illustrated this position remarkably well. Set in the interwar 1920s, the story follows an amiable fourteen-year-old war orphan, Yves Tréguier, as he is pulled, gravity-like, through an orphanage to a reformatory and at last, at the brutal core of the novel, to a penal colony. Abused and mistreated in a Dickensian hell, Tréguier repeatedly attempts escape only to be punished harshly upon his recapture. In each institution, one by one, Tréguier loses his few friends through escape, transfer, or suicide. With no family or friends, he is abandoned to his fate inside the juvenile prison system, where gambling, thieving, and fistfighting rule, until at last he kills in self-defense. He has entered these state institutions guilty of being an orphan, but he ends as a murderer. Reluctantly, Tréguier is remade into a criminal, fulfilling the system's premature condemnation. The penal institution was a factory that specialized in the production of criminals. Le Breton's sympathetic portrayal of a youth trapped in the quicksand of delinquent incarceration epitomized the reforming sensibility that had inspired legislators to adopt the Ordinance of 1945.[36]

As a boy, Le Breton had spent several years in a reformatory, and he dedicated *The High Walls* to his friends there. But his attitude marks a striking contrast to the more renowned delinquent-turned-writer, Jean Genet. Genet *celebrated* his transformation from orphan to delinquent; he embraced villainy and transgression as liberating and cathartic. For Genet, the juvenile penal system of reformatories, jails, and penal colonies was the nostalgic homeplace where he had matured into social outlaw. He was even known to have declared that his true mother was Mettray, the institution that was closed in 1939 after a lengthy journalistic exposé resulted in the publication of a scathing testimonial entitled *Maisons de supplices* (*Torture Houses*).[37] The reforms of the postwar period were anathema to Genet's ideas of the beauty and virtue in child criminality; they sought to eliminate the very conditions that had created him, and, therefore, quite logically in his mind, he opposed them. Genet supported the oppression of the unreformed penal colony *because* it turned youngsters into hardened criminals.

In 1947 Genet was asked by Fernand Pouey to prepare a broadcast for Pouey's radio program *Carte Blanche*. Genet wrote a script denouncing the ongoing reforms and improvements to the juvenile justice system because, he said, the harsh cruelties of internment transformed the child into the criminal and, hence, into the suffering poet. He admired the penal colony as a manifestation of the child's "violence, strength, and virility." It was a necessary step toward heroism, and "these cruelties had to be born . . . out of the passion of these children for evil." In reference to the reforms, he proclaimed: "As for me, I have chosen; I will be on the side of crime. And I'll help children not to regain your houses, your factories, your schools, your laws and holy sacraments, but to violate them." Not surprisingly, the broadcast of Genet's polemic was cancelled by the authorities, but in 1949 he published the censored text, in book form, as *L'Enfant criminel* (The Criminal Child).[38] The absurdity of Genet's claim that the tyrannical treatment of delinquents was heroic and desirable must be recognized in part as an intentional provocation. Genet's need to validate his own past and endorse a masculinist morality based on the aesthetics of evil put him in the ridiculous position of advocating for the cruel abuse of juveniles. His was a unique voice of opposition in the overwhelming postwar consensus advocating reform, and his objections did nothing to stop the unwavering momentum.

In the fall of 1945 the Ministry of Justice made the Department of Supervised Education (Direction de l'Education Surveillée), under the direction of Jean-Louis Costa, an independent department to administer the new re-education program.[39] The department would not only operate the new treatment system for delinquents that replaced the penal system of 1912, it would also be in charge of "children at risk" (*en danger moral*, or *moralement abandonné*). This was a concept, outlined in previous legislation, that identified potentially troubled children and adolescents. The idea of the morally abandoned child had entered the institutional framework of France during the Third Republic. A series of laws, predominantly that of July 24, 1889,[40] had been established to combat the ill-effects of poor and/or abusive parenting, which could cause a lapse in the moral standards and personal habits of the young, and which, in the end, could result in deviancy and criminality in adults. In the late nineteenth century, the family had emerged as a critical site for the state to form a secular yet morally astute republican society; the new legislation gave the government the power to regulate family matters by entering the household and removing children identified as being "at risk."[41] In 1945, the new Department for Supervised Education was not only responsible for setting young wrongdoers on the correct course, but also for rescuing potential wrongdoers as well.

In addition to combating juvenile crime, the goal of the new department was to realize a series of positive reforms in "judicial, social, and pedagogical domains."[42] It worked in tandem with the new juvenile court system, administering its auxiliary services. It conducted inquiries, examinations, and investigations; updated and expanded the system of shelters (*centres d'accueil*), the observation centers (*centres d'observation*), and the institutions of rehabilitation (*rééducation*); and it coordinated the probation network (*liberté surveillée*). The impetus behind supervised education was to separate these new institutions from the jurisdiction of the Penitentiary Department and break definitively with the "repressive" tradition of punishment and move toward a therapeutic system.[43]

The first step in this process was observation. Once a minor was brought before the tribunal via police arrest, difficulties at school, or persistent trouble-making, an investigation would begin into the background and character of

the wrongdoer in an attempt to explain the causes of his social maladjust-
ment so as to determine the appropriate solution. According to the Ministry
of Justice, the court was "to proceed with an in-depth inquiry on behalf of
the minor, notably on the material and moral situation of the family and
on the character and history of the youth, because it is important to know,
more than the reproachful hard facts, the minor's true personality, which will
determine the measures taken in his interest."[44] The idea behind the entire
process was to try to understand the youth, to recognize delinquent behavior
as the result of problems of character due to failed socialization, and to determine the best means for correction.

Depending on the case, as the investigation proceeded the minor would
be housed at an observation center (*centre d'observation*, or *centre d'acceuil*),
or he would be allowed to continue his daily life within his family or under
a guardian (*en milieu ouvert*). But in either instance the procedures were
largely the same: social workers investigated family and neighborhood, psychiatrists and psychologists interviewed and tested the minor, social workers inquired at schools, and doctors conducted medical examinations. The
inquiry ended with a tally of character traits, family history, daily activities,
and personal habits. The duration of the investigation varied according to
the difficulty of the case, but generally if the perpetrator remained in the
family or with a guardian it lasted three months, whereas if he was resi-
dent in one of the centers it tended to be shorter.[45] The observation centers
were located in those places that had the most acute rates of juvenile crime,
typically in urban areas. In addition to Paris, Lyon, and Marseilles, centers
were planned for Toulouse, Rennes, and Lille. A reception center was to
be placed within each civil department, to work as a temporary shelter and
examination center.[46] The culmination of the entire observation process resulted in a recommendation to the court for the appropriate form of "reeducation." Many of these procedures had been in practice for years in a variety
of forms, but the new system made them a matter of strict policy.[47]

The means of reeducation were designed to vary according to the parameters of each case. Once the period of observation had resulted in a completed study, the minor's case was returned to the court for a judicial ruling
of the appropriate treatment, based on an assessment of the severity of the
problem. Whenever possible, the judge would set up a program of counseling that left the minor in his family's custody, which was known as *liberté*

surveillée, or "supervised freedom." Court-appointed volunteers continued with the counseling of the delinquent, and were used "to assure, in principle, the surveillance of minors."[48] Keeping a watchful eye, they furnished reports to the court each trimester, relating the situation and progress of the delinquent in terms of his or her rehabilitation. The volunteers worked in conjunction with professionals to monitor and direct the youngsters under their tutelage. The idea was that they would make certain that appointments were kept, households were wholesome, and the state was informed, though in practice it seldom worked out that way. Generally, volunteers came from the ranks of the liberal professions, or were social workers or primary teachers. But in large urban areas it was sometimes difficult to place volunteers, so priests were often given charge of cases there.[49] Although the program was concentrated in cities, delinquency was not just an urban phenomenon. In December 1954, of 13,227 minors in the *liberté surveillée* program nationwide, 3,459 were in rural areas, and of the 5,376 adult volunteers, 2,186 of them worked in the countryside.[50] This means that the program had one volunteer for every 2.5 juveniles.

Liberté surveillée was a temporary solution conceptualized in part as continual observation but also as a kind of probation. The inquiry established the "character" of the minor, and the judge's decision depended on the good faith of the adolescent to stay out of trouble. The judge could, at any time, revoke his decision and take more severe measures. To qualify for *liberté surveillée*, the home environment could not present any grave difficulties; indeed, the family was to be considered "perfectible," and the social milieu in which the child continued to live could not be deemed harmful. By 1958, the program was considered to have been something of a success. Parisian judge Jean Chazal, in his work *L'Enfance délinquante*, estimated that the *liberté surveillée* program's rate of success was 71 percent, with a failure rate of 9.5 percent and an unconfirmed rate of 19.5 percent.[51]

For many cases, the court determined there was a need for intervention, and so removed the delinquent from his home and temporarily placed him in an institution for reeducation. The term "reeducation" applied to public institutions of *éducation surveillée*, but also to other organizations, public and private, that worked to reform the delinquent outside his family milieu. Approximately 10 percent of juvenile delinquents, most of whom were over the age of seventeen, were annually deemed as unreformable and sentenced to a term of incarceration.[52] The primary task of the new institutions of supervised education was to substitute new methods of character reeducation—emotional and moral development, professional training, scholastic education, physical education, and directed leisure activities, such as scouting—for conventional methods of punishment and incarceration. Ultimately, the goal of reeducation was the harmonious readaptation of the juvenile delinquent to society. For that reason, the institutions divided their charges into groups of approximately twenty delinquents, who together would learn the value of participation and solidarity within a peer community. This interaction was designed to build trust between individuals, a sense of obligation and duty to others, and a basic understanding of the dynamics of group living.[53]

After minors had been divided into groups according to gender and age, placement criteria depended on the results of the observation period. Delinquents were assigned according to the severity of their cases or the "perversity" of the individual. There were five public institutions for boys—Saint-Jodard, Saint-Maurice, Saint-Hilaire, Belle-Ile-en-Mer, and Aniane—which handled 75–80 percent of all the cases.[54] The three institutions for girls were Brécourt, Cadillac, and Clermont. The institutions differed according to the average age of the minors they accepted, the type of professional training offered, and the level of security they offered, based on the assessed degree of reformability of the delinquents. Minors were categorized as being either "reformable," "rather difficult," "difficult," "very difficult," or "unreformable," and were then placed in the corresponding institution, with Saint-Jodard and Aniane occupying opposite ends of the spectrum from not-so-bad, younger boys to very bad, older boys. With the exception of Saint-Jodard, all the institutions were former agricultural colonies that dated from the nineteenth century. It was an old idea: remove the urban delinquent from the city and get him into the rural, robust life of the country. Yet by the mid-twentieth century, young people required urban labor skills. Converting the facilities of these former penitential farms entailed a great many improvements to support all the activities outlined for the new program of reeducation and represented another facet of France's willingness to invest in its young people.

Unlike penitential incarceration, reeducation was not designed to punish the miscreant, but to reform him and make him into a productive citizen of France. Because most delinquents were male, professional training was as vital as traditional schooling. Because notions of the productive citizen were gendered as male, reeducation programs for girls lagged behind; they continued to promote "traditional" household skills such as sewing. (Importantly, for girls delinquency was overtly conceptualized in sexual terms, which I address in the following chapter.) Jean-Louis Costa considered professional training "to be the basis of reeducation in all the institutions," because not only did it give young delinquents "a taste of work, a boost of will and perseverance, but above all it constitute[d] the best means of preparing them for their social placement."[55] This "placement" assumed a future of manual labor, and therefore it was important that the young man learn a wage-earning skill that would "permit him to acquire a sense of human dignity and to inculcate within him the habits and lifestyle of a useful citizen."[56] The Department of Supervised Education hoped to "convert" the young delinquent into an "honest adult." It was assumed that minors would spend only limited time in the reeducation facilities. Their terms averaged only two to three years, usually until they reached the age of majority,[57] so the system was set up to progressively move the young men from institution to professional school, and then on to a halfway house before their final release into society. In April 1948, Aide des Jeunes à la Reconstruction (AJAR) in Besançon even accepted some young delinquents into its reconstruction program. In consideration of society, AJAR felt it was important to think about "the needs of the national economy and not contribute to unemployment."[58] Accordingly, many of these delinquents left the AJAR program with a Certificat d'Aptitude Professionnelle or a Certificat d'Aptitude aux Métiers in a skilled trade such as cabinetry, plumbing, or masonry. In 1950, of the 225 who took certificate exams, 167 received degrees. Thus, public institutions were housing close to two thousand minors by 1950, compared to nine hundred in 1945, but there were approximately seven thousand other delinquents annually who were classified for reeducation but who were conspicuously absent from the rolls of the institutions.[59]

Most of the young mischief-makers were placed within private institutions that were dedicated to housing and reforming delinquents. Due to the lack of public institutions, 75 percent of delinquents sentenced by the juvenile court were placed in private reformatories, which meant that the new system of reeducation relied on these establishments to institute its reforms. Most of the private homes were sponsored by philanthropic societies, both religious and secular, that had been founded in the late nineteenth century to safeguard the welfare of children; still others were privately owned by for-profit entrepreneurs. Both types of institutions received significant subsidies from the state for each juvenile placed by the court; however, after 1945, in order to receive these funds, the state subjected the homes to new reeducation guidelines.[60] Notably, the 1945 Ordinance came about because some of the charitable programs had already been implementing new conceptions of treatment, rather than punishment. Jean-Louis Costa credited private initiative with largely inspiring the new law (the law of 1850 for agricultural colonies was promulgated in a similar fashion).[61] But ensuring that the private homes (their number fluctuated around 150 during the Fourth Republic) adhered to the new principles of reeducation would prove to be difficult. Ultimately, the Department of Supervised Education had difficulty in bringing the private institutions under their control and in monitoring their day-to-day programs—until, that is, the public scandal of Serge Tonelli and the Petites Ailes institution forced the government to take action.

The Problem of Adults

As the Petites Ailes scandal emphasized to the public and the reeducation program reiterated in policy, the responsibility for misbehavior did not reside with the young, but rather it was to be found in personality problems, familial negligence, or societal incompetence. Young mischief-makers were not inherently evil, but had been conditioned by their debauched environment. In the course of the Petites Ailes debates, Senator Charles Morel pointed out that modern society had a tendency to separate the family from its chief duty and obligation to children, and that intervention by a "third party," the state, was particularly necessary for children at risk. Morel noted, "Almost always, childhood offenses are the consequences of an unfortunate life of which he is not responsible." It is "in the interest of France" that the state intervene when "parents are indigent in their noble mission." Morel continued, "The family is too often incapable of assuring by itself this special education, nor does it always understand the benefit and need."[62] Senator Marcel Mollé urged the government to expand its network of institutions, because too often "children are left in their family due to a lack of space." In a 1950 report, government officials estimated that at least 300,000, and perhaps as many as 500,000 young people were "at risk" or in "moral danger" in postwar France, and therefore in need of government intervention.[63] It was clear that the family milieu could be considered a harmful environment that could produce juvenile crime and placed children in moral danger. The revue *Enfance*, an academic journal of psychology, pedagogy, and sociology, maintained that "a child's character disorder should be defined as a function of his family milieu."[64] But if young people were misbehaving members of hazardous families, then it was specifically the adult family members, the parents, who were problematic. Indeed, a law proposal in 1952 suggested that parents should be prosecuted if a minor's "future is compromised by [their] indignity or incapacity."[65]

As already mentioned, the reform law of 1945 had assumed a causal relationship between the family, the environment, and delinquency. Because reeducation was based on the assumed failure of the family to correctly socialize the child, Article 8 of the new law stated that a period of observation of the child should focus on "the material and moral situation of the family."[66] Problems at home were often attributed to growing up in single-parent households, as a result of either separation or death, but working mothers, unclean or insalubrious homes, and even "alcoholic or syphilitic heredity" were also cited as contributing to the child's delinquency. Such problems appeared most prominently in urban working-class homes and in the rural outreaches of the provinces.[67] Of course, the effects of the war were also taken into account, especially the black market and the immoral influence of the Germans and, later, the Americans. But mostly the war was considered in terms of its effect on the family: separation due to flight, deportation, or death; hardship due to rationed food, ruined housing, or disrupted education. "It is well known that 80–90 percent of juvenile delinquents come from separated families," claimed a 1951 government study, which also found that the government's "administration of minors is more and more a paternal one."[68] This conclusion, however, was based on conventional wisdom and anecdotal evidence rather than on the contemporary research data, which did not support such a claim.[69] Still, the supposed absent figure within the family was conceptualized, both literally and figuratively, as a paternal one. It was not merely the breakup of families or the weakening of parental authority that was the problem, but specifically the absence or lack of a *paternal* authority. Increasingly, the state envisioned itself as a surrogate father whose job was to protect, regulate, and discipline the young.[70]

Alfred Potier, a magistrate from the Ministry of Justice, advised that when confronted with delinquency, "society should be like the father faced with the ordinary misbehavior of his child," and should base its punishment on an edifying reprimand. According to Potier, society has the interest of the child as its "supreme objective." Furthermore, he pointed out, "the difference between familial education and social education is that the interest of the family should be sacrificed to the interest of the child, while the last actually coincides with the interests of society." For Potier, what was best for the young was best for society, and what was best for society was best for the young. The future of both society and the young were conflated as being mutually efficacious. "It is this interest of society that demands to transform or complete inadequate education" so that the juvenile delinquent can "start again on the correct path and become an honest citizen and worker. Thus a full recuperation takes place to the benefit of society."[71]

Such assumptions regarding the state's right to intervene in family affairs originated in the second half of the nineteenth century, when legislation was passed by the Third Republic establishing the government's ability to regulate family life. Children and young people became the prominent objects of both public philanthropy and state initiative in the 1870s and 1880s, as philanthropic societies and associations sought to get children out of factories, into schools, and inculcated as a part of a new moral order.[72] These groups brought the issue of children at risk and in moral danger to the forefront of public concern, which led to necessary progressive social policies that effectively curbed the harm, abuse, and neglect of children. One result of this effort to protect children's welfare was the reconceptualization of the child as the most essential part of the family, its raison d'être.[73] The family was reorganized around the interest of the child, since the (male) child represented the future citizen, worker, and soldier. In terms of the law, parental authority was supervised by the state. The Third Republic could distribute and rescind this authority by virtue of laws, such as the previously mentioned law of July 24, 1889, also known as the law on the termination of paternal authority, which provided for the protection of maltreated or morally abandoned children. Furthermore, the state's authority, according to the law, was gendered; it was specifically "paternal," rather than merely "parental." The concept of the moral endangerment of children at the hands of their parents and the legal formulations of the Third Republic were designed to combat the decline of the "domestic civilizing process."[74] Parenthood was displaced from being a naturalized right to one of social responsibility. In the patriarchal household, as the arbiter of familial discipline, the father was ultimately responsible. Consequently, it is not surprising that intervention by the state was often interpreted as benevolent fatherly tutelage.

But the family represented only the most immediate corrupting influence for young people. Outside the door to the family home lay the temptations of the street, neighborhood, and city. Jean Chazal wrote that delinquency was a problem for socio-psychological study rather than criminology. It arose out of the "family and social conditions" that formed the network of relationships between "the child and his family, ethnic, social, economic, scholastic, and/or professional groups."[75] The community as a whole, not just shoddy parenting, was responsible for the poor character of young people. It was the "individual and social factors of milieu that enticed them incessantly."[76] In one measure to get children off the streets, the state strengthened truancy laws, by providing more power to truancy officers and a new system of bureaucratic control over parents to ensure that their children were in school.[77]

Outside the schoolyard, the state attempted to control the activities of young people by restricting their access to noxious influences. In 1953 the National Assembly passed a new ordinance that restricted access to bars and other establishments serving alcohol. Importantly, the law did not prohibit alcoholic consumption by minors, as that had been in place since 1917. Rather, it aimed at keeping young people under sixteen from witnessing the consumption of alcohol and the inevitable occasions of drunkenness that occurred in establishments intended primarily for drink. Senator Marcelle Delabie urged the passage of this measure, to ensure "the physically and morally healthy development of youth," upon which "the future of our country depends."[78] According to Deputy Jean Cayeux, who introduced the legislation, too often young people were unable to resist temptation, and restricted access to this "social evil" would protect young people from falling into the jeopardy of delinquency.[79] It is not odd that the state sought to limit the young's exposure to alcohol and its fellow traveler, the alcoholic.

Familial alcoholism, not surprisingly, was considered one of the essential factors rendering households prone to delinquency. Some estimates claimed that as many as three-quarters of juvenile delinquents had at least one alcoholic parent.[80] Pierre Mendès-France, famous as a milk drinker, had attacked alcoholism during his tenure in office by removing subsidies and proposing new taxes for the alcohol industry.[81] In 1959 the measures restricting access to pernicious amusements were expanded to include cabarets, dance clubs, gaming houses, theaters, and hotels, or any establishment that offered "entertainment or spectacles harmful to morality,"[82] a problem the Ministry of Public Health and Population considered "the most delicate" in protecting youth.[83]

These efforts to mask adult pastimes from the watchful eyes of young innocents implicitly condemned these activities as reproachful. It was not enough to prevent minors from participating in adult activities; they had to be totally concealed to ensure proper moral upbringing. Similarly, the disposition toward concealment resulted in substantial censorship of publications. A law to regulate sales of juvenile literature in 1949 aimed to curb the harmful effects of comic books (see chapter 6 for a full discussion). There was an effort to demarcate the boundaries of what constituted an adult lifestyle from that of an adolescent. The state increasingly used its powers to intervene in areas that had previously been the domain of parents.

Bad, ineffective parenting was seen by many as a specific symptom of a larger moral crisis, one that affected all of adult society. Doctor Marcus-Jeisler, in her 1947 report on the effects of the war on young people, insisted that the "general demoralization dated from well before the war." The war may have augmented the problems of juvenile crime, but the groundwork had been laid by a corrupt and immoral adult generation. To resolve the problems of young people, it was necessary that adults seek a "revalorization of honesty." According to Marcus-Jeisler, "It is absolutely necessary that we impel adults to give the right example. It is at this price that we will have a strong and decent youth."[84] A priest involved with counseling adolescents was asked by *Elle* magazine to identify the causes of juvenile delinquency. He responded, "In the first place, they are familial," but he continued by accusing the older generation of having lost its moral authority generally. "Our times are crazy," he said. "How do you expect kids to keep some stability in a world where the sense of values is turned upside down?"

Paul Baudet, a lawyer, responded similarly, by admonishing adult society: "It is necessary to restore the confidence of the young: confidence in their parents, confidence in their educators, confidence in well-founded moral values, confidence in the future. Adolescents today not only ask to believe in someone or something, but not to be fooled. They require a complete harmony between words and actions." For, "Adolescents will reform when adults reform themselves first."[85]

Perhaps the best example of this attitude that permeated France is a cinematic one. Popular culture does not strictly determine public point of view, but it does tend to translate and reflect aspects of collective sensibility. Furthermore, a successful film or novel is one that has clearly tapped into an expectation or a mentality that permeates the society, and in the end it serves to both create and perpetuate this disposition. Few films from this period had greater success than François Truffaut's feature debut, *Les Quatre cents coups* (*The 400 Blows*). Critically, the film was a smash: in 1959 Truffaut won Best Director at Cannes, and the film itself garnered Best Foreign Film from the New York Film Critics, a Medal of Honor from the British Film Institute, and the Oscar for Best Foreign Language Film. Financially, the film was a hit as well, playing in France and around the world to captivated audiences and parting the curtain for New Wave cinema's astonishing debut. Like other New Wave directors, Truffaut was a young man, twenty-seven, when he filmed *The 400 Blows*, so this film represented the vision or voice of a young person. Though he denied that the film was autobiographical, in 1947 Truffaut had been arrested, at his father's request (a reminder that paternal authority did still exist), and sent to a reeducation center at Villejuif.[86]

As Truffaut has explained, the film explores the "dreadful gap between the world of adolescents and that of adults."[87] The film follows Antoine Doinel (Jean-Pierre Léaud), a likable thirteen-year-old, through his daily routine of school and home, of chores and amusement, of scorn and neglect. The opening scene at school, an institution designed to facilitate the adaptation of the young into society, establishes the dynamic between youth and adult that is consistent throughout the film. A disgruntled schoolmaster nags and berates his students in his meager efforts to educate them. "Poor France! What a future!" he laments, unable to see himself as part of the problem. At home, as the only child of a couple that would rather have none, Antoine is unsettled and cheerless. The problem is not that Antoine is mistreated, but that "he isn't treated at all."[88] His father refers to him simply as "the kid," and his mother treats him lovingly only after Antoine catches her kissing another man. Displaying more affectation than affection, she wants Antoine to be complicit in her adulterous secret.

Between the dread of school and the disregard of home, Antoine resigns himself contentedly to the asylum of the street, with its absence of adult authority. He and his friend René run about Paris committing small transgressions and petty sins. Unable to sell a stolen typewriter, Antoine is caught returning it to his father's office. It is his father who then turns him in to the police. In a pivotal scene, Antoine responds to the questions posed by an off-screen psychologist while he is being detained at a *centre d'observation*. Looking directly into the camera, Antoine testifies before us, the jury, exposing the negligence of his parents. To confirm our verdict, Truffaut brings Antoine's mother to visit, where she declares that neither she nor her husband cares about Antoine any longer and that they have abandoned him to the system. Antoine later escapes, however, making his way to the sea and, ostensibly, toward his freedom and a different future (Figure 10). This summary may make the film seem heavy-handed, melodramatic, or simplistic, but it is not. There are no alcoholic rants or beatings, no screams or sobs or dramatic confrontations; there is simply a heavy malaise weighing down on young Antoine. In its condemnation of adults and its valorization of the young, ultimately the film is not very subtle.

This meaning was not lost on Truffaut's contemporaries, and admiration for the implicit message of the film crossed all political lines. Louis Chavet, of *Le Figaro*, maintained that the protagonist of the film was "not a monster and committed only venial mistakes." After all, "he had excuses," notably his parents.[89] Simone Dubreuilh, of *Liberation*, said that Antoine was "a victim, but a victim of foolish circumstance, of adult fear." According to her, Antoine's refusal to submit to his destiny liberated him from social constraint through the device of petty crime.[90] *The 400 Blows*, then, represents the testimony of a mistreated and misunderstood youth surviving the rigors of adolescence in spite of adult dereliction. Antoine Doinel, like Le Breton's Yves Tréguier, is the Delinquent-Hero. Both characters present sympathetic portrayals of young defiants chafing against the invisible strictures and rules of an unjust and unfeeling adult world. The Delinquent-Hero is a resistor rejecting the adulterated society of his elders. He is a romanticized and

Figure 10. Famous closing shot of *The 400 Blows* (1959) with Antoine Doinel, the Delinquent-Hero, at the seashore. Christophe L Documentation.

sympathetic hero living a life on the margin. Movies, novels, and popular amusements allow an audience to participate innocuously in the risks and dangers of youth. One can collectively identify with such characters as the ultra-cool, suave gangster Michel, for example, in Jean-Luc Godard's *A Bout de souffle* (*Breathless*, 1959) as he hot-wires sports cars and eludes police.

The Spectacle of Delinquency

The thrill of theft and the excitement of petty crime exhilarated audiences in Robert Bresson's 1959 classic film *Pickpocket*. The film follows Michel, an unemployed young man who chooses to support himself by pilfering the pockets of unwitting strangers. Michel prowls through the crowds of the Metro and the racetrack, surreptitiously studying his prey and plotting his strategy. We share his nervous tension as he presses up against a woman so as to position his fingers with patience and supple deliberation inside her purse. Camouflaged by the crowd around him, he slowly and steadily removes her wallet while maintaining a blank stare that belies the rapid beating of his heart and the slick movement of his hands. The thrill of detection and the enticement of danger compel Michel to bolder and bolder deeds. "I thought I was mastering the world," he confesses. The film is dominated by physical movement, by the prowess and finesse of street thieves, rather than the banter of dialogue. In an amazing sequence, Michel works a train station with two others, demonstrating the timing, grace, and choreography of hands slipping adroitly into coat pockets, passing wallets beneath folded newspapers, and deftly removing watches from wrists. Like magicians, the young pickpockets perform a ballet of confident hand movements. As a protagonist, Michel is neither sympathetic nor disagreeable. We sense that he steals by compulsion, that he deliberately and self-consciously tries to operate outside the conventions of morality. Inevitably, Michel is arrested and imprisoned. Bresson does not celebrate this lifestyle so much as he presents it as a matter of fact. The viewer does not cheer for Michel as a romantic hero, but rather we become complicit in the titillation of the crime and the seductive lure of thieving as we excitedly catch our breath in rapt attention with each new pocket picked.

This fascination with the baser side of humanity not only captivated the hoi polloi of the cinema house, it charmed the intellectual and cultural aesthete as well. In postwar France, Jean Genet became the darling of the intelligentsia. With Jean Cocteau and Jean-Paul Sartre as patrons, Genet maneuvered through the highest circles of the Parisian literati without the credentialed accoutrements of high society. A self-proclaimed dirty little thief who left school at the age of twelve, Genet used his writings to philosophically reimagine the world, rejecting moral standards and "reversing traditional hierarchies of value and meaning." He wrote five novels between 1942 and 1947, four of which were fictionalized memoirs depicting his scabrous life as a young thief, prostitute, and vagabond. These works, published clandestinely, circulated within the small literary circles of postwar France, provoking immense speculation about the nature of good and evil, right and wrong, virtue and vice—all themes of particular resonance in the wake of the war and resistance/collaboration.[91]

Born in 1910, Genet was abandoned by his mother and subsequently raised by foster parents. At age thirteen, he ran away from an apprenticeship as a typographer and began a life of crime. Regularly arrested for theft and vagabondage, the young Genet was repeatedly incarcerated in such infamous prisons as La Petite-Roquette, Fresnes, and Mettray, among many, many others. As a soldier (the army regularly recruited at penal colonies such as Mettray), Genet traveled across France and Europe, but again he could not resist the temptation to desert and live the vagabond's life of evasion and deception. His novels are primarily constructed from his experiences as a young vagrant and criminal, and they contain near pornographic passages of his sexual encounters. Not only a thief and vagabond, Genet was also a homosexual, which further defined him as a deviant, both socially and sexually. His novels revel in lurid detail while presenting a tale of his youth as a self-proclaimed pariah. *Notre-Dame de Fleurs* (*Our Lady of the Flowers*) drew on his childhood, *Miracle de la Rose* (*Miracle of the Rose*) on his incarceration at Mettray, *Journal du voleur* (*The Thief's Journal*) on his vagrant drifting, and *Pompes funèbres* (*Funeral Rites*) on his love affairs during the war.[92]

Although Genet would not achieve popular success until the international triumph of his plays—*Le Balcon* (*The Balcony*), *Les Nègres, clownerie* (*The Blacks, A Clown Show*), and *Les Paravents* (*The Screens*)—in the late fifties and early sixties, Jean-Paul Sartre would take it upon himself to proclaim Genet's genius, in his 1952 paean *Saint Genet: Comédien et martyr* (*Saint Genet: Actor and Martyr*), published as a book-length introduction to Genet's collected works issued by Gallimard.[93] Part literary criticism, part biography, and part hagiography, *Saint Genet* served as a philosophical treatise extolling the integrity of criminality as a virtuous state of being. Labeled a thief and a delinquent by society, Genet accepted these terms as transformative and, in the end, sacred. In his writing, Genet sought an inversion of the moral order, a subversion of standard propriety and a sanctification of evil and betrayal. For Sartre and his protégés, Jean Genet became the supreme anti-hero, the thinking man's Delinquent-Hero.

In a book-length essay published as *L'Enfant criminel* (The Criminal Child), Genet pointed out the contradiction between French society's admiration for art and literature that revered crime and its scornful condemnation of criminals themselves: "Your literature, your fine arts, your after-dinner entertainments celebrate crime. The talent of your poets has glorified the criminal whom you hate in life." Fictional crime was sanitary, but for Genet the true heroes were the young brutes in the street coming to terms with their foul actions. He reproached the French: "You admit heroism only when it is tamed. You ignore heroism in its true nature." Extolling the virtue of the delinquent as hero, he maintained that "nothing will replace the se-duction of the outlaw," and that, in reference to the spirit of reform, "there are no remedies, I hope, against this heroism."[94] Indeed, while the French public insatiably absorbed films and novels about delinquents and crime, a morbid fascination of disbelief and disgust colored their experience of real juvenile crime. Unable to look away, the public was transfixed by the brutal reality of juvenile crimes reported in the media.

Violence held the greatest appeal, and most of the juvenile media sensa-tions had murder as a common denominator. At times, the murders might be the result of panic from a theft gone wrong, as in the case from Valence; at other times, an unsavory act of passion. But those cases that demonstrated a calculated disregard for life, a cold unkindness to the victims, or a pre-meditated plot of trickery were the ones that captivated the public. The murder of Alain Guyader was just such a case, and it held sway over the pub-lic imagination throughout the 1950s. It would become a reference point for future juvenile crimes and an example of the monstrosity of the young.[95]

Alain Guyader was the unofficial leader of a group of *lycée* students from the well-to-do 16th arrondissement of Paris. The club was made up of seven members—six boys and a girl—who played an imaginary game of spying and conspiracy, of drug running and gun dealing. As a group, they would day-dream scenarios of diplomatic intrigue, Russian invasion, or daring escapes to Morocco. Allegedly, Guyader was the most imaginative at these games, bragging at school about the large amounts of American dollars he had gar-nered from the black market or from international contacts he had made through arms dealing. On Thursday, November 18, 1948, in Guyader's ab-sence, the group voted to condemn him to death as a traitorous scoundrel. Undoubtedly, for some in the group, the condemnation was just another part of the game, a way to have a laugh at Guyader's expense. But for three of them, the game would end in a conspiracy to commit murder.[96]

Guyader was seventeen and was described as "tall," "athletic," and "brilliant." His murderer, Claude Panconi, eighteen, was by contrast "tormented," "anxious," and "bitterly jealous." Bernard Petit, Panconi's seventeen-year-old accomplice, carried a "cold hatred" for Guyader, and Nicole (whose surname was withheld from all public records), sixteen, played the girlfriend role, pitting the boys against one another. First Nicole persuaded Guyader to write a letter to his parents announcing his departure for Canada; then Panconi invited Guyader for a walk in the park at the Bois de La Malnoue the following Thursday; and finally Petit stole a revolver from his father, a police inspector, and gave it to Panconi. On Thursday, December 9, Guyader and Panconi met at the edge of Paris and took a bus to the park. Once in the woods, Panconi shot Guyader in the back, removed his wallet, and left him for dead. He was not dead, however, and managed to get to a nearby highway, where he was picked up, taken to a hospital, and questioned by police before dying in surgery.[97]

Although Guyader did not implicate Claude Panconi, he did, for some unknown reason, mention the name of Bernard Petit, which put the police on the trail of the three conspirators, who were arrested the following day. "L'Affaire Guyader" immediately fascinated the French public. The affair seemed to be an affront to France itself, the co-conspirators' actions an offense and an outrage. Their conduct, "inspired by a scabrous imagination, ha[d] overstepped the bounds of shamelessness." They had "coldly decided to eliminate Alain Guyader, for whom Petit felt a ferocious hatred." The deed itself was "more atrocious than we can even believe." These "three brats" deserved much more than "a spank on the bottom and no dessert."[98]

In May 1951, the case went to trial. *Le Monde* called it the "Procès des J3," a reference to both the war and the Roger Ferdinand play. Petit and Panconi were tried as adults, whereas Nicole was sent to juvenile court (thus, her family name was withheld). There was a need to explain the wickedness of the crime, to understand the motivation behind such cold brutality in such young people. Psychologists declared them to be mentally sound—that is, they were not pathological. One reporter asked, "But the incentive of these abominable acts, was it greed, jealousy, hatred, contrary love?" Were these the new "enfants terribles"? "The Guyader Affair escapes the rules of traditional psychology. It confounds human justice when it attempts to apply its criteria."[99] The reporter concluded that, sadly, these youths represented "an epoch." They were "a new kind of youth, typical of the postwar period."[100] Guyader had bragged about the double life he led as a studious good-boy and a fearful street thug while others in the little group played make-believe espionage.

Was this all just a silly, childish game gone horribly wrong? André Le Gall, a psychologist, explained that the whole group was obsessed with crime and playing the criminal. Guyader was the most formidable at this game of brag and bluster, and therefore, for Panconi to kill Guyader was a way to legitimize himself, both in impressing Nicole and the others, but also in realizing the myth of the bad-boy.[101] Claude Panconi was sentenced to ten years in prison, Bernard Petit to five years, and Nicole to three years of juvenile incarceration. Upon their release, years later, Claude and Nicole married.

The Guyader Affair resonated throughout the decade and the story was glamorized in the 1954 film *Avant le déluge (Before the Flood)*.[102] Other crimes by young people also made headlines, such as the "Murderers of Saint-Cloud," Jean-Claude Vivier and Jacques Sermeus, both twenty, who lived by theft, burglary, and hold-up, and who eventually killed a couple walking their dog in December 1956. There were also "The Angers Three," three boys from "good" families in Angers who killed a sleeping-train conductor for his wallet in May of 1956. *Le Monde* even maintained that the 1950 attempted robbery and murder of Vincent Scheld in Valence had been "inspired and enheartened by the band of students who murdered young Guyader" in 1948.[103] The media helped to make these young criminals notable and newsworthy. A stream of sensational journalism made famous the exploits of young criminals and further stirred an excitable public. The sense of excitement, exploit, and media frenzy that reverberated around the young murderers was captured in a subplot of Louis Malle's first feature film, *Ascenseur pour l'échafaud* (literally, Elevator to the Gallows; released with the English title *Frantic*, 1957). The film depicted Julien and Veronique, two young delinquents who boldly kill some German tourists for their sleek Mercedes gull-wing sports car. Julien and Veronique represent the reckless danger of certain youth who are willing to capriciously kill for a speedy joyride. Back at their flat in Paris, the young murderers gleefully imagine the sensational headlines that will detail their audacious crime. They dream of notorious celebrity.

A Certain Youth

The portrayal of menacing youth on the movie screen and the infamy of newspaper headlines affected popular sensibility. A tension developed in the public discourse between sympathy for delinquents in the abstract and fear of actually encountering them in the flesh. As newspapers reported the nasty details of delinquent crime, concern for the moral and material threat posed by such young thugs mounted and public interest in all things delinquent escalated, which in turn created demand for more stories of wild youth. It was a self-perpetuating vicious circle of alarm, or as James Gilbert has said in reference to this phenomenon in America, a cycle of outrage.[104] A proliferation of books, with titles like *Nos Enfants sont-ils des monstres?* (*Our Children, Are They Monsters?* 1959), warned against criminal and vulgar youth. Jean Chazal's 1958 work, *L'Enfance délinquante* (Juvenile Delinquency), which has been cited throughout this chapter, was written as part of the Que sais-je? (What Do I Know?) series of brief instructive paperbacks geared for a popular audience. Even *Elle* magazine devoted an exposé to the problem of delinquency, with "Why Are Adolescents Becoming Murderers?" The article warned that "the problem of juvenile delinquency is becoming one of the most grave issues, perhaps the most, of our troubled time. It is nearly impossible to open a newspaper without discovering a new offense by an adolescent criminal." The piece closed by asking, "Are we responsible?"[105]

Unable to explain away the harsh realities of violent crime, France searched for answers to justify what it perceived to be a crisis of moral values. This concern smacked of class prejudice, for it was specifically the criminality of the young bourgeoisie that most perplexed the public, though the majority of delinquents were from the working class. If delinquency was the unfortunate result of poor family relations and an impoverishing environment, how does one explain the troublesome youngsters who come from good families and an upstanding social class? The stories that most often made headlines—the Guyader Affair and the Angers Three—were aberrations to the delinquency equation of "bad parents" plus "bad milieu" equals "bad kids." The lack of a plausible explanation for the delinquency of the young bourgeoisie led many to attribute their behavior to a general malaise, a sickness—"mal de jeunesse"—that had infected young people and threatened to corrupt them. Two films captured this sense of malaise and disaffection that was believed to be endemic among bourgeois adolescents and that turned them into no-good do-nothings, or worse. Both films caused quite a stir.

The first was Jacques Becker's *Rendez-vous de juillet* (*July Rendezvous*), the 1949 winner of the Prix Louis Delluc and recipient of the French Critics'

Prix Méliès in 1950. Becker was a well-established and venerated actor/ director from the prewar years who was already canonized in French cinema. With *July Rendezvous*, he hoped to present "a painting of modern youth"; it was the film of a mature filmmaker about the generation that comes after him. Reminiscent of the *zazous*, the anti-Fascist youth of Occupied France, the film's teenagers spend the summer of 1948 together in the cellars of the Left Bank, listening to jazz, frenetically dancing, and generally carousing. Moving from café to *cave*, they haunt the clubs and coffeehouses of Saint-Germain-des-Prés, reflecting on their vague aspirations to escape their staid, humdrum lives. There is nothing egregiously amoral about them, apart from a little hedonism and a budding bohemianism. Perhaps they are a bit too American in their casualness and pastimes; they even get around town in a U.S. Army surplus amphibious car, which they use effectively to avoid traffic by crossing the Seine wherever they choose. The young people in the film lack any great emotional pain or cheerful exuberance: couples form, break up, and re-form, and the group continues on unabated. The characters' family backgrounds form a diverse cross-section of modern France, and include a butcher, a professor, a factory worker, and a haut-bourgeois heir. Yet there is no great conflict between the protagonists; instead, there is a warm affection that comes from a sense of camaraderie, a mutual regard based on a common age. The magazine *La Laterne* noted that the film marked "the phenomenon of absolute rupture of current youth with their elders. A gap forming between the two generations."[106] Confirming this interpretation, the filmmaker himself commented, "I loathe my generation. . . . The young are more pure, more unselfish than their elders."[107] Others in the public, however, were offended by the lyrical tone and breezy style of the film, and vehemently rejected the idea that its characters were representative of an entire generation. One critic maintained, "The young of *Rendez-vous de juillet* represent and can only represent themselves. They are isolated in their artificial world; before us, without end, they dance, dance, dance with frenetic obstinacy as if they hope to make something of themselves in a futile dispense of energy! They never appear to live a single second of real life—the pains, hopes, and struggles of the other French their age. They stand apart."[108]

Although Becker's young characters are not delinquents per se, they do project a disaffection and a rebelliousness that rankled a part of the French public. Part of this was a growing mistrust of the Left Bank milieu and its association with the radical intellectuals of the postwar period. Saint-Germain-des-Prés was seen as corrupting the good young bourgeois of France. The Left Bank jazz clubs, such as Le Tabou or Le Club Saint-Germain, and the boulevard cafés, such as Le Napoléon or Le Deux Magots, were the suspected meeting places for estranged and sullen adolescents. The young writer and jazz trumpeter Boris Vian, for example, was associated with this Left Bank scene and accused of corrupting the young. In 1946 Vian had published a supposed translation of *I Spit on Your Grave*, a hard-boiled noir novel by the American writer Vernon Sullivan. But Vernon Sullivan was merely a pseudonym for Vian, and the novel had never been published first in English. The violence and explicit sex scenes in *J'irai cracher sur vos tombes* caused a scandal in the press and launched the book as a best seller. In the spring of 1947, a copy of the book was found beside a murder victim: a man had killed his mistress and then himself in a manner copied from the novel. The book was open at the relevant page, with the description of the murder underlined. In 1950, after a long trial, Vian was fined 100,000 francs and the book was banned in France, confirming the country's fears of the notorious influence of the Saint-Germain-des-Prés neighborhood on French society.[109]

Soon after, the young novelist Bernard Frank published *Les Rats* (1953), taking his title from a common nickname for the "existential" youths and students who frequented the cellars of the Left Bank. Frank's novel portrays a group of young, pseudo-intellectual wannabes who drink whiskey in cellar bars filled with gaming tables, engage in witty repartee, and pair off for casual sex. They discuss the merits of Sartre and Merleau-Ponty while sharing cigarettes in alleyways before returning home to their wealthy neighborhoods in the west of Paris. "Ennui" is a consequential word throughout this book, as the characters lack a sense of satisfaction or fulfillment from their intellectual nihilism. But Bernard Frank holds his characters at a contemptuous distance; he clearly was not trying to present a sympathetic portrait of wayward and misguided youth, and neither does he blame nor venerate the older generation. In the end, his book is itself an exercise in the nihilism of the age, demonstrating a perplexing disposition of sneering mockery.

Although *Les Rats* does not depict its characters as criminals, it does capture the sense of transgression and rebellion that France believed to be pervading the middle-class young who frequented Saint-Germain-des-Prés. As an example, in March 1953, Gérard Dupriez, nineteen, killed his parents after lunch one afternoon. He bludgeoned his mother at the kitchen table, first with a club, then a kitchen knife, and finally with a hatchet. Next, he moved to his parents' bedroom, where he hacked apart his napping father in similar fashion. The family was very wealthy, from the Ile Saint-Louis, and Gérard had no wants or needs unfulfilled. Unsurprisingly, the police could find no reasonable explanation for such a brutal crime. However, the newspapers reported that Gérard was "interested in psychoanalysis and often visited a strange professor who habituated the cafés of Saint-Germain-des-Prés." The implication was clear. Unable to explain Gérard's crime, people looked to the Left Bank as a repository of suspicious ideas and behavior. A neighborhood of debauched hedonism, Saint-Germain-des-Prés implied something transgressive and deviant. Another example: in 1954, Alain Montevardi, the nineteen-year-old son of an industrialist, killed his father's mistress and dumped her in the Marne River. Although he had committed the crime elsewhere, it was dubiously noted that Alain was known to "frequent Saint-Germain-des-Prés."[110] For France, the Left Bank increasingly represented a hall of initiation into a harried lifestyle of sinister rebellion and murderous barbarity for "certain youth."

A decade after the release of *July Rendezvous*, a second film portrayed the youth of the Left Bank in terms of amoral excess and was met with remarkable public scandal. *Les Tricheurs* (*The Cheaters*, 1958) was directed by Marcel Carné, a legend of French cinema who was responsible for such classic films as *Hôtel du Nord* (1938) and *Enfants du paradis* (*Children of Paradise*, 1946), among others. *The Cheaters* won the Grand Prix du Cinéma for 1958, a controversial choice, and it was the highest grossing motion picture of the 1958–59 season. The film became the center of a great public debate about the morality of young people in France, and no doubt this controversy increased its receipts at the box office and was responsible, in part, for its great success. In fact, the film was marketed to stir public debate. For example, the publicity poster (see Figure 11) foregrounds its young stars, as a hedonistic party takes place behind them. A textual insert reads: "A film that all youth are going to see and that will become obligatory for parents!" The film's success was not merely due to alarmist marketing, however, as it addressed genuine concerns of the French public, old and young alike. The story line follows Bob, a university student and the son of a wealthy industrialist, as he meets and befriends Alain, an Ecole Normale dropout without a fixed address but with a ready toothbrush. On impulse, Bob helps Alain shoplift a jazz record and the two become friends. Alain's nihilism and anti-conformist angst intrigue Bob, and soon he is attending parties with other like-minded youngsters. He meets and sleeps with Clo, a young heiress who lives for self-gratification, but Bob is more attracted to Mic, the daughter of a petit bourgeois family, with whom he has sex the following day. Bob and Mic (whom some considered an ersatz Brigitte Bardot) fall in love, but are unable to admit it to themselves or each other because the code of their kind is cautiously noncommittal. For them, love is just a vapid bourgeois constraint that interferes with hedonism and excess. The primary concern of their life is the debauched party where they drink whiskey, listen to American jazz, and engage in casual sex. They plot petty crimes, extort money for sex, and revel in drunken promiscuity. Bob and Mic continue to deny their

Figure 11. Publicity poster for *The Cheaters* (*Les Tricheurs*), 1958. The insert reads: "A film that all youth are going to see and that will become obligatory for parents!" Christophe L Documentation.

feelings for one another until Bob, at last, pursues her, declaring his love as she speeds off in her white Jaguar, into an oncoming truck. Following her death, the hospital's attending physician asks Mic's brother Roger, "But what is wrong with these kids? For heaven's sake, what is the matter with them?" Roger responds, "Young people have fifty years of mess behind them . . . and no doubt fifty more ahead. But it's like that everywhere."

The furor that accompanied the film's release in October 1958 would continue well into 1959. "Rarely does a film begin its career in such an atmosphere of passion," commented the journalist Michel Capdenac. He admired the film, because its "images profoundly plunged into the reality of our times, exposing an abscess of youth's malady."[111] The weekly newsmagazine *L'Express* published a special issue dedicated to *Les Tricheurs* and its subject matter (see Figure 12). Françoise Giroud, the magazine's editor-in-chief, maintained that Marcel Carné had revealed "an essential dimension of the universe of the young: boredom and inaction." The controversy that this film was sure to ignite simply made it "an event." Given Roger's statement

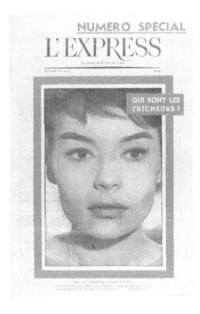

Figure 12. Special issue of *L'Express* (October 16, 1958), asking "Who Are the Cheaters?" and featuring the main character Mic from *Les Tricheurs* on its cover.

at the end of the film, which seemed to absolve the "cheaters" from any accountability, *L'Express* asked Carné, who was fifty-two at the time, if he "considered the conditions of our time responsible for the lifestyle of these young people?" He responded, "Undeniably. I frequent Saint-Germain-des-Prés and have had on occasion an opportunity to know certain individuals. The principal characters of this film exist, I know them."[112]

The Cheaters was banned in the Vaud for presenting an "idle and debauched youth," in an "immoral and unhealthy film" that was ultimately "dangerous for young people."[113] In Nice, the mayor initially banned the film in response to more than fifty complaints from family associations. After viewing the film, however, he agreed to screen it, but only for those over eighteen years of age. He stationed police outside the cinema to screen the spectators as they arrived.[114] *France Catholique* published a biting editorial condemning Carné and his film. His depiction of the "depravation of the young" was "exceptional, even for Paris." He irresponsibly threatened to undermine the moral authority of his audience, because the "evocative power of the cinematic image" combined with the "carnal power of the film" would have lingering effects, "subconsciously." If Carné wanted to reveal the problems of young people, "was it necessary to poison 9/10 of the audience to make an illustration for administrators, educators," or whomever?[115]

Young people themselves, of both left and right political persuasions, rejected Carné's vision as well. In October, the weekly paper *L'Humanité-Dimanche* organized young Communist students and workers for a round-table discussion with Marcel Carné to voice their objections to his film. They told Carné that they were not *tricheurs*, or cheaters, and that they resented the "false idea of French youth" the film gave "by its tendency to generalize." As young Communists, they were hard-working, diligent individuals of the best moral fiber, though they were willing to concede the possibility of such depravity among bourgeois youth.[116] In December, the Catholic Center of French Intellectuals organized its own public debate about the film. Jacques Madaule conceded that Carné had shown "an authentic vision of French youth," but he suggested that it was a very specific group of young people, "une certaine jeunesse." Others noted that young people can venture into delinquency just as a way of showing off, for "self-valorization," but that their sort had nothing in common "with the spirit and dedication of good young people."[117]

In a lengthy editorial, Etienne Fuzellier of *Education Nationale* defended Carné and *The Cheaters* in the face of the critics. He agreed that *The Cheaters* represented only a small fraction of the young in France, and only the urban young at that, but he argued that the film could reveal pertinent issues for debate and that, therefore, it was an "important film" worth seeing. Specifically, the film had touched upon topics that suffered from "the indifference or blindness of parents," such as sexual libertinism and diminishing honesty. According to Fuzellier, Carné had perfectly shown "three predominant characteristics of contemporary youth." First was the "apocalyptic sense" young people felt, of living in a world with an uncertain future. Second was their "herd instinct," or the need to function within a group. And third was their desire to not think, their need for distraction. "Sex . . . alcohol, movies and jazz," he said, "are the first of these habits, these passions, these narcotics."[118]

Carné conceded at the outset that he was not trying to "condemn" French youth, nor was he implying that all the young in France were disenchanted nihilists. Rather, he explained in an interview for *Les Lettres Françaises*, "I asked myself why, in France, we have this problem of disoriented youth, of these 'children of disorder' as I first thought to call them, who lack enthusiasm, conviction and ideals. Understand, these young people do not represent all youth, nor all students, nor all of the Latin Quarter or Saint-Germain-des-Prés."[119] In another interview, Carné elaborated, "It is a 'certain youth' that I have shown in the film, a tiny minority of French youth." The characters of the film "represent certain types of this milieu" of Saint-Germain-des-Prés.[120] If *Les Tricheurs* represented just a "certain youth," a "tiny minority" of little significance, then France's visceral reaction seems overblown and unwarranted. The consensus that the characters in this film were unique curiosities was incongruent with the overwhelming response it received. The baggage of the past decade's concern with young delinquents, with amoral and endangered adolescents, was being carried into the imagining of youth generally, as a social group in total, and that was problematic because it contradicted the narrative of youth as innocent and as the redemptive future of France.

Many seemed to be troubled by the fact that these immoral delinquents, these cheaters or pretenders, had come out of what the French had defined in their legislative efforts and government programs as an "ideal" environment: stable and proper households; clean, uncorrupted neighborhoods;

and upstanding, proficient schools. *The Cheaters*, and the recent sensational crimes in the newspapers, challenged the assumption that it was negative conditioning and a bad milieu that created bad kids. If the young, even delinquents, were as inherently good and salvageable as public policy and public sensibility believed, then those youth who were beyond the realm of understanding or explanation, those like the characters in *Les Tricheurs*, needed to be separated from the category of youth generally. Not only were they not representative of the young, or youth as a social group, but they were not even representative of delinquency either. The youth in these specific cases represented "a certain youth"; media depictions of young disaffection and bitterness were only valid for "a certain youth." "Une certaine jeunesse" became a conceptual device to alleviate the threat from the ubiquitous presence of the young, a way of locating the menacing problem in an indefinite elsewhere that operated somewhere beyond the perimeter of propriety. To speak of "a certain youth" was to speak in shorthand, to say that there were some depraved youngsters whose acts could not be explained away by bad parenting or a noxious milieu. Their social malevolence was born of something altogether different; they *did not* represent youth as a whole, but were an unfortunate aberration, a nasty minority.[121]

Carné and others pointed out in their discussions of, and responses to, *The Cheaters* that those who had seen the film or read the newspaper reports of real crime believed that the characters they encountered were of their time. They could not imagine Claude Panconi, Gérard Dupriez, or the Angers Three in any other epoch, though earlier examples are abundant throughout the modern period. Still, one journalist wrote, in response to the film, that: "Certainly the milieu we've been shown really exists, it is a world only five or ten years old. . . . The young generation is, if not lost, at least distracted, because it has only known a world of disorder, a world of war."[122] Despite the profound continuities with the interwar period and Vichy era, there was a willful belief that the postwar world was different, altered, unique. But the supposed rupture of 1945 was perhaps more a mental construct than a material reality. In this frame of mind, because of the experience of the war and the Occupation, the prewar world was rendered unrecognizable, perhaps unknowable, and hopefully irreplicable. France wanted to believe that its society after World War II was demonstrably different. In this line of thinking the Liberation had ushered in a new era, a new time, the singularity of which had left a mark on the young who matured in it. This deliberate rupture served as a motivating opportunity, a chance to reform France, to start over, to start anew.

Therefore, the year of the Liberation was as well a year of possibility. A new constitution had been drafted to significantly differentiate France's system of government from that of Vichy, though it largely reverted back to that of the Third Republic. Great public works projects were initiated in the name of postwar reconstruction: new schools, buildings, roads, bridges, hospitals, and tenements were built. But for society as a whole, youth among all social groups best represented the anticipated potential of postwar France.

The legislators who drafted the Ordinance of 1945 that altered France's juvenile justice system had hoped that by managing and reforming youth the new delinquency law would help to regulate social tensions generally and thus "happily resolve problems of the social order."[123] The new system gave the courts judicial power to reshape the families, neighborhoods, and social environments of the young. The state tried to impose social norms through its teams of inspectors and investigators. There was an implicit postulate behind the idea of reeducation: that there existed a cultural norm, a homogeneity of family morality and Frenchness that the state sought to impose on its population. By intervening in the lives of juvenile delinquents, the state hoped to standardize its young population by refashioning its flawed members. In this way, future discord or social problems could be avoided by normalizing and homogenizing the anomalous adult while he or she was still impressionably young.

Youth as a concept was advanced without a class element: youth was the future; they would be the modernizers, idealized citizens. But delinquency undermined this conceit and actually heightened the class problem of youth. Reeducation was in many ways about expunging class from the social category of youth, and was based upon the values, principles, and assumptions of a broadening middle class absorbing the lower orders. Class could be removed from the category of youth by removing delinquency from the young. Eliding class differences produced youth as a normative social group, at a time when class conflict continued to reverberate, particularly after the mass strikes of 1947. The problem, then, was that delinquency, in many ways, began to represent youth generally, particularly when the public was confronted with middle-class delinquents. One way around this metonymy, of letting the delinquent stand for youth in totality, was to speak vaguely of "a certain youth," an indeterminate phrase that grouped together all the truly *bad* elements of youth and that served as a youthful bogeyman. Not all youth were delinquents, but not all delinquents were "a certain youth" either.

Reeducation, with its notion of the reformability of delinquent youth, participated, on its own level, in the collective task of reconstruction. Since young males were imagined as the future workers, leaders, and actors of society, the programs of reeducation sought to prepare delinquent young men for the responsibilities of productive citizenship. At the same time, young women continued to be imagined as future mothers (see Chapter 5). Through the improvement of its young, France would improve itself. The program of reeducation sought to elevate problem youth and the popular milieu to a bourgeois normality. A juvenile court judge in Nancy confirmed this idea when he noted that "80 percent of juvenile delinquents come from the popular classes. Our task is to clean up the climate in which their young live through our instructive judgments. . . . The evolution of the proletarian milieu, their ascension to the responsibilities of leadership in the nation, is a reality in which I believe along with many others." He went on to explain that these adolescents "will have, in the future of the country, a mission to replenish [and] a responsibility to assume."[124] Perhaps part of the frenzy surrounding the morality of the characters of *Les Tricheurs* is that they came from exactly the kind of environment that policymakers defined as the ideal, the prototypical home that avoided the conditions that created delinquency. These characters were from "good" bourgeois families, had access to education and opportunity, and yet they were abominably nihilistic and amoral. By categorizing them as "a certain youth," France was able to minimize the challenge to the accepted norms of cultural reconfiguration they represented.

Questions of good/bad and right/wrong had a particular significance for postwar France. The war and the Occupation had not only wrecked France in the material sense, it had left the deep emotional scars of Nazi collaboration as well. Unwilling to deal directly with issues of adult moral complicity, France channeled the question of moral reform into its discussion of the young, who, by their lack of lived experience, held no responsibility for the disgrace of Vichy. If the delinquent was a victim, then maybe France was as well. If a delinquent could be reformed, then perhaps so could France.

Jean Cocteau, in *Diary of a Film*, an account of the 1945–46 filming of his magical interpretation of *La Belle et la bête* (*Beauty and the Beast*), maintained that the film, for him, was an allegory of France at the Liberation. The suffering of the Beast corresponded to that of France during the war, yet the Beast, in the end, is redeemed. Thus, the Beast overcomes his disagreeable childhood, the cause of his adult beastliness.[125] Similarly, postwar concern for the juvenile delinquent functioned as the perfect metaphor for France to deliberate on the moral crisis of society at large, to approach questions of victimization as opposed to culpability, and to create opportunities for cultural rehabilitation. As with the Beast, the possibility of redemption and rehabilitation lay within. The delinquent, whether a victim or a threat, was ultimately reformable. Reeducation sought to improve upon the present for the promise of the future while avoiding the problems of the past.

CHAPTER 5

Sex and the Cynical Girl

On March 17, 1954, in the northern French city of Caen, an angry crowd of three hundred demonstrators attacked the Majestic Cinema during a Wednesday night film screening of *Le Blé en herbe* (*Ripening Seed*).[1] A brawl ensued as local police, supported by members of the CRS riot police, intervened to protect the cinema house from the menace of the mob. Soon after, the mayor of Caen negotiated with the manager of the Majestic to modify the cinema's program in the "interest of public order." Likewise, in nearby Rouen and Bayeux, similar rallies of unruly protest disrupted screenings of the same film, threatening violence and forcing local authorities in Rouen to forbid anyone under the age of eighteen to see the film, while in Bayeux its screening was aborted altogether. The previous Sunday, March 14, Bishop Picaud of Bayeux had demanded that a proclamation be read in all the churches of his diocese. It concluded: "We [the church] formally forbid all the faithful of the diocese to go see the film *Ripening Seed* wherever it may be shown. We demand them to obey dutifully and firmly in a spirit of discipline and honesty. It is necessary to show that a Christian knows to condemn that which corrupts the soul of society."[2] In Rouen, Archbishop Martin expanded the denunciation when he added, "Everyone knows that [the film] is a profoundly immoral and unhealthy work. It has not only provoked disapproval from Catholics, but that of all honest people, regardless of religious distinction."[3]

The standard screening license for the film, issued by the French government, had approved it for all audiences, yet throughout France magistrates established restrictions for its screening, based on their own local authority. In Biarritz it was forbidden for minors under eighteen, in Bouches-du-Rhône and Troyes for minors under sixteen. The Mayor of Troyes explained that, "due to its subject and character, the film is of a nature that provokes regrettable demonstrations dangerous to the public order." He issued the age restriction in order "to repress the attacks against public tranquility and to assure the maintenance of good order." Rather than try to control any morally incensed crowds, local authorities used the threat to public order created by demonstrators against the film to restrict its showings or close it altogether. The Association of Film Creators defended *Ripening Seed* and fought the restrictions, which they said were infringements on the right to free expression, guaranteed by the French Constitution, but their bid for a protective court order was unsuccessful.[4] It was reported by the newspaper *L'Humanité* that a Communist deputy had also demanded that the government take immediate action to prevent "reactionary groups" from hindering screenings of the film.[5]

Ripening Seed is set in the 1920s on the Breton coast, a popular summer vacation area, and revolves around the friendship of Phil and Vinca, sixteen and fifteen, whose families share a beach house each summer. Inseparable, Phil and Vinca are best friends, and they obviously share an unspoken love, though because of their age they are uncertain of what that means and unsure of what to do about it. Unable to interpret their feelings, or at the very least not daring to declare them, they behave with mild aggression toward one another. Their adolescent fear and uncertainty is incapacitating and renders each of them irritable. Enter Madame Dalleray, the "Lady in White," an older woman in her forties with great sophistication and a superb automobile, who has come to the coast for a brief respite from the bustle of Paris. At once, Phil is infatuated by the flirtatious charms and seductive manner of the older woman, and he creates excuses to visit her beach house. Soon, she initiates Phil in the act of love, if not its sentiment, and after having sex,

Phil, seeing himself in the mirror, proclaims, "I don't recognize myself." "You are sixteen years old and one night," she glibly responds. Gradually, with this rite of passage, the awkwardness of adolescence leaves the boy, and his spry step is replaced by the self-possessed gait of manhood, a change that does not go unnoticed by Vinca. The affair continues for a brief period, until Madame Dalleray at last ends it, invoking Phil's love for Vinca: "You come here for what you dare not ask of her. Go on. I believe that I have done well for you. And for her." Thus resolved, Phil returns to Vinca, and in a moonlit garden he shares with her his newly acquired sexual experience, thereby restoring the equilibrium to their relationship. Thus, the film traces the arc of an adolescent relationship over the course of one summer vacation, culminating in Phil and Vinca's sexual coupling.

Ripening Seed was directed by Claude Autant-Lara and was based upon a 1923 novel of the same name by Colette. Autant-Lara had previously explored a similar theme in *Le Diable au corps* (*Devil in the Flesh*, 1947), about a schoolboy's passion for a young married woman. That film was a critical smash (and is still considered one of the best films of postwar French cinema), but the film's salacious theme did provoke some controversy, though mild in comparison to the tumultuous outcry against *Ripening Seed*. Autant-Lara began working on *Ripening Seed* immediately after completing *Devil in the Flesh*, but due to interference from moral authorities it was not released until seven years later, in 1954. The Cartel of Moral and Social Action judged that the film's "nefarious moral repercussions on the youth of our country cannot be denied." They interfered with Autant-Lara's financing, petitioned the National Center of Cinematography to quash the project, and even convinced members of the right-wing Mouvement Republicain Populaire (MRP) party to use their political influence.[6] Although these obstacles did delay the film's production, they did not halt it.

Yet the tone of the film is truly innocuous; in fact, by today's standards, it is treacly sentimentalism. Although the off-screen sexual activity implied by the plot cannot be doubted, the film's approach to sex is more curious than lustful, lacking nudity and explicit acts or language. The sweet reticence displayed by Phil and Vinca is amusing in its innocence and charming in its tenderness. One favorable review described the film as appropriately showing "the anguish of adolescents standing before the revelation of their physical desire," which was, admittedly, "a delicate problem," but one that the film "treats poetically, with infinite tact and discretion."[7] Conversely, *Paris Comoedia* referred to the film as "deplorable" and "pornographic."[8]

Significantly, what was so provocative, or "pornographic," about the film was not the sex, generally, but the sexual activity of Vinca, specifically. It was one thing for an adolescent boy to lose his virginity—objectionable to some, to be sure, but considered an inevitable circumstance all the same, a rite of passage. It was quite another thing altogether for a girl of fifteen to willfully relinquish her virtue. That was scandalous, sordid, and shameful, and threatened to "corrupt the soul of society," as Bishop Picaud put it. Vinca's choice to become sexually active triggered an explosion of outrage against the movie by challenging notions of chastity for adolescent girls. Notably, the newspaper *Le Matin* had first published Colette's novel *Ripening Seed* as a serial between July 1922 and March 1923, but the paper's editors decided not to publish the final episodes of the book: the emotional climax of Phil and Vinca's sexual union. It was acceptable for readers to follow Phil's discreet affair with Madame Dalleray, but intolerable for them to be exposed to young Vinca's decision to have sex.[9]

Enemies of the film worried about the "nefarious moral repercussions" on the young, the immoral impact of sexual example, fictitious or otherwise. According to a tract distributed by demonstrators at Rouen, the film's proposition of sex between Phil and Vinca "presented an atmosphere of vice as a necessary eventuality of nature."[10] Traditionally, boys were expected to experiment sexually, whereas girls were implored to remain chaste until marriage. The film's acknowledgment of sexual activity for an adolescent girl was so improper and repugnant that it had inspired a crowd of demonstrators to riot. This preoccupation with Vinca's sexual virtue reveals assumptions about French society's prescriptive norms of gender and sex for the young—specifically, that young women's sexual desires and activities were taboo subjects not to be trifled with. As the movie *Ripening Seed* and the response to it demonstrated, the acknowledgment of sexual independence for young women emerging in the postwar period challenged accepted sensibilities of adolescent chastity by introducing sex for personal pleasure rather than for reproduction. Much of France, however, resisted this change, seeking to maintain the traditional gender roles of sex for the young. Sexual reproduction had been a dominant national issue in France for nearly a century, and the tacit approval of sex outside marriage, outside procreation, for self-gratification, and without seeming consequences challenged ideas about behavioral expectations for young women as they had been traditionally defined in French society. The issue of sexual propriety and moral accountability became a point of conflict and change for the social categories of gender and age in postwar France.

As a social group, young women in France had historically been defined by their ordained future as wives and mothers. If the social institutions, legal framework, economic circumstances, and cultural traditions conceived of young men as France's future leaders, workers, and citizens—that is, if they were socially defined as the fated actors of society—then the place of young women was predicated upon their biological capacity to reproduce. Maternity, strictly supervised within the patriarchal authority of marriage, was considered a social function, a civic duty. Reduced to her biology, to her sex, a woman's physiological destiny was fulfilled by maternity. With this ultimate understanding of women as sexual beings, the regulation of sex for young women became of paramount concern: in the first instance, upon an adolescent girl's sexual maturity—to prevent it; and in the second instance, upon her marriage—to encourage it. Because women were socially defined by their sexuality, social controversy about young women in postwar France manifested itself in the terms of sex. Yet, as Colette's work and this film demonstrate, there was a counterdiscourse as well. Unsurprisingly, sexuality became the arena in which young women asserted their autonomy, which resulted in a redefinition of traditional conceptions of gender and sex for the young, while also providing the footing for the sexual liberation that would be associated with the 1960s. More broadly, the sexual activity of young women was tied to a supposed worldview marked by a weary cynicism that was interpreted as symptomatic of a larger pessimism threatening to undermine not only the normative social value of youth, but also the project of rejuvenation in France generally.

Young Women in French Society

Around 1800, France had been the most densely populated nation in Europe. Yet by mid-century, the medical profession noted, there had been a steady incremental decline in the country's birth rate. By the end of the century, France had the lowest birth rate in the world; in some years, the number of deaths actually exceeded the number of births. A growing concern about depopulation was framed in terms of France's apparent decline in diplomatic and economic power, in relation to such rising powers as the United States and Germany. Particularly following France's swift military defeat at the hands of the Germans in 1870, politicians, physicians, intellectuals, journalists, demographers, and social scientists expressed alarm at the country's inability to produce vast numbers of babies—a situation, they believed, that was having a detrimental effect on France's economic and military standing in the international community. To maintain its hegemony, the French nation needed to replenish and maintain a robust population, full of new workers and soldiers.

Throughout the period of the Third Republic (1870–1940), the state intervened in the reproductive life of the nation, in an attempt to stimulate its birth rate. This state pronatalism took the form of inquests, commissions, legal reforms, tax reforms, social welfare policies, legislation, church leagues, charity groups, and media campaigns. By 1922, there were at least seventy-eight organizations sponsoring pronatal measures in France. However, only those measures that reduced infant and child mortality seemed to have had any impact on population growth. Despite state intervention, France was simply not reproducing quickly enough.[11]

Women were largely blamed for this, for not fulfilling their maternal duties to take care of children or for avoiding pregnancy altogether. There were some critics, such as the physician Jacques Bertillon, who blamed men by attacking their virility, but ultimately the burden of maternity fell to women.[12] As such, women became the targets of pronatalist campaigns. Women's wage work was regulated, even discouraged, in order to give them more time at home. The Catholic Church, through a papal encyclical of 1891, had proclaimed motherhood and domestic work to be woman's "natural" destiny. Civic groups in France had established societies to foster hygienic practices for mothers and infants. Schools set up programs to educate girls on the particulars of maternity. The government discouraged and eventually outlawed contraception, making its use an act of civil disobedience. By 1920, the state was celebrating Mother's Day by giving medals—bronze, silver, and gold—to the mothers of large families. The government also punished abortion with increasingly harsher sentences, until at last in 1942 the Vichy regime made abortion a crime against the state rather than mere murder or an affront to morality; as treason, abortion was punishable by death.[13]

Women's civil, economic, and political status in modern France was conceptualized in terms of motherhood. Their role in society was to bear children. Since the French Revolution, women had been seen as lacking the physical, intellectual, and moral capacity for full participation in republican politics. The Civil Code promulgated in 1804, during Napoleon's dictatorship, established the legal foundation for French patriarchy. Article 213 stated that women must obey their husbands, while Article 1124 defined the condition of women as minors before the law. Women were subject to the legal guardianship of men, first by their fathers and later by their husbands. This legal status continued throughout the nineteenth century as a series of legal decisions established precedents that emboldened the state in its efforts to exclude women from politics. Woman was made for domestic duties rather than public functions, for the family, not for politics. However, by the late nineteenth century, due to France's renewed interest in women's maternal duties for the nation, there was a growing understanding of the political significance of women as mothers.

Recognizing this, some feminists and women's activists began to argue for measures to reform women's legal and civic status.[14] The government's new emphasis on maternity and the social function of women as mothers of the republic offered strategic inroads for activists to argue for social, legal, and economic reforms that would benefit women and elevate their civil status. Women won some piecemeal legislation and social welfare reforms, such as the 1909 Maternity Protection Law, but their goal and focus remained squarely on motherhood as a claim to citizenship. Notwithstanding these small gains, women would not be granted the vote until 1944, by decree of General de Gaulle's provisional government, two decades after most other Western nations had enfranchised women. The 1946 Constitution of the Fourth Republic confirmed women's suffrage and at last guaranteed equal rights for women before the law, though social roles for women were still defined in terms of marriage and motherhood.[15] Thus, it is notable that the centrality of woman's sexual participation in society was emphasized across the political spectrum, by defenders of male hegemony who wished to embolden the workforce and the military, as well as by radical feminists who sought political enfranchisement and legal equality.

As women were at last beginning to achieve equal rights before the law, the French intellectual and author Simone de Beauvoir wrote a book about how women's place in society had been historically constructed, and provided a sharp commentary on that construction from a contemporary woman's point of view. In *The Second Sex*, Beauvoir famously proclaimed that "one is not born, but rather becomes, a woman." Published in 1949, Beauvoir's lengthy tome examined the biologic, economic, historic, philosophic, religious, literary, and social subordination of woman to man. One of the primary themes of *The Second Sex* was Beauvoir's radical argument that there was nothing "natural" about woman's inferior rank in society, since it had been historically determined by men for their own benefit. Society's legal, social, and economic institutions were organized around the principle of male primacy, and, as society perpetuated itself, men and women were conditioned to accept this specious principle as Truth. Beauvoir proposed that the sustained socialization of the sexes originated in a prejudicial interpretation of biological function, in the male/female sexual difference determined by sexual reproduction, which defined man as active subject and woman as passive object. Therefore, reduced to her physiology, a woman's body becomes "not a thing" but "a situation" that limits how she is able to experience the world.[16]

In the second part of her study, Beauvoir examined the ways in which a young woman was conditioned to participate in her own subordination, as "a destiny imposed upon her by her teachers and by society." Upon reaching sexual maturity during adolescence, she is taught to make herself a sexual object, for it is by attracting men and charming her suitors that she can secure the stability of a good marriage, deriving "her worth not from her own efforts, but from a capricious approval." It is at adolescence that society demands that she "renounce her sovereignty" and cease to be an "autonomous individual," by making herself subject to male desire. Yet as her body transforms and men take notice of her figure, commenting on her anatomy and pursuing her with libidinal interest, she is required to deny her own sexual impulse and maintain a virginal purity. Society requires young women to be sexual objects, at the same time that it denies them a sexual outlet. Marriage is the only socially sanctioned way for a woman to keep her dignity and at the same time find sexual fulfillment. So young women are trapped within two socially sanctioned options: remain chaste, struggling against sexual urges and desires, or marry and have reproductive sex for the nation's prosperity.[17]

Interestingly, Simone de Beauvoir published her landmark study at the very time when it appeared that young women in France were beginning to assert an autonomy based upon sexual activity, an independence based on the pursuit of sexual pleasure. Because France grounded its expectations of gender for young women upon their future sexual roles as wives and mothers, sexuality became the most visible site of rebellion against social custom. Furthermore, the sexual definition of women established a framework for the discussion of young women generally, which led to the interpretation of girls' issues in ways distinct from that of boys. Thus, what began as an issue of sexuality ended as one of gender.

Sexual Delinquency

The preoccupation with the sexual behavior of young women characterized the concern for the female juvenile delinquent, which was in contrast to that of the male delinquent. The female delinquent was almost always discussed, if she was discussed at all, in terms of prostitution. The silence surrounding female juvenile delinquency is notable when one considers the extent to which France obsessed about delinquency generally.[18] The 1945 ordinance that transformed the juvenile justice system did not specifically mention female delinquents at all. Perhaps it is not surprising that young women were subsumed under the universal rubric of male delinquency. Yet during the postwar period girls accounted for, on average, 20–25 percent of all juvenile court cases.[19] In *L'Enfance délinquante*, Jean Chazal devoted only a handful of paragraphs to female delinquency; a fifty-page report to the United Nations in 1949 included less than one page of material about girl delinquents; and the Ministry of Justice's 1951 report on juvenile delinquency considered the plight of young women in a single paragraph.

When it was addressed, female delinquency was equated with prostitution. In 1946 the government estimated that since the war's outset, prostitution rates for female minors had multiplied by a factor of ten.[20] The Ministry of Justice stated plainly that "prostitution . . . characterizes feminine juvenile delinquency."[21] Delinquent girls were evaluated in terms of their sexual activity. They were arrested for other crimes as well, yet the focus remained squarely fixed upon their sexual behavior, real or imagined. For example, cases of vagabondage for boys and girls were roughly equivalent: in 1949, there were 869 cases for boys and 707 for girls; in 1950, there were 654 and 640, respectively.[22] But unlike cases involving boys, cases of female vagabondage assumed or implied criminal sexual acts. Some specialists even interpreted prostitution as "a special form" of vagabondage,[23] or even as "a habitual complication."[24] This meant that if a female vagabond did prostitute herself, she merely met expectations. The likelihood that girls who had neither parental guidance, a fixed address, or a fixed income would turn to prostitution as a viable means of survival is, of course, significant, but more important here is the stipulation that prostitution was the *only* way that young women garnered attention in the larger discussion of delinquency in general. For France, the codes of criminality for young women were bound fundamentally by their perceived sexual practices.

Doctor Le Moal, a psychologist, expressed the greatest concern for the effect that sex-for-money had on the moral and emotional development of young women. Because the practice of prostitution was "the exact opposite of the normal sexual act," it "depreciated" that which was "best and most fundamental" for a young woman: "her femininity." Le Moal suggested that "[woman's femininity] sinks into the orgy, demeaning and savoring the acrid pleasure of its own destruction in vulgar eroticism." Accordingly, prostitution perverted a young woman's image of men and of "authentic love," with consequences that, Le Moal believed, had clear long-term effects on society as a whole. As a possible remedy, Le Moal argued for sexual education to be an integral part of the reeducation program for delinquent girls, to ensure their emotional, sexual, and moral development—an aspect of reeducation, not surprisingly, that the specialists did not consider necessary for male juvenile delinquents.[25] General sex education for juveniles would not be realized in France until the 1970s.[26] Despite the efforts of André Berge at the Psychopedagogic Center of the Academy of Paris, who published a treatise arguing for sexual education in 1952, the subject remained taboo.[27] Allowing sexual education would have implied a recognition of young people's sexuality and sexual practices, which was a hotly contested notion in France in the 1950s.

Because of France's position on sex education, Le Moal's proposal was not adopted. Still, the reeducation program for girls at Cadillac and Clermont was significantly different from that for boys at Aniane or St. Jodard. For example, counselors were exclusively female and of very high moral standards because it was believed that girls, more than boys, tended to identify with role models. Girls were organized into groups of eight to ten members, as opposed to groups of twenty to thirty for the boys; it was thought that the smaller-sized group served as "a model of a large family," whose female counselor, with whom the girls were expected to identify, "play[ed] the role of mother." Although they were also taught skills for "feminine work," the ultimate "goal of group life [was] to give the minors a thorough education for the family and household."[28] Furthermore, female delinquents were not considered good candidates for supervised counseling in their home environment (*liberté surveillée*) because it was felt that they would have poor role models at home, or because of the high risk of recidivism for young prostitutes.[29] In fact, the entire ethos behind the reeducation system placed a greater value on boys than girls, as is shown by how the program was implemented. Well into the 1950s, reform in the girls' institutions lagged far behind that in the boys', and they remained far worse in terms of physical condition and repressiveness.[30] If the goal of reeducation for boys was based upon encouraging their preparation for a future as workers and citizens of the greater society, for girls it was based upon ensuring their capacity to reproduce, to act as mothers within the familial household. Hence, the gendered sexual capacity and/or behavior of young women defined their experiences within the reeducation system in ways distinct from that of boys.

Popular conceptions of the female juvenile delinquent reflected this distinction as well. During the Alain Guyader murder trial in 1949,[31] the media made the three defendants, Claude, Bernard, and Nicole, into icons for misdirected youth. Claude and Bernard were depicted as cold, petty, and jealous malcontents who lived in an imaginary world of spies, intrigue, and high crime. The murder of Guyader by Claude and Bernard was depicted as a case of regrettable play-acting turned real. Nicole, however, was imagined differently. Not having participated in the murder itself, she was depicted as the knowing accomplice, a temptress and the object of rival sentiment within the small group of boys. As one journalist said, "At sixteen, she played the cinema vamp among six boys, amusing herself with the jealousy of one against the other."[32] It was implied that she used her feminine powers to manipulate and tease the others into a pitched frenzy. The newspapers described her as having the "air of a vamp" and as a "precocious starlet of childish loves."[33] One journalist described her as "a little housemaid" who "smirked and acted the coquette" before the media cameras.[34] The pervasiveness of such sentiment was so strong that during the trial Nicole's attorney presented medical testimony to prove her virginity, as a demonstration of her virtue.[35] In the end, Nicole received a much lighter sentence than her co-conspirators, but the way in which she was characterized by the press and society, in their use of the sexually charged vocabulary of the moviehouse—"vamp," "coquette," "starlet"—must be considered significant. In the postwar period, popular culture was an arena increasingly associated with the young via youth's consumption of film, music, and books, as well as the growing representation of young people within these media. These concepts operated within the popular culture and bled into other areas of society as well, helping to establish the terms by which the young were discussed while at the same time creating a forum for the discussion of young people in general, all of which, in its turn, structured the social group of youth as a whole.

In the public mind, popular culture most clearly illustrated the menacing threat of sexual degeneration, as the spirited response to *Ripening Seed* demonstrated. The sexuality of young women, as embodied by the young, sensual film star Brigitte Bardot, came to the forefront of public concern. A provocative young dancer, Bardot provoked a scandal in 1956 and 1957 with her aggressive and pouting sensuality in the hugely successful *Et Dieu créa la femme* (*And God Created Woman*). This followed the controversy surrounding the critically successful and immensely popular novel *Bonjour tristesse*, whose author, Françoise Sagan, was only eighteen at the time of its publication in 1954. Sagan's frank depiction of sixteen-year-old Cécile's pursuit of a sexual tryst continued the themes of Colette by challenging accepted sensibilities of gender and sex for the young. Importantly, the author's age was much more scandalous than that of the protagonist; that an eighteen-year-old girl had written such material was shameful and improper. The predatory sexuality of Bardot and Sagan was anathema to the conception of wholesome girls as future mothers. The significance of these scandals lies in the prescriptive behavior applied to categories of gender *and* age. The heart of the issue resides in the fact that they were not only female, they were young.

Brigitte Bardot: La Femme-Enfant

At the height of her career in the late 1950s, Brigitte Bardot was worth more to France as an export commodity than all the country's Renault automobiles combined. The magazine *Cinémonde* calculated that by 1958 she had accounted for one million lines in France's daily newspapers and two million in the weeklies, while her photograph had appeared nearly thirty thousand times.[36] Brigitte Bardot was the first international sex symbol to emerge from the postwar generation, and in the fifties she introduced the informal, naturalized sex appeal of tousled hair and rumpled bed sheets that would become associated with the sexual liberation of the sixties. Marilyn Monroe was ten years older than Bardot, and her on-screen sexuality of naive bubble-headedness was markedly different from Bardot's brazen aggressiveness. Bardot was condemned by some as scandalous and obscene, and celebrated by others as a vanguard of sexual autonomy for the young, and specifically for young women. As an icon of burgeoning sexuality, she generated a storm of controversy in a whirlwind of contention. *Le Figaro* referred to her as "the scandal in three dimensions," and *L'Express* called her "the perverse ingénue." Meanwhile, Edgar Morin, in the review *Arguments*, qualified Bardot's love scenes as the "only truly good news of modern times," and critic Tony Crawley characterized her as "James Dean in bra and panties"—although she would be most memorable without either.[37]

Brigitte Bardot was born in Paris on September 28, 1934, to Louis and Anne-Marie Bardot. The eldest of two daughters, she was born into a solidly bourgeois family that spent weekends at the family chalet in Louveciennes near Versailles, summers on the beaches of Biarritz, and winter vacations at Meribel in the French Alps. Louis managed substantial assets, running the family's chemical firm north of the city, to which he commuted from the posh neighborhoods of western Paris. As a girl, Brigitte attended private schools for well-bred young ladies and took personal dance lessons. In 1947 she auditioned and was accepted to the National Conservatory of Music and Dance on her first attempt. There, she became an accomplished young ballerina with a promising future. Soon, however, her maturing body interfered with those plans, as she grew taller and developed womanly hips and a full bosom—impractical for a dancer but most effective for a sex symbol.[38]

In the summer of 1949, *Elle* magazine featured the fourteen-year-old Brigitte as the emblematic young French woman. Editor-in-chief Hélène Lazareff was a friend of the Bardot family and convinced Brigitte's parents to allow her to grace the magazine's cover. Bardot was pictured in the family living room, smiling pleasantly as her mother knelt to adjust her mauve taffeta dress. A year later, at age fifteen, she again appeared on the cover of *Elle*. A photo spread inside once more included her fashionable mother and pointed out that Brigitte was a dutiful daughter, the ideal young French woman, the prototypical young lady from a proper bourgeois background that emphasized chastity, charity, and maternity.[39] It was the *Elle* cover that brought her to the attention of Roger Vadim. Vadim, her future husband and film director, was at that time a young assistant to the filmmaker Marc Allegret; he would eventually whisk her away into the world of cinema. The irony is clear: discovered as the supreme representative of the moral young French woman, pretty and pleasant, Bardot would in a matter of years come to represent the unfettered, insolent sexual spitfire, immoral and immodest, who confronted the very precepts of bourgeois society she had so innately possessed.

Throughout the early fifties, Bardot became a mainstay of the popular press. She continued appearing on covers for *Elle* and was often seen in *Paris-Match*, to this day an icon of photojournalism and exemplar of the paparazzi. Though she was neither a movie star nor a runway model, Bardot's celebrity grew. Not a part of the film industry's publicity machine, she was nevertheless a photogenic sensation. At the 1953 Cannes film festival, she dominated the attention of photographers, offering up provocative poses in a revealing bikini, and as a result upstaged many of the renowned film stars who were seeking publicity for their new movies. Meanwhile, Bardot had begun her own venture into film, orchestrated by husband Vadim, with small parts in mostly forgettable films that made much of the pretty girl with the remarkable figure.[40]

By 1956 she had appeared in sixteen films, but it was the release of *And God Created Woman* that made Brigitte Bardot a superstar, and her initials, BB, a term of common usage. Written by her husband Roger Vadim, *And God Created Woman* was his feature directorial debut and was conceived from the outset as a star-making vehicle for showcasing Bardot's sizzling sex appeal. It opened in France in December 1956 to poor reviews and even poorer attendance. The film was teetering on the edge of financial ruin when it became a smash hit in the United States, eventually grossing four million dollars at the American box office, an astronomical figure in the late 1950s for an obscure foreign film. Committees for the Protection of Morals were organized in more than a hundred cities across the United States; police confiscated prints of the film and arrested cinema managers, while the courts issued their verdict on the film's suitability.[41] The infamy generated by this moral outrage spurred the film's success, and more than six months after its initial release it became a hit in France as well, a *succès de scandale*. With quivering anticipation, audiences around the world then flocked to the cinema seeking to see the "real thing": sex personified.

The plot of *And God Created Woman* follows Juliette, an orphaned young woman who exudes an effortless sex appeal and is desired by all the local men, young and old alike. She sunbathes nude and walks around barefoot in summer dresses, having sex whenever, wherever, and with whomever she desires. Men attempt to seduce her, control her, even buy her affections, but Juliette will have none of it. Sexual conquest is to be on her terms. Set in Saint Tropez, at that time a small fishing village on the Mediterranean coast, the movie is full of balmy sea breezes and the shiny brilliance of the summer sun. Our first glimpse of Bardot is of her naked body lying in the radiance of the sun's warm glow, her tawny blond hair strewn against honey-brown skin. Thus, from the outset, Vadim establishes the film's subject: ostensibly about Juliette's search for fulfillment, sexual and otherwise, in truth the film is about Bardot's uncompromising sexual power bound within the fleshy curves of her body.

Pursued by the rich widower Carradine (Curt Jurgens), Juliette gets involved with the three Tardieu sons, who struggle to maintain a boat-building business. Attracted to the brawny eldest son, Antoine (Christian Marquand), she eventually marries the shy, earnest middle brother, Michel (Jean-Louis Tritignant). Juliette is well meaning and attempts to be a good wife, but she struggles with the conflict between her conscience and her demanding sexual appetite. Soon, she cuckolds her husband by having sex with his older brother, in an erotic beach scene full of clinging, wet clothes, sticky sand, and a very self-satisfied Juliette. In fact, the plot is neither important nor is it particularly interesting, although Vadim's abstract filming style effectively converts the audience from simple viewers to titillated voyeurs. The allure, significance, and controversy of the film lie squarely with Bardot's portrayal of young sexuality untrammeled by moral hang-ups.

Bardot's training as a dancer gave her grace, balance, and an ease of movement that was languid and sultry, while her straight posture and upright carriage lent an air of smug confidence. Her vulgar pout, full figure, and unkempt hair bestowed wild insolence to her youthful sexuality. Her beauty was not glamorous; what she lacked in the extravagant ornamentation of gowns and jewelry, she compensated for with brazen nakedness and a "roller-coaster of contours and curves." Her unbridled approach to sex aroused male desire. As one biographer put it, "Bardot strips, teases, pouts, dances, writhes, rocks, rolls: a constant invitation to coitus."[42] A sex symbol was born.

Although men may have been drawn to BB's seductiveness, that does not mean they were kindly disposed toward her. For most women, Bardot merely represented an impudent trollop, a slutty vixen. There was something dangerous about her sexual honesty, something powerfully immoral and perverse. In 1957, when three young scoundrels from good families robbed and murdered a sleeping train conductor in Angers (see Chapter 4), a local parent-teachers association denounced Bardot to their mayor. It was she, they insisted, who was responsible for the crime. *And God Created Woman* had been screened in Angers and Bardot's sultry perversion had immediately corrupted the local young, they claimed.[43] In Britain, a woman was granted divorce on the grounds that her husband preferred watching Bardot films to sleeping with his wife.[44] In 1959, Simone de Beauvoir proclaimed that "almost everyone is ready to regard BB as the very monument of immorality."[45] *L'Express* declared that, "with *And God Created Woman*, the ingénue has become perverse. Eve has been given the undulations and malevolence of the serpent."[46]

While the fallout from *And God Created Woman* continued, the release of another Bardot film intensified the controversy. The provocative *En cas de malheur* (*Love Is My Profession*, 1958) was the newest release of director Autant-Lara, who had a few years before released *Ripening Seed*. In the film, Bardot plays the part of Yvette, a young woman of very low virtue who prostitutes herself with indifference and who attempts a foolish jewel theft that ends in the injury of an old woman. For her trial, Yvette approaches the venerable barrister Gobillot (played by Jean Gabin), a celebrated member of the *grand bourgeoisie*, and offers to pay him in trade. That is, in response to Gobillot's question of how she will pay, Yvette boldly raises her short dress to reveal (to him from the front, to us from behind) a lack of underwear but an abundance of assets nonetheless. Soon, Yvette becomes Gobillot's young mistress, for whom he provides an apartment and a maid. As Gobillot becomes increasingly obsessed with the desirable Yvette, he abandons his position and prestige. In effect, the story is about the respectable elder Gobillot emancipating himself from the strictures of polite society in pursuit of the rootless, amoral, and youthful Yvette.

On the whole, the film was a critical success, with Bardot's performance particularly noted.[47] The young critic François Truffaut considered it "one of Autant-Lara's best films," proving Bardot's capabilities as a talented actress, although Truffaut thought she had been "magnificent" in *And God Created Woman* as well.[48] Others, like Max Favalelli, described Autant-Lara's effort as "a good, solid film," but lamented its chosen subject matter.[49] Even the conservative newspaper *France Catholique*, while panning the film as mostly "facile eroticism, calculated impudence, and verbal audacity," went out of its way to praise Bardot as having "demonstrated a talent and scenic quality until now unknown."[50] The critic Jean d'Yvoire, however, could not tolerate the challenges presented by the film and remarked in shrill tones that in the film, "all is dirty and sordid." In his excoriating review, he observed: "Dirty is the heroine, not only for her purely animal behavior but for her smell of filth, of dirty linen," "Sordid is this generation," and "Sad is the abasement of the grand bourgeois which counts as a social corruption." "The film's interior truth," he went on, "reveals its decadence."[51] *Love Is My Profession* aroused furious protests because it attacked the social order, challenged sexual taboos, and crossed boundaries of moral tradition by showing a young, lower-class woman manipulating and corrupting an older, upper-class man.[52]

What really rankled Bardot's critics was not what she revealed physically, but the wicked attitude toward sex she exemplified mentally. Nudity and implied sexual relations were not at all novel in French cinema, but a sexually predatory young woman was. Vadim had merely sought to show "a young woman whose taste for pleasure was limited neither by morality nor social taboos."[53] Morality and social taboos were there precisely to keep sexually playful or aggressive young women in line. In fact, it was not so much that

Bardot defied moral categories as that she passed them by without notice. For her characters, distinctions between good and bad did not exist. Or, as Simone de Beauvoir wrote, "BB is neither perverse nor rebellious nor immoral and that is why morality does not have a chance with her. BB does not try to scandalize, she has no demands to make; she is no more conscious of her rights than of her duties."[54]

A response by Vadim to the hoopla that surrounded *And God Created Woman* elaborated on Bardot's provocative ability to disturb:

> People pretended to be shocked by Brigitte's nudity and unabashed sensuality when, in fact, they were attacking a film that spoke without hypocrisy of a woman's right to enjoy sex, a right up to that point reserved for men. It wasn't Brigitte's sunbathing in the nude that enraged "decent" people. It was the scene where Brigitte makes love with her husband after the religious ceremony, while her parents and friends wait for her in the dining room. It was an amused Brigitte without complexes, appearing in her dressing gown, her lips puffy from lovemaking, picking a few apples and chicken legs to feed her lover—for even though married she treated her husband like her lover and not her master.[55]

It was her "male" attitude toward sex, then, that was particularly troubling. Simone de Beauvoir analyzed Bardot as being "as much hunter as she is prey" in the game of love: "The male is an object to her, just as she is to him. And that is precisely what wounds masculine pride."[56] Jane Fonda would later characterize *And God Created Woman* as a cinematic landmark for women's liberation. "She may have been portrayed as a beautiful sex object, but Brigitte Bardot ruled the roost," Fonda proclaimed. "She kicked out any man she was tired of and invited in any man she wanted. She lived like a man in Vadim's films."[57]

This type of behavior was anathema to the prescriptive norms of sexuality for women. Sexual dichotomy dictated that men should play the part of the aggressor, determining the time, place, and the partner, whereas women, docile and supplicating, passively accepted the propositions. Unable to break out of these binary categories, France interpreted Bardot's sexuality as being masculine, "like a man," and hence as highly transgressive and challenging to the patriarchy's status quo. Bardot's sexuality challenged male power and dominance in sexual relations. Her "masculine" approach to sex upset cultural conceits of gender, while her age rattled ideas of chastity and propriety for the young. Indeed, at the end of *And God Created Woman*, the Carradine character ruefully observes, "The girl is made to destroy men," thus emphasizing both the gendered and generational problem that she posed.

Above all, though, Bardot's appeal and controversy derived from her untamed youthfulness. The vamp and *femme fatale* were not new to cinema—one need only think of Mae West or Marlene Dietrich—yet the combination of the *enfant terrible* and the *femme fatale* shockingly mixed childlike candor with torrid sensuality. Edgar Morin described Bardot's face as capable of only two expressions, childishness and eroticism, making her "the sexiest of baby stars, and the babiest of sexy stars."[58] By artfully combining the *ingénue* and the vamp, Bardot revealed an uncomplicated attitude toward sex that manifested desire as impulse, or, simply, appetite (see Figures 13 and 14). The Americans coined the term "Bardolatry" to describe this mixing of innocence with sex; in England she was referred to as a "sex kitten," and

Figure 13. Bardot was capable of two expressions: the first, childishness—here, playfully on the beach in 1956 . . .

in France BB became known as the *femme-enfant*. Her nickname, based on her initials, appropriately enough is, of course, pronounced "*bébé*." Bardot represented a troubling transgression, a quandary that was readily evident in the hyphenated articulation of *femme-enfant*, or "woman-child."

By 1959, the Bardot phenomenon was so widespread that Simone de Beauvoir was compelled to analyze it, which she did in her excellent essay "Brigitte Bardot and the Lolita Syndrome." Pointing out the recent trend demonstrated by Vladimir Nabokov's novel *Lolita*, first published in Paris in 1955, before becoming a best seller in Britain and the United States, Beauvoir declared the triumph of the woman-child with Bardot's ascendancy. Because "BB has not been marked by experience . . . she is without memory, without a past, and, thanks to this ignorance, she retains the perfect innocence that is attributed to a mythical childhood," and "though she retains the limpidity of childhood, she has also preserved its mystery." BB's age established sexual desire unencumbered by the burdens of adulthood or the weight of a past; her lack of lived experience provided a sense of unadul-

Figure 14. . . . and the second, eroticism—here, seductively on the beach in *And God Created Woman*, also 1956. Agence Keystone and Christophe L Documentation.

terated purity to the sexual act, unfettered by society's traditions. Bardot's ascendancy and representation meant that "she embodies the credo that certain young people of our time are opposing safe values, vain hopes and irksome constraint." Moreover, as a young person, as a member of the postwar generation, "BB springs from and expresses the immorality of an age."[59]

Bardot's essence of youthfulness was bound up with and made representative of a larger trend of sexual autonomy and moral cynicism for postwar youth as a whole. François Truffaut declared that "Brigitte Bardot is a girl absolutely representative of her epoque,"[60] whose films "typified our generation" because they were "amoral—refusing current morality without proposing another in its place."[61] In *Cahiers du Cinéma*, Claude de Givray agreed, saying that BB was "a product of our era, enabling our time to invade the film screen."[62] This trend of moral and sexual cynicism had revealed itself most prominently in recent French literature, most notably from the young author Françoise Sagan. Bardot and Sagan became the exemplars of this transition, through their work in film and print and due to their membership in the *nouvelle vague* generation. Thrust into the position of generational representatives, Bardot and Sagan found the crisis of sexual autonomy for young women whirling about them, like the energy between two iconic positions, one the voluptuous sex kitten, the other the jaded intellectual.

Contemporaries, of course, did not miss this connection. *L'Express* noted that Brigitte Bardot's characters had an "immoral appeal like the heroine of *Bonjour tristesse*."[63] Michel Perez noted, in his review for *And God Created Woman*, that in terms of the film's tone and character he was reminded of the young novelist Françoise Sagan.[64] Simone de Beauvoir wrote that if the contention "is to assert one is man's fellow and equal, to recognize that between woman and him there is mutual desire and pleasure, Brigitte is thereby akin to the heroines of Françoise Sagan."[65] And Georges Hourdin extravagantly compared the two of them to Greek goddesses, invoking for them a worshipful following. He contended that for the new generation Brigitte Bardot was "Venus," whose power derived from being "a woman of generous form," and that Françoise Sagan was "Minerva, possessing the secret of wisdom."[66] Hourdin's appeal to mythology seems overwrought, yet the influence of Bardot and Sagan on 1950s French culture was seen as an obvious harbinger, either a good or a bad omen, depending on one's point of view. These cultural sensations merited Hourdin's grand proclamation because the phenomenon surrounding both surpassed the substantive actuality of each. They had entered the imagined realm of icons, of representative myths.

Françoise Sagan: The Charming Little Monster

Like Bardot, Françoise Sagan was a product of the Right Bank Parisian bourgeoisie. The youngest of three children, she was born as Françoise Quoirez on June 21, 1935, nine months after Bardot, in the small town of Carjac. Located in the Department of Lot, Carjac was the home of her mother's family, whose strict sense of tradition dictated that all the Quoirez children must be born in the same bed at the family's country home in the south of France, to which the family returned each summer for vacation. Though not wealthy, Sagan's family was propertied and enjoyed the advantages of estate income, enabling them to live in the fashionable districts of West Paris, where Françoise grew up. She attended a series of private academies, due to her remarkable skill in getting expelled for unruly conduct not befitting a young lady. Once, at age twelve, instead of telling her parents of her most recent expulsion, she roamed the streets of Paris for three months, consuming volumes of French literature. Like BB, the bookish Françoise had a happy and contented childhood surrounded by a thoroughly bourgeois family. In 1952 she received her baccalauréat degree and began preparatory classes for entrance to the Sorbonne. She subsequently failed those examinations in 1953.[67]

While studying for her entrance exams, Françoise had begun to write *Bonjour tristesse*. As she explained, "I'd convinced all my friends that I was writing a novel and I told so many lies that I finally had to write it."[68] She wrote the short novel in approximately eight weeks and sent it out to publishers, adopting the pseudonym "Sagan" from Marcel Proust's duchess of the same name. At the end of that year, the publishing house Julliard responded. *Bonjour tristesse* was released in the spring of 1954 and won the Prix des Critiques in May, an unprecedented accomplishment for an eighteen-year-old girl (see Figure 15). The short novel became a literary phenomenon in postwar France and thrust the young Sagan into the scrutiny of the literary limelight. In France alone, the novel sold one million copies in its first year,

Figure 15. The young Françoise Sagan at the reception for her 1954 Prix des Critiques for her novel *Bonjour tristesse*. Agence Keystone.

and by the early 1960s *Bonjour tristesse* had been translated into twenty-three languages, with sales exceeding four million copies worldwide.[69]

The Prix des Critiques, awarded in May 1954, generated controversy around the young writer. In response to the award, François Mauriac, the doyen of French letters, famously described Sagan as "a charming little monster" and a "shocking little girl," while simultaneously admiring her graceful skill as a writer.[70] Indeed, even the prize committee was torn between the striking talent revealed in *Bonjour tristesse* and its seeming "amorality." While the committee "agreed on her talent, they were uncertain about recommending this immoral book to the larger public," a book that artfully projected its adolescent protagonist Cécile as, according to the committee, "a monster." They described *Bonjour tristesse* as "a masterpiece of cynicism and cruelty," and Sagan's talent as "undeniable," yet they also noted that "such indifference to good and evil at so tender an age sends a chill down one's back."[71]

Sagan's novel is set, coincidentally, on the Mediterranean coast at Saint Tropez, where seventeen-year-old Cécile, the novel's heroine and narrator, spends her summer vacation at a beach house with her widowed father, Raymond. However, the power dynamic in this family has been inverted. Throughout the novel, Cécile manipulates her libertine father and his lovers with beguiling chicanery masked as youthful naiveté. The adults have neither moral authority nor parental inclination, and they offer little in the way of wisdom or guidance, with the exception of the motherly Anne, whom, accordingly, Cécile views as an obstacle. The fiercely independent Cécile plots and schemes to maneuver those around her into positions beneficial to her purposes, whatever they may be. That is not to say that she is plainly evil, just dangerously self-indulgent. In addition, there is Cyril, a young man spending his summer nearby, in the next cove, whom Cécile charms, teases, and gradually manipulates until he is lost in love and wishes to marry. Cécile does not share his expectations, although she is very pleased to meet him in the pine woods or in the bow of a small sailboat for sexual rendezvous, once having at last rid herself of her virginity, one of her goals for the summer. Throughout the novel, Cécile operates within the seeming confines of patriarchy, as a daughter and woman who is acquiescing to her father and her lover, while she actually subtly challenges and undermines these conventions by recognizing their limitations and by maneuvering within them to satisfy her own desires. This untroubled duplicity in one so young is what critics found so shocking and "monstrous."

Another strong element of Sagan's novel, and the books to follow, was its dolorous tone. Sagan's characters seem to yearn for something beyond sex and fast living, something akin to fulfillment, that always remains elusive. Her characters seem enervated, drained of happiness despite their love of pleasure and easy self-gratification, or perhaps because of it. Indeed, *Bonjour tristesse* opens with these words from Cécile: "A strange melancholy pervades me to which I hesitate to give the grave and beautiful name of sorrow."[72] The title *Bonjour tristesse* itself translates as "Hello, sadness." A heavy malaise and dispirited gloominess infects Sagan's young characters, emboldening them with a sharp cynicism; as Cécile comments, "Cynicism always enchanted me; gave me a delightful feeling of self-assurance and self-approbation."[73] Sagan's characters maintain a lassitude and a weariness usually accumulated over years and years of disappointment. Moments of delight and joy are ephemeral within a constancy of ennui and lethargy. One reviewer noted that Sagan's characters were at least ten years ahead of their grandmothers in understanding the disappointments of life, while another pointed out that "the cynicism one finds in *Bonjour tristesse* is astonishing because it comes so naturally to one so young."[74]

Sagan's next three novels continued with similar themes of wealthy and wearied young people. Although not remarkable best sellers, like *Bonjour tristesse* had been, *Un Certain sourire* (*A Certain Smile*, 1956), *Dans un mois, dans un an* (*Those without Shadows*, 1957), and *Aimez-vous Brahms?* (1959) sold several hundred thousand copies each, due in part to the burgeoning market for cheap paperbacks. These works were primarily short, terse romances that examined the lives of well-off yet cynical young Parisians immersed in casual love affairs. Whiskey, nightclubs, fast cars, and easy sex predominated, yet these stereotypically masculine interests were pursued with vigor by the novels' young heroines, without seeming consequences. Hence, Sagan's characters challenged conventional notions of desire, pleasure, and sexual expectation for young women. Her characters were neither burdened nor limited by the usual feminine duties to family or men, nor were they punished for their transgressions.[75] Sagan's characters were able to indulge themselves free from the usual constraints of patriarchy and the consequences of biology.

Beyond the radical tone of her books, it was the indisputable success of Sagan's novels that brought her such acclaim and such scrutiny. The notoriety generated by *Bonjour tristesse* of course fed Sagan's literary triumph, and because of it Sagan and her novels wielded tremendous influence. Even she described her achievement as "a phenomenon of the sociologic kind," beyond any easy explanation.[76] For postwar France, she had struck a chord that resonated with the vibrancy of youth, not only because her books were preoccupied with the young, but also because she herself had emerged from among that same youth, lending her very person a mark of authenticity. Thus, it was her young age that particularly rattled the public, and it was her thoughts as a young person that interested them. It was as a young woman, as the voice of youth generally, that Sagan was elevated to the position of generational spokesperson. She was credited with the ability to reveal the dirty secrets and unpleasant truths about the contemporary world and its emerging "new wave" generation. Georges Hourdin announced, "Without doubt Françoise Sagan has expressed spontaneously, unconsciously, some grand truths concerning the young of our time."[77] Others maintained that she was "a powerful witness of our era."[78] In 1957 Madeleine Chapsal of *L'Express* begrudgingly acknowledged that Sagan "personified, unfortunately, more than any other writer, the youth of today."[79]

Sagan became a staple of the press as the appointed voice of the social group of youth. The media reveled in her blunt cynicism, displayed in countless interviews ranging from short newspaper quotations to full-length features in magazines to television appearances. Her opinion was sought on any issue involving young people, whether it was delinquency, censorship, Algeria, politics, music, movies, or cars. When asked in 1957 if she felt she represented the young, Sagan coyly responded, "That's madness. I am the standard-bearer for no one. That doesn't interest me. I'm twenty-two, that's true, but I do not represent the young woman of today."[80] Whether her reluctance was genuine or not, it was France, not she, that anointed her as the emissary of the young and credited her with the capacity for revelatory insight.

By 1958, a mere four years after *Bonjour tristesse* was published, there were already three book-length studies of the "Sagan phenomenon," in addition to the thousands of articles in print. In their dissections of this young woman, her novels, and their meaning, some writers condemned her and others defended her. Georges Hourdin, an eminent Parisian psychologist and a resolute Catholic, wrote *Le Cas Françoise Sagan*, in which he described her books as not merely symbolic, but "revelatory." While Hourdin noted that some critics "have found her and her success indecent," he believed that it was, "above all, significant," because Sagan had revealed the corrupt and rotten state of modern France. Hourdin responded favorably to Sagan, her talent, and her themes, yet he used her profound success and the subject matter she wrote about to point out the endemic dilemma of French morality. Sagan had revealed it, touched on it, exposed it, and that is why she had had such grand success. Hourdin believed Sagan's novels had shown how far away from religion France had drifted, that modern society had caused mankind to move away from its rightful place beside God. Sagan was not to blame for this, and neither were the young generally, Hourdin believed, because they were merely the inheritors of a godless society: "I think that the difficulties of adolescence are terribly aggravated when the adolescent finds himself before divided and disgraced parents." Hourdin further described the postwar generation as one "without parents," as "orphans" whose elders, with their immoral complicity, had failed them. He used the "undeniable social significance" of Sagan and her books to urge France back toward God. The lesson to be learned from Sagan, Hourdin believed, was that French adults needed to seek redemption for their past and present in order to save the future for their children.[81]

Later in 1958 Gérard Mourgue published *Françoise Sagan* as a response to Hourdin. In the book's preface, Pierre de Boisdeffre declared that Sagan was emblematic of the era. "In a world without values, without goals, without justification, the only criteria left is the authenticity of experience," he wrote, adding, "she is a powerful witness of her time, she incarnates the vacuity, dispersion, despair." However, Boisdeffre maintained that Sagan was "certainly not" the voice of French youth in their totality. She merely represented a "bourgeois fraction, like Brigitte Bardot." Although he felt she was not the supreme representative of the young, he saw her as a soothsayer for her time. While Mourgue's book largely agreed with Hourdin's in his defense of her novels and in his explanations of their success, in terms of the supposed truths they revealed, he did not interpret her books as a cry for help, as morality tales that exhibited France's need for evangelical redemption. Rather, he celebrated her novels because they "touch a vital subject of civilized life. They stand as the markers of a new conception of morality." For Mourgue, Sagan's works were signposts of a new era free from the constraints and contradictions of bourgeois moral tradition. Sagan had shown that "our freedom is a fable," that society was ruled by obscure forces beyond man's control. In defense of the iconoclasm of the young, Mourgue invoked images of World War II and of France's ongoing conflict in Algeria: "If today's young no longer follow the rules of traditional morality, perhaps it is to protest against a society whose fruits are concentration camps, atomic bombs, and torture. It is useless to demand these children to give esteem to the parents who are degraded before them." Sagan and her novels were often interpreted as expressing the young person's feelings about the moral impotence of adult society and as being a resounding declaration of independence from it.[82]

If Bardot became the pinup, the poster girl for the postwar generation's sexual autonomy, then Sagan became its jaded prodigy, the diffident intellectual mouthpiece for youthful independence, sexual and otherwise. Not only their respective fictional efforts, in film and in print, spurred these judgments, however; the personal lives of both Bardot and Sagan also became subjects of great scrutiny and speculation. Indeed, their lifestyles only exacerbated the myths that were developing around each of them, blurring the lines between fact and fiction, reality and myth.

During the filming of *And God Created Woman*, Bardot left her husband, Vadim, for her co-star, Jean-Louis Trintignant. A string of lovers followed, as BB seemed to consume men as others might automobiles, holding on to one for a year or so before exchanging it for the next model. Bardot spent her time away from the movie camera traipsing about on beaches and flaunting her magnificent figure before the lenses of the paparazzi. In the early 1960s she shocked France by essentially abandoning her newborn son Nicholas to his father, her second ex-husband, Jacques Charrier. BB's rejection of motherhood struck many in France as an absolute demonstration of her depravity, and it fed the myth of Bardot as a sexual animal interested only in the pleasures of self-gratification and accepting none of the responsibilities.[83]

Sagan, likewise, became the *enfant terrible* of French society. The press hounded her every move, often criticizing her improper behavior. Sagan was renowned for staying out all night partying. She was an accomplished drinker of whiskey who frequented Parisian nightclubs for very late nights of jazz and dancing. She was often spotted speeding around in her sports car, thrilled by the fast movement and fast living that her new wealth provided. Sagan was also an avid gambler, and the press reported on her astounding losses at the roulette wheel, chastising her for such extravagant waste. As she wearily attested, "Money, whiskey, cars, that's all anyone ever talked to me about. I was getting three or four insulting letters a week. Some said I was a disgusting, perverted girl who spent her days—nights, rather—doing all sorts of horrible things."[84] Some believed that her lifestyle had finally caught up with her in April 1957, when she flipped her Aston Martin on the way to Saint Tropez. Many thought that Sagan, with eleven broken ribs, shattered legs, a fractured skull, and a subsequent addiction to morphine (described in her book *Toxique*), had received a just comeuppance. This was because of what Sagan had come to represent, not only through her writing, but also through her real-life exploits. She later reflected, "I became a commodity, a thing, the Sagan myth, the Sagan phenomenon."[85] Neither Sagan nor Bardot could escape the myths of their personas, which overshadowed and intruded upon their private lives. As the ordained representatives of youth, they both reaped the rewards and suffered the consequences of their symbolic celebrity.

The Crisis of Youth

The attitude of reckless abandon with which Bardot and Sagan chose to live their lives fit the public's perception of the *mal de jeunesse* or *mal du siècle* phenomenon that had predominated postwar thinking about the young.[86] This idea interpreted the burdens of recent history as a hardship weighing down upon the new generation, crushing youthful vigor, enthusiasm, and optimism. The alleged crisis, *la crise de la jeunesse*, implied that the young were infected with a melancholy illness, with a cynical nihilism that threatened to disrupt the happy idyll of being young. Professor J.-P. Reynaud described it as "a specific confusion with which we see contemporary youth struggle." This confusion, this "distress," leaves the social group of youth unable to behave according to "traditional morality or with a clear vision of the world, but instead, [youth] feels abandoned to itself, like an orphan, without roots, without ancestors, without guides, free, no doubt, but free like a ship adrift." Most disturbing of all, Reynaud maintained, was that as a result of this crisis, "youth have ceased to live at all" and "have suspended their existence a little like the old philosophers declared that they had suspended their judgment."[87] In a special issue of *Foi Education* dedicated to the *mal du siècle* phenomenon, one article claimed that young people's "judgment on society is all the more severe because they feel themselves to be the victims of an incredible machination." Yet, at the same time, they "refuse to accept this condition" and rail against it with "imperfect and unsuitable behavior in all aspects of life. It is as if they have lost the sense of becoming, the concept of individual progress through the course of existence."[88] Another article from *Foi Education* declared that as a result of an "atmosphere of dreariness and fear," youth's "attitude is characterized by a refusal, a negation of all values, collective and individual, a denunciation of current hypocrisies."[89] A few years later, in 1957, just as *nouvelle vague* was creating a sensation, *Cahiers Pédagogiques* published a special issue dedicated to the "crisis of youth," which interrogated professionals, specialists, and the young about the phenomenon in a search for explanations and solutions.[90] It was felt that the *mal de jeunesse* was an ailment that manifested itself in antisocial, apathetic, maladjusted, cynical, and pessimistic behavior by the young.

Françoise Sagan and her novels were alternately criticized and commended as prime examples of the *mal du siècle*, or *mal de jeunesse*, phenomenon. Although Hourdin agreed with Sagan's characterization of the postwar malaise, he claimed that many young people had expressed to him that they resented Sagan's work as yet another "expression of a new *mal du siècle*" that was not representative of them at all.[91] Thierry Maulnier, in his review of *A Certain Smile*, castigated Sagan for her "superficial and comfortable *mal du siècle*," conceived, he believed, as an artificial device to sell large quantities of books. Her characters suffered from ennui, but of the "best kind, a conformist ennui." Maulnier had wearied of the brouhaha surrounding dispossessed adolescents, whom he viewed as nothing more than isolated complainers with a proclivity for melodrama.[92] François Nourissier, in a book whose argument was utterly hostile to the young, *Les Chiens à fouetter*, railed against the cynical literature of Sagan and others and the trend toward cheerless juvenile complaining. Young people under twenty were nothing more than cranks who knew nothing of the world or of true suffering, he declared.[93] Others writers, such as Reynaud, used Sagan as an illustration of the very real phenomenon of a postwar malaise that encouraged the young to reject traditional lifestyles. He noted that "to live as in the novels of Françoise Sagan is exactly to cease to live," and that "for once, this spirit of chagrin was perfectly just."[94]

This malaise was intimately connected to, and even inspired, the abandon with which Sagan's characters approached their sex lives, and it was consistent with one aspect of Doctor Le Moal's analysis of sex among delinquent vagabonds. Le Moal conceded that the sexual activity of the young could at times be a willful choice rather than an unfortunate circumstance. He noted that the "existential adolescent" of Saint-Germain-des-Prés can, "in her vagabond life find the occasion to affirm her contempt for bourgeois traditions and conformism." This was all a part of what he considered the "philosophical crisis of adolescence"[95] or, in other words, a *mal de jeunesse*. Coincidentally, Sagan herself had begun frequenting the cellar clubs of Saint-Germain when she was fifteen, enjoying the fashionable bohemianism that was the hallmark of the burgeoning Left Bank and the dismay of the proper Right Bank.

The "existential adolescent" predisposition of the late 1940s served as the forerunner of the 1950s *mal de jeunesse*. Existential philosophy gained broad intellectual and popular acceptance in the postwar period due to the prevalent philosophical disenchantment that followed World War II. As the horrors of the war continued to be revealed, the rational metaphysical bases for understanding the world were undermined. The war had revealed the world to be absurd and incomprehensible. Existentialism's primary exponent, Jean-Paul Sartre, advocated that in such a meaningless world each individual must find his or her own meaning through personal activity. Making choices and acting on them was, according to Sartre, the only way to give meaning to one's life; that is, people are essentially what they make of themselves—a person's existence precedes the realization of his or her essence. Ultimately, Sartre and Beauvoir were advocating a value system based upon an individual's commitment to bettering him/herself outside the sanction of traditional belief systems such as religion. It was a philosophy based upon freedom and choice, and a belief in the individual's capacity for self-realization. Although most of France never fully grasped the detailed philosophical substructure of existentialism, and certainly most did not bother to study the subtleties of its precepts or principles, existentialism experienced a remarkable vogue in postwar France. And none were perceived to have been more affected or influenced by the fad of existentialism than the young.

Existentialism's popular appeal was more about attitude than philosophical rumination; it represented a particular mood or disposition that was characterized by disenchantment and disillusionment. The ambiguities of existentialism meant it was capable of being used as a tagline to describe everything from art and music to dress and style. By denying traditional belief systems, acknowledging the meaninglessness of the world, and insisting on the individual's freedom and self-obligation, existentialism appeared to advocate a cynically jaded, self-indulgent, and self-gratifying conceit that harbored a blatant disregard for tradition. "Existential" became a label applied to the bohemian young who frequented the cellar clubs of Saint-Germain-des-Prés and subsequently inspired media scrutiny that detailed the alleged exploits of these hedonists.

The exposé that launched this phenomenon was a 1947 illustrated feature in the sensationalist newspaper *Samedi-Soir*, which announced with chagrin, "This is how the troglodytes of Saint-Germain-des-Prés live." Beside a photograph featuring a young Roger Vadim and a younger Juliette Gréco, who both looked forlorn as they stood atop a stone stairwell that descended into darkness behind them, the article began: "Do not look for the existentialists at the Café de Flore. They have taken refuge in the cellars. It is there that the existentialists drink, dance, and love, awaiting the atomic bomb for which they all perversely long." The article described these "existentialists" as extremely poor though from good bourgeois families, and as between the ages of sixteen and twenty-two, though "existential apprentices" could be as young as fourteen. Typically, they were vagabonds who never knew in the morning where they would sleep that night. Without a fixed domicile, they stayed up late into the night carousing and dancing at clubs and bars where they drank on credit or on someone else's tab until the early hours of the morning when, at last, they would exit with someone for the night. The "existential graffiti" that these sullen youths scribbled in phone booths and on bathroom walls dealt with macabre subjects, such as unhappiness, death, and suicide, with a morbid humor. The journalist Robert Jacques was "struck by their young pale faces, withered expressions, and despondency of each gesture."[96]

The "veritable sanctuary of the new generation" was Le Tabou, a tiny, tunnel-like after-hours cellar club on rue Christine that Jacques described as "the most harmful of places."[97] Le Tabou had only been open for a short while when the *Samedi-Soir* article appeared, and apparently the club's promoter, Anne-Marie Cazalis, had been responsible for the exposé, as well as for labeling the young people who frequented the club as "existentialists," though of course they had no real connection to the philosophical movement. Dark, dank, narrow, and low-ceilinged, Le Tabou became a sensation of frenetic energy, as the young danced *le jitterbug* and *le boogie-woogie* to the beat of live New Orleans jazz (see Figure 16). It was closed less than a year after opening, due to vociferous complaints from the neighborhood. The wild revelry simply relocated, however, across the quarter to Le Club Saint-Germain, where bebop was the jazz style and the dancing was even more chaotic and furious. In addition, late-night partyers could seek out Le Vieux-Columbier, Le Bar Vert, Le Méphisto, Le Catalan, L'Abbaye, or La Rose-Rouge, among several other clubs, for jazz, dancing, and heavy drinking. In the late 1940s the Saint-Germain quarter of Paris was not only the center of literary-artistic endeavor where intellectuals gathered in cafés to

Figure 16. A night of jazz and revelry in the cellar club Le Tabou in Saint-Germain-des-Prés, 1946. Agence Rapho-Top, Doisneau.

write and argue, but it was the core of the burgeoning cult of hedonism that characterized the all-night partying of an emerging French youth culture.[98]

The fury of media attention smacked of scandal, which heightened the popularity of these clubs while at the same time stimulating moral outrage for the corruption of the young, for which many held Sartre responsible even though he did not, as a practice, frequent the cellar clubs. Sartre's well-known association with the quarter, his reputation as a notorious womanizer, and his advocacy of the existentialist philosophy made him a perfect target for the critics. The newspaper *Inter*, describing the behavior of youth as "scabrous and scatological," argued that "Sartre is largely complicit in the vice and human ugliness" through his "pornographic literature."[99] *Dernière Heure*, in Algiers, reported that the quarter had become the meeting place for "declining pleasures, endorsed, God knows why, by Jean-Paul Sartre and existentialism."[100] *La Gazette des Lettres* compared the writings of Sartre with those of D. H. Lawrence, the author of *Lady Chatterley's Lover*.[101] *Le Monde* described the young as "beasts led by their instincts" and by "falsehoods," who admired Sartre as their "master."[102] Immediately following the publication of *The Second Sex*, in May 1949, François Mauriac, writing in *Le Figaro*, condemned Simone de Beauvoir for her "pornographic" writings and for the deleterious effect she, and existentialism, would have on the young. A week later, he castigated Sartrian thought generally for the proliferation of sexuality that was appearing in French literature. This "eroticism" represented a danger not only to literature generally, but to the young in particular. Throughout that summer, in the pages of *Le Figaro Littéraire*, Mauriac called upon young people to condemn the existentialists and the sexual overtones of contemporary literature. The response to his call to arms did not condemn, however, but mostly dismissed the issue as unimportant and as having very little influence on their, the young's, well-being and intellectual development.[103] In the tense political and intellectual climate of the postwar period, the public perception of the corrupted young running wild in the permissive atmosphere of Saint-Germain provided an opportunity to attack Sartre and his colleagues.[104]

Still, the perceived sexual practices of the young "existentialists" preoccupied the newspapers, who continued to print sensational stories about them. The first negative article, in *Samedi-Soir* in May 1947, had implied that through their indigent lifestyle, "existential adolescents" indulged in unbridled sex and that they engaged sexual partners with the same abandon that they chose dance partners.[105] *La Presse* claimed that the cellar clubs "harbored a strange and aggressive bacchanalia."[106] *Flash* ran a headline announcing that "Saint-Germain-des-Prés Makes Too Much Love!"[107] Furthermore, the oversexed, cynical, and nihilistic existential adolescent was most often represented as an anonymous girl. Dressed in the standard existential uniform of a black sweater, black shirt, and black pants, the young existential girl "lives in filth and invites you to drink and pay for her."[108] *La Presse* recommended that to end a late evening one should go to the cellar clubs "to meet overexcited young women."[109] These young women "are the dregs of Paris: a curious mildew of hatred, jealousy, stupidity, and the most vulgar sexuality. Such is the face of the existentialists. Such is the credo of their life."[110]

The media attention actually created a notorious celebrity for two of the young female "existentialists," Anne-Marie Cazalis and Juliette Gréco, who together became known as the "muses of Saint-Germain-des-Prés," and who, along with the young actor Marc Doelnitz, were responsible for promoting Le Tabou and, later, Le Club Saint-Germain. Cazalis, an attractive redhead with brown eyes, had won the 1946 Prix Paul Valéry for poetry at the young age of twenty-five, and was adept at promoting the quarter and herself. But the face, and the voice, that truly came to represent the Left Bank existential adolescent was Juliette Gréco, Cazalis's notorious playmate and protégée. Gréco had come to Saint-Germain from Montpellier in 1943, when she was fifteen. Her acting career in the theaters of Saint-Germain never took off, but when the nightlife of the quarter became a scene, her pretty face, long, straight dark brown hair, dark brown eyes, and attire of black turtleneck and trousers made her the photogenic epitome of the young "existential." She appeared so often in the popular press that people stopped her on the street to ask for her autograph.[111] Gréco turned this celebrity to her advantage, and by the age of twenty-one she had established what would become a very successful singing career by putting famous poems to music and touring the country with Claude Luter's jazz band. Her young voice and visage became a staple of the 1950s popular music scene.

Undercurrents of Sexual Perversion

The idea of a debauched sexuality as a part of moral abandon, however, became the primary reference point for the public's view of the 1940s "existential adolescent." In the decade that followed, at a time when youthful sexuality was still considered by many to be a taboo subject, Bardot and Sagan presented and represented sexually promiscuous youth to the collective consciousness. Although in 1947 the government had established a committee to explore the possibilities for sexual education in public schools, the committee's report left no place for such a measure in 1950s France.[112] To implement sexual education in French schools would have meant an official acknowledgment of the young's sexuality. Officially, France did not recognize that young people could have sexual desires or sexual practices. The political struggles about sex in postwar France whirled around the issue of modern contraception, and the sexuality of the young was not a priority. Even when the pill was legalized, in 1967, women under the age of twenty-one had to procure written consent from a parent or guardian to acquire it.[113]

Notably, the major studies conducted in the 1950s to learn more about young people from their own point of view tiptoed around the subject of sex. The two major studies of the young, those directed by Robert Kanters in 1951 and Françoise Giroud in 1957, both ignored the sexual practices of young people in their questionnaires.[114] While they asked the young about their studies, leisure activities, relationship with parents, and opinions on religion, politics, and money, Kanters and Giroud both avoided any direct questions about sexuality. They did each allude to sex, by asking young people for their opinions on marriage, cohabitation, children, sexual education, and abortion (Kanters), as well as love and fidelity (Giroud), but neither researcher asked directly about sexual practices. While we learn that there was a lack of consensus among the young on the appropriateness of abortion, cohabitation, or sexual education, and that generally the young expected men to be less faithful than women, ascertaining the numbers of young who were sexually active remained guesswork. One study conducted in the final months of 1961 did at last broach the subject, if hesitantly. It found that by the age of twenty, 8 out of 10 young men and 5 out of 10 young women had had sex before marriage, and it thus concluded that, among the young, "chastity was no longer fashionable." However, the study also concluded that the "sexual liberation of the woman," as depicted in newspapers, film, and literature, had been overstated, because the data showed a clear inequality in the attitudes and practices of sex for young men and women.[115] Yet the fact that the study even considered sexual activity in its inquiry is indicative of a shift in perspective, and the numbers did reveal that more young people were having sex before marriage than were not.

In contrast to the apparent silence surrounding the young and sex in these surveys, a 1955 exposé on French youth, written for *Time* magazine by Stanley Karnow, depicted them as "immoral" by Anglo Saxon sexual standards: "French kids mush it up in doorways, in the Métro, in cafes, during mealtime, and after coffee." Karnow even passed on the rule of thumb that "if you kiss a girl on the lips, you go to bed with her," and he quoted a twenty-three-year-old girl as proclaiming, "We don't talk—we do."[116] While Karnow's emphasis on the libidinous sex lives of the young French was almost certainly exaggerated, it is interesting to note that his examples focused on the permissiveness of young women, as if they were the gatekeepers to free love. Regardless of the actual numbers of the young having sex, the public responded to Karnow's depiction of sexually active young women with fierce protest. As noted earlier, after the *Time* article appeared, Karnow was condemned in the Parisian press for generally maligning French youth.[117]

Given the uproar that had been created by the film *Ripening Seed*, by Brigitte Bardot, and by Françoise Sagan, it is clear that the issue of sex and the young continued to creep into the popular culture and popular discourse, even though it was a taboo subject that official France did not want to address. Some sought to open up the discussion, while others sought to silence it, but it was a losing battle. For example, in three successful films from young directors of the New Wave cinema, the morality and sexual practices of the young were challenged: Louis Malle's *Les Amants* (*The Lovers*, 1958) followed a young woman (Jeanne Moreau) as she sought sexual fulfillment through a series of lovers, first among them her young husband; François Truffaut's third feature, *Jules et Jim* (1962), revolved around a ménage à trois consisting of two young men and a woman (again, Jeanne Moreau) who sought an alternative lifestyle together outside the boundaries of traditional society; and Jacques Rozier's *Adieu Philippine* (1963) pitted two young women as the consenting lovers of an army conscript about to leave for Algeria. Moreover, in 1954, the novel *L'Histoire d'O* (*The Story of O*) was published to great scandal. It combined the style and scope of great literature, but with the explicit detail of pornography. *The Story of O* was neither about, nor written by, a young person, but the fact that it had been authored by a woman, writing under the pseudonym Pauline Réage, amplified the scandal of its publication. What's more, the sadomasochistic themes of *The Story of O* were set within a student/teacher paradigm: O becomes the sexual apprentice of her lover-master, a dynamic that emphasizes the power relationship between a young pupil and her adult mentor. O's sexual subordination is based upon both a gendered and an age hierarchy, of the male adult authority sternly disciplining and edifying his young female charge. The idea that an upright, upper-class woman by day could enjoy wild, perverse sex by night ran counter to traditional notions of woman as the repository of purity and morality. Despite the apparent domestic tranquility of the 1950s, then, there was a strong undercurrent of transgressive sex, which surfaced only on occasion to provoke scandal.

The challenge to traditional male sex roles represented by the predatory sexuality of Bardot and the rest was exacerbated by the threat to masculinity represented by homosexuality. More than the sexually aggressive woman, the homosexual threatened male virility from within the gendered ranks. The pronatalist campaigns of the late nineteenth and early twentieth centuries had defined the homosexual as not only an affront to moral propriety but as a treacherous rogue who would undermine France's efforts to boost the birth rate and hence damage France's national prestige. Through his sexual acts, the homosexual not only betrayed his gender and his society, but his nation as well. In postwar France, the supreme representative of the transgressive homosexual was, of course, Jean Genet, who, in his writings, resolutely linked his homosexuality with being young.

Genet was the darling of the intelligentsia in postwar France, and he had garnered marvelous critical acclaim for his autobiographic novels published clandestinely between 1942 and 1947. Although his novels were underground sensations and not initially popular sellers, Genet's reputation grew throughout the 1950s, and the legacy of his novels expanded following the success of his plays. Genet accepted his homosexuality as a quality that furthered his rejection of society. He celebrated and esteemed it as profane and oppositional. He defined the homosexual as "a man who by his very nature is out of step with the world, who refuses to enter into the system that organizes the entire world."[118]

Three of his novels—*Our Lady of the Flowers*, *Miracle of the Rose*, and *The Thief's Journal*—chronicled his personal experience as a vagabond, delinquent, and homosexual reveling in the youthful ardor of amorality. These autobiographical novels bound together the passions of being young with a love of treachery. Of *The Thief's Journal*, Genet's most famous novel, the author remarked that he was "assembling these notes for a few young men," and that "betrayal, theft and homosexuality are the basic subjects of this book. There is a relationship among them which, though not always apparent, at least, it seems to me, recognizes a kind of vascular exchange between my taste for betrayal and theft and my loves." Thus, as a young man embracing homosexuality, theft, and crime, he had "resolutely rejected a world which had rejected [him]."[119] Genet very purposely took the alterity represented by the homosexual and the criminal and emphasized its juxtaposition to mainstream French society, thereby rejecting bourgeois moral codes.

This link connecting sexual delinquency with criminal delinquency was not uncommon. Genet's confession of his love for all things treacherous confirmed a preconceived notion of the homosexual as deviant and as a threatening force to behavioral norms. For example, Jean Chazal, in his study on juvenile delinquency, documented a connection between the aberrant antisocial behavior of the delinquent and that of the homosexual, suggesting that the perversion of the criminal act combined with that of the sexual act provided an erotic charge for the young delinquent.[120] Genet and Chazal were each concerned with the homosexuality of the young; Genet celebrated it, Chazal scorned it, but both noted its transgressive qualities and the potential hazard it represented for France. Interestingly, it was not until 1942, under the Vichy government, that France established an explicit legal distinction between homosexual and heterosexual acts. The law, which was kept in place by the Fourth Republic, established separate ages of sexual majority for homosexual and heterosexual acts, twenty-one and fifteen, respectively, on the premise that homosexual acts distinctly corrupted, perverted, and victimized the young.[121]

Not all representations of youthful homosexuality in postwar France depicted it in the intentional guise of gross perversion and criminal deviancy. Roger Peyrefitte's first novel, *Les Amitiés particulières* (*Special Friendships*), scandalized France in 1945 with its story of the homosexual love affair between Georges and Alexandre, two boys in a strict Roman Catholic boarding school in the mountains of Languedoc. Set in 1930, the narrative recounts the bittersweet coming-of-age story of two teenage boys whose passion for each other becomes more intimate than the headmaster can tolerate, and ends tragically in the suicide of Alexandre. The novel won the Prix Théophraste Renaudot, had enough popular success to merit a minor scandal, and was eventually made into a movie twenty years later. Some of Peyrefitte's later novels, such as *Mademoiselle de Murville* (1947) and *Les Amours singulières* (1949), continued his exploration of sexuality among the young, though not exclusively of a homosexual nature.

Clandestine liaisons among sleeping schoolmates in boarding-school dormitories also typified the writings of Violette Leduc. Often considered the female counterpart to Jean Genet in both subject matter and style, Leduc wrote autobiographical novels that recounted her illegitimate birth, her ugliness, her strained relationships, and her bitter losses at love. Championed by Simone de Beauvoir, as Genet had been by Jean-Paul Sartre, Leduc's earliest works, *L'Asphyxie* (1946) and *L'Affamée* (1948), earned her the esteem of a small coterie of influential writers, which garnered her a publishing contract with Gallimard. Leduc wrote unflinchingly about her homosexuality, which had blossomed within the confines of a girls' boarding school. In her third novel, *Ravages* (1955), she wrote about the nervous excitement she had felt in slipping past sleeping girls in the dead of night to engage in sexual intimacy with her waiting lover. Gallimard balked, however, at publishing the more explicit accounts of her life's loves, and removed the offensive episodes, which were later published as *Thérèse et Isabelle* in 1966. Leduc's masterpiece, *La Bâtarde* (*The Bastard*), was published to great acclaim and notoriety in 1964. It was a complete recollection of Leduc's life until the war's end when she had begun her writing career, and it included a detailed account of her days as a lesbian schoolgirl.[122]

If Leduc was considered a counterpart to Genet, Françoise Mallet-Joris was often considered the sisterly complement to Sagan. Mallet-Joris had much more success than Leduc, though nothing that compared to the astounding achievement of Sagan with *Bonjour tristesse*. Still, the critical and financial success of her first novel, *Le Rempart des béguines* (*The Illusionist*), in 1951, allowed Mallet-Joris to concentrate on her writing, which resulted in a Prix des Librairies de France in 1956, a Prix Fémina in 1958, and a Prix René Juillard in 1963. A young author, Mallet-Joris was twenty-one at the time *The Illusionist* was published. Her novel traces the coming-of-age story of Hélène Noris, a fifteen-year-old schoolgirl living in Gers with her wealthy widowed father René, who maintains a mistress—a very similar setup to that in Sagan's *Bonjour tristesse*. Bored and frustrated, Hélène directs her rebellion against family and community by refusing to play the role assigned to her by society. However, she is not at all the confident manipulator that Sagan's Cécile is; rather, Hélène lets her passions direct her and she falls under the spell of the beguiling Tamara, her father's mistress, with whom she maintains a tempestuous and torrid secret love affair. Ironically, when René telephones Tamara to propose marriage, she is, unknown to him, in bed with his naked daughter.

The betrayal of Tamara, who marries René though she does not love him, empowers Hélène; it teaches her to steel her emotions and transforms her into a clever and calculating young woman. In a 1955 sequel entitled *La*

Chambre rouge (*The Red Room*), Mallet-Joris tells the story of how Hélène completes her sexual education by taking a male lover, allowing herself to accept only desire as a legitimate and useful emotion. She works toward bringing about the downfall of Tamara, with whom she had fallen madly in love as an obsessive teenager, and she essentially reshapes herself into a fiercely independent young woman capable of shrewd calculation. The similarities of this work to that of Françoise Sagan are obvious, and the two women were sometimes interviewed together as up-and-coming young female writers who both depicted the despair and anguish of their generation, of "a certain youth" in postwar France.[123]

The primary difference between the two, of course, is in Sagan's heterosexual characters, in contrast to Mallet-Joris's bisexual ones. However, in the third major study of the "Sagan phenomenon," a psycho-sexual deconstruction of *Bonjour tristesse*, Jean Lignière claimed to detect a hidden pattern of lesbianism and incest in her novel. In *Françoise Sagan et le succès* (1957), he maintained that the dynamic between the characters of *Bonjour tristesse* was predicated upon their unconscious sexual desire for one another. Lignière claims that Anne is really a lesbian, as is Cécile, and that the tension between them derives from their unspoken passion for one another. Meanwhile, Cécile also harbors sexual desires for her father, Raymond, and, likewise, he for her. Lignière believes that, "between the words," Sagan was sending a message to her readers—a subtext of sexual struggle set within the confines of the "eternal feminine." Undoubtedly, *Bonjour tristesse* is full of sexual tension and erotic overtones, yet Lignière's incestuous and Sapphic interpretation remains unconvincing and somewhat bizarre. However, his search for a deeper understanding of the sexual conflict inherent in the maturation of a young woman, as extreme as that interpretation might be, does resonate with the fixation on the young in terms of sex.[124]

The Sexual Transgression of Young Women

However marginal some of these last literary examples may be, and without disputing that they found neither a broad audience nor wide influence, it is still significant that they emerged in the specific context of postwar France, as they underscore the tension generated around the issue of sexual propriety for the young. In this context, there are numerous examples of sexual trans-gression that had a broad impact on French society: juvenile prostitution, the existential adolescent, and the great success of Bardot and Sagan. Because sex for the young was a taboo subject, France was at odds over the emerging public sexuality of youth, and demonstrated this anxiety in particular with regard to young women.

France had experienced a similar phenomenon in the wake of the First World War: first, pronatalist campaigns had been intensified in an effort to compensate for the human losses of the war; second, the cultural release of the Roaring Twenties brought a concern for the moral well-being of France; and third, these combined anxieties were often manifested in animosity to-ward independent women, and specifically, the "new woman," the "flapper," and the "gamine."[125] While the parallels are striking, it would be wrong to assume that 1920s France and 1950s France bore the same marks of these related phenomena. Though both were postwar eras, the historical contexts differed markedly.

France lost far fewer young men to battle in the Second World War than it did in the First, and immediately following the war in 1945 there was an explosion in births, the *bébé-boom* that was sustained through the 1950s. This demographic phenomenon reduced the state's pressure on adult women to reproduce. Moreover, as much as France claimed to be a victor in World War II, in truth it had been swiftly defeated and subse-quently occupied by the Nazis for most of the war, making it complicit with Nazi rancor through the collaboration of the Vichy government. Hence, the reconstruction after World War II took on a particularly moral tone in addition to a material one.

In 1945, in the tolerant atmosphere of celebration, the usual rules of chastity for young middle-class women were temporarily suspended as some young women saw the soldiers as "liberators" worthy of generous gratitude. Furthermore, at Liberation, the role of women as resistors was ignored, whereas women who had collaborated were condemned in public rituals across France that emphasized their unacceptable sexual relations. Women were more often accused of sexual collaboration, *collaboration hori-zontale*, than of any other form. The usual punishment, of public humilia-tion—of women with their heads shaved and paraded naked through jeering crowds—left a lasting image of the shame of the Occupation and of the moral complicity of the war years.[126] Furthermore, these women were often young. For example, in Calvados, fifty-four minor women were punished by the courts for sexual impropriety with Germans.[127] It seems that part of the postwar concern about the sexual activity of young women was a response to the war itself and the legacy of sexual wantonness it left behind. The repetitive display of images of amoral young women served as a reminder of the war years that echoed down through the postwar era, making total recovery problematic. As Simone de Beauvoir put it, "The war was over; it remained on our hands like a great, unwanted corpse, and there was no place on earth to bury it."[128]

As the decade of the 1950s drew to a close, and along with it, the Fourth Republic, the potential of sexual intimacy to stir up memories of the war was most poetically evoked in the award-winning film *Hiroshima, mon amour* (1959), by Alain Resnais. Just a few years earlier, in *Nuit et brouillard* (*Night and Fog*, 1955), Resnais had forced France, and the rest of the world, to confront the Holocaust. In *Hiroshima, Mon Amour*, he and scenarist Marguerite Duras tell the complex story of a casual love affair between a French actress and a Japanese architect in the Hiroshima of 1959. Resnais and Duras reveal very little about either of the characters, who remain nameless; they seem more interested in the way sex creates an intimate space in which truth, memory, and regret can be conjured. At the war's end, the young French woman had been guilty of *collaboration horizontale* in Nevers, while the young Japanese man had returned home to a devastated Hiroshima. Very much a tone poem rather than a linear narrative, *Hiroshima, Mon Amour* intercuts and interconnects the years 1945 and 1959 to juxtapose the quiet tranquility of present sexual encounters with the unpleasant volatility of past wartime memories. A philosophical melancholy pervades the film, and its theme of coming to terms with the past crescendos as the couple's love affair dissolves. The past, it seems, had not simply gone away, but had resurfaced to trouble the present.

In addition to the complicated memory of the war and the propriety of gender, the film brought to the surface the underlying issue of sexual codes of conduct determined by class. Traditionally, there had been a long-standing implicit association between working-class women and promiscuity. Societal ideas about promiscuity generally allowed for, even if they did not approve of, licentiousness among poor and working-class women. A poor woman's reliance on prostitution, for example, might seem understandable if not acceptable—an unfortunate result of circumstance. In contrast, the bourgeois woman, pious and proper, was held to be the moral backbone of society, the repository and standard-bearer of the social code. The tradition of social reform and charitable activities among bourgeois women derived from the idea that they were responsible for safeguarding the moral well-being of French society through their example and guidance—an idea that was also integral to woman's role as mother.[129] Mothering meant more than producing offspring; it meant inculcating the next generation with moral precepts through edification and virtuous example.

For a woman, maintaining moral credibility was tantamount to a civic responsibility; it was intimately tied to her state-sanctioned function as mother of the republic. She was expected not only to populate the nation, but to provide virtuous continuity through the transfer of a moral tradition. Whereas young men were defined according to their future as leaders, soldiers, and workers, young women were defined according to their role as future mothers and benevolent guardians of morality. For a woman, then, citizenship was intimately bound up with sexual practice. She was to be virtuous and chaste before marriage, and to sexually reproduce thereafter, while at the same time maintaining the nation's cultural standards of morality.

Often, the young filmmakers in the 1950s were criticized for their singular concern with the middle class, who were depicted as being "bourgeois in their acts, their speech, their reactions, and their revolts"; hence, the unsavory behavior of the young depicted in the films I have discussed was all the more subversive for their being bourgeois, as was the case with Marcel Carné's *The Cheaters*.[130] Bardot and Sagan both emerged from proper bourgeois backgrounds, yet their films and novels depicted an amoral bourgeois youth transgressing the boundaries of class. The sexual licentiousness of Bardot and Sagan, or of existential adolescents, was all the more troubling and upsetting for its rejection of social standards for middle-class women. That young bourgeois women should be portrayed as bawdy, promiscuous, wild, and alienated upset conceptions of class distinction, while their predatory sexuality, their approaching sex "as a man," threatened conceptions of masculinity and challenged cultural conceits of gender.

Precocious sexual activity was not only a threat to male sex roles, it also threatened to undermine femininity. Docteur Le Moal's worry for the consequences of sex on the emotional development of young female delinquents characterized the concern for the virtue of young women in general. The blurring of sexual categories threatened to disrupt both the gendered and generational organization of societal roles. Even if the portrayal of sexually precocious young women in movies, novels, and the press was merely on the level of the symbolic—that is, even if it was not tangibly real—the anxiety it generated represented a transition in the collective imagination, in society's attitudes toward sex, the young, and gender.

Society habitually gendered the social group of youth as masculine, which meant that young women were usually talked about in the particular rather than the universal. Yet two young women, Brigitte Bardot and Françoise Sagan, were thrust into the position of mythic icons for postwar French youth. BB, as the photographed body, and Sagan, as the interviewed brain, were acknowledged as representatives of the postwar generation in its entirety, not just of young women. This reversal, in which young women were made to represent young men, can be explained in terms of sex. If young women were traditionally defined or determined by their sexual capacities, and specifically by their ability to reproduce, then it is not surprising that young women were made to stand for the transitional sexual empowerment of new social codes. As a result, young women's sexual transgression metonymically stood for the moral rebellion of youth generally, which the public feared.

Yet the obsessive worry about sex and the young was not simply about prudery. If the juvenile delinquent problematized the idealized representation of young males in postwar France, then it was young females, depicted as sexually promiscuous or cynically jaded libertines, who problematized the idealized representation of young women. Over and over again, the sexual activity of young women was tied to a particular worldview, to an attitude characterized by a wearied skepticism of tradition and a bitter rejection of inherited belief systems—an image that remains a standard caricature of French youth. The nihilism of the existential adolescent, the forlorn hopelessness of the vagabond prostitute, the cynicism of Sagan, the brazen disregard of Bardot, the scourge of the *mal de jeunesse*—these attitudes made the hoped-for renaissance of France problematic. The sexual behavior of young women was only the most visible symptom of a greater, more pervasive disillusionment threatening the temperament of young France. The optimism of the Liberation had turned into pessimism a mere decade later. The world had not been remade. If youth was the future of France and this was the youth of France, then France was in trouble.

Pierre Voldemar, in a commentary on the *mal de jeunesse*, made this connection plain. He said that the public's preoccupation with the *mal de jeunesse* was more like a *mal du public*. Expressed through a concern for the young and a fear of youth, France was itself "implicated in this affair." Voldemar pointed out that France repeatedly professed that to better the young "the solutions are simple: send them to summer camps, place others in reformatories, the rest should have some fresh air, build athletic fields, educate parents, post agents at the cinema box office, monitor the press, censor publications." But, he warned, France was completely off-track, "because youth does not form a separate race from you, it doesn't obey different laws . . . it resembles you, and that is all!" France wanted to reassure itself by "proclaiming the rise of a revolutionary youth, adventurous youth, and anti-conformist youth," but, Voldemar argued, "[youth] is like us and that is the bad omen."[131] Just as the enemies of Sartre used the supposed corruption of the young as a weapon of attack, when adult France talked about youth they were usually talking indirectly about themselves. The momentum of concern for the problem of youth—whether a juvenile delinquent or a sexually promiscuous libertine—coincided with the steady disillusionment of French society since the Liberation. By the mid- to late fifties, despite its many successes since the war, France was suffering from problems that seemed intractable: the intransigencies of the Fourth Republic, the escalation of colonial wars of independence, the volatility of superpower adversaries, and the crush of an urban population without adequate housing or schools. The utopian hope and promise of the Liberation remained unfulfilled. The public's fascination with the sexual cynicism of young women was largely a result of the social category of youth operating as a barometer for French society generally, with the hope and threat of the young rising and falling with the prevailing social conditions.

The conception of youth as a normative social group eliding differences of class and gender was undermined by the impertinence of the delinquent and the libertine. Yet the paradox of youth acting as both hope and threat is central to reinforcing traditional age hierarchies of power. All the while, adults were bemoaning that these wayward youngsters were products of

SEX AND THE CYNICAL GIRL **231**

their time, that the young were not at fault, that the problems stemmed from the society in which the young found themselves, and that it was the adults who must fix the young. The construction of the category "youth" is typically undertaken by the old, both conceptually and sociologically. The old were the ones who had created the problem of problem youth, and yet they considered themselves the ones who must fix the problem of problem youth. Thus, despite the rhetoric to the contrary, it was the old who were actually recuperating their position and reinscribing typical age hierarchies. Throughout the postwar period we can see how the old produced and idealized the social group of youth, all the while subverting it with their own anxieties related particularly to the agency of the young. On the verge of the 1960s, young people, like Bardot and Sagan, seemed to be taking over this youth discourse, or at the very least complicating it and making it their own, which was just what was so troubling and problematic.

CHAPTER 6

Tarzan Under Attack

Since the Second World War, the comic book has emerged in the West as a form of popular literature that appeals to both children and adults. The comic book hero has leapt from the pages of periodicals, as an icon in the art of Roy Lichtenstein and Andy Warhol, and as a celebrated genre of Hollywood film and television. However, it would be a mistake to believe that comics are a purely American obsession. In France, the comic book maintains a position of prominence as an artistic and literary medium. A survey conducted by *Le Monde* in 1982 revealed that comics made up 7 percent of all reading matter in France. Furthermore, it showed that comics were more likely to be read by those of higher education or socioeconomic status than by those of lower. Indeed, in France, in public approval and popularity, the comic book occupies a space matched only in the United States and Japan, and in critical appreciation, it is perhaps unmatched. It operates as an esteemed element of popular culture that has literary and artistic appeal to young and old alike. Today, there is a section of the Ministry of Culture devoted to comics, a comics commission within the National Center for Letters, as well as an annual comics salon and archival institute for the study of comics at Angoulême.[1]

Although comics are pop-cultural merchandise that is consumed and collected by adults, the primary audience for comics has been and remains the young. Yet the history of the comic book reveals a tension regarding its suitability for minors. In the West, after the Second World War, campaigns were waged against comics that were deemed to have content inappropriate for young people. These moral outcries resulted in legislation, first in France and then later in Austria, Germany, Britain, and the United States.[2] The first of these campaigns, in France, culminated in a law of July 16, 1949, establishing a Commission for the Oversight and Control of Publications for Children and Adolescents. Yet this campaign, ostensibly about comics, was not specifically about comics at all, but rather about competing conceptions of society and youth in postwar France.

The Moral Reconstruction of Youth

Initially, the reform of juvenile publications grew out of the perceived need for a general moral reconstruction of France after the troubled years of the Second World War. Some vituperative attacks even proclaimed that "the juvenile press of 1938 made ready the treachery of 1940."[3] Louis Raillon hoped to rally educators to the moral reconstitution of the nation. He maintained that the best way to initiate national change was to alter the noxious influence on the young of demoralizing reading material; reforming the reading matter of juveniles would do no less than "prepare and develop the soul of France."[4] In a warning to parents, André Fournel explicitly linked the reform of juvenile publications to the project of reconstruction more generally by demanding that "France, who tends to its reconstruction in all other domains, needs to consider the moral reconstruction of its young generations."[5] In other words, intervening in the reading habits of young people would ensure "a solid education that would form citizens conscious of their duties and all their civic and personal responsibilities."[6] Uniting around the interests of young people and the reformation of their reading habits was a way to start anew for "the future of France."[7]

Comic books were, in fact, a medium with significant access to the young people of France. The kind of information and the tone of messages conveyed in this medium were paramount to the efforts of moral rejuvenation, in part because of the scale of distribution of comics. Throughout the Fourth Republic many *journaux de jeudi* (released on Thursdays) and *petit format* comic books had higher rates of circulation than leading newspapers. For example, in 1957 *Le Journal de Mickey* alone had a circulation of 633,000, whereas *Le Figaro* had a circulation of 486,500, and *Le Monde*, 211,500.[8] Thus, depending on the content, comic books could be either an undermining threat or a viable tool in the efforts to shape and mold the young into an ideal citizenry for France.

The Fourth Republic was concerned about what it perceived to be the moral degeneration of France, as reflected in the country's defeat, occupation, and collaboration, as well as the subsequent damage the high rate of juvenile delinquency could have on France's future. Notably, the legislation overseeing comic books emerged from the Assembly's special commission appointed to study the high rate of juvenile delinquency.[9] The National Assembly passed the law of July 16, 1949, to protect France's young from debauchery, delinquency, and corruption, and, significantly, to protect the country from its own maladjusted youth. Deputy Paul Gosset stated that the legislator's duty was to prevent "the publication of texts and images not conforming to morality and contrary to the governing principle of the training and education of French youth." Moreover, he emphasized, "the problem of preparing them for their work as citizens is a public responsibility."[10] Thus, what guided the legislation was the government's belief in its own duty to shape and construct the identity of French youth into what it believed to be most valuable for France's future.

The legacy of the Second World War featured prominently within the Assembly debates in January and July of 1949, and the experience and conduct of the French during the war helped shape the legislation. For instance, it is significant that during the debates the words "cowardice" (*la lâcheté*) and "hatred" (*la haine*) were added to the paragraph outlining the unfavorable characteristics that would indicate whether a publication warranted censure. In its final form, the article stipulated that publications "should not contain any illustration, any narrative, any chronicle, any heading, or any insertion that favorably presents banditry, falsehoods, thievery, idleness, *cowardice*,

hatred, debauchery or any criminal acts or misdemeanors of a nature demoralizing to children or youth."[11] That neither of these minor amendments
was met with any opposition from the floor shows that the Assembly sought
to use the legislation as a way to create a citizenry among its youth that was
imbued with a moral sense of what it meant to be French, an attitude that
was shaped by the disagreeable experience of the Second World War.[12]

Comic Books in France

The concern for the effect of comics on youth stemmed from the interpretation of their content, as well as from the very nature of the medium, which
relied on the bold power of iconic images. Though comics had emerged at
the turn of the century and had reached a mass audience by the 1930s, they
were still considered to be relatively new and thus potentially dangerous.
Many believed images could be powerfully influential on young, impression-
able minds because pictures, unlike writing, can be decoded and interpreted
without specialized knowledge. Comics were derided for their repetition of
images that "hypnotized" and "intoxicated" youngsters while simultaneously
promoting illiteracy by coaxing young readers away from storybooks.

Comics rely on sequential images to tell their stories graphically rather
than textually. Whereas the images in film occupy the same screen space in
a narrative sequence, with one image replacing the next, comics use spatially
juxtaposed images to convey narrative structure. This distinction is significant because it is the empty space *between* the pictorial frames that allows the
comic book reader to focus on the completion of an action in his or her own
mind. In comics, the reader can deliberate and brood on individual panels.
Thus, comic books require human imagination to interpret and transform
their panels into a meaningful narrative structure. In comic books, therefore, violent or sexual acts are created in the mind of the reader more than
they are on the page, or, for film, on the screen.[13] More problematically, the
popularity of comic books in France ensured their wide readership and distribution because they were portable and could be shared and read repeatedly, at home, at school, or on the playground.

Comic strips emerged in France at the same time as elsewhere in the
West, at the turn of the century. Until the mid-1930s, French comics usually

appeared in weekly illustrated papers for children, along with short stories, fairy tales, and articles, a format that extended back into the nineteenth century. This configuration radically changed, however, with the introduction of *Le Journal de Mickey*, first published in France in October 1934.[14] Its format was twice as large as the traditional illustrated paper (roughly the size of an American tabloid paper), and it was comprised almost entirely of serial comic strips, most of them of American origin, such as "Mickey Mouse" or "Jungle Jim." *Le Journal de Mickey* immediately dominated the French market, crushing its competitors in circulation and forcing rival publishers to adopt a similar format, style, and content. By the late 1930s, the best-selling and most revered comics in France were the heroic adventure comics of "Tarzan," "Flash Gordon," "Mandrake the Magician," and "Red Rider."[15] The French industry was left reeling from the popularity of American comics, and it struggled to match the quality and market appeal of the designs, styles, and story lines that were being imported; the industry even sought protectionist legislation, unsuccessfully.[16]

During the Occupation of France, Germany had banned American comics, a move that, in fact, helped to solidify the sputtering French industry. In the Vichy South, however, American comics continued to be available, as long as the U.S. government maintained a position of neutrality.[17] In the immediate postwar period, a number of French comics were launched, or relaunched, some of which capitalized on the reputation of the Resistance, and they became quite popular among the young of France.[18] Although *Tarzan* and the *Journal de Mickey* (not relaunched until 1952) would continue to be extremely popular, imported American comics never regained their dominant prewar market share. Indeed, the postwar period is often seen as a golden age for French comics.[19]

Nevertheless, following the Liberation of France and the subsequent end of the war, American publishers poured a backlog of comic books into France and Europe, which was greedily consumed by the young. This deluge of American comics created political opposition from both the left and right in France, as concern mounted regarding France's cultural hegemony in the young's reading material. The Communist Party opposed these comics because they presented values counter to Stalinist orthodoxy; that is, the party disapproved of the mighty individual champion who violently and heroically would defeat scores of enemies to ensure the triumph of liberty, freedom, and the American way. Meanwhile, the Catholic social democrats of the Mouvement Republicain Populaire (MRP) opposed these comics because they supposedly undermined the construction of a new moral, national, and, specifically, French identity. Thus, industry protectionists, public morality groups, pedagogues, and political parties all joined together in an uneasy alliance in the campaign for the 1949 law.[20]

Cold War Politics: A Third Way or Anti-Americanism?

In its first years, the Fourth Republic was politically and intellectually dominated by these two political groups, as each desired to build a new and better France out of the ashes of the old. Even though the Communists had been forced out of the Tripartite coalition in 1947, they remained the largest party in the National Assembly and generated support from 25 percent of the electorate. The Communist/Gaullist rivalry formed the two poles between which the line of the Fourth Republic's cultural policy tended to be strung. Both groups maintained a leery attitude toward American intervention, which they viewed as an insidious threat to French hegemony. America did indeed seem to be everywhere in the late 1940s—from GIs stationed in France, to Marshall Plan advisors, to NATO diplomats, to American products and businesses. In view of this, the law of July 16, 1949, represented a moral concern for juvenile literature intertwined with a concern for American vulgarity influencing the worldview of French youth and the succession of French *civilisation*. Yet it is significant that the Assembly rejected motions to specifically name American publications as the objects of the legislation. This issue had been raised repeatedly by the Communist Party and successively defeated by the Assembly.

These two seemingly opposed political parties, the Communists and the Catholic MRP (which included many Gaullists), worked together to develop an initial bill designed to protect French publications.[21] The bill, whose aim was to prohibit all foreign comic strips, was presented to the National Assembly in 1948. It took up the cause of writers and draftsmen by seeking economic protection for this floundering French industry, as an indirect way to attack material of foreign origin on an ideological basis. This initial bill, however, was deemed to be too extreme and was rejected due to its harsh condemnation of all foreign material. The Catholic MRP party then revised the proposed legislation. Its bill emphasized the moral considerations of the young and established a watchdog committee with the power to censure and threaten prosecution.[22] The revised bill shows that the debate was really a domestic one, more about France itself than about America in France. To be sure, however, anti-Americanism remained a significant element of this domestic debate.

Indeed, on July 2, 1949, the Communist Party actually voted against the final bill, despite its support for the project in general and its sponsorship of the original legislation. René Thullier warned the Assembly that if the legislation failed to ban all foreign work then the Communist Party would not only abstain, it would actually vote against the bill that it had helped to produce. The Communists argued for the suppression of all imported material, regardless of content, on the dual grounds of the corruption of youth and the need to ensure employment for French writers and draftsmen. Such a measure, according to Thullier, would raise the quality of French publications due to the substandard, inferior, and profane work of the Americans.[23]

The debate surrounding the explicit censorship of foreign, specifically American, material emerged in January 1949, when the bill was first presented to the National Assembly. André Pierrard of the Communist Party savaged American comics and, in particular, the publisher of *Opera Mundi*, Paul Winkler, who imported material from King Features Syndicate. Pierrard claimed that "all the publications unhealthy for our children come from America and exclusively America," and that Winkler "controlled the juvenile press in our country." Pierrard charged that Winkler was a capitalist of the worst kind who greedily profited from the demoralization of French youth via "the great Hitlerophile press of America!" The problem was bigger than just that of comics and youth, however. Pierrard hinted at the larger cultural project underway when he said, "It is not only *Tarzan* and *Zorro* that should be changed; it is society itself that should be changed!"[24]

Winkler responded coolly and directly to Pierrard's attacks with a letter addressed and sent to each Assembly deputy detailing Pierrard's exaggerations and outright falsehoods, which were legion. Of the fifty-nine periodical publications for youth, *Opera Mundi* provided material for only three. Furthermore, Winkler pointed out that his company did not import *Tarzan*, *Zorro*, or *Red Rider*, the comics that had been specifically named in the

Assembly debate, but rather he imported Walt Disney's *Mickey Mouse*, which was "universally recognized to be of the highest moral value." As far as undermining the French industry, Winkler pointed out that his company actually exported a number of French comics, such as *Les Trois Mousquetaires*, to other markets. Next, Winkler noted that many of the most violent and sexualized comics were actually of French origin, though they might be set amidst the "gangsters of Chicago." Finally, Winkler suggested that the censorship of foreign comics in France only served to undermine the influence of French thought in the larger world, and thus threatened France's great intellectual tradition and sophisticated reputation, the very *civilisation* that the legislation sought to protect.[25]

The vitriolic attacks on America did not cease after the bill's passage, and they were not confined to Communist extremists nor to the Assembly floor. Partly at issue was the predominance of American products in the French market. It was true that comics of American origin were the most popular comics in France and they enjoyed the largest circulations. Even among comic papers of mostly French origin, the American strips were the most popular.[26] In 1950, a member of the new Commission for the Control of Juvenile Publications claimed that American publishers dictated to French editors what material could be altered and what material must remain intact. He essentially suggested that, as an economic power, imperial America was controlling the reading material of French youth.[27] Other critics were more plain: "Through open commerce and the fiction of free enterprise, the conscience of childhood is poisoned to the profit of Yankee imperialism."[28]

This "poison" was that of mass American consumer culture spoiling the great tradition of French *civilisation*. Many critics lamented the glamorous "easy life" portrayed in American comics and films as a "universe without any material problems," thus complicating France's lingering material hardship in the wake of the war. The multiplicity of these images of luxury "progressively intoxicated the adolescent with visions of an artificial world."[29] As a result, critics feared, the youth of France learn that to achieve the "good life" one steals, swindles, and kills without a moral conscience, as evidenced in the unfortunate Guyader Affair of 1948 or the J-3 de Valence, both of which were reminiscent of the wartime black market. Even a serious intellectual review like *Les Temps Modernes* made the absurd claim that "the

American generation born after 1930 does not know how to read," due to the essential "substitution of text by image" in popular culture.[30]

The campaign against American comics played itself out amid the hottest moments of the early Cold War: the Berlin Airlift, the Korean conflict, McCarthyism, the Rosenberg trial and execution, the rearmament of Germany, the Soviets' demonstration of their nuclear capability, and the struggle over the *coca-colonisation* of France by American capitalism. Although the strident anti-American sentiment was led by the Communist Party and its fellow travelers, who viewed American comics, with their exoneration of the violent individual superhero, as promoting "Fascistic themes," centrists and Atlanticists as well hoped that France would maintain an independent national policy free from American domination. Thus, although not everyone supporting the measures against comic books could be characterized as anti-American, resistance to the capitalist behemoth and the desire for French hegemony and an independent national identity in the wake of Nazi, and then Allied, invasion and occupation did inform the debates about foreign comics and the practice of cultural consumption.

Yet this was not simply rampant anti-Americanism. These critics wanted the young to grow up as particularly French, not universally American or German or Italian or whatever. An opinion poll from the mid-1950s showed that most people in France did not consider the United States to be a cultural threat, merely a political and strategic one.[31] Italian comics were similar in style, content, and popularity to American ones and were also a target of the legislation, though they were directly cited much less often. Wildly popular Belgian comics, however, such as *Tintin*, *Spirou*, *Lucky Luke*, and, later, *Les Stroumphs* (*The Smurfs*), were not condemned, most likely due to their Francophone character. In fact, many considered these comics French, even though they were produced in Belgium for the French market. Importantly, however, the content of these comics was not objectionable, and, quite frankly, they participated within the French cultural project more easily.

The attack on American comics was only one part of a larger, ongoing debate about French youth and the bad influence comics had on them. That some seized upon this issue is understandable, significant, and very much consistent with the historical moment. It is also significant, however, that the National Assembly voted *not* to target American comics specifically. In fact, the only editor ever prosecuted under the 1949 law published comics of

French origin exclusively. Nevertheless, French publishers were encouraged to drop American material, especially translated versions of American comic books such as *Superman*, *The Phantom*, *Tarzan*, or *Flash Gordon* (known in France as *Guy L'Eclair*).[32]

A Moral Panic?

The moral outcry damning comic books for their nefarious influence on the young also raged in the French press. This media campaign against comics not only anticipated and stimulated the Assembly legislation but continued on for years even after the new law was promulgated. The review *La Croisade de la Presse*, which published the Assembly proceedings, was founded with the very mission of reforming juvenile publications. By the late 1940s, the crusade to reform juvenile publications rallied increasingly around the problem of juvenile delinquency. Compared to figures before the war, the number of juvenile court cases immediately after the war had doubled. "If [comic books] are not the essential source of the juvenile delinquent," one critic wrote, "they too often furnish him with the model. The detonator is not the explosive, but it has a responsibility in the explosion."[33] Likewise, Jean Chazal, the prominent *juge des enfants* of Paris, claimed to recognize an undeniable connection between the content of comic books and the wrongdoers who made their way before him in the new juvenile justice system. Particularly susceptible to such images, Chazal maintained, were the young of the working class, whose moral fiber was rendered "fragile" by their unfortunate milieu and whom the new "reeducation" system sought to make more middle class.[34] The long chain of juvenile crimes that had captured the public eye in the postwar period helped maintain an ongoing debate about problem youth. In fact, this fixation with juvenile delinquency suggests that the delinquent was perceived to be as much, if not more, of a threat to France's future than was America. Thus, the concern and outrage for comic books was, in part, an element of a larger ongoing obsession with postwar delinquency and its potential deleterious effect on France's future.

In 1947 the journal *Educateurs* sponsored a five-part series to evaluate the quality of juvenile publications. To its dismay, the series reported that some papers, such as *Pic et Nic*, had "a crime per page!!!" Of the twenty-four publications reviewed, fourteen were condemned outright as dangerous to the morality of youth.[35] In a *Combat* editorial, Louis Pauwels asked publishers, "How many children do you kill each week?" He counted, on average, twenty-three murders for every eight pages, including victims of busted guts, cut throats, strangulation, and machine-gun fire.[36] *Combat* even noted that comic books were the favorite reading material of imprisoned criminals.[37] The simple conclusion was that violence and criminality in comics inspired the same behavior in children, such as the regrettable incident of a ten-year-old boy in Melun who accidentally killed his friend with a loaded .22 caliber pistol while playing "Zorro."[38] In 1948, the prefect of the Rhône sent the Ministry of Interior the Ballandras report, a study, sponsored by local family associations, that detailed the state of juvenile publications and concluded, "It is above all on [youth's] moral sense that this criminal prose exerts its greatest damage."[39]

In light of the rise in delinquency rates and the ongoing media frenzy, the Ministry of the Interior began to consider juvenile publications and the need "to preserve the morality of children and adolescents."[40] In fact, in conjunction with the Ministry of Education, the government sponsored an exhibition on the juvenile press in the summer of 1948 to show the public the dreadful state of juvenile publications and the need for moral intervention.[41] Because of its success in Paris, the exhibit then traveled throughout the provinces. In 1949 the Communists organized their own exhibit, which toured the Parisian *banlieues* and outlying factories. Not to be outdone, a Catholic group, also in 1949, sent a traveling exhibition of ideal and wicked juvenile literature through several French parishes.[42] In 1951 three filmmakers put together a short film entitled "They Kill on Each Page," which circulated in France and Europe for screenings before educators, student and parent associations, social workers, doctors, and youth organizations. The film graphically depicted the worst examples of violent and sexual images in order to drum up moral outrage and support for the protection of the young from depraved and licentious reading material.[43]

Along with the late-1940s delinquency issue came the simultaneous and related concern for sexuality of the early 1950s. Like the juvenile press, films, publicity posters, and the media were condemned for "saturating the general atmosphere with an eroticism" that exerted "a harmful influence on pubescent youth."[44] At times, critics combined their analysis of the sexual and violent imagery of the comic book, such as with the Italian superwoman import *Blond Panther*. This superwoman's aggressive sexuality was displayed "in a general atmosphere of brutality . . . sadism, and sexual perversion." Indeed, Blond Panther was interpreted as a voluptuous dominatrix: "Booted and armed with a whip, she engages in acts of violence that yield nothing to her masculine colleagues."[45] These heroines, "with their painted nails, provocative breasts, and their legs in the air," set a terrible example for young French women and created dangerous expectations for young French men.[46] The imagery of "silky mane[s] of hair, large saucer eyes, sweeping eyelashes, enormous sensual mouth[s], provocative breasts, long uncovered legs, and doll-face[s]" brought "eroticism to the cradle."[47]

In 1949 *Les Temps Modernes* published a translated essay by the American Gershorn Legman on the psychopathology of comics, and in 1955 it published translated excerpts of Frederic Wertham's *Seduction of the Innocent*, which shows the growing international consensus about the dangers of comics for youth. With shrieking alarmism, Legman outlined the perverse sexual universe of comic books by detailing the homosexual, sadistic, and masochistic themes prevalent in them. These sexualized images "incite masturbation" and create unhealthy appetites in young unformed libidos, while perverting the norms of sexual and gender roles. For example, Superman had "ridiculously swollen genitals," and "the lesbian" Wonder Woman "desired to dominate males."[48] Thus, comic books not only created a sexually charged atmosphere dangerous to immature libidos, but they also transgressed appropriate gender roles.

The Abbé Pihan, a member of the commission and a Catholic publisher, lamented the transgressive nature of female gender roles in comics. Women were either depicted as a point of struggle between men or as "a superwoman who fights against men, with cruelty and an absence of feminine sensibility." Moreover, "mothers and wives do not really exist" in the comic book universe, a deficiency that "is particularly grave" for girls.[49] Sexuality and gender roles became a growing concern in the commission's work more generally. In 1954 and again in 1958, a subcommission sought an expansion for Article 14, which listed the unfavorable characteristics warranting government intervention. Commission members wanted to include homosexuality, lesbianism, sadism, and masochism, in order "to defend youth against precocious eroticism, sexual obsession, sexual excess, and sexual deviations." This "perturbation" of youthful desire and sexual energy created "erotic impulses" and a "sexualized" environment that "debase[d] the moral and virile potential of the entire population."[50] Through editorials, articles, interviews, and polemics, members of the commission became active participants in the more general public discourse that condemned the state of juvenile publications and defined gender roles.[51] In fact, the commission conceived its duty to be that of maintaining and normalizing the social order for young people.

The Commission

Even though Communist deputies objected to the final legislation as being too lenient toward America, the law of July 16, 1949, passed easily, with 422 votes in favor and 181 against. The law created a commission of twenty-eight members, symbolically including a husband and wife, to oversee juvenile publications. Though not empowered to ban publications outright, the commission could discourage publishers from running certain strips and could recommend prosecution of offending publishers to the French Attorney General. One of its duties was to differentiate "adult" publications from "juvenile" ones. The law stated that "it is forbidden under penalty . . . to promote, to give, or to sell to minors under eighteen, publications of a nature dangerous for youth, by reason of their licentious or pornographic character, of their immoral character, or of their criminal character."[52]

The Commission for the Oversight and Control of Publications for Children and Adolescents met for the first time on March 2, 1950. Notable among its twenty-eight members were Jean-Louis Costa, the director of the new "reeducation" program from the Ministry of Justice; Michel Le Bourdelles, a high-ranking *juge des enfants* from the juvenile justice system; Father Jean Pihan, the head of the Catholic comic books *Coeurs Vaillants* and *Âmes Vaillantes*; Jean Chappelle, an independent Lyonnais editor; and Alain Saint-Ogan, the creator of *Zig et Puce* and head of the draftsman union. Other members included representatives from youth organizations, family interest groups, government departments, and local magistrates. René Mayer, the Keeper of the Seals, opened the commission's inaugural meeting by confirming its great need and outlining its purpose and also describing the legislation's design and elucidating its fundamental principles. Mayer recalled the widespread concern for juvenile delinquency and the deleterious effects on the young of over a decade's worth of upheaval: economic depression, military defeat, Occupation, and material hardship. Above all, he said, the commission's responsibility was to the "public welfare, which turns now toward the interests of youth. You must help youth find the inspiration that will assure its fidelity to the ideals of a national and republican tradition." Thus, the commission's ultimate project was to re-create French citizenship in the wake of Fascism.[53]

The commission had two basic responsibilities: to identify and prevent the sale of adult publications, such as pornography, to minors, and to improve the quality and content of juvenile publications, notably comic books. The first responsibility was rather simple and straightforward; the second, however, was complicated and ambiguous. All publishers were obligated by law to deposit periodical issues with the commission's archival collection. In 1950, its first year, the commission examined 42 publications that it identified as restricted for sale to adults only. Meanwhile, there were 127 juvenile periodicals (29 weekly, 20 bi-monthly, and 78 monthly) provided for inspection.[54]

The commission's strategy to improve juvenile publications was, in theory, more preventive than repressive. After reviewing several issues of a particular comic book or publication, the commission would send a report of its findings to the publisher. These reports were of four types: praise for the educative quality and moral tone of the publication; general recommendations for improvement; a warning to modify the publication or suffer reprisal; and an official sanction demanding the editor to extensively modify the comic book or strip, cease publication, or suffer prosecution under Article 2 for the demoralization of youth. The final two types of warnings also stipulated that the editor must appear before the commission to discuss the details of the case and to develop a timetable for the suggested improvements. A publication, in general, was granted a three-month compliance period to make necessary changes before the commission would resort to such measures as recommending prosecution by the Attorney General. Thus, the commission entered into a dialogue with editors, however one-sided, to improve the moral tone of juvenile reading material. In the end, though, the editors, not the commission members, were responsible for making the appropriate changes in their publications. Hence, the commission's powers were not, strictly speaking, censorial. In its first year, the commission issued sixteen warnings and thirty-five sanctions, for a total of fifty-one publications considered to be in violation of the new law. Over the course of that first year, the commission met with twenty-nine different editors (several editors published more than one periodical under review). By the end of 1950, twenty-nine publications had already disappeared, seven had suspended publication, and others were scrambling to make improvements amenable to the commission.[55]

In the official account of its activities, the commission outlined twenty-three general considerations for the improvement of the juvenile press. In addition to the obvious concerns for violent and erotic content, other themes emerged that seem pertinent in the context of postwar France. Notably, the commission was worried by the prevalent tone of pessimism in comic books, because, for young people, optimism was "vital" and a "primordial need" for "hope and yearning." The commission noted that this pessimism left young people with a malaise and despair for the future, which could, potentially, ensure just such a future for France. Furthermore, the distinction between good and evil was often blurred, rendering a confused sense of morality, appropriate behavior, and recognition of right and wrong. Likewise, the distinction between fantasy and reality was obscured, leading young imaginations into an "absolutely false universe" with a misapprehension of "plausibility" in regard to the laws of science. The commission feared that the ambiguity of comic books would confuse young readers and would leave them ungrounded in the realities of daily life and ill prepared to participate within it.

The commission also worried that the complexity of the human condition was undermined in comics as well. In most comics, there was "an atrophy of emotion" along with an "equaled atrophy of intellect." The characters of comic books were too often emotionally "motivated by hate" and intellectually dominated by "instinct" rather than reason. Because of the simplification of its characters and the violent end so many of them met, the comic book denied their "human dignity," did not convey "a respect for human life," and encouraged readers "to accept human massacre as a normal incident of any endeavor." Instead, young readers should learn "the sentiment of human solidarity" and "community," which was so important in the wake of recent tragedies.[56]

The commission's catalogue of deficiencies showed that it was most concerned about shaping youth into an idealized social body prepared for the responsibilities and duties of adult daily life and ready to accept the mantle of France's future. This expressed need for optimism, for clear differentiation between right and wrong, for plausible reality, for intellectual and emotional balance, and for the values of cooperation, community, and social solidarity are indicative of the larger efforts of cultural reconstruction and rejuvenation in the fifteen years following the war.

To help guide the industry, the commission developed a standard of elementary recommendations for editors to improve their publications. Even the recreational press, said the commission, needed to recognize that it had an educational responsibility to the young of France. Comic books should "avoid excessive fantasy," "remain logical," and should not contradict the "laws of science." No happy result should be obtained "without effort, work, and intelligence." There should not just be action or conflict between two parties, but "a place for labor, for the pursuit of an ideal, for struggle against the elements, [and] for work." "Vulgarity and rudeness" should be proscribed. "Scenes of horror, torture, and bloodiness" should be avoided, as should characters who are "hideous, monstrous, or deformed" or women with "provocative attitudes." Characters should be shown in a "familial, professional, and social milieu." Heroes should never commit "reprehensible acts." They should abstain from "summary justice," "help the weak and oppressed," and use "intelligence rather than force." Finally, comics should increase their amount of written text, should have no errors of syntax, spelling, or grammar, should avoid onomatopoeia, and should adjust the drawn image to avoid "tortured and tensed lines" or "shrill colors."[57] It seems that, in essence, the commission was asking editors to deny the very nature of comics, in substance and style, in their desire to promote a society of responsible workers and citizens living in a rational and national collective harmony. In effect, the law and the commission sought to codify social customs for the social order through the medium of juvenile literature, as exemplified by the incredible assault on the Lord of the Jungle, or *L'Affaire Tarzan*.

The Tarzan Affair

The first conspicuously significant target for the commission was the comic book *Tarzan*. By the early 1950s, *Tarzan* enjoyed a huge weekly circulation of approximately 300,000 issues, twice that of its closest competitor, *Vaillant*, and easily the largest in France. *Tintin*, for example, had a circulation of only 76,000. Of course, *Tarzan* had the marketing advantage of a popular ongoing Hollywood film series. In its first few months of existence, the commission identified *Tarzan* as its "no. 1" priority. Due to its wide circulation, the commission considered *Tarzan* to be the "guiding periodical" of the undesirable juvenile press, serving as a kind of "prototype that more or less directly influences the other publications."[58] Thus, by attacking *Tarzan*, the largest, most visible, and, evidently, the most offensive of comics, the commission hoped to demonstrate its determination to set a standard for the industry at large.

Tarzan was the most popular comic book in France, and one of American origin, and featured a seminude, animalistic superhero. The commission's determination to attack *Tarzan* coincided with a broad campaign in the French media criticizing the content of the comic book, bemoaning its ill effects on French youth, and pressuring its publisher to pull *Tarzan* from circulation. Commission members participated in this public inquisition by writing books and articles attacking *Tarzan*. The commission and its supporters accused the comic hero, created by Edgar Rice Burroughs and drawn by Hal Foster and, later, Burne Hogarth, of all kinds of transgressions of a sexual, animal, and savage nature. Cino Del Duca, the head of Editions Mondiales, the publishing house responsible for the translation and French publication of *Tarzan*, fought back, attempting both to stem the wave of protest as well as to make minor modifications amenable to the commission. In the end, however, these tactics merely served to delay the inevitable. In 1952, Editions Mondiales pulled *Tarzan* from circulation, to avoid legal prosecution under Article 2 of the 1949 law, pertaining to the demoralization of youth. With the exception of a few months of publication in 1953, *Tarzan* would not reappear as an independent publication in France for over a decade.

Tarzan had first appeared in France in the publication *Hop la!* in 1937. The serial quickly gained popularity and evolved into its own weekly publication, which was suspended in September 1941. After the war, Cino Del Duca relaunched *Tarzan* in 1946 to great success, but the drumbeat of journalistic outcry began soon after. For example, in its 1947 study of the juvenile press, the respected journal *Educateurs* singled out *Tarzan* as especially "dangerous" for young people.[59] As pressure mounted, Cino Del

Duca opted to end publication due to the overwhelming public support the commission enjoyed in its efforts to condemn *Tarzan* in the early 1950s. In its final, 1952 issue bidding "Adieu to Tarzan," the editorial management defied "anyone to find a single attitude of Tarzan that was counter to the regulations." Moreover, the editors wrote, "We will always consider Tarzan to be an honest, loyal, courageous, just, and irreproachable man."[60]

Still, between 1949 and 1952, specialists in professional revues as well as the popular press had thrashed *Tarzan*.[61] *Tarzan* was described as a "public danger," a "national catastrophe," and an "evil." The comic was blamed for the 1947 killing, in the Loire Valley, of a five-year-old boy by a twelve-year-old boy, after a stack of *Tarzan* comics had been found in the latter's home. In 1950, one father lamented that he worked long hours in a factory and could not adequately supervise his thirteen-year-old son who had accidentally killed a nine-year-old boy. Offering an explanation, the tearful father revealed a pile of *Tarzan* comics his son had purchased on a weekly basis. *Tarzan* was even denounced for causing broken bones by inspiring lads to swing Tarzan-style from tree branch to tree branch.[62] Unfortunately for the ape-man, the only defender of *Tarzan* was the publishing house itself.[63]

The editorial management of *Tarzan* responded with an open letter, published in April 1950. They maintained that *Tarzan* had been targeted simply because it was the most popular and most important publication of the juvenile press, and they referred to the widespread criticism as "the ransom of success." They accused the commission of heading a conspiracy that focused the public's attention solely on *Tarzan*, when there were, in fact, other truly harmful publications that warranted censure. "How could *Tarzan*," they asked, "corrupt the moral and human development of juveniles," or "cause their perversion"? *Tarzan*, rather, incarnated "all the best qualities of a modern hero: admittedly, physical strength and love of a healthy outdoor life, but also honesty, sincerity, and defense of the weak and oppressed." They accused *Tarzan*'s critics of "hypocrisy" and described their attacks as "irresponsible" and inspired by either "malevolence" or "ignorance."[64] This editorial defense of *Tarzan* only inspired a renewed and even more vitriolic counteroffensive, however.[65]

The quasi-nude sexual representations in *Tarzan* were the most obvious and visible point of attack. Tarzan himself wore only a shockingly small animal skin over a physique that bulged muscularly (see Figure 17), but even more licentious and dangerously provocative were the female characters, who were suggestively "undressed," indicating "the insistence of the draftsman to underline the sex and breasts of principal characters."[66] The sensual curves, prominent breasts, long legs, torn skirts, and suggestive attitudes of the female characters offered young readers a comic-book version of the "pinup"[67] that was "dangerous for the imaginations of twelve- to fifteen-year-old boys."[68] Critics charged that the voluptuous female form perverted the decency of the young male readership, wickedly distorting their morality. Editions Mondiales had already attempted to appease its critics on these matters by covering young Tarzan's bare bottom with leafy wraps (see Figure 18). The publisher had even removed or erased its women character's breasts altogether, in an effort to de-sexualize the iconography of the female anatomy (see Figure 19). Similar measures can be seen in *Guy L'Eclair*, where editors concealed female curves beneath long gowns (Figure 20) and even extricated a female love interest from the hero's arms altogether (Figure 21). Editors across the industry adapted comics by altering the female form as a means of salvaging their right to publish in France.

Tarzan's propensity for violence and the use of muscular brute force to resolve problems and overcome difficulties in the treacherous jungle was an example of "super-animality," as exemplified by the "inarticulate cry of victory" he let loose after each triumph.[69] Tarzan was "brutal force exalted" and "a panegyric for excessive muscular strength," as opposed to an archetype for clever thinking.[70] Even the size of his head was criticized as being too small for his bulky frame, indicating an intentional emphasis on an underdeveloped intelligence and an overdeveloped physique. His body was not made of flesh, which "suffers, bruises, and submits," but of a "new metal" that defied damage; his "nudity" served as his "armor."[71] This invincibility was considered to encourage reckless behavior on the part of young readers—notably those young boys falling out of treetops. Likewise, Tarzan's recurrent combat encouraged violent behavior in children, as evidenced by the deadly tragedies that had occurred among youngsters at play.

More difficult to alter, however, was the very premise of the character of Tarzan that troubled the commission and other critics. He lacked "sophisticated ambition" and "rarely engaged modern society."[72] Tarzan had no

Figure 17. Tarzan was identified as "Enemy no. 1" by the commission. Tarzan © UFS.

Figure 18. In response to criticism, French editors covered young Tarzan's bare bottom with a leafy wrap. Tarzan © UFS.

Figure 19. French editors even removed breasts to desexualize the iconography of the female anatomy. Tarzan © UFS.

Figure 20. In *Guy l'Eclair* (*Flash Gordon*), French editors covered the seminude female form in long flowing gowns. © King Features Syndicated.

Figure 21. Guy l'Eclair's love interest was even removed entirely from his embrace. © King Features Syndicated.

professional or familial milieu, no education or cadre of peers; in short, he did not participate as a member of society and he did not offer the young a valuable archetype in this measure. His detractors lamented that Tarzan preferred to roam the isolated jungle rather than commune with others within a modern social framework. Tarzan thrived outside social networks and civil institutions. Likewise, he was not committed to democracy. "If children voted," two members of the commission maintained, "Tarzan would be president of the world," and, worse still, "He would become a dictator."[73] Apparently, what many critics in France found so troubling about Tarzan was that he was inherently and by definition a reactionary as he responded to contingent crises in the jungle. Tarzan's continual struggle was again and again to restore order and reestablish the carefully balanced equilibrium, or "law of the jungle." Thus, he did not advocate nor promote social progress, a point counter to the interventionist social engineering of the postwar welfare state.[74]

Tarzan's animal instinct rejected reason and rationality and thrived in a primitive representation of the world that lacked the cultured mores of civil society. "Let Tarzan solve a problem of differential calculus," one editor sniffed, "or ask him to analyze a page of Valéry!"[75] It made no difference if Tarzan was noble; he was still a savage. Tarzan appeared "as the incarnation of precivilized man whose animality remains intact." He was "the symbol of a humanity that refuses and defies thought." Simply put, Tarzan was unthinking and uncivilized. He represented a "formidable revolt against the rational precedence of our civilization."[76] His rejection of reason and reliance on violent impulse challenged the basis of the civilized world. Through Tarzan, "the animal is opposed to the man and the jungle to the civilization, implying that one of these two terms symbolizes artificiality, falsity, and the unreal; it is, roughly, civilization that is presented as artificial."[77] True enough. When Edgar Rice Burroughs created the character in 1912, Tarzan was indeed offered as a criticism and intended to show that the civilized world had gone soft.

Ironically, in the original novel Tarzan was "civilized" by a Frenchman, a Lieutenant D'Arnot. D'Arnot taught Tarzan the codes and etiquette of civilized behavior, until the mighty ape-man emerged as a refined, charming gentleman. Monsieur Tarzan resided in Paris, socialized in the best circles, and spoke English with a French accent! In the comics, however, Tarzan remained in the jungle, and in 1950, in the midst of France's rejuvenation, comic-book Tarzan represented a threat to the very precepts of civility, morality, and community that France had been championing since the troubles of the Second World War.[78] In fact, France had long considered itself the guardian of the Western tradition of *civilisation*, more generally.[79] Thus, not only was the comic-book Tarzan not clothed enough, he was, more problematically, not even French enough.

With few exceptions, the topic of the inherent racism in *Tarzan* remained largely neglected and unexplored by critics. The Committee of Defense for North-Africans, however, did send a letter to the management of Editions Mondiales condemning the "racist propaganda" against Africans found in *Tarzan*. "We are astonished," they wrote, "to see a children's publication distill racist poison so insidiously."[80] In fact, it was not until November 1954 that Article 2 of the 1949 law was amended to include "ethnic prejudices" in its extended list of the unfavorable characteristics that were demoralizing youth.[81] Nevertheless, in 1952 Tarzan's most egregious faults, and the grievances repeatedly waged against the Lord of the Jungle, were not simply that *Tarzan* was an American product, but that it ran counter to the complicated strategies of cultural reconstruction in postwar France. Essentially, the Mighty Ape-Man undermined the effort in France to remake and reform its young along national, moral, and rational lines.

In Defense of Comics

It is remarkable that there were so few defenders of Tarzan or of comics generally in the public debates regarding their appropriateness as reading material for young people. Even the obvious issue of freedom of the press was easily set aside, despite objections.[82] The primary consumers of comic books—the young—were, of course, largely unable to participate in the ongoing polemics, having no access to either the legislature or the media. Meanwhile, the producers of comic books were in a precarious position. If opposed to the law and the commission, they would be viewed as obviously biased by their desires for broad circulation and high profits, to the detriment of France's youth. Conversely, others from the industry supported the law and the commission as a way to provide job security for local draftsmen, as well as a means to reduce the market share of competitors. However, one member of the commission, Jean Chappelle, himself an editor from Lyon, seems to have been reasonable in his assessment of comic books. While acknowledging that there were some extreme examples of poor judgment on the part of editors, he defended the industry and comics to the commission by pointing out that, while "it is possible that juvenile delinquents read comic books," there are, "in effect, millions of other children who read comic books, and these millions of other boys and girls do not steal, hurt others, or kill their grandmothers." Moreover, he said, "the causes of bad behavior in young people are thus much deeper than the simple reading of comics."[83] Chappelle also warned that the recreational press was just for that, recreation, and need not be made into instruments of pedagogy. With so many titles disappearing from circulation, the commission threatened the industry's footing while giving an open hand to the already powerful political (Communist) and religious (Catholic) press, a policy that Chappelle resented.[84]

A 1949 political carton from *Le Figaro Littéraire* does offer some popular criticism of the Assembly debates (see Figure 22). The cartoon's title, "The Purge of the Children's Press," is an obvious reference to the recent purge of Vichy collaborators. The elderly and grimacing Keeper of the Seals and Minister of Justice, André Marie, enters a courtroom, followed by the equally old and haughty Minister of National Education, Yvon Delbos. They advance toward a rostrum so antiquated that it is covered in cobwebs. Standing in the dock to be confronted by the people's justice are the bewildered Breton housemaid Bécassine, the rather frank, no-nonsense Buffalo Bill (a popular comic of French origin, though set in the American West), les Pieds Nickelés, a slobbering Donald Duck, and an impassive Tarzan with his hands clasped politely behind his back. Clearly, the cartoonist, Jean Effel, intends to mock the government's attack on comics. Importantly, however, he has included among the accused popular French comics as well as American ones, indicating what he sees as the potential danger of the new legislation to exaggerate the menace of juvenile literature.[85]

The most sophisticated critic of the commission and of the general brouhaha surrounding comic books was Pierre Fouilhe, a social science researcher from the prestigious CNRS institute. Fouilhe published a number of articles and even an entire book on the subject of juvenile periodicals. In *Journaux d'enfants, journaux pour rire?* (1955), Fouilhe recounted the history of the comic book and the superhero, noting that both had emerged in the 1930s

L'EPURATION DE LA PRESSE ENFANTINE

(De gauche à droite : MM. Marie, Delbos, Mlle Bécassine, MM. Buffalo Bill, les Pieds Nickelés,
Donald et Tarzan.)

(Dessin de Jean Effel.)

Figure 22. Jean Effel's political cartoon from *Le Figaro Littéraire* offered some popular
criticism on the 1949 Assembly debates. Courtesy of *Le Figaro.*

at a time of crisis, when the escapist nature of literature allowed the hero
to come to the rescue of those in trouble. This imaginative escapism was
precisely what young people needed, he claimed. Fouilhe argued that comic
books were, in practice, instruments that furthered a child's development
through imaginative play: "By reading comics, children find a way to live out,
in the imaginary, dramatic situations, and to assume the role of the hero."
The real and the imagined are not confused or blurred for a young person,
Fouilhe argued, because this imaginary playacting is a crucial element of
child development, one that occurs with or without comic books. Moreover,
he said, comics may actually be an ideal mechanism for child development,
because images are processed more easily than text, and it is through images that children begin to comprehend and enter social reality. Thus, young

people are quite capable of and quite accustomed to distinguishing between reality and representation, between fact and fantasy, and they are able to negotiate the real and the imaginary.[86] Far from being endangered by comic books, said Fouilhe, young people are actually enriched by them.

There was no hard evidence of any connection between comic books and juvenile delinquency. For several years, Fouilhe had been calling for an extensive empirical study to investigate this supposed link.[87] He castigated the juvenile judge Jean Chazal for declaring that there was a causal relationship without "citing any concrete case" but instead relying on conventional wisdom and personal anecdote. Fouilhe archly noted that "wine leads a number of drinkers to commit crimes each year. Should we outlaw wine? And yet it is relatively easy to determine the influence of alcohol on the execution of crime." Finally, he emphasized the legal weaknesses of the commission, which had no real power to enforce its oversight or control. He pointed out that the commission relied on consultation because it was incapable of demonstrating legally the demoralization of youth by an offending publication.[88] Though Fouilhe's criticisms were valid, they were not heeded. He was greatly outnumbered by the educators, judges, politicians, and family groups who found that the harmfulness of comic books was a self-evident and obvious truth.[89]

The Prosecution of Pierre Mouchot

As Pierre Fouilhe so rightly surmised, demonstrating the direct link between comic-book reading and delinquent behavior was difficult, if not impossible. Legally verifying the supposed "demoralizing" effects of comics on youth was, in practice, burdensome, as evidenced by the repeated prosecution of the publisher Pierre Mouchot. From 1954 until 1961, in a series of eight court decisions, Pierre Mouchot was prosecuted under Article 2 of the 1949 law, which stipulated that a publication "should not contain any illustration, any narrative, any chronicle, any heading, or any insertion that favorably presents banditry, falsehoods, thievery, idleness, cowardice, hatred, debauchery, or any criminal acts or misdemeanors of a nature demoralizing to children or youth."[90] Although Cino Del Duca and others had been threatened with prosecution on the basis of Article 2, those publishers had either made changes amenable to the commission or, as Del Duca did with *Tarzan*, had opted to cease publication altogether. Mouchot, however, refused to acquiesce, and he remains to this day the only publisher prosecuted under Article 2 for publishing material intended for juveniles that was "demoralizing to youth."

Pierre Mouchot, known as "Chott," was a Lyon author, draftsman, and publisher who in 1946 launched *Fantax*, an influential and successful comic of French origin that combined noir storytelling with exotic adventure and featured a masked superhero who tended toward excessive violence and cruelty. Recognizing what was to come from the new legislation, Mouchot pulled his comic from publication in late 1949, after its thirty-ninth issue.[91] Perhaps Mouchot hoped that this evident act of good faith would gain him clemency from the commission for future publications. It did not. In 1954, Mouchot was prosecuted in the Lyon tribunal for the 1950–54 publication of *Big Bill le Casseur* and *P'tit Gars*.[92] The first comic had as its hero a masked and muscled cowboy-adventurer of the American West who meted out "eye-for-an-eye" justice with savage vengeance. The second comic, *P'tit Gars*, featured a young adventurer who explored the exotic jungles of Africa with frequent violent encounters. Importantly, neither comic was of foreign origin; both were fully French, though heavily influenced in style and content by American and Italian comics—so much so, in fact, that Mouchot was frequently accused of plagiarism.

The commission recommended indictment of Mouchot to the French attorney general in 1953, after Mouchot's repeated refusals to adhere to the commission's mandates and warnings. Joining the state prosecution was a civil suit on behalf of the Union Départmentale des Associations Familiales du Rhône, whose national organization held a seat on the commission and who had produced the Ballandras report a few years earlier. The prosecution maintained that Mouchot's violation of the 1949 law was of a material, subjective, and intentional nature. First, his publications presented noxious content of a nature demoralizing to youth; second, his publications presented this material in a favorable light; and third, Mouchot, as publisher and author, had committed these digressions with full knowledge of the law.[93] Mouchot's defense rested primarily on each comic book issue's moralizing conclusion, or "*le happy-end*." That is, in the conclusion of each comic, evil was vanquished and justice triumphed, thus showing good as a more powerful and noble force than evil. Unable to determine what effect, exactly, these comics had on French youth, the Lyon tribunal acquitted Mouchot on March 4, 1955. The prosecution persevered, however, and appealed the ruling.

The Lyon Court of Appeal upheld Mouchot's acquittal in February 1956, while at the same time castigating him for his bad taste and "assuredly regrettable" publications, of a nature that probably "troubled the sleep of its young readers, if not also their elders."[94] But in January 1957 the Supreme Court of Appeal annulled both acquittals and sent the case to Grenoble for a new trial. In December 1957 that court also acquitted Mouchot. But in March 1959 the Supreme Court of Appeal annulled that ruling as well and then sent the case to Dijon for yet another trial. Once again, Mouchot was acquitted. And once again, this ruling was annulled and the case sent to Angers. There, on January 12, 1961, Mouchot was at last convicted of demoralizing the young, given a one-month suspended sentence, and fined 500 (new) francs. The Union Départmentale des Associations Familiales du Rhône was awarded 50 (new) francs in damages.[95] Although the financial penalty was nominal, the years of court battles and legal fees had sapped Mouchot's finances and left him near bankruptcy. In fact, although he continued to publish throughout the ordeal, Mouchot had sold Les Editions Pierre Mouchot in August 1960, just a few months before his conviction.[96]

The difficulty of convicting Mouchot frustrated advocates of the commission and undermined the effectiveness of the new law. *Votre Enfant* lamented that the rulings in Mouchot's favor "distressingly underlined the ineffectiveness of the law," allowing "sadism and terror to reign supreme" and demonstrating that editors "risked nothing great" in violating the law.[97] *La Croix* complained that the "Lyon court missed an opportunity to render a great service to French families."[98] Despite Mouchot's recurring courtroom victories, the Supreme Court of Appeal was clearly sympathetic to the commission's raison d'être and by its repeated annulments of his acquittals ensured Mouchot's eventual conviction.

The juridical issue in this case was how to define the qualifier "favorably," because the legislature had provided "no easy criteria" with which to establish such a vague principle. The Supreme Court of Appeal wrote that it was "most regrettable" that the law gave "license to editors without scruples to profit off the demoralization of youth by taking the simple precaution of providing a moralizing conclusion."[99] Each of Mouchot's acquittals came

from the prosecution's inability to show conclusively that he had demoralized the young through the depiction of criminal or immoral acts shown in
a favorable light. With each annulment, the Supreme Court of Appeal demanded that subsequent courts conduct a detailed investigation, both analyzing the comics and determining their effect on the "imagination of young
readers." The Supreme Court of Appeal instructed the Angers judge that
his mission would be to determine whether Mouchot's publications were a
healthy diversion for young readers, appealing to their taste for adventure,
or "if, on the contrary, there developed in their nature a path toward bad
instincts and perverse passions." This determination was within the court's
power, the Supreme Court said, because "the legislators' intention entrusted
the sagacity and good sense of judges."[100]

In essence, the Angers court was charged with bringing this long battle to
a conclusion by, at last, convicting Mouchot. In fact, the Angers court ruled
that the happy endings of Mouchot's comics did not "balance" the "scenes
of violence, acts of crime, and visions of horror" found within them. Rather,
the court found in his comics "an uninterrupted succession of scenes of murder, pillage, and violence of all kinds." However, after seven years and eight
court decisions, Mouchot's conviction was more symbolic than punitive, as
evidenced by the one-month suspended prison sentence and modest fine.
One commentator concluded that the previous rulings in Mouchot's favor
had been "judged on the facts," whereas the Angers ruling was "judged on
the consequences." However, he also pointed out that all the studies examining the effects of comics had been predisposed in their conclusions because
they had been conducted on delinquent youth or on those in psychiatric
hospitals, and rarely, if ever, on average, well-adjusted children.[101] While
Mouchot's conviction was, ostensibly, a victory for the commission and the
1949 law, the seven-year wrangle had revealed legal weaknesses in the law
and ensured that there would be no similar prosecutions in the near future.

The Commission's Legacy

Despite the difficulties of the Mouchot case, by the end of the 1950s the
commission was considered to have been quite a success in its moral crusade
to protect French youth from the nefarious effects of suspect periodicals.

Between 1951 and 1954, the commission received, on average, two thousand issues annually, of 23 weekly, 25 bimonthly, and 105 monthly periodicals. In that same time period, the commission had issued 135 simple recommendations, 45 warnings, and 41 sanctions.[102] The comic book industry had, for the most part, made alterations acceptable to the commission. Many of the "worst" publications, such as *Tarzan* and *Le Fantôme du Bengale* (*The Phantom*), had ceased publication altogether, and Mouchot was being prosecuted in Lyon for his defiance. However, in its 1955 report the commission identified some new concerns it had for juvenile publications. Notable was the "at least implicit racism" in many comics, that may be "perhaps generally unconscious" but "unacceptable" nonetheless. Keeping with its emphasis on technocratic rationality, the commission also worried about the increasing prevalence of horoscopes in juvenile publications, which were "absolutely anti-educational by suggesting that behavior can be influenced by occult factors." Finally, there was a new concern for the multiplying portrayals in comic books of the Second World War, depictions that demeaned the war's awesome relevance and "insulted the patriots and resistors of all nationalities, especially for those who knew the horrors of torture and deportation."[103] This subject, the commission believed, was too profound to be dealt with adequately in such an unsophisticated form of media.

Because the "worst" publications had disappeared, the commission refrained from issuing warnings and sanctions after 1955, although it still had such measures at its disposal. Instead, the commission relied on the "good faith" of editors and issued recommendations for improvement. Of the 173 periodicals it reviewed, on average, from 1955 through 1957, about 50 publications a year received such recommendations.[104] The other primary responsibility of the commission—to prevent the sale of adult (pornographic) publications to minors under the age of eighteen—was a great success and much more easily accomplished and enforced than the "moral" improvement of juvenile publications. From 1950 to 1958, the commission identified 651 publications that it forbade for sale to minors. In that same period, thirty-six vendors were convicted of selling forbidden material to those under eighteen, and an individual in Colmar was convicted for simply showing pornographic material to the young.[105]

The commission wanted to extend its reach and compound its good work to protect French youth. In the late 1950s, it lobbied the government to extend its responsibilities to include the romance novels of the *presse du coeur* that targeted adolescent girls. These seemingly "inoffensive" stories, in fact, "duped" young women into desiring fabulous and luxurious lives that created "troubled feelings" and "tortuous envy" among them. They encouraged young women to desire a social status and lifestyle beyond their reach, leaving them "emotionally confused."[106] Even worse, they excited sexual desire and amorous longings at an age when there should be none. As early as 1954, the commission had sought control over this genre, which "reduced relations between young men and young women to the sole objective of amorous seduction."[107] In 1958 the commission was granted jurisdiction over all publications for youth, not just periodicals. A subcommission for the *presse du coeur* was soon established, as was one for the *presse de l'horreur*, short novels of scary tales that were marketed to adolescent boys and that "compromised the mental health of its readers." As the 1960s began, the commission even sought jurisdiction over the "licentious records" of rock 'n' roll and over the media that broadcast them, radio and the expanding medium of television.[108] Moreover, for several years, the commission had been lobbying the government for authority to regulate the film industry more strictly and to remove lewd advertisements from cinema houses and sidewalk kiosks as well. This was a part of the larger impulse, dating from the Liberation and spanning the Fourth Republic, to regulate film for the moral protection of the young.

The Related Danger of Film

As with comic books, the power of the cinematic image was deemed deleterious to the young and incongruous with the project of cultural rejuvenation. In 1945 the French government had established a commission to regulate the film industry and dissolve wartime censorship. Its duties had included awarding screening visas, charging taxes, and setting standards for film imports. Although the ordinance that created the commission established the awarding of separate screening licenses for those films deemed appropriate only for those over sixteen years of age (a system that had been in place before the war), it did not substantially establish any further measures of control.[109] Part of the ordinance's logic was, in fact, to take power away from local officials who might interfere in film screenings, and grant that power exclusively to the national board.[110] However, as the concern for delinquent and demoralized youth escalated, the cinema house, like the comic book, came under increasing attack, as the coordinated campaign and protests against *Ripening Seed* demonstrated.

In 1949 Armand Lanoux published the results of his personal investigation, which condemned the frequency with which young people patronized the cinema. He estimated that it was the "pre-delinquents" who went to the movies most often, on average six times a month, and even as often as fifteen times a week. He cited the disturbing nightmares of boys and girls as examples of the wicked and unsettling influence of film. While he avoided thrusting total blame upon the film industry for the high rates of juvenile delinquency, Lanoux did conclude that "the existence of a real relationship between the abuse of the cinema and child criminality can no longer be denied."[111] Notably, in his estimation, "most influential" and "most dangerous" for the imaginations of the young French were the films from the wildly popular Tarzan series.[112]

Also in 1949, Michel Le Bourdelles, a judge from the juvenile justice system and a future member of the Commission for the Oversight and Control of Juvenile Publications, published an article in which he depicted young boys and girls as addicts who would steal from parents and strangers in order to pay the admission price for a cinematic fix. The cinema served as a school, he said, teaching young brutes to steal, burgle, and murder through the repetitious example of the images on the screen. The influence of film on delinquency was "a fact." It "demoralizes and mentally weakens" the young. Worse still, adolescent boys have their "precocious eroticism excited by scenes of passion, nudity, and amorous adventures," and seek "to realize these same scenes with their feminine friends who accompany them." In fact, "films are above all demoralizing for girls," because they excite their desire for a life of glamour by promising "cars, jewels, and nightclubs." Le Bourdelles stated flatly that, for young women, "sexual adventure" and "prostitution" were "the culmination of going to the movies." According to Le Bourdelles, a judicial authority, "the cinema is at the root of infinite cases of runaways, juvenile prostitutes, precocious perversions, and the worsening instability and mental impairment of young people." Thus, film "censorship should be supported, expanded, and strengthened."[113]

As with comics, the emerging furor over film was based upon a belief in the powerful impact of the iconic image on young minds. Critics described both film and comic books as having a hypnotic effect on vulnerable imaginations. "The cinema," some said, "exerts a powerful attraction on youth," for whom there "exists a dangerous need to see films that have 'bewitched' them, even the same film repeatedly."[114] The young were described as becoming "drunk" or "intoxicated," as well as "excited" and "perverted," by the repetition of the graphic imagery of film and comics. This "repetitive nature of film constitutes a toxic environment engendering the demoralization, despair, and delinquency of youth."[115] And the perverse imagery even spilled out onto the sidewalk, in the form of publicity posters and movie advertisements.

The journal *Ciné Jeunes*, founded by the French Committee of Cinema for Youth in 1955 to provide a forum for the problematic effects of cinema on the young, began a campaign to regulate film publicity, which too frequently "appealed to the most base instincts of man," such as "violence, crime, sadism, and pornography." The children of France were "without defense before these images so dangerous to their unsettled equilibrium." Most egregious was the public "exhibition of attractive breasts" and "hands tensed on nude shoulders," displayed on movie posters to titillate and seduce audiences into the darkened cinema houses. "Our children have the right to walk on the sidewalks," the editors declared, and not be exposed to "crime, violence, and pornography in the public way."[116] Even the commission for the control of juvenile publications lamented the ubiquity in public of the lewd film posters.[117]

In Casablanca, in 1953, a priest rallied a public protest against the suggestive publicity photos advertising the film *Manina, la fille sans voile* (known in the United States as *The Girl in the Bikini*), which featured the unknown, nubile young beauty whose name was written above in enormous letters: "Brigitte Bardot." Louis Bardot, the seventeen-year-old's father, was not amused, and he brought suit to prevent the misleading posters from being used in Paris and was even granted permission to have the film edited. On the poster, BB appears to be entirely nude, though in the film she is not, but wears, rather, a very revealing bikini. Thus, even before her fame, the iconic image of Bardot's sexuality was causing a ruckus, by endangering the moral conscious of the young.[118] The larger campaign to remove lewd posters from public view was successful and resulted in a 1955 ordinance.[119] However, while the display of publicity stills and movie posters was reformed, there still remained the issue of film content.

The Commission for the Control of the Film Industry was not significantly altered until the late 1950s, despite legal initiatives to do so. Naturally, the film industry itself dragged its feet in responding to criticism or in taking measures that might restrict its potential audience. An interest group, the National Association of Cinema for Children and Youth (ANCEJ), was formed to pressure the industry to increase the number of films appropriate for a young audience. In reference to stricter controls and censorship, which they supported, the group proclaimed, "It does not suffice to forbid, it is necessary to replace."[120] Throughout the 1950s, the commission declared, on average, only twelve French films (including four Bardot films) and thirteen foreign films a year as inappropriate for those under sixteen years of age.[121] In 1959 the French government ordered a new commission to study and reform the regulation of films, citing, of course, the "demoralization of youth and the growth of delinquency caused in great part by the cinema."[122] This was a common refrain, accepted as axiomatic though still unproven. Interestingly, movies about young people, such as Marcel Carné's *The Cheaters*, Claude Autant-Lara's *Ripening Seed*, and *La Femme et le pantin* (a Bardot film) were all cited as examples of films that should have been restricted to adult audiences but were not.[123] It was even suggested that the new commission be modeled on the Commission for the Control of Juvenile Publications, which, in the end, it was.[124] Finally, in January 1961, a new ordinance restricted the access of minors to the cinema by creating three new screening license categories: films deemed suitable for all ages, those suitable for ages 13 and over, and those for ages 18 and over.[125] Thus, in the name of rejuvenation and the moral protection of the young, the comics commission's insistence on the furtherance of its mission was extended into various other media.

The commission continues to exist, and it presently monitors all juvenile publications in France, yet it remains controversial for the industry.[126] Still, comic books in France have undergone a renaissance and rehabilitation, despite or maybe because of the 1949 legislation. In the 1960s, not only did René Goscinny and Albert Uderzo's feisty little Gaul *Astérix* emerge, but so did Jean-Claude Forest's space-age sex-vixen *Barbarella*, who was modeled, incidentally, on Brigitte Bardot. The latter is indicative of a shift toward the growing market for adult comics. One side effect of the 1949 law was to differentiate the markets for juvenile and adult comics, emphasizing the distinction between youth and adults as social groups. Many elements of comics deemed inappropriate for the young—sex, violence, fantasy, visual rather than textual emphasis—became highly developed in, and characteristic of, adult comics. *Barbarella* and its imitators simply targeted a narrower market and accepted their status as adult publications. The underground, or adult, comics emerged as a viable market for artists and editors as the spread of television in the 1960s caused a slump in the juvenile market.[127]

Youth and Cultural Reconstruction

In the fifteen years following the Second World War, *Tarzan*, Mouchot, and the others fell victim to the complicated strategies of cultural reconstruction in France. Most obviously, as an American product, *Tarzan* was caught in the politics of the emerging Cold War at the peak of Communist political power in France. The attack on American comics was in part a protectionist response to stabilize France's own industry as it floundered against foreign competition. It was also motivated in part by politicians seeking to demonstrate a renewed French hegemony over domestic policy in the context of Nazi and then American interference. Most obviously, politicians and pedagogues did not want French children to grow up influenced by "American" dispositions of a crude, unsophisticated, and individualistic materialism. They feared that the consumption of American comic books would result in the Americanization of French youth.

Yet both the Tarzan Affair and the prosecution of Lyonnais publisher Pierre Mouchot show that the campaign against comics and the new law for the oversight and control of juvenile publications were not simply signs of rampant anti-Americanism either. More importantly, *Tarzan* and Mouchot were attacked for the specific nature of their comic book content, which ran counter to the cultural reconstruction rhetoric of the postwar period. By controlling comic books, and film as well, France hoped to produce, in some capacity, the development of a domestic moral character in its young. Reducing American influence in comics was merely one measure in the larger reassertion of a specifically "French" social construction of youth that sought to emphasize community, social and civic responsibility, morality, integrity, and France's cultural *civilisation*—all issues responding relevantly to France's troubled recent past.

Like such programs as the Youth Civic Service, the *travailleuse familiales*, the Youth and Culture Houses, or the Formation Prémilitaire, the commission's work on comic books sought to shape and mold French youth into a morally upright, idealized social body capable of accepting its future mantle of adult citizenship in a technocratic modernity. The commission's recommendations to editors repeatedly emphasized norms of gender, class, and rationality that formed the basis of the social order. They emphasized the collectivity of society as opposed to triumphant individualism, and social harmony as opposed to social conflict. In short, the commission, like other programs and projects targeting the young, emphasized the future communal welfare of France.

At the same time, public worries over youthful criminality and sexuality that seemed to threaten the welfare of France helped to direct the criticisms hurled at comic books. Reeducating juvenile delinquents meant accounting for and overcoming a failed socialization. Likewise, eliminating violence and crime from comic books meant eliminating the reminiscences of a violent past and displacing delinquent impulses. Desexualizing the images of comics both preserved the fragile libidos of male adolescents while providing chaste female role models for girls. In the conservative cultural climate of the 1950s, cleaning up comic books of immorality coincided with the moral elevation of France more generally, as new ordinances restricted such adult activities as drinking, dancing, and carousing from the watchful eyes of the young, as well as prevented the sale of pornographic publications to anyone under the age of eighteen.

This campaign, and the subsequent evolution of the comic book in France, reveal broader themes, of France's struggle to create a new national identity following the devastation and destruction of the Second World War, and of a particular desire to influence the cultural construction of French youth. While recent scholarship has traced the "moralization" of the juvenile press by carefully contextualizing its development in the postwar period, we learn how many adults in France imagined cultural reconstruction as well as the conceptualization of youth as a social body participating within it. Thus, the controversy surrounding juvenile publications coincided with the other thematic issues dominating discussions of youth and the young, namely reconstruction, technocracy, citizenship, delinquency, and sexuality.[128]

In this context, the July 16, 1949, law was only one small measure in a larger national project of rejuvenation that revamped the juvenile justice system, retooled the national education system, and culturally prioritized the young at a time of national recovery. Through these deliberations, of which the comic book was but a part, the social group of youth was being produced and reified by French society at large. As a cultural artifact, the comic book became a site of intervention by the state and society to help manage the identity of its youth, the future citizens of France. Most significantly, in the wake of the war and amid the eleven million births of the *bébé-boom*, the young became a key social body, to be mobilized, managed, and directed for the cultural resurrection and reconstruction of France, and who, subsequently, would have a profound impact on French society in the 1960s.

From Hope to Threat

In 1959 Charles de Gaulle's new government, the Fifth Republic, published *The Young Face of France*, which highlighted the postwar social policies that had stressed youthfulness and innovation in France's cultural reconstruction in the midst of postwar optimism. According to this publication, France was now "the most dynamic country in the old continent" because it possessed the largest number of young people in Europe. "Self reliant and outgoing," it concluded, "these young people are keenly interested in the problems of their time. The young face of France is turned with confidence toward the future."[1] Fifteen years after the Liberation, adults still classified youth as the social group that would solve problems and improve France. Though Gaullism gloried in France's past heritage and tradition as a "great power," the newly realized Fifth Republic immediately tried to capitalize on the burgeoning presence of a new mass social group and the underlying concept of youthfulness that had dominated the Fourth Republic's rejuvenation.[2]

The Young Face of France was published in English, primarily for an American audience. In 1965 the French consulate in New York published another promotional piece in English, *France and the Rising Generation*, which again celebrated the young of France and emphasized the link between French youth and a vital, modern nation. Both publications featured hundreds of photographs of shiny bright faces, ranging from young schoolchildren in play clothes to twenty-something technocrats in business suits and lab coats, from young athletes at play to hobbyists painting, singing, or performing in plays. The text emphasized the educational expertise, physical fitness, and cultural fluency that young people in France demonstrated, a result of postwar social engineering. For the new government, youth represented France's activity, progress, advancement, vigor, and vitality. Therefore, it sought to associate itself with this social body, at least as an effective promotional strategy.[3]

Because a rejuvenated France fit well into de Gaulle's program for a triumphant return to French grandeur in international relations, de Gaulle's new government mobilized the category of youth as emblematic of France's robust progress. The Fifth Republic appeared eager to exploit the dynamism and liveliness of the young abroad as the new government sought to establish its own legitimacy and distinction. As the 1960s opened, the new government tried to identify itself with the rising tide of the New Wave, the very social body that Fourth Republic society had prioritized through social and political institutions. Youth and youthfulness had indeed become a social model. Yet despite the stability and prosperity of the 1960s, and the more prominent role the young began to play in public life, youth as a social body and cultural concept would profoundly clash with de Gaulle and the Fifth Republic in a very substantial way as the decade closed.

One remarkable element in de Gaulle's return to power—that is, in the collapse of the Fourth Republic's Constitution and system of government—was the equanimity with which most of the French public faced it. There was the notable exception of some young people, who protested the 1958 inauguration of the new Constitution at the Place de la République with placards that equated the new powers of the president to Fascism and that denounced de Gaulle as a dictator. The police charged down the rue Turbigo; the young put up barricades in defense.[4] The moment passed without much more ado, though the protest of youth against de Gaulle and the

Algerian war would escalate and, of course, there would be the events of May a decade later.

The decline of the Fourth Republic had been clear for some time. Its inability to maintain continuity in the highest offices of government, and its inability to effectively control the *colons* and the French military in Algeria had exacerbated the weaknesses of a fragile parliamentary system and rendered it impotent. Yet despite this dramatic shift in power, there was no great rupture. The whole enterprise was marked much more by a resigned continuity than an anxious discontinuity. In fact, the government stability that de Gaulle and the Fifth Republic enjoyed in the 1960s brought to light the remarkable successes of the Fourth Republic's economic, diplomatic, and social policies. Much of what the Fifth Republic claimed as its triumphs it owed to the Fourth Republic, which had effectively steered France through the reconstruction, modernized the country's economy and infrastructure, and established a broad social safety net. De Gaulle inherited a booming economy, an influential position in the United Nations, NATO, and the new European Community, and an expanding population with a rapidly rising standard of living. Despite the crumbling empire, and with the significant exception of the worsening Algerian crisis, France was in fairly good shape.

Likewise, in terms of youth, the transition from the 1950s to the 1960s was one of tremendous continuity. The Fourth Republic's policies and programs concerning the young were not abandoned, but maintained and expanded. In 1958, in the Fifth Republic, the High Commission for Youth Affairs was made into an autonomous body (adding sports and recreation to its responsibilities); then, in 1963, it became an independent department; and finally, in 1966, it was transformed into the new Ministry for Youth and Sports. The Youth and Culture Houses (MJC) program continued to expand exponentially and came under the purview of municipal government control and state subsidy across France, as did the national network of youth hostels. The moral protectionist impulse continued through the regulation of reading material and film content for young people, though the difficulties of the Mouchot case took some of the heat out of this fire. The *rééducation* program of the juvenile justice system was deemed a great success and given increased funding and resources, even though there remained delinquency alarmists.

Studies of French youth more generally continued to abound in the 1960s, as they had in the 1950s.[5] Their subject matter included, as a contrast to the Gaullist propaganda of triumphant youth (youth as hope), the persistent theme of menacing youth (youth as threat).[6] The plethora of studies reveals that throughout the postwar period the category of youth had served as a matrix for adult France to consider and dwell upon all sorts of topics. Because youth served as a common denominator that crossed boundaries of class, gender, race, and region, it provided a convenient prism through which adult France could think about the past, the present, and the future; about urbanization, modernization, and technocratic progress; about morality, criminality, and virtue; about nationality, cultural identity, and citizenship; and about changing structures of class and gender roles. In short, the category of youth was a point of convergence where adult France could deliberate indirectly on itself and on France more broadly in every way imaginable.

Yet there was great ambivalence in this process of rejuvenation as well. This was because youth was never an "either/or," but always an "as well as": not angel *or* devil, not hope *or* threat, but angel *and* devil, hope *and* threat. The symbolic form of youth was capable of flexibility, compromise, and contradiction, which made it ideally suited for the purpose of cultural rejuvenation after the Second World War. The most potent symbols are by their very nature multivalent and unstable. They are powerful precisely because they can be interpreted in multiple ways. In the case of youth, its power lay in the fact that it attracted to itself both hope and fear, both the dream of regeneration and the fascination of degeneration. The concept of youth was so highly idealized in postwar France that it was equally subject to excesses of condemnation when it failed to live up to grand expectations. The promise and problem of youth created a distinctly interwoven dilemma for adult France, producing a dynamic tension that remained unresolved at the close of the decade.[7]

A wonderful illustration of this tension is found in Raymond Queneau's best-selling novel, *Zazie dans le metro*. The 1959 novel and the subsequent Louis Malle film (1960) are considered classics of New Wave literature and film. Zazie is an impish and foul-mouthed but very likable eleven-year-old visiting her eccentric transvestite uncle Gabriel for a day and a half in Paris, where Zazie desperately desires to ride the Metro, though it is closed due to a strike. Instead, she seeks out other forms of amusement offered by Paris. Zazie is an androgynous tomboy who likes all things American, drinks only Coca-Cola, and desires nothing more than a pair of blue jeans. Though a precocious troublemaker, she is nonetheless adorable. Zazie is a scoundrel ragamuffin who makes mischief, and in the midst of her absurdist misadventures across Paris, the adult characters banter wittily in the playful argot of the street. Because Zazie is irreverent and cheeky, yet amusing and likable, the adults simply do not know how to handle her or what to make of her, and they spend much of their time reflecting and conferring on this conundrum with one another. The adult gaze is squarely fixed on Zazie, as they try to decide if she is more angel or devil. Zazie, for her part, pays no attention to their concerns, though she remarks candidly on some awkward truths, particularly sexual ones. Interestingly, upon Zazie's return from her day in Paris, her mother asks, "Well, did you enjoy yourself?" "All right," says Zazie. "Did you see the Metro?" "No." "What have you done then?" "I've aged," Zazie responds petulantly.[8] As the center of attention, Zazie harbors a sense of autonomy derived from the scrutiny of adults and the accumulation of experience.

The young themselves were becoming more vocal and more visible in French public life, predominantly through an emerging youth culture that began to overwhelm French popular culture.[9] In October 1959 two jazz lovers, Daniel Filipacchi and Frank Tenot, launched the weekly program *Salut les copains!* on the commercial radio station Europe No. 1. *Salut les copains!* was crucial in the development of the national (and international) French youth culture of the 1960s by providing a public forum for the young, both to perform and to consume as a mass social body. Initially, *Salut les copains!* featured jazz, but very soon it reverted to the pop standards of rock 'n' roll, a music style that became known in France as *yé-yé*.[10]

The popularity of *Salut les copains!* grew slowly but steadily, and, increasingly, young people in France, Belgium, and Switzerland came to see the program as "their" show, because it was for them, about them, and included them. As the program grew in popularity, it more often featured conversations with and by young people, and based its programming on questionnaires and listener responses to emphasize the participation of its young audience. Request lines were opened, giving voice to youth from across class and geographic barriers, and young listeners were brought into the studio to participate as members of a live audience. "The important thing," Filipacchi said, "was to demonstrate to those who seemed not to know it, that youth is not an illness and that teenagers are not necessarily mental defectives or hysterics."[11]

The popularity and allure of the *yé-yé* youth culture was publicly verified in the summer of 1963. *Salut les copains!* organized an open-air concert at the Place de La Nation in eastern Paris for the night of June 22. With the pompadoured Johnny Hallyday headlining, concert organizers anticipated a large crowd of about 30,000 young people. Instead, more than 150,000 showed up to listen, dance, sing along, commiserate, mingle, and socialize— a remarkable number for a pop concert in the early 1960s. The young fans climbed trees, scaled lampposts, and clambered atop one another to get a view of the stage and the crowd. One historian has called the *nuit des copains* "a veritable collective baptism of an age class," emphasizing the aggregate whole of youth as a social class and the sense of community and cohesion demonstrated by the young acting as the collective of youth at this mass celebration. The *nuit des copains* sparked excitement in the faraway reaches of provincial France and reverberated even for those young people who had been unable to attend. It sanctified and exalted the new youth pop culture and operated as a reference point for years to come.[12]

The music festival also sparked a flurry of commentary in the French press that continued the good youth/bad youth dichotomy. There was something decidedly troubling about 150,000 young people gathered together without the direct supervision of adults. Most commentators denounced the *nuit des copains* as an improper example of youth gone wild, though it was in fact a joyful party and not an angry riot. As elsewhere, rock music in France was frowned upon by adults as being coarse, vulgar, and substandard. Furthermore, like jazz, it had emerged out of American black culture and was thus seen as threatening to the "Frenchness" of French youth and France more generally. *Paris Presse* wrote, "There are laws, police, and courts. It's time to make use of them before the savages of the Place de la Nation turn the nation's future upside down." *Le Figaro*, concerned by the music's power to elicit a collective response, asked, "What difference is there between the twist . . . and Hitler's speeches in the Reichstag, apart from the music?" However, in a series of articles for *Le Monde*, Edgar Morin, ever the cheerleader for the young, applauded and celebrated the exciting demonstration of youthful enthusiasm and mass identity.[13]

The visibility of a discernible youth culture developed dramatically in the 1960s in tandem with and via the visual media. Of course, many of the popular New Wave films displayed the habits, behaviors, slang, style, and preoccupations of French youth for both young and old audiences. These films revealed, reproduced, and, in some measure, standardized the emerging youth culture. Likewise, and more importantly, the emergence of television as a mass medium in France heightened this visibility on a national scale. In 1950 there had been fewer than 10,000 televisions in French households; by 1960, there were 1,300,000, and by 1970 there were over 11 million. The new sixties telejournalism paid special attention to youth, young people, and youth culture. News magazine shows such as *Cinq colonnes à la une*, *Face à face*, and *Zoom* devoted many segments to young people in France, from exposés on the popularity of stars such as Johnny Hallyday to features detailing the *rééducation* program that was teaching juvenile delinquents vocational trades. By the mid-sixties, some television shows began to focus on youth exclusively, as both subject matter and audience. In 1964 the series *Seize millions de jeunes* featured interviews with young people between the ages of sixteen and twenty-four, seeking their opinions on life, politics, love, and the like. In 1966 *L'Avenir est à vous* sought to understand the complex relationship between children and parents, and, by extension, between youth and adults in France more generally. Later, in 1967, the same producers who had brought France *Seize millions de jeunes* created *Bouton rouge*, another show that targeted a young audience through their popular culture in music, dance, and style. The producers hoped to show young people as they were, not how adults thought they should be. In fact, *Bouton rouge* was inundated with letters from parents and educators scandalized by the appearance of young "long-hairs" on television.[14] The new youth pop culture gave the young a greater sense of agency and collective identity, while aggravating the sense of antagonism with adults.

This new youth culture's national scale, visible prevalence, and relative consistency across boundaries of class, gender, and geography helped to solidify a sense of community among the young French. That is not to say that the young and their cultural practices were homogenous or unvarying, but there was a very discernible national trend. In 1967 Edgar Morin published the sociologic study *Commune en France: La Métamorphose de Plodémet*, which traced the transformation of a small community in Brittany over the

decade of the 1960s. In the study, Morin recounted how the rural young
of Plodémet had "the same equipment, the same passwords . . . the same
antennae, the same culture as the urban young."[15] He expounded on the
societal transformation from rural to urban, from old to young, from local
to national, that the new youth culture of the 1960s had come to represent
for France more generally. According to Morin, popular culture had become the common denominator uniting young people from the Normandy
beaches to the Provençal foothills, from the Strasbourg *lycées* to the Au-
vergne farms, thus creating a national community of youth with its own
characteristic rituals and practices distinct from those of adults.

The policies and programs, studies and discussions, and activities and
movements for, about, and by the young since 1945 had created the social
space for this new youth culture to emerge. The focus and concentration
on young people in France's cultural reconstruction—in new programs like
the Youth and Culture Houses, in the political rhetoric of Pierre Mendès-
France, in the moral protectionist legislation, in the revamped juvenile justice system, and in the vast number of studies contemplating the impact
of the baby boom—created a massive public discourse about youth in the
1950s. Moreover, the "existential" young, who stayed out all night jamming
and dancing to jazz in the cellars of Saint-Germain-des-Prés, the lifestyle
and works of Françoise Sagan and Brigitte Bardot, the films about, for, and
by the *nouvelle vague*, and the media's preoccupation with the activities and
lifestyles of young people opened the door for the prominent role played by
youth in the next decade.

The voluminous studies of the young in France had shown that, like any
mass social group, youth as an aggregate was comprised of a broad assort-
ment of attitudes, dispositions, beliefs, convictions, activities, habits, and
behaviors. Nevertheless, the very inquests that had revealed the diversities
continued to interpret and represent French youth as a homogenous whole
with common traits and characteristics. Homogeneity, though, is neither a
requirement nor a condition for the existence of a social group. The definitions and characteristics attributed to a group—what, ostensibly, gives it distinction in the larger social body—is the result and reification of an ongoing
negotiation and struggle about what a group is or should be. A social group
is called into being because people believe in its existence. Adults were as
responsible as young people, and possibly more so, for setting youth off as

a separate mass social body. Even as adults deliberated, studied, chastised, and celebrated youth, the young themselves were living their lives and producing their own sense of identity. Thus, the identity formation of youth as a social group was a broad, diffuse, and, at times, conflicting process that manifested itself not only culturally, but socially, politically, and legally as well. For the young themselves, this was a social experience of a cultural category. Youth as an idea or cultural category was distinct from the young people who may or may not have identified or been identified as members of the group "youth."

In one sense, what became visible in postwar France was a renewed emphasis on youth as a mass social group. In general, the concept of youth as an intermediary life-stage, the notion of youth as a transition stage of the individual between childhood and adulthood, is largely a modern invention and was firmly in place by the end of the nineteenth century. Yet, over the course of the twentieth century, and most visibly since the Second World War, the idea of youth has been substantially recast to represent a mass social group, rendering its meaning as an individual's life-stage secondary. The concept of youth was consolidated in the postwar period as that of a mass social body participating in and constitutive of larger society politically, economically, and culturally. The notion of youth as intermediary has expanded accordingly beyond the individual's life-stage; now youth functions as an intermediary between social classes, genders, age groups, epochs, and nations.

That is not to say, however, that youth as a concept is a uniquely French phenomenon. What I have traced here is the development, in the French context, of a process that is identifiable in the postwar West generally. Yes, some of what was driving this preoccupation with youth as a source of revitalization and as a source of worry was happening for broad reasons—demographic baby booms, the expansion of education, technocratic modernization, the emergence of new forms of popular culture and media—but the particular inflection these processes took in France had its roots in longer-term French developments, such as the preoccupation with pronatalism or concern for the loss of grandeur and national identity, but especially in the experience of defeat, war, and the Occupation.

In France, the concept and social category youth, which was so much discussed and debated in the immediate postwar years, actually anticipated the demographic dominance of the young as a social group at the end of the

1950s and into the 1960s. That is, the revitalizationist discourse that predominated in France's project of rejuvenation, and the centrality of youth to this process, preceded and precipitated the formation of the social body of youth by preparing the young to take on the mantle of youth. In fact, this rhetorical conceptualization had been building since the turn of the century.[16] The discourse itself functioned as an anticipation that helped youth become a mass social group once the demographic bump of the baby boom came into effect at the end of the Fourth Republic.

By the 1960s, youth in France was represented as a mass social group with particular political, social, and cultural characteristics. While youth was not an entirely homogenous social body, this age category became an organizing principle for a social body's aggregate identity as it was defined dialogically by old and young France. Social groups tend to reflect hierarchies, such as old and young, rich and poor, male and female, rulers and ruled. Like other groups defined by race, class, or gender, those defined by age are based upon the distribution and division of power. In short, the age categories of "adult" and "youth" impose limits and produce an order for one another. Therefore, it should not be surprising that, at times, these mass social groups based on hierarchies of power will come into conflict with one another. This conflict is not simply the result of a "generation gap," but of the production of social groups and the distribution of power.

In part, the events of 1968 were about this young/old, youth/adult conflict. Charles de Gaulle and his government were the absolute epitome of stiff, intransigent, withered, and stubborn old age. De Gaulle—a grayed, wrinkled nationalist and authoritarian veteran of World War II—was the supreme symbol of the past in the present. The students in the Latin Quarter played off this in their posters, banners, and slogans, mocking de Gaulle's age and his absolutist dictatorial manner by repeatedly comparing him to Louis XIV, Napoleon Bonaparte, and Adolf Hitler. In his defense, de Gaulle famously retorted that these young people were simply ungrateful "bedshitters" incapable of appreciating how good they had it thanks to him, which was satirized in the poster "Be young and shut up" (see Figure 23).

In *The Young Face of France* and *France and the Rising Generation*, de Gaulle's own government had trumpeted the dynamic power of young France in remaking old France. The idea of youth as the harbinger of change, radical or not, had permeated the postwar period, from the rhetoric of the recon-

Figure 23. In this poster from 1968, de Gaulle muzzles a protester and commands, "Be young and shut up." Anonymous.

struction in the 1940s, through the public concern for the *mal du siècle* in the 1950s, to the protests and radicalization of the 1960s. The cantankerous Fifth Republic tended to respond unsympathetically to the proposals and concerns raised by young people themselves.[17] If the 1950s were characterized by the young's sullen passivity in politics and civic life, then over the course of the 1960s, with the Algerian war as a turning point, we can see an increased mindfulness of politics and political activity culminating in the rebellions of 1968.[18] Perhaps this was in part the result of French society using the category of youth for the project of rejuvenation, which encouraged the young to participate in civil society at the same time that it intentionally excluded them due to their age. Notably, one 1968 poster is a picture of a paving stone, the projectile of choice for protestors, with the caption, "Under 21 here is your voting ballot."

The repeated use of brute police force to deal with disgruntled students and striking workers throughout the 1960s, and especially in 1968, brought unavoidable comparisons to Fascism, Nazis, and the Vichy collaborators. As was the case throughout Europe, it was the police and not the protesting students who instigated violence throughout the 1960s. In scenes reminiscent of the troubled past, the state, through its police forces, violently repressed its own citizenry. The young protesters of 1968 repeatedly brought these continuities to light, which they said showed that despite the booming economy and social policies of the welfare state, not so much had changed. After all, the power structure, from government to big business, was still dominated by the very same people that had been running the country at the time of the Liberation in 1944: de Gaulle and his cronies.

In a sense, young people in 1968 were demanding the future that had been promised to youth in 1948. After Liberation and at the founding of the Fourth Republic, France had been optimistically enamored of the opportunity of starting over. The thrust of the Resistance charter and the goals of the leftist Tripartite Coalition had been to create a more socially just and equitable society that truly exemplified fraternity, equality, and liberty. A motivating spirit behind the reconstruction was the messianic belief that France could surmount material and structural limitations if it only exercised the vision and will to imagine and realize a better society. This reformist impulse idealized the future and placed France's youth at its center. Yet by the 1960s the idealistic optimism of the Liberation had dissipated, the reconstruction had been completed, and youth had become more of a threat than a hope, as it wielded the potential to disrupt the social order rather than rejuvenate it.

The Fourth and Fifth Republics had fought bloody wars to subjugate colonial subjects, and had employed brutal police force to subdue its own citizens. Gaullism was a political philosophy of order and tradition as opposed to reform and change. And because it based its vision of France on the grandeur of the past, Gaullism refused to explore France's complicity with Vichy Fascism or the Holocaust.[19] Young protesters in 1968 called attention to this disparity between the postwar vision and the Gaullist reality. They demanded the changes and reforms they had been taught to expect and to initiate as a social body.

In the library of works about the events of 1968, the explanations for its causes remain inadequate. Almost all the literature expounds on the effects and consequences of the rebellion, which are vast and significant, to be sure. In part, this is because the explosion of 1968 is so difficult to explain. Although there had been active student unrest throughout the 1960s, as late as the end of April 1968 no one was able to foresee what was to come in a couple of weeks. Times were good; France was stable and prosperous. In fact, *L'Express* ran a feature article that expounded on the growing youth unrest in other countries and commented on the relative tranquility of France.[20] While explaining 1968, or even the role of youth in it, is beyond the scope of this book, the implications of my larger conclusions for those events merit comment.

Most often, May '68 is simply chalked up to a generational conflict. The term "1968 generation" is bandied about as being self-explanatory, and the May conflict is viewed as a struggle between young and old generations, between children and parents. But the self-congratulatory generational interpretations overemphasize the role of a narrowly defined age cohort, almost to the point of implying a predestined fate.[21] The generation of 1968 needs to be seen as the result of a specific identity construction for the larger social group of youth—which, in 1968, this "generation" constituted. True, the twenty-year-old in 1948 was not the twenty-year-old in 1958, nor the twenty-year-old in 1968. Yet it is imperative to recognize the long-term conceptualizations of age-based social groups, even as the exact individuals, or generations, associated with that social group were in perpetual flux. The category of youth as a social body, and its meaning and role in society, maintained a continuity even as its membership changed. Therefore, another way to view the events of 1968 is to see them as having roots in the postwar cultural reconstruction that promoted and emphasized the rejuvenation of France via youth. Hence, the "generation of '68" (or, more accurately, those protestors claiming youth as a form of political legitimacy), whether New Wave or baby-boomer, can be seen as a product of this identity formation as it inherited and advanced through all the programs, policies, and social discourses for and about the young during the Fourth Republic and continuing into the Fifth.

Notably, the students in the Latin Quarter were using the idea of youth, as it had unfolded in the postwar period, to their advantage. "Professors, you make us grow old" was one such graffiti indictment. The government and the public were very receptive to the discourse of youth as revolution. Adult France had indoctrinated itself to think of young people as actors and to see historical progress in terms of generational renewal—notions they had been instrumental in developing since 1945. In effect, they had been taken prisoner by their own revitalizationist rhetorics. This might explain, in some measure, the belated response of the government and the bemused fascination of the public throughout May. In a 1968 political cartoon, established politicians are portrayed as jumping on the youth bandwagon, as François Mitterand has declared himself a "nouveau jeune" (see Figure 24).

Nor was the 1968 protester necessarily twenty years old. The events of 1968 demonstrated that youth could be an ideological foundation for political identity and political protest because of the variability of its definition. Perhaps this elasticity even strengthened youth's base. The youth of 1968 were not just university students, but *lycée* and vocational students, faculty, professionals, and workers whose ages ranged from the early teens to the late thirties. In May 1968, the very act of violent protest made one a part of the collectivity of youth because the rebellion itself was being defined as young, whether that was an accurate description or not. The "youth" movement was not a single, unified social group acting in concert during

Figure 24. In this political cartoon from *Paris-Presse*, October 8, 1968, established politicians are shown jumping on the youth bandwagon as François Mitterand declares himself "nouveau jeune" with his shirt.

the events of May. Among the student protesters themselves, chaos reigned. There was no programmatic revolutionary consensus among them, an actuality that anarchists like Daniel Cohn-Bendit gleefully encouraged.[22] Likewise, many young people sat out the whole thing, preferring to watch the bedlam on television from the safety of their own homes, while others even organized in opposition. Nevertheless, this act of revolution confirmed the cultural concept as social identity. "For the first time youth really existed," proclaimed the Situationists, whose ideas repackaged those of the Uprising Youth of the 1950s.[23]

This is not to deny the very real political grievances of 1968 and the significance of historical circumstance: 1968 was neither an inevitable nor an exclusive uprising of youth. In mid-May, ten million workers went on strike and occupied factories across the country. This represented over one-third of the entire French labor force. Led by enthusiastic young workers, and in spite of disapproval from the older union bosses, the labor strikes were far larger and broader in scope than those of 1936 or 1947, and they were exercised without the organizational support of the official unions controlled by the Communist Party. Yet the enormity of this worker unrest has often fallen out of the basic narrative of 1968. The rebellion of 1968 happened without the leadership, machinations, or assistance of organized political parties or labor unions. It was truly a popular uprising, of massive proportions, expressing deep discontent. In fact, during the conflict five workers were killed in police actions, whereas only two students were. And yet, focus and historical attention has steadfastly been placed on the rioting students.[24]

Because of the unique and consequential participation of the young in this uprising, 1968 has been easily dismissed as lacking real political significance. By emphasizing the rebelling students from middle-class backgrounds and by characterizing May 1968 as a callow adolescent rebellion, the government and others, most famously Raymond Aron, were able to effectively depoliticize it.[25] Because the idea of youth is socially produced and given significance (usually) by adults, it can equally be rendered insignificant by adults.[26] Nevertheless, it is true that one thing that makes the events of May 1968 so unique historically is the authoritative role played by youth in such a broad and grand uprising. Thus, at the same time that the idea of youth was used by some to depoliticize 1968, 1968 also helped to repoliticize the concept of youth as revolutionary.[27]

The cultural reconstruction of France after the Second World War placed the idea of youth at the center of its social rejuvenation. Youth had become an ideology, one way of looking at the world. As an object of public and private policies and social discourses, young people were educated, directed, shaped, and molded within this ideology to constitute the ideal citizenry of a reformed France. Young people were empowered to believe that they were responsible for and capable of initiating change within and for French society. In part, 1968 was a spontaneous expression of this empowered identity. Tired of waiting for reform, youth attempted revolution, albeit without a coherent ideology, direction, plan, or leadership, and with very mixed results. French youth fought against the state and the society it was supposed to constitute. As it turned out, the social category of youth did represent both a hope and a threat for French society.

Notes

1. Françoise Giroud, "La Nouvelle Vague," *L'Express*, 5 December 1957, 2; Giroud, *La Nouvelle Vague*, 9.

2. Jean-Marie Despinette, "La Jeunesse est à l'ordre du jour," *Educateurs*, January–February 1955, 44.

3. In 1954 President Pierre Mendès-France, who emphasized that young people were a crucial element of his constituency, even referred to his administration as "Le New Deal." See chapter 3 for more on Pierre Mendès-France and his "call to youth."

4. See Pomfret, "'A Muse for the Masses'"; Hellman, *The Communitarian Third Way*; and Fox, "Rejuvenating France."

5. For a detailed account of the Liberation of Paris, from which my summary is drawn, see Beever and Cooper, *Paris after the Liberation*. Other works on the Liberation include Kedward and Wood, *The Liberation of France*; and Footitt and Simmonds, *The Politics of Liberation*.

6. As quoted in Beever and Cooper, *Paris after the Liberation*, 57.

7. On the Occupation, see Jackson, *France: The Dark Years*; Oustby, *Occupation*; Le Betorf, *La Vie parisienne sous l'Occupation*; Azéma, *From Munich to the Liberation*; and Sweets, *Choices in Vichy France*.

8. On the Vichy regime, see Paxton, *Vichy France*; Azéma and Wieviorka, *Vichy, 1940–1944*; and Dreyfus, *Histoire de Vichy*. On collaboration, see Burrin, *France under the Germans*; Gordon, *Collaboration in France during the Second World War*; and Ory, *Les Collaborateurs 1940–1945*. For a description of how France's economy was integrated into the German war effort and helped pay for the Occupation, see Milward, *The New Order and the French Economy*.

9. On the Resistance, see Kedward, *Resistance in Vichy France*; Kedward and Austin, *Vichy France and the Resistance*; and Dank, *The French against the French*.

10. However, the *épuration sauvage*, or "unofficial purge," only accounted for approximately 10,000 summary executions across the country, a figure hardly compa-

rable to the total of 280,000 French killed by the Germans and Vichy over the course of the war. For months after the Liberation, known collaborators died suspicious, "accidental" deaths; another 767 people were officially executed following trial, and thousands more were jailed. On the purges, see Novick, *The Resistance versus Vichy*; and Lottman, *The Purge*.

11. On the development of generational theories and ideas in the early twentieth century, see Wohl, *The Generation of 1914*.

12. The work of Karl Mannheim makes a distinct comparison of generation and class as analytic models; see his "The Problem of Generations."

13. For example, in Jean-François Sirinelli's latest work, he defines the baby-boom generation strictly as those born between the end of the war in 1945 and 1953, yet the demographic phenomenon of the baby boom begins in late 1943 and extends into the late 1950s (see Sirinelli, *Les Baby-boomers*). On the arbitrary nature of the distinctions between age categories, see Bourdieu, "Youth Is Just a Word."

14. Some generational histories include Spitzer, *The French Generation of 1820*; Wohl, *The Generation of 1914*; Sirinelli, *Générations intellectuelles*; Crête and Favre, *Générations et politiques*; and Roseman, *Generations in Conflict*. On the 1968 generation, see Hamon and Rotman, *Génération*; and, most recently, Sirinelli, *Les Baby-boomers*. Also see the special issues of *Daedalus* and *Vingtième Siècle*, "Generations" and "Les Générations," respectively.

15. See, for example, Feuer, *The Conflict of Generations*.

16. Sirinelli, *Les Baby-boomers*, 17.

17. On the difficulties of generational histories, see Renouard, "La Notion de génération en histoire"; Spitzer, "The Historical Problem of Generations"; Jaeger, "Generations in History"; and Kriegel, "Generational Difference: The History of an Idea."

18. For example, Alan B. Spitzer's work on generation is among the best in erudition, analysis, and research, yet his careful study *The French Generation of 1820* is based on a mere 183 subjects, all of whom were white, male, privileged, and in the upper-class elite. These young men were significant and influential, and many contemporaries did indeed conceptualize them as constituting a generation, but are they representative of their French coevals?

19. The *zazous* were wartime "swing youth" who resisted the Nazis and thwarted Fascism by having all-night parties, listening to jazz, growing long hair, and committing petty crimes. The *blousons noirs* were pseudo-gang types in fake black-leather jackets who were prone to delinquency but mostly hung out on street corners in the late fifties and early sixties. *Yéyé*, however, was a true phenomenon of national proportions in the early 1960s. *Yéyé* kids listened to pop music, bought teen magazines, and danced to *Le Twist*—a Johnny Hallyday remake of the Chubby Checker hit. On French youth subcultures, see Loiseau, *Les Zazous*; Louis, *Skinheads, Taggers, Zulus & Co.*; Mauger, *Hippies, loubards, zoulous*; Bollon, *Morale du masque*; Rioux, "Les zazous"; and Barsamain, *L'Age d'or du yéyé*.

20. Most notable are Stanley Cohen and Dick Hebdige from the Centre of Contemporary Cultural Studies in Birmingham, or, more recently, the Youth Culture research project led by Johan Fornäs and Göran Bolin in Sweden. Most works on youth subcultures have focused on the intersection of style, rock 'n' roll, and rituals of rebellion in the United States and Britain. Some key studies include Hebdige, *Subculture*; Hall and Jefferson, *Resistance through Rituals*; Brake, *The Sociology of Youth Culture and Youth Subcultures*; Frith, *Sound Effects*; Nava, *Changing Cultures*; McRobbie, *Feminism and Youth Culture*; and Fornäs and Bolin, *Youth Culture in Late Modernity*.

21. Ariès, *Centuries of Childhood*; and Gillis, *Youth and History*. See also Crubellier, *L'Enfance et la jeunesse dans la société française*; and Galland, *Les Jeunes*.

22. Weiner, *Enfants Terribles*, 10; and Weiner, "Youth," 279.

23. Rioux, *The Fourth Republic*, 444, 356.

CHAPTER I. YOUTH OF TODAY, FRANCE OF TOMORROW

1. Some of this attitude was the result of the youthful optimism and energy that had infused the Resistance through the growing participation of the young. Particularly after the forced labor program for Germany announced by Laval in 1942, scores of young men fled their communities and swelled the ranks of the Maquis, the bands of resistance fighters who roamed the woods of rural France. For more on the participation of the young in the Resistance, see Granet, *Les Jeunes dans la Résistance*. The charter is published as appendix B in Novick, *The Resistance versus Vichy*, 198–201.

2. Albert Camus, *Combat*, 21 August 1944, reproduced in Camus, *Between Hell and Reason*, 40.

3. Jean-Paul Sartre, Editorial, *Les Temps Modernes*, 1 October 1945.

4. Beauvoir, *Force of Circumstance*, vol. 1, *After the War*, 4.

5. For more on how societies turn military defeats into moral victories and opportunities for change, see Schivelbusch, *The Culture of Defeat*.

6. Beauvoir, *Force of Circumstance*, vol. 1, *After the War*, 8.

7. See Shennan, *Rethinking France*; and Cowans, "Visions of the Postwar." The Popular Front came to power in 1936 as a broad coalition of left-wing forces led by socialist Léon Blum. The threat of Fascism sweeping through Europe and troubling France inspired a union of leftists to govern France based upon a reformist program designed to improve the quality of life for the French masses. But the difficulties of the Depression, combined with the Popular Front's faulty financial policies, diminished support for the regime. Soon, the various political bodies of the coalition began to splinter, as some wished to slow reform while others demanded to hasten it. By 1938, the Popular Front coalition had broken apart. Many of Vichy's innovations, notably those policies directed at families, the development of the young, and a state-managed economy, laid the foundation for the postwar modernization of France's governing institutions.

8. The Third Republic as a political system had been in something of a crisis in the years before the war. France had become, in Stanley Hoffmann's words, a "stalemate society" stagnated in a social, political, and economic equilibrium that obstructed change and produced immobilism (see Hoffmann, "The Effects of World War II on French Society and Politics"; and his "Paradoxes of the French Political Community").

9. Cowans, "Visions of the Postwar," 93.

10. Jacquier-Bruère, *Refaire la France*, preface, 83, 176.

11. Bloch, *Strange Defeat*, 175.

12. There was nearly a unanimous agreement to abandon the institutions and leaders that had governed France before and during the war, as evidenced by the October 1945 referendum in which a whopping 96 percent of the voters opposed a return to the Third Republic. Although there was a rededication to the fundamental values of republicanism—democracy, liberty, social equality, justice—there was no related devotion to the governmental institutions of the prewar republic.

13. Beauvoir, *Force of Circumstance*, vol. 1, *After the War*, 9.

14. Mounier, "La Jeunesse comme mythe et la jeunesse comme réalité," 143, 144. For Mounier's interwar nonconformism, see Hellman, *The Communitarian Third Way*.

15. Jean Planchais, "Pour une politique cohérent de la jeunesse," *Le Monde*, 3 May 1946, 5.

16. Raymond Millet, "Visites aux jeunes d'aujourd'hui: VII—Bilan et conclusion," *Le Monde*, 2 April 1948, 4.

17. "Memorandum of conversation between Douglas MacArthur and General Delmas-Chabon [*sic*], 27 September 1944," in U.S. National Archives, Record Group 59, 851.00 (Doc. no. 9-2711), as quoted in Shennan, *Rethinking France*, 51.

18. These numbers are taken from McMillan, *Twentieth-Century France*, 168; for more on the postwar baby boom, see chapter 17 in Rioux, *The Fourth Republic*; and Sirinelli, *Les Baby-boomers*.

19. Jacquier-Bruère, *Refaire la France*, 19.

20. Jean-Pierre Azéma, "Faire face aux déstructions de la guerre de 40," in *Reconstructions et modernisation*, 38.

21. Mary Louise Roberts has expertly shown how the postwar tensions of social and cultural change became bound up with concerns of female identity: the challenging behavior of the "modern woman" represented the war's upheaval and, conversely, the domestic ideal of the mother stood for prewar stability. As a nation, Roberts argues, France fought the changes represented by the "modern woman" by promoting a maternal and domestic function for women, and thus France "looked backwards to the future" (Roberts, *Civilization without Sexes*, 217).

22. The Belle Epoque continued to take on mythic meaning in the years that followed. Even after the Second World War there was a noticeable nostalgia for the era preceding the upheaval and devastation of the two world wars, most noticeably

in popular culture. However, it was less an urge to return to the past than it was a sentimental regard (see Jouhaud, "La 'Belle Epoque' et le cinéma").

23. For an elaboration on the 1920s French desire and attempts to return to the political, social, and economic conditions of the prewar era, see Becker and Berstein, *Victoire et frustrations*; and see chapter 4, "Folklore of the People's Paris," in Rearick, *The French in Love and War*.

24. Annette Becker, "Le Culte du souvenir après la grande guerre: Les monument aux morts," in *Reconstructions et modernisation*. See also Sherman, *The Construction of Memory in Interwar France*; and Antoine Prost, "Monuments to the Dead," in *Realms of Memory*, vol. 2, *Traditions*, 307–32.

25. Jay Winter's book is largely in response to the "modernist" interpretation of World War I that sees the war as an accelerating phase in the ascent of literary and cultural modernism (see Winter, *Sites of Memory, Sites of Mourning*, 228; see also Winter, "Forms of Kinship and Remembrance in the Aftermath of the Great War").

26. These losses can be subdivided into 170,000 military casualties, 150,000 civilians, and 280,000 "displaced persons." Each of these figures can be further subdivided to demonstrate the diversity of the French wartime experience. The six weeks of battle in May–June 1940 resulted in 100,000 military deaths; the campaigns in Africa and Italy, 8,000 and 8,500, respectively; and the Normandy invasion through the German surrender in May 1945 had 15,200 casualties. Interestingly, there were 40,000 more military casualties on the Eastern Front, where 130,000 French citizens fought in the German Wehrmacht, but these figures are officially included in the displaced persons category, which also includes 75,000 Jews, 60,000 other victims of deportation, 21,000 deaths among prisoners of war, and a small number of civilian workers deported to Germany. Civilian losses included 60,000 deaths from air raids, 26,000 victims of incidental military operations, and 10,000 executions. The variety of these numbers demonstrates the complex amalgam of war-related losses in France, which stands as a striking contrast to the circumstances of World War I losses, which had a remarkable consistency due to the prolonged stalemate of trench warfare on the Western Front between 1914 and 1918. These numbers are taken from Lagrou, *The Legacy of Nazi Occupation*.

27. Lagrou, *The Legacy of Nazi Occupation*.

28. Wohl, *The Generation of 1914*.

29. Péguy, *Notre jeunesse*.

30. On the Agathon survey and the prewar generation, see Bénéton, "La génération de 1912–1914"; Cohen, "Heroes and Dilettantes"; and "France: The Young Men of Today," in Wohl, *The Generation of 1914*, 5–41.

31. See Ozouf, "Regeneration."

32. Interestingly, the average age of the Legislative Assembly was only twenty-six when many of these texts were drafted.

33. For a summary of the generational concept in the French Revolution, see

Nora, "Generation"; for more specific studies, see Nicolas, "Génération 1789"; and Baecque, "La Révolution française et les âges de la vie."

34. Many of that century's revolutions, such as those of 1848, had youth insurrection at the core. Additionally, there were the young Romantics, the German Burschenschaften, France's reformist generation of 1820, and Mazzini's Young Italy and its continent-wide variants.

35. See Moretti, *The Way of the World*.

36. See, for example, Pomfret, *Young People and the European City*.

37. See Sergio Luzzatto, "Young Rebels and Revolutionaries, 1789–1917," in *A History of Young People in the West*, 2:174–231.

38. For more on the development of the interwar concept of the young as France's "New Men" or youth as revolutionary, see Hellman, *The Communitarian Third Way*; also Whitney, "The Politics of Youth"; and Fox, "Rejuvenating France."

39. The most obvious and successful examples, of course, are the Italian Fascists and German Nazis and the legion of like-minded political groups across Europe. The Fascists managed to use youth very effectively, as both a metaphor and a tool, enabling the party to represent Fascism as the youthful vigor of historical destiny at the same time that it deployed young enthusiasts to do the party's bidding. See Luisa Passerini, "Youth as a Metaphor for Social Change: Fascist Italy and America in the 1950s," in *A History of Young People in the West*, 2:281–340; and Eric Michaud, "Soldiers of an Idea: Young People under the Third Reich," ibid., 2:257–80.

40. See Whitney, "The Politics of Youth."

41. Troyansky, "Generational Discourse in the French Revolution."

42. They rejected the traditional form of novels as an obsolete product of the nineteenth century and argued for a new literary aesthetic devoid of plot, character, story, or chronology. Unsurprisingly, because of its difficult style, the "anti-novel," as it was also known, did not enjoy a broad readership—indeed, many who employed the term "new novel" did so pejoratively. Yet it did appeal to intellectuals because of its theoretical rigor infused with an avant-garde approach to writing, an approach interpreted as an undeniable yearning for change, for something different (see Babcock, *The New Novel in France*; and Britton, *The Nouveau Roman*).

43. Barthes, "Littérature objective."

44. Having no relation to the Anglo-American phenomenon of the same name, French New Criticism aimed to reveal the coded ideologies buried within textual narratives by applying Marxist, existential, psychoanalytic, or phenomenological analytic frameworks, for example. As its influence grew, by the mid-1960s this new criticism found itself in heated opposition to traditional criticism, or what Roland Barthes called *university criticism*, with which the New Criticism sought to break. For a description of these two critical schools, see Barthes, "Les Deux critiques"; for the "traditional" point of view, see Picard, *Nouvelle critique ou nouvelle imposture*.

45. Renaud Matignon, "Enquête de Renaud Matignaud: Depuis vingt ans la littérature française se remet sans cesse en question," *Arts*, 23 July 1963, 3.

46. See Marly, *Christian Dior*. For an analysis of the role high fashion played in the economic and symbolic recovery of France after World War II, focusing on the operators, designers, business managers, journalists, tastemakers, models, and workers who participated in the industry's prominent rise, and including a detailed account of Maison Dior's success, see Campbell, "High Fashion and the Reconstruction of Postwar France."

47. Garrier, *Histoire sociale et culturelle du vin*, 320–22.

48. Among the myriad titles concerned with New Wave cinema, see Monaco, *The New Wave*; Douin, *La Nouvelle Vague 25 ans après*; and chapter 13 in Williams, *Republic of Images*. For more on the connection between the *nouvelle vague* generation and New Wave film, see Gurrieri, "New Waves."

49. As a result of these efforts, the breakdown of those who responded was 44 percent workers, 24 percent bourgeoisie, and 23 percent agricultural workers (Françoise Giroud, "La Nouvelle Vague," *L'Express*, 5 December 1957, 19).

50. Giroud, *La Nouvelle Vague*, 9.

51. Giroud, "La Nouvelle Vague," *L'Express*, 5 December 1957, 2.

52. Fourth Republic politicians, however, still did not rely on or utilize polling for making policy or tapping into public opinion (see Cowans, "Fear and Loathing in Paris").

53. For the complete statistical breakdown, see Giroud, *La Nouvelle Vague*, 331–37.

54. Henri Lefebvre, "La Jeunesse aurait-elle découvert le bonheur?" *L'Express*, 19 December 1957, 10–11.

55. Alfred Sauvy, "La Jeunesse et le pouvoir," *L'Express*, 2 January 1958, 8.

56. Georges Hourdin, "Enquête: Dieu et la jeunesse," *L'Express*, 15 January 1959, 25–26.

57. Giroud, *La Nouvelle Vague*.

58. André Parinaud, "La Génération des J3 à la conquête de Paris," *Arts*, 12 February–9 April 1958.

59. Ibid., 1.

60. This trend is more fully explored in Gurrieri, "New Waves."

61. François Mauriac, Editorial, *Le Figaro*, 30 May 1949.

62. The series was published each week from July 25 to August 6 in *Le Figaro Littéraire*.

63. Kanters and Sigaux, *Vingt ans en 1951*.

64. Raymond Millet, "Visite aux jeunes aujourd'hui," *Le Monde*, 23 March–2 April 1948; "Jeunesse qui es-tu?" *La Nef*, March 1955; and Duquesne and IFOP, *Les 16–24 ans*.

65. Henri Perruchot, "Jeunesse d'aujourd'hui, France de demain," *Les Nouvelles Littéraires*, 3 January, 14 and 28 February, 21 March, 25 April, 30 May, 11 July, 1, 8, 15, 22, and 29 August, and 19 September 1957; Perruchot, *La France et sa jeunesse*.

66. Stanley Karnow, "France: The Younger Generation," *Time*, 30 May 1955, 32.

67. As quoted in Karnow, *Paris in the Fifties*, 237.

68. Henri Lefebvre, "La Jeunesse aurait-elle découvert le bonheur?" *L'Express*, 19 December 1957, 10.

69. Shennan, *Rethinking France*.

70. Rousso, *The Vichy Syndrome*.

71. Beauvoir, *Force of Circumstance*, vol. 1, *After the War*, 4.

72. Ibid., vol. 2, *Hard Times*, 158.

73. André Monteil, "Forum de L'Express," *L'Express*, 15 May 1954, 6.

74. Alfred Sauvy, "La France va-t-elle renouveler?" *L'Express*, 23 October 1954, 4.

75. Francis Perrin, "La France va-t-elle renouveler? Répond," *L'Express*, 6 November 1954, 4.

76. Louis Armand, "Jeunesse qui es-tu?" *La Nef*, March 1955, 45, 50.

77. Kanters and Sigaux, *Vingt ans en 1951*, 9, 10.

78. Françoise Giroud, "La Nouvelle Vague," *L'Express*, 5 December 1957, 19.

79. Georges Hourdin, "Enquête: Dieu et la jeunesse," *L'Express*, 15 January 1959, 25.

80. Jacques Laurent, "Sagan et les vieillards," *Arts*, 11–17 April 1956, 1.

81. See Chapter 5 for an exploration of the cynicism perceived to be infecting the young.

82. J.-P. Reynaud, "Un professor parle du mal du siècle," *L'Express*, 2 August 1957, 16.

83. F. Gay, "Peut-on encore éduquer la jeunesse," *Foi Education*, May 1952, 74.

84. Pierre Voldemar, "Y a-t-il un mal de jeunesse?" *Jeune Europe*, 15 April 1954, 7.

85. Mireille Baumgartner, "Mal du siècle 1952 et jeunes générations," *Foi Education*, May 1952, 83, 85.

86. André Labarthe, "Préparons des français pour l'an 2000," and "Jeunesse qui es-tu?" *La Nef*, March 1955, 7–8.

87. Jean-Jacques Servan-Schreiber, "La Jeunesse devant l'avenir," *L'Express*, 22 May 1954, 7.

88. "Les Jeunes écrivent à PMF," *L'Express*, 30 October 1954, 5. PMF did create a high commission for youth during his tenure in office that would later evolve into the Ministry of Youth and Popular Education under the Fifth Republic; this is discussed in chapter 3.

89. In early 1955 it changed its name to Union de la Jeunesse.

90. The manifesto was subsequently revised, in 1966, to launch a new polemical journal and political organization, *Le Front de la Jeunesse*, although *Front de la Jeunesse* had been an on-again, off-again polemical review edited by another *lettriste* and Isou fellow-traveler, Maurice Lemaître. Isidore Isou, a Romanian artist in postwar Paris, had launched the "Lettrist" movement in 1947, also with a manifesto (he would later write, in 1966, a manifesto demanding the shake-up of architectural forms as well). The Lettrists were artists who, appropriately, put the letter at the center of their artistic endeavors, whether it be poetry, literature, painting, or film. Today, the Let-

trists are seen as forerunners to the Situationists, and, in fact, a young Guy Debord joined the Lettrists in 1951 (see Home, *The Assault on Culture*).

91. Isou, "Les Manifestes du soulèvement de la jeunesse," 5, 8.

92. Baecque, *La Nouvelle Vague*, 47.

93. Yolande du Luart, "Je hais la jeunesse," *Soulèvement de la Jeunesse*, June 1952, 3.

94. "Chroniques des enfants martyrs," *Soulèvement de la Jeunesse*, June 1952, 4.

95. "La Jeunesse embrigadée," *Soulèvement de la Jeunesse*, June 1952, 6–7.

96. Yolande du Luart, "La Destruction, seule possibilité de construire," *Soulèvement de la Jeunesse*, October 1952, 3.

97. Yolande du Luart, "La Dynamique du progrès," *Soulèvement de la Jeunesse*, December 1952, 4.

98. Front page headline, *Soulèvement de la Jeunesse*, March 1953.

99. *Soulèvement de la Jeunesse*, March 1953, 12.

100. Claude Nemaux, "L'Heure de la jeunesse," *Soulèvement de la Jeunesse*, December 1954, 7.

101. Marc O, "Etant et le Devenir," *Soulèvement de la Jeunesse*, March 1953, 11.

102. There was a resurgence of the Uprising Youth movement in the mid- to late 1960s. For an account of their activities and ideas during 1968 from the point of view of Isidore Isou, see his *La Stratégie du soulèvement de la jeunesse*.

103. "Toutes les femmes n'en font vraiment qu'a leur tête," *Elle*, 5 January 1953, 10–11.

104. Jacques Perret, "Le Syndicat des enfants terribles," *Arts*, 12–18 June 1952, 1, 7.

105. Specifically, the 1966 pamphlet "Ten Days that Shook the University—The Situationists at Strasbourg" (found in *Beneath the Paving Stones*, 9–27); and, from 1967, Raoul Veneigem's *The Revolution of Everyday Life*.

106. Pierre Voldemar, "Y a-t-il un mal de jeunesse?" *Jeune Europe*, April 1954, 7.

107. Roger Vadim, "Les Jeunes préparent une surprise," *L'Express*, 7 May 1957.

108. Reprinted in *La Génération du twist et la presse française*, 5; and quoted in Marwick, *The Sixties*, 99.

109. Sauvy, *La Montée des jeunes*, 115.

110. Sauvy, *La Montée des jeunes*.

111. Ibid., 114, 156, 251.

112. Morin, *The Stars*, 123.

113. Morin, *L'Esprit du temps*, 207, 206, 220.

114. Other works included Jousselin, *Jeunesse, fait social méconnu*; Perruchot, *La France et sa jeunesse*; Rousselet, *Jeunesse aujourd'hui*; Peyrade, *Jeunes hommes*; Lapierre and Noizet, *Le Civisme des jeunes*; Vieujean, *Jeunesse aux millions de visages*.

115. Ariès, *Centuries of Childhood*.

116. Nora, "General Introduction: Between Memory and History," 1:6.

117. Camus, *Between Hell and Reason*, 133, 121, 125. Camus' editorials from November 1946 expound on his idea of relative utopia.

118. For a detailed analysis on political symbolism, see Kertzer, *Ritual, Politics, and Power.*

CHAPTER 2. MANAGING A MODERNIZED FRANCE

1. Kindleberger, "The Postwar Resurgence of the French Economy."

2. Unable to dictate the terms of the new constitution, Charles de Gaulle, head of the provisional government, had spurned politics altogether and retired to the country, leaving the field open to these parties. In the first national election, each of the parties (all had been active in the Resistance) garnered approximately 25 percent of the vote and formed a governing coalition to preside over the parliamentary system of government established by the new constitution.

3. This term is used by William I. Hitchcock in *France Restored: Cold War Diplomacy and the Quest for Leadership in Europe, 1944–1954.*

4. See Kuisel, *Capitalism and the State in Modern France.*

5. On the Monnet Plan, see Mioche, *Le Plan Monnet*; on nationalizations, see Andrieu, Le Van, and Prost, *Les Nationalisations de la Libération*; on postwar economic stability, see Maier, "The Two Postwar Eras and the Conditions for Stability in Twentieth-Century Western Europe."

6. See Wakeman, *Modernizing the Provincial City*; Ross, *Fast Cars, Clean Bodies*; and Hecht, *The Radiance of France.*

7. These numbers are taken from *Reconstructions et modernisation*; for a further detailed breakdown of the damages and destruction of the Second World War, see Voldman, *La Reconstruction des villes françaises de 1940 à 1954,* 17–40.

8. Voldman, *La Reconstruction des villes françaises.*

9. As quoted in Jean Luquet, "Qui a reconstruit la France?" in *Reconstructions et modernisation,* 84.

10. French comic books are more like magazines that maintain several serial comics in each issue, rather than each issue being dedicated to a single serial such as "Batman" or "Superman," as is the case in the United States. See Chapter 6 for more on comic books in France.

11. *Coeurs Vaillants,* no. 1, 1945, 8.

12. Catholic intellectuals had played an important role in interwar efforts to create a "new" (often stridently antimaterialist) social order, one that would ultimately depend on the organization and commitment of a new civic-minded youth (see Hellman, *The Communitarian Third Way*).

13. "Plus de 60,000!" *Coeurs Vaillants,* no. 3, 1946, 2; see also *Coeurs Vaillants,* no. 6, 1946, and *Coeurs Vaillants,* no. 8, 1946.

14. Raymond Millet, "Visites aux jeunes d'aujourd'hui; VII—Bilan and conclusion," *Le Monde,* 2 April 1948, 4.

15. Among the myriad of youth groups working for the reconstruction were Jeunesse Française Libre, Jeunesse Libération, Jeunesse Secours, Jeunesse Service,

Nouvelle Jeunesse Française, Organisation Civile et Militaire des Jeunes, Service Civique de la Jeunesse, Les Equipes d'Entr'Aide Sociale, Les Equipes d'Entr'Aide Ouvrière, Jeunesse et Reconstruction, Aide des Jeunes à la Reconstruction, and, of course, Scoutisme.

16. "Jeunesse Française Libre," AN F44/107/15.

17. "Jeunesse Secours," AN F44/107/17.

18. "Nouvelle Jeunesse Française," AN F44/107/22.

19. "Service Civique de la Jeunesse," AN F44/108/25bis.

20. Association Equipes d'Entr'Aide Ouvrière, "Statuts," p. 1, AN F44/106/12.

21. Camarades de la Liberté, "Points de départ," pp. 11, 13, 16, AN F44/106/03.

22. Association Equipes d'Entr'Aide Ouvrière, "Statuts," p. 4, AN F44/106/12.

23. Most service groups working for the recovery had emerged through the participation of young people in the Resistance. For example, La Nouvelle Jeunesse Française, Jeunes de la Libération Nationale, Jeunes de la Résistance, Jeunesse-Libération, Organisation Civile et Militaire des Jeunes, and Service Civique de la Jeunesse were all Resistance groups that reorganized their activities for the reconstruction. Four of these groups combined in the fall of 1945 to form Camarades de la Liberté, a militant organization of six thousand members that espoused a left-wing rhetoric committed to socialist revolution; they professed that the transformative renewal of France could only be achieved through the ascendant power of youth within the reconstruction—"the new men for a new France." Organisation Civile et Militaire des Jeunes, the young division of a prominent Resistance group, was a militant right-wing group claiming twelve thousand members dedicated to the continuation of the war in Germany and to the military preparation of the young, yet it carefully declared its dedication to the CNR charter and its willingness to cooperate "with all the movements and parties recognized by the CNR," even the Communists, in pursuit of a "profound social revolution" (see Camarades de la Liberté, "Points de départ," AN F44/106/03; and La Nouvelle Jeunesse Française, "Ne Jamais Faillir" and "Qu'est-ce que la Nouvelle Jeunesse Française," AN F44/107/22; see also the pamphlets "Organisation Civile et Militaire des Jeunes" and "L'O.C.M.J. et la Préparation Militaire," pp. 4, 5, AN F44/108/23).

24. "Le Comité Directeur du Service Civique de la Jeunesse," 11 May 1945, p. 1, AN F44/108/25bis.

25. See M. Rous, "Rapport sur la necessité d'un Service Civique de la Jeunesse," AN F44/108/25bis.

26. "Le Comité Directeur du Service Civique de la Jeunesse," 11 May 1945, p. 1, AN F44/108/25bis. There is a great complexity to the transformation of these organizations and actors, who were struggling to dissociate themselves from Vichy even before the Liberation while maintaining an emphasis on shaping the young to serve France that extended back to the interwar period (see Hellman, *The Communitarian Third Way*).

27. For more on these movements, see Halls, *The Youth of Vichy France*.

28. Voldman, *La Reconstruction des villes françaises*, 77.

29. The program was set up for young people aged sixteen to twenty-five, though the majority were no older than twenty and the number of young women participating was roughly equal to that of young men. Although there were significant numbers from the bourgeoisie and rural peasantry, the social background of those participating was predominantly working class. Many were sympathetic to the Communists, but they did not dominate the organization.

30. "Rapport sur une enquête effectuée auprés du Service Civique de la Jeunesse," November 1945, AN F44/108/25bis.

31. "Rapports d'activité du Service Civique de la Jeunesse," September 1945, AN F44/108/25bis.

32. The JOC was created in the 1920s as a countermeasure to the growing influence of the Jeunesse Communiste (JC) movement. For a detailed account of this rivalry and the political mobilization of youth in interwar France, see Whitney, "The Politics of Youth."

33. "Etat actuel des differents organisations du Service Civique," 26 February 1945, p. 2, AN F44/104/04.

34. "Les Equipes d'Entr'Aide Ouvrière: Bilan des activités et projets," 1945, AN F44/106/12; and "Association Equipes d'Entr'Aide Ouvrière: Statuts," AN F44/106/12.

35. "Equipes d'Entr'Aide Ouvrière," AN F44/106/12; and "Les Equipes d'Entr'Aide Ouvrière: Bilan des activités et projets," 1945, AN F44/106/12.

36. "Rapports d'activité du Service Civique de la Jeunesse," September 1945, AN F44/108/25bis.

37. "Rapport sur les activités des mouvements de jeunesse féminine et leurs service civiques, 1944–1945," AN F44/53/5; "Les jeunes filles de l'OCMJ," February 1945, AN F44/108/23.

38. "Contribution de la Jeunesse Féminine à la Reconstruction du Pays," AN F44/104/04.

39. "Le Président du gouvernement à messieurs les Ministres," 20 March 1945, AN F44/120.

40. Le directeur des Mouvements de Jeunesse et d'Education Populaire circulaire, "Utilisation des services bénévoles de la jeunesse française," 10 July 1946, AN F44/104/04.

41. In the spring of 1945, at the urging of Jean Guéhenno, the Director of Youth Movements and Popular Education (a new government department in the Ministry of Education), Service Civique, Equipes d'Entr'Aide Sociale, and Equipes d'Entr'Aide Ouvrière formed a coordinating committee to unite their reconstruction efforts by avoiding needless overlap, organizing large common projects, establishing long-term goals, and serving as an intermediary to government ministries and other service groups such as the Red Cross. This furthered the ethos of coop-

eration, while each group maintained its autonomy in this administrative hierarchy. Other preexisting groups, such as the Scouts or Jeunesses Socialists, were encouraged to participate in reconstruction via these groups, which, in fact, they already had done or were doing. In the summer of 1945, the government approved over ten million francs in subsidies to be divided among these three service groups, with most earmarked for Service Civique (see "Bases d'Accord pour la constitution des Comités de Coordination des Services Civiques," 15 March 1945, AN F44/104/04; and "Réunion du 19 juín 1945 Comité de Coordination des Services Civiques," AN F44/104/04).

42. See "Le Directeur des Mouvements de Jeunesse et d'Education Populaire à Monsieur le Directeur Général de l'Education Physique et des Sports," 18 May 1946, AN F44/53/6; Le Directeur des Mouvements de Jeunesse et d'Education Populaire aux inspecteurs principaux et les présidents des mouvements, "Aides des Jeunes à la Reconstruction," 20 May 1946, AN F44/120; Le Directeur des Mouvements de Jeunesse et d'Education Populaire circulaire, "Utilisation des services bénévoles de la jeunesse française," 10 July 1946, AN F44/104/04; "Aides des Jeunes à la Reconstruction: Réglement Intérieur," 26 June 1946, "Projets des Statuts" and "Rapport sur le fonctionnement de l'AJAR," both March 1948, and "Notes sur l'Aide des Jeunes à la Reconstruction," CAC: 840231, art. 187.

43. Le Directeur des Mouvements de Jeunesse et d'Education Populaire aux Inspecteurs Principaux des Mouvements de Jeunesse et d'Education Populaire, "Aide des Jeunes à la Reconstruction (informations complémentaires)," 10 July 1946, AN F44/120.

44. "Les étudiants reconstruiront-ils?" *Le Monde*, 5 August 1946, 5.

45. "Notes sur l'Aide des Jeunes à la Reconstruction," 1947, p. 3, CAC: 840231, art. 187.

46. "Rapport sur le Fonctionnement de l'AJAR," March 1948, pp. 2, 3, 4, CAC: 840231, art. 187.

47. "Rapport du Directeur Technique: Situation de l'AJAR," 5 March 1948; and Le Ministre des Finances et des Affaires Economiques à Le Ministre de la Reconstruction et de l'Urbanisme, "Aide des Jeunes à la Reconstruction," 3 April 1948, CAC: 840231, art. 187.

48. See Hellman, *The Communitarian Third Way*.

49. Guinot, *Formation professionnelle et travailleurs qualifiés depuis 1789*, 267–70.

50. See Friedmann, *Problèmes humains du machinisme industriel*.

51. Charlot and Figeat, *Histoire de la formation des ouvriers*, 341.

52. See Voldman, *La Reconstruction des villes françaises*.

53. See chapters 1 and 2 in Day, *Schools and Work*; also chapters 3 and 4 of part 3 in Charlot and Figeat, *Histoire de la formation des ouvriers*.

54. Paul Langevin, "Culture et Humanités," *La Pensée et l'Action*, October–December 1944, 25–31.

55. Commission Ministerielle d'Etude, *La Réforme de l'Enseignement*, 8.

56. The commission recommended extending mandatory schooling from age fourteen to age eighteen, and called for dividing the curriculum into three cycles. Primary education would begin at age three, last until age eleven, and be comprised of a common curriculum. The commission's most influential recommendation was a common middle school lasting from age eleven to fifteen, in which each student would be carefully evaluated for skills and abilities and recommended, or "streamed," into the third cycle. There, from age fifteen to eighteen, a specialized education would correspond to a particular degree in a vocation—technical, intellectual, or otherwise—which would be awarded after examinations. Even *lycée* students seeking a *baccalauréat* and further education at the *grandes écoles* would emerge through this streaming process, which would ideally promote an equality of access. The various technical and vocational schools would be fully absorbed and integrated into the educational system as a whole, whose national curriculum ultimately would reflect a technical humanism. Moreover, the commission emphasized that this education should be free and that stipends should be provided to offset the impact to household economies of keeping students in school longer. Likewise, a massive investment in facilities and program development would be required to accommodate the influx of vast numbers into the student body (see Commission Ministerielle d'Etude, *La Réforme de l'Enseignement*, 10–15; in addition, there is a detailed analysis in Charlot and Figeat, *Histoire de la formation des ouvriers*, 363–69).

57. Rioux, *The Fourth Republic*, 415.

58. Ibid., 411–22. For more details on the Berthouin reforms, see Charlot and Figeat, *Histoire de la formation des ouvriers*, 369–81.

59. Day, *Schools and Work*, 62–63.

60. Ibid., 120–25.

61. Margeurite Othon, "Métiers feminine . . . Horizons élargis . . . ," *Technique, Arts, Sciences*, October 1946, 10–11.

62. For an extended discussion of educating young women, see Weiner, *Enfants Terribles*.

63. Marie Novalis, " . . . la jeune fille qui veut arriver," *Elle*, 27 February 1956, 34–37.

64. Crouzet, *Bachelières ou jeunes filles?* 9, 324.

65. "Maman dans l'embarras faites-vous aider!" *Marie France*, 31 May 1946, 5.

66. See Sauvy and Debré, *Des français pour la France*.

67. Mademoiselle Gousset, "Le Point de vue des aides familiales," *Information Sociales*, 1 February 1949, 155.

68. "Jeunes filles apportez votre aide," *Marie France*, 31 May 1946, 5.

69. Ibid.

70. Ibid.

71. Bonamy, "Pour une histoire des Travailleuse Familiales rurales et populaires"; see also Bonamy, *La Travailleuse Familiale*.

72. "Jeunes Filles apportez votre aide," *Marie France*, 31 May 1946, 5.

73. Marguerite Germain de Montauzan, "Où trouver la solution du problème de l'assistance à la mère de famille," *Pour la Vie*, November 1947, 5.

74. "La chance d'être Travailleuse Familiales," *Travailleuses Familiales*, November 1960, 2.

75. Henriette Viollet, "Pour venire en aide aux mere de famille," *Pour la Vie*, July–August 1947, 24.

76. Marguerite Germain de Montauzan, "Le service familiale des jeunes filles," *Pour la Vie*, December 1947, 13–14.

77. "L'Enseignement ménager dans l'enseignement technique, rapport 1958," CAC: 770393, art. 2.

78. "Dossier relative aux examens et à la deliverance de la certificat travailleuse familiale, 1949–1960," CAC: 760177, art. 71.

79. "Maman dans l'embarras faites-vous aider!" *Marie France*, 31 May 1946, 5.

80. Mademoiselle Gousset, "Le point de vue des aides familiales," *Information Sociales*, 1 February 1949, 156.

81. J. Jacquemin, "Les Travailleuses Familiales," *Art Ménager et Culinaires*, June 1951, 59.

82. Neret, *Les Carrières féminines*, 122.

83. Mademoiselle Gousset, "Le point de vue des aides familiales," *Information Sociales*, 1 February 1949, 157.

84. Miller, "Reconstructing the Nation in the Regions."

85. *The Condition of Women in France, 1945 to the Present.*

86. Laroque, *La Politique française en France depuis 1945*.

87. See Weiner, *Enfants Terribles*; and Duchen, "Occupation Housewife."

88. Mademoiselle Morin, "L'Enseignement Ménager dans le Service Social," *Information Sociales*, 15 March 1948, 310–22.

89. See Edwards, "The Science of Domesticity."

90. For example, see Compain, *La Science de la Maison*; *Sciences appliqués*; and Bernège, *De la méthode ménagère*.

91. Mathiot, *Comment enseigner l'éducation ménagère*.

92. CAC: 770393.

93. "Le Concours national d'enseignement ménager," *Informations Sociales*, 15 March 1949, 366–76.

94. Lebrigand, "Les Archives du Salon des Arts Ménagers." See also Frost, "Machine Liberation"; and Furlough, "Selling the American Way in Interwar France."

95. "Le Concours national d'enseignement ménager," *Informations Sociales*, 15 March 1949, 378–81.

96. Annette Sauger, "Les Fées du logis vous parlent," *Arts Ménagers*, March 1952, 99–101.

97. Duchen, "Occupation Housewife," 1–12.

98. See *Travailleuses Familiales*, October 1956–November 1960.

99. See collected applications from the mid-1950s, CAC: 760179, art. 11.

100. "Enquête sur les effectifs de travailleuses familiales et les conditions de recruitment, 1957," CAC: 760177, art. 31; and "L'Enseignement ménager dans l'enseignement technique, rapport 1958," CAC: 770393, art. 2.

101. See Bonamy, *La Travailleuse Familiale*.

102. CAC: 770393, art. 3.

103. "Extension à Algérie des textes concernant les travailleuses familiales," CAC: 770393, art. 4.

104. See chapter 2 in Ross, *Fast Cars, Clean Bodies*.

105. See Marguerite Germain de Montauzan, "Où trouver la solution du problème de l'assistance à la mère de famille," *Pour la Vie*, November 1947, 17–18.

106. Ross, *Fast Cars, Clean Bodies*, 7.

107. Closon, *Un Homme nouveau*; and Wakeman, *Modernizing the Provincial City*, 3.

108. Boltanski, *The Making of a Class*, 95. On "technopolitics" and "technopolitical regimes," see Hecht, *The Radiance of France*.

109. Ross, *Fast Cars, Clean Bodies*, 165–75.

110. Boltanski, *The Making of a Class*, 118.

111. As quoted in Hecht, *The Radiance of France*, 226.

112. Armand and Drancourt, *Plaidoyer pour l'avenir*, 218–20.

113. See Hellman, *The Communitarian Third Way*.

114. Jacques Veuillet, "La Leçon d'électricité dans un parc," *Contacts Electriques*, March–April 1957, 6–17.

115. "Présentation," *Technique, Arts, Sciences*, October 1946, 3.

116. Gaston Berger, "Culture, qualité, liberté," *Prospective*, no. 4, 1959, 2.

117. Jacques de Bourdon-Busset, "Au rond-point de l'avenir," *Prospective*, no. 4, 1959, 16.

118. For more on "prospective thinking," see Hecht, *The Radiance of France*, 43–50.

119. "Ordinnance n. 45-2283, du 9 octobre 1945," in *Journal officiel de la République Française: Lois et décrets* [hereafter cited as *Lois et décrets*].

120. "Comment on devaint haut fonctionnaire," *France Illustration*, 13 October 1951, 383–89.

121. Roger Dardenne, "Faire des fonctionnaires, mais surtout des hommes," *France Illustration*, 13 October 1951, 388–89; F. C., "Les Buts et les méthodes de l'Ecole Nationale d'Administration," *Le Monde*, 9 October 1946, 5.

122. Pierre Racine, "La Formation humaine des jeunes fonctionnaires: L'Exemple de l'Ecole Nationale d'Administration," p. 12, in Conférence prononcée au cours du cycle d'information, "Le Facteur humaine dans les Administrations Publiques," 15–20 October 1951, BNF 4-R-6476-73.

123. Debré, *Trois républiques pour une France*, 367–83.

124. On the cadres of Uriage, see Hellman, *The Knight-Monks of Vichy France*.

125. "Comment on devient haut fonctionnaire," *France Illustration*, 13 October 1951, 383–89.

126. For a detailed sociologic and professional portrait of ENA alumni, see Bodiguet, *Les Anciens élèves de l'ENA*; for a larger critical overview of the ENA, see Kessler, *La Politique de la haute fonction publique*.

127. Le Béguec, "Les Premiers pas de la République des énarques."

128. Le Béguec, "Pierre Mendès-France et la technocratie."

129. "Orientation et formation des ingénieurs et cadres supérieurs," *Le Peuple*, April 1957, 7.

130. Sylvain Moran, "Enseignement technique et scientifique inadapté: Nous manquons d'ingénieurs et de technicians," *Force Ouvrière*, April 1957, 6–7.

131. See chapter 4 in Hecht, *The Radiance of France*.

132. These were the Association des Jeune Cadres and the Centre National des Jeune Cadres (see Gabrysiak, *Cadres qui êtes-vous?* 240).

133. Crozier, *The World of the Office Worker*, 110–11.

134. While the technocrat had been championed in the 1950s, he became vilified in the 1960s as the soulless yes-man bureaucrat of corporate France. The term "technocrat" itself had become a derogatory epithet, and debates about the merits of technocracy were ongoing. Many, like PMF, argued that technocracy's reliance on the expert created an elite clique and undermined democracy. Ironically, Gaullists had in fact condemned the Fourth Republic for being too technocratic, yet it was during the Fifth Republic that technocrats thrived (see Hecht, *The Radiance of France*).

135. Though they disagree on many of the details, there is a point of agreement here among scholars. See Hecht, *The Radiance of France*; Kuisel, *Seducing the French*; and Ross, *Fast Cars, Clean Bodies*.

136. The idealization of youth to transcend these sorts of differences through their work and service is pertinent at the turn of the century as well; see Pomfret, "Representations of Adolescence in the Modern City."

137. Rioux, *The Fourth Republic*, 317–21.

CHAPTER 3. MAKING THE FUTURE FRENCH CITIZEN

1. Centre de Coordination et de Synthèse des Etudes sur la Reconstruction, "Formation de la Jeunesse," p. 19, AN F44/53/2.

2. Jean Blanzat, "Etat moral de la jeunesse française," 1945, pp. 1–11, AN F44/52/4.

3. "Les Mouvements de jeunesse et de culture populaire: Problème jeunesse-culture," p. 4, AN F44/52/4.

4. See Furet and Ozouf, *Reading and Writing*; and Weber, *Peasants into Frenchmen*.

5. See Alain Schnapp, "Images of Young People in the Greek City-State," in *A History of Young People in the West*, 1:12–50.

6. Ministère de l'Education Nationale, "Exposé des motifs du projet de décret portant institution d'un Comité interministerial de la Jeunesse," 9 January 1945, AN F60/1047.

7. "Rapport à Monsieur le Ministre," 1945, AN F44/52/4.

8. "Rapport Générale sur les problèmes de la jeunesse," July 1947, p. 3, AN F44/52/4.

9. See Rioux, *The Fourth Republic*, 436.

10. As quoted in Werth, *The Lost Statesman*, 8.

11. For more on this French politician, see Lacouture, *Pierre Mendès-France*; and Werth, *The Lost Statesman*.

12. Giroud, "La Fondation de 'L'Express.'"

13. Pierre Mendès-France, "Appels à la jeunesse," *L'Express*, 22 May 1954, 8–10.

14. Radio broadcast of 10 July 1954, as quoted in Werth, *The Lost Statesman*, 122.

15. Mendès-France, *A Modern French Republic*, 177.

16. Batigny, "Pierre Mendès-France et les jeunes," 149.

17. Measuring his appeal to youth is difficult. Though he certainly appealed to many, particularly university students, he was unable to draw large numbers of young people into the Radical Party, so his successful influence on the young must be considered as qualified (see Batigny, "Pierre Mendès-France et les jeunes, 151–52).

18. "Les Jeunes écrivent à PMF," *L'Express*, 30 October 1954, 5.

19. "Ministère de la Jeunesse," *Soulèvement de la Jeunesse*, November 1954, 11 (capitalization is original to text).

20. André Moynet, "Voici le role des jeunes," *L'Express*, 20 November 1954, 4.

21. Jean-Marie Despinette, "La Jeunesse est à l'ordre du jour," *Educateurs*, January–February 1955, 44–48.

22. Georges Izard, "Faut-il passer à l'action?" *L'Express*, 26 February 1955, 3.

23. *L'Express*, 9 July 1955, 11.

24. Batigny, "Pierre Mendès-France et les jeunes," 154.

25. It was renamed in 1955 Le Salon de la Jeune Peinture; see Parent and Perrot, *Le Salon de la Jeune Peinture*.

26. "Les Peintres Temoins de Leur Temps: La Jeunesse" (exhibition catalog), vol. 9 of the *Musée Galliera* (1960), BHVP no. 711718.

27. Ministère de l'Information, "La Culture Populaire en France," notes documentaires et études, n. 233, 12 February 1946, p. 5, AN F44/52/4.

28. Direction des Mouvements de Jeunesse et d'Education populaire, "Organisation Generale de la Direction," p. 1, AN F44/53/4.

29. "Rapport Générale sur l'Activité de la Direction des Mouvements de Jeu-

nesse et d'Education populaire depuis la Libération," 1946, p. 2, AN F44/52/4; and "Service Civiques," pp. 1–3, AN F44/53/5.

30. "Rapport sur les mouvements de jeunesse et l'éducation populaire," 1946, AN F44/52/4.

31. Looseley, *The Politics of Fun*, 15–17. On the Popular Front, see Jackson, *The Popular Front in France*.

32. Rioux, *The Fourth Republic*, 435.

33. Jean Vilar, "La Jeunesse aime le courage," *L'Express*, 5 June 1954, 12. For more on Vilar and the Théâtre National Populaire, see Loyer, *Le Théâtre citoyen de Jean Vilar*.

34. See Rigby, "The Reconstruction of Culture."

35. Looseley, *The Politics of Fun*, 14.

36. Hellman, *The Communitarian Third Way*, 171–74; see also Nord, "The Legacy of Jeune France."

37. See Chabrol, "L'ambition de 'Jeune France'"; and Looseley, *The Politics of Fun*, 18–21.

38. "La Maisons des Jeunes," AN F44/64/1.

39. "Notice sur les Maisons de la Jeunesse, Région Ardennes-Picardie" (booklet), pp. 1–2, AN F44/68/9.

40. M. Olivier-Martin, La Secrétaire Générale de la Jeunesse à Mes. Les Délégués Régionaux de la Jeunesse, Les Délégués Départmental, les Chefs Régionaux et Départmental des Equipes Nationales, September 18, 1943, AN F44/62/3.

41. La République des Jeunes, Association Fédérative des Maisons des Jeunes, "Liste des associations départmentales," 31 October 1945, AN F44/64/1.

42. "Les maisons de jeunes ont un statut," *Le Monde*, 17 January 1948, 4.

43. Organisations d'Education Populaire, "Maisons des Jeunes et de la Culture," indice decimal 374.6, June 1947, AN F44/53/3.

44. La République des Jeunes, Association Fédérative des Maisons des Jeunes, "Réglements intérieur," 1945, AN F44/64/5.

45. André Philip to M. le Ministre de l'Education Nationale, "Rapport Moral," 1 August 1946, 2, CAC: 790592, art. 1; FFMJC Assemblée Générale, "Rapport Moral," 29 March 1953, pp. 32–33, CAC: 790592, art. 1.

46. Gilbert Ganne, "Les Jeunes et leur maisons," *Les Nouvelles Littéraires*, 1 September 1955, 2; FFMJC Assemblée Générale, "Rapport Moral 1955," 13 May 1956, p. 7, CAC: 790592, art. 1.

47. Robert Guillou, "Les Maisons des Jeunes et de la Culture, Un exemple: Vincennes," *Les Cahiers Français*, January 1956, 21–23.

48. There were MJCs in the Ivory Coast, Upper Volta, Guinea, and Senegal.

49. In 1952 those numbers had been 24,058, 13,728, and 227,599.

50. FFMJC Assemblée Générale, "Rapport D'Activité—1958," 17 and 18 May 1959, pp. 1–8, CAC: 790592, art. 1. The eight Maisons de Culture set up by André Malraux in the 1960s were different from the MJCs, in that they were government-

sponsored arts centers that presented high-quality professional performances in large regional cities. They were not for local amateur participation, the development of skills and appreciation, or for the young; rather they were for the diffusion of high artistic Parisian professionalism (see Lebovics, *Mona Lisa's Escort*).

51. See the FFMJC General Assembly reports, at CAC: 790592, art. 1.

52. Ministère de L'Education Nationale, "Rapport générale sur l'activité de la Direction des mouvements de jeunesse et d'éducation populaire depuis la libération," 1946, pp. 5–6, AN F44/52/4.

53. Centre de Coordination et de Synthèse des Etudes sur la Reconstruction, "Formation de la Jeunesse," pp. 8–9, AN F44/53/2.

54. "Reconstruction à Caen," *Pas à Pas*, April 1954, 3.

55. See Whitney, "The Politics of Youth."

56. M. André Philip to M. le Ministre de l'Education Nationale, "Rapport Moral," 1 August 1946, pp. 1–2, CAC: 790592, art. 1.

57. "Les Maisons des Jeunes et de la Culture," *Pas à Pas*, Special Issue, 1955, 1.

58. Raymond Millet, "Visites aux jeunes d'aujourd'hui; VII—L'Arbre de science," *Le Monde*, 31 March 1948, 2.

59. Gilbert Ganne, "Les Jeunes et leur maisons," *Les Nouvelles Littéraires*, 1 September 1955, 2.

60. FFMJC Assemblée Générale, "Rapport Morale—1955," 13 May 1956, p. 53, CAC: 790592, art. 1.

61. Ibid.

62. André Raillet, "Primauté de la culture," *Pas à Pas*, November 1953, 18–20.

63. Raymond Berrurier, "L'Education populaire et les maisons des jeunes," *Pas à Pas*, June 1956, 4–5.

64. FFMJC Assemblée Générale, "Rapport Morale," 29 March 1953, pp. 36–37, CAC: 790592, art. 1.

65. FFMJC Assemblée Générale, "Rapport Morale—1955," 13 May 1956, p. 23, CAC: 790592, art. 1.

66. Gilbert Ganne, "Les Jeunes et leur maisons," *Les Nouvelles Littéraires*, 1 September 1955, 2.

67. "Les Maisons des jeunes et de la culture," *La Documentation Française Illustré*, April 1965.

68. For a full discussion of the assimilationist character of French citizenship, see Brubaker, *Citizenship and Nationhood in France and Germany*; for debates about what the nature of this assimilationist national identity should be, see Lebovics, *True France*.

69. André Philip to M. Le Ministre de l'Education Nationale, "Rapport Moral," 1 August 1946, p. 8, CAC: 790592, art. 1.

70. Bourdieu and Passeron, *The Inheritors*.

71. Penaud, "Mémoire de stage," *ENA Promotion*, December 1966, p. 16, BHVP no. 140 399.

72. "Les mouvements de jeunesse et de culture populaire," 1947, p. 2, AN F44/52/4.

73. Centre de Coordination et de Synthèse des Etudes sur la Reconstruction, Commission Enseignement, "Formation de la Jeunesse," [1946?], p. 3, AN F44/53/2.

74. Ibid., p. 2.

75. As quoted in Holveck, "Jeune Alsace," 219.

76. Centre de Coordination et de Synthèse des Etudes sur la Reconstruction, Commission Enseignement, "Formation de la Jeunesse," [1946?], pp. 14–15, AN F44/53/2.

77. Moyens Généraux d'Education Populaire, "Cinéma: Cinémathèque de la direction générale de la jeunesse et des sports," July 1952, pp. 1–7, AN F44/53/8.

78. "Le choix de films au ciné-club des jeunes," pp. 1–2, AN F44/107/01bis.

79. Rioux, *The Fourth Republic*, 440.

80. Baecque, *La Nouvelle Vague*, 29.

81. Raymond Millet, "Visites aux jeunes d'aujourd'hui; VII—L'Arbre de science," *Le Monde*, 31 March 1948, 1–2.

82. Ministère de l'Information, "La Culture Populaire en France," notes documentaires et études, n. 233, 12 February 1946, p. 4, AN F44/52/4.

83. The two youth hostel organizations were La Ligue Française des Auberges de la Jeunesse, founded by Marc Sangnier, and Le Centre Laïque des Auberges de la Jeunesse, led by Léo Lagrange.

84. Direction des Mouvements de Jeunesse et d'Education Populaire, "Les Auberges de Jeunesse," 1947, AN F44/105/01.

85. For an exhaustive account of this history, see the two-volume thesis by Lucette Heller-Goldenberg, "Histoire des Auberges de Jeunesse en France des origins à la Libération (1929–1945)."

86. "Statistiques de FNAJ," AN F44/105/04.

87. La Fédération Nationale des Auberges de Jeunesse, "Auberges de la Jeunesse et Ajistes," 1951, pp. 3, 9, AN F44/105/04.

88. Ministère de la Jeunesse, des Arts, et des Lettres, "Rapport générale sur les problèmes de la jeunesse," 1947, p. 41, AN F44/52/4.

89. "Instruction concernant le fonctionnement et les normes d'aménagement des auberges de la jeunesse," 1949, AN F44/105/01.

90. "Statistiques de FNAJ," AN F44/105/04.

91. Le Directeur des Mouvements de Jeunesse et d'Education Populaire, "Organisation de la Croisade de l'Air Pur 1945," 4 April 1945, AN F44/120.

92. For a thorough and detailed history of the *colonies de vacances*, see Downs, *Childhood in the Promised Land*. In a careful analysis, Downs traces the evolution and expansion of these programs, giving attention to the larger political and social contexts of France in the first half of the twentieth century. See also Pomfret, *Young People and the European City*.

93. Ministère de la Santé Publique et Ministère de l'Education Nationale, report of 18 May 1945, AN F44/120.

94. "Texte des Voeux de la Commission des Colonies de Vacances du 14 June 1948," AN F44/72/1.

95. Louis Raillon, "Le Phénomène 'colonies de vacances,'" *Educateurs*, January–February 1949, 1.

96. Raymond Millet, "Visites aux jeunes d'aujourd'hui; VII—L'Arbre de science," *Le Monde*, 31 March 1948, 4.

97. Rationing had greatly limited the diet and nutritional needs of growing bodies. In October 1944, an examination of thirteen- and fourteen-year-olds in Lyon revealed that they were 19 percent under normal weight. During the war, the infant mortality rate rose from 66 per 1,000 to 75 per 1,000. In 1938, less than half of tubercular deaths were among fifteen-to-thirty-years-olds, but during the war that figure rose to over 60 percent. Alcoholism and the attendant health problems had actually declined among the young during the war, probably due to German confiscation of French alcohol, but it was still considered a serious problem. Finally, venereal disease had spread widely in France, with an estimated one million cases of syphilis; this, as well, was prevalent among youth, particularly young prostitutes (Commission d'Etudes des Problèmes de la Jeunesse, "Rapport générale sur les problèmes de la jeunesse," 9 July 1947, pp. 9–11, 14, AN F44/52/4).

98. "Ordonnance du 28 août 1945," s.v. "Les Associations sportives," in *Lois et décrets*.

99. For an overview of the development of sport in France, see Holt, *Sport and Society in Modern France*; for an evaluation of the Fourth Republic's policies on sport for youth, see Amar, *Nés pour courir*.

100. Amar, *Nés pour courir*, 8.

101. Congrès National du Sport et du Plein Air, "Bulletin de Press," March 1946, AN F44/70/2.

102. "Rapport sur l'activité du congrès," 2 October 1946, AN F44/70/4.

103. Congrès National du Sport et du Plein Air, AN F44/70/1.

104. Congrès National du Sport et du Plein Air, "Rapport de la 6e commission: Le Sport et la Femme," pp. 1–6, AN F44/70/1.

105. Holt, *Sport and Society*, 207.

106. Direction Générale de la Jeunesse et des Sports, "Education Physique et Sportive Education Populaire," p. 5, AN F44/52/4.

107. Amar, *Nés pour courir*, 52.

108. Le Directeur des Mouvements de Jeunesse et d'Education Populaire to les Inspecteurs, "Formation prémilitaire des jeunes de la classe 1944," 22 February 1945, AN F44/120.

109. Le Ministre de l'Education Nationale aux Présidents des Mouvements de Jeunesse, "Circulaire n. 76" and "Program de Projet," 30 November 1945, AN F44/53/1.

110. "Position défendue dans les travaux du congrès de la formation prémilitaire en December 1945 par l'Association catholique de la jeunesse française et par la Fédération gymnastique et sportive des patronages de France," CAC: 860446, art. 12; and "Conclusions présentées en séance le samedi 15 décembre, à 9h.30 au nom de toutes les Fédérations sportives françaises de la commission sportive du CNR et de la CGT par J. Guimier," p. 7, AN F44/70/2.

111. Commission d'Etudes et de Coordination entre le Ministère des Armées et le Ministère de l'Education Nationale, première séance, "Exposé fait par monsieur Roux directeur générale de l'éducation physique et des sports," 23 October 1946, p. 3, VIN 4Q/85-2.

112. See "Notice sur La Formation Prémilitaire," December 1945, CAC: 860446, art. 12; and Ministère de la Guerre, "La Formation Prémilitaire," VIN 7T/314-3.

113. "Programme d'entraînement des jeunes gens astreints aux deux premières années de formation prémilitaire," *Bureau Officiel de l'Education Nationale* 38 (12 September 1946): 1148–56, AN F44/68/7.

114. See Ministère des Armées, "Instructions ministérielles relatives au service prémilitaire," August 1946, CAC: 860446, art. 12.

115. Ministère des Armées, "Notice sur la Formation Prémilitaire," December 1945, 5, CAC: 860446, art. 12.

116. Centre de Coordination et de Synthèse des Etudes sur la Reconstruction, "Commission enseignement: Education et culture populaire," pp. 5, 11–12, AN F44/53/2; on the proposal for a national service for girls, see the essay by Marguerite Germain de Montauzon, "Ou trouver la solution du problème de l'assistance à la mére de famille" (*Pour la Vie*, November 1947, 4–19).

117. Ministère de la Jeunesse, des Arts, et des Sports, "Rapport générale sur les problèmes de la jeunesse," 9 July 1947, p. 29, AN F44/52/4.

118. "Note sur les rapports de l'Armée et de la jeunesse," 1947, AN F44/73/2.

119. See Sabina Lorgia, "The Military Experience," in *A History of Young People in the West*, 2:11–36.

120. For a comparison of post–World War II conscription in Britain, the United States, and France, see Flynn, "Conscription and Equity in Western Democracies"; for a detailed overview of the French military as an institution since 1945, see Martin, *Warriors to Managers*.

121. Groupe d'Education Contemporaine (Section Inter-Armes), "L'Education dans le cadre des armées," 1946–1947, pp. 1–11, CAC: 860446, art. 12.

122. Ibid., 12–15.

123. "Qu'est-ce que la commission armées-jeunesse?" 5 March 1956, VIN 16R/6-1.

124. For a broad, detailed overview of the war, see Horne, *A Savage War of Peace*.

125. "Jeunesse: Conflit avec le général," *L'Express*, 4 January 1957, 6.

126. See the periodical collection of *Fascicules Armée-Jeunesse*, at BNF, 8-FW-1235.

127. For an account of how resistance to the Algerian War related to the French experience of World War II, see Evans, *The Memory of Resistance.*

128. Alleg, *The Question*; and *The Gangrene.*

129. Rioux, *The Fourth Republic*, 268.

130. Hamon and Rotman, *Les Porteurs de valises*, 48–51.

131. Vidal-Naquet, *Torture*, 40, 139; chapter 9, "Confusion in the Nation," is specifically about young conscripts and the youth of France.

132. Grall, *La Génération du djebel*; see also Lemalet, *Lettres d'Algérie*. The numbers come from Jauffret, *Soldats en Algérie*, 79–80.

133. J.-M. Domenach, "Demoralisation de la jeunesse," *L'Express*, 29 March 1957, 4.

134. GEROJEP was made up of all of the major youth organizations, including the various scouting groups, large Catholic groups, athletic associations, student unions, and popular education organizations such as the Federation of MJCs, the Federation of Ciné-Clubs, *Peuple et Culture*, and the hostel federation.

135. "Cinquante mouvements de jeunesse expriment leur volonté de voir cesser la guerre d'Algérie," *Le Monde*, 4 June 1960, 1.

136. See Sabot, *Le Syndicalisme étudiant et la guerre d'algérie.*

137. Whitfield, "The Rise of Student Political Power and the Fall of French Imperialism in North Africa"; and Evans, *The Memory of Resistance.*

138. Likewise, there was not a single woman in a French government between 1949 and 1959, and throughout the 1950s women made up, on average, less than 2 percent of the National Assembly and Senate (Duchen, *Women's Rights and Women's Lives in France*, 53, 58).

139. Françoise Sagan, "La Jeune fille et la grandeur," *L'Express*, 16 June 1960. This work is reprinted in its entirety in Beauvoir and Halimi, *Djamila Boupacha.*

140. Rioux, *The Fourth Republic.*

141. On intellectual opposition to the war, see Schalk, *War and the Ivory Tower.*

142. For more on Hurst and Jeune Résistance, see Evans, *The Memory of Resistance.*

143. As quoted in Hamon and Rotman, *Les Porteurs de valises*, 220.

144. "Patriotisme 57," VIN 16R/6-3.

145. Ibid., p. 1.

CHAPTER 4. REHABILITATING DELINQUENT FRANCE

1. "Le 'Gang des J-3' de Valence," *Le Monde*, 1 February 1950, 7.

2. J-3 refers to a wartime system of categorization for rationing. Roughly, E was for infants to age 6; J1 for ages 7–10; J2, 10–13; J3, 13–21; and A, adult. There were additional categories for pregnant women, workers in essential industries, farmers, old-age pensioners, and so on.

3. "Le 'Gang des J-3' de Valence," *Le Monde*, 1 February 1950, 7.

4. He used the term *pour jouer*, which can mean "to play," "to act," or "to gamble," plus it can have sexual connotations as well; however, nothing in the article indicates which meaning the boy meant, and he may have intended multiple meanings.

5. Jean Couvreur, "Les Jurés de la Drôme ont sévèrement condamné les J-3 de Valence," *Le Monde*, 4 February 1950, 6.

6. "Le Directeur des 'Petites Ailes' porte plainte en diffamation," *Le Monde*, 4 March 1948, 5; "Le Douleureux procès des 'Petites Ailes' s'est ouvert à Pontoise," *Le Monde*, 22 July 1948, 4; "Le Code Napoleon n'a pas prévu les montres . . . ," *Le Monde*, 23 July 1948, 5; "Trois ans de prison aux epoux Monnier dans le procès des Petites Ailes," *Le Monde*, 24 July 1948, 5.

7. Assemblée Nationale, Procès-verbal de la séance du 4 novembre 1949; "Rapport fait au nom de la Commission de la famille, de la population, et de la Santé publique sur le projet de loi relatif aux maisons d'enfants a caractère sanitaire ou de rééducation motrice et aux établissements privés reçevant des mineurs atteints de déficiences sensorielles ou psychiques, de troubles du caractère ou de comportement, délinquants ou en danger moral," by M. Gallet [hereafter cited as Gallet Report], p. 4; and Assemblée Nationale, Procès-verbal de la séance du 24 novembre 1949, "Avis présente au nom de la commission de la justice et de législation sur le projet de loi," by M. Louis Rollin [hereafter cited as Rollin Report], pp. 2, 3, both in AN F60/1411. For more on how the experts of the 1940s built their professional credibility, asserted their authority, and gained power over institutions, see Chauvière, *Enfance inadaptée.*

8. Gallet Report, pp. 3, 5; Rollin Report, pp. 2, 3.

9. Schaber, "Rapport: Les Enfants en Danger Moral et Social" [1957–59?], p. 7, AN F44/103.

10. See chapter 3 in Fishman, *The Battle for Children*. Fishman's work is an excellent resource for the social and legal history of delinquency and juvenile justice in modern France. She combines thorough synthetic information on the nineteenth century with her own research on the twentieth century, arguing that the most vigorous reform and greatest change occurred during the Vichy regime.

11. Chazal, *L'Enfance délinquante*, 6; and Bidaux and Depouilly, "Rapport sur l'organisation et le fonctionnement des services et organismes charges de problèmes de l'Education surveillée," 1961, CAC: 910333, art. 15. These two sources are separately incomplete for the years 1939–58. I have interspersed the rates together. There are some numerical discrepancies between the two sources, but they are minor and do not alter the overall trend from year to year. Chazal's was the most complete source, so his has been listed first.

12. Chazal, *L'Enfance délinquante*, 5–6.

13. Docteur Georges Heuyer, "Psychopathologie de l'enfance victime de la guerre," *Sauvegarde* 17 (January 1948): 3.

14. Jean Sarrailh, "Jeunesse, qui es-tu?: Etudiants 1955," *La Nef*, March 1955, 39.

15. His pen name was Roger-Ferdinand and he wrote prolifically through the 1930s to the 1950s, for both the stage and screen (see Ferdinand, *Les 'J 3' ou La Nouvelle Ecole*; and Ferdinand, *Ils ont vingt ans*).

16. Docteur Simone Marcus-Jeisler, "Réponse à l'enquête sur les effets psychologiques de la guerre sur les enfants et jeunes gens en France," *Sauvegarde* 9 (March 1947): 8–9.

17. See Fishman, "Absent Fathers and Family Breakdown."

18. Simone Marcus-Jeisler, "Réponse . . . ," *Sauvegarde* 9 (March 1947): 4, 6.

19. Ibid., 7, 5, 10.

20. Ibid., 6.

21. Ibid., 6, 8, 9.

22. "Exposé des motifs du projet d'ordonnance relative à l'enfance délinquant," 22 January 1945, p. 1, AN F60/1052.

23. "Prisons et Prisonniers: Le problème de la délinquance juvénile en France," from "vol. 9 (1er trimestre 1951)" of an unnamed publication, p. 97, CAC: 910333, art. 18.

24. "Exposé des motifs du projet d'ordonnance relative à l'enfance délinquant," 22 January 1945, p. 1, AN F60/1052.

25. *Livre blanc sur la jeunesse*, pt. 6, *Inadaptation sociale et délinquance des jeunes* (Ministère de la Justice, 1967), CAC: 910333, art. 3.

26. *La Délinquance juvénile en France*, Notes et études documentaires, no. 1.423 (19 January 1951), p. 18, CAC: 91033, art. 3; Fishman, *The Battle for Children*.

27. *La Délinquance juvénile en France*, Notes et études documentaires, n. 1.423 (19 January 1951), pp. 6–7, CAC: 910333, art. 3; Fishman, *The Battle for Children*.

28. Fishman, "Juvenile Delinquency as a 'Condition,'" 92, 93, 98.

29. See chapters 5 and 6 in Fishman, *The Battle for Children*.

30. Bailleau, *Les Jeunes face à la justice pénale*, 12. For a breakdown of juvenile criminality during the Vichy regime and a survey of the state's response, see Fishman, "Youth in Vichy France."

31. Bailleau, *Les Jeunes face à la justice pénale*, 36.

32. For an explicit comparative analysis of the 1942 and 1945 proposals, see chapter 6 in Fishman, *The Battle for Children*.

33. Magistrat Alfred Potier, "L'Enfance délinquant" (rapport de la Ministère de la Justice, Direction de l'Education Surveillée, 1953), p. 1, CAC: 910333, art. 3.

34. "La Session des Juges des Enfants et Directeurs de la Population" (Vaucresson: Centre de Formation et d'Etude de l'Education Surveillée, 6–11 July 1959), p. 11, CAC: 910333, art. 1.

35. "Prisons et Prisonniers: Le problème de la délinquance juvénile en France," from "vol. 9 (1er trimestre 1951)" of an unnamed publication, p. 99, CAC: 910333, art. 18.

36. Le Breton, *Les Hauts murs*.

37. Champagne, "Jean Genet in the Delinquent Colony of Mettray"; White, *Genet: A Biography*, 7, 70; Danan, *Maisons de supplices.*

38. Genet, *L'Enfant criminel*, 17, 16, 26.

39. See "Ordonnance du 1er septembre 1945," in *Lois et décrets.*

40. See also "Loi du 19 avril 1898," "Loi du 11 avril 1980," and "Décret du 30 octobre 1935," in *Lois et décrets.*

41. Schafer, *Children in Moral Danger and the Problem of Government in Third Republic France*, 10. For how this policy carried into the twentieth century, see Childers, *Fathers, Families, and the State in France.*

42. Jean-Louis Costa, "Plan de réforme des services de l'Education surveillée et les institutions protectrices de l'Enfance en danger morale" (Direction de l'Education surveillée, April 1946), p. 4, CAC: 910333, art. 3.

43. Ibid.

44. "Exposé des motifs du projet d'ordonnance relative a l'enfance delinquant," 22 January 1945, p. 3, AN F60/1052.

45. "Ordonnance du 2 février 1945 relative à l'enfance délinquante," in *Lois et décrets*; and *Livre blanc sur le jeunesse*, pt. 6, *Inadaptation sociale et délinquance des jeunes*, pp. 23–24, CAC: 910333, art. 3.

46. Jean-Louis Costa, "Plan de réforme des services de l'Education surveillée et les institutions protectrices de l'Enfance en danger morale" (Direction de l'Education surveillée, April 1946), pp. 56, 61–63, CAC: 910333, art. 3.

47. See Fishman, *The Battle for Children.*

48. Jean-Louis Costa, "Plan de réforme des services de l'Education surveillée et les institutions protectrices de l'Enfance en danger morale" (Direction de l'Education surveillée, April 1946), p. 43, CAC: 910333, art. 3.

49. Michèle Communaux, "Rapport sur La Liberté Surveillée" (Institut des Sciences et Techniques Humaines, June 1958), p. 13, CAC: 910333, art. 4.

50. "La Liberté Surveillée en milieu rural" (Centre de formation et d'études de l'éducation surveillée, February 1956), pp. 43–44, CAC: 910333, art. 4.

51. Michèle Communaux, "Rapport sur La Liberté Surveillée" (Institut des Sciences et Techniques Humaines, June 1958), pp. 14–15, CAC: 910333, art. 4.

52. In 1952, of 14,624 minors judged, 1,405 were sent to prison; see Magistrat Alfred Potier, "L'Enfance Délinquante" (Rapport de la Ministère de la Justice, Direction de l'Education Surveillée 1953), p. 2, CAC: 910333, art. 3.

53. Costa, "Plan de réforme . . . ," 68, CAC: 910333, art. 3; and *Livre blanc sur la jeunesse*, pt. 6, *Inadaptation sociale et délinquance des jeunes* (Ministère de la Justice, 1967), p. 25, CAC: 910333, art. 3.

54. Chazal, *L'Enfance délinquante*, 8.

55. Jean-Louis Costa, "Plan de réforme des services de l'Education surveillée et les institutions protectrices de l'Enfance en danger morale" (Direction de l'Education surveillée, April 1946), p. 70, CAC: 910333, art. 3.

56. *La Délinquance juvénile en France*, Notes et études documentaires, n. 1.423 (19 January 1951), p. 23, CAC: 910333, art. 3.

57. Robert Lecourt, "Rapport sur la situation de la justice en France à la fin de l'Année Judiciaire, 1948–1949," p. 70, CAC: 910333, art. 3.

58. *La Délinquance juvénile en France*, Notes et études documentaires, n. 1.423 (19 January 1951), p. 24, CAC: 910333, art. 3.

59. Ibid., pp. 27, 25.

60. "Ordonnance n. 45-1845 du 18 août 1945," in *Lois et décrets*.

61. Jean-Louis Costa, "Plan de réforme des services de l'Education surveillée et les institutions protectrices de l'Enfance en danger morale" (Direction de l'Education surveillée, April 1946), p. 103, CAC: 910333, art. 3.

62. Senateur Charles Morel, "Avis présent au nom de la Commission de l'éducation nationale, des beaux-arts, des sports, de la jeunesse et des loisirs sur le projet de loi, adopté par l'Assemblée Nationale rélatif aux établissemenst privés . . ." (Conseil de la République, procès-verbal de la séance du 22 juin 1950), p. 2, AN F60/1411.

63. Senateur Marcel Mollé, "Rapport fait au nom de la Commission de la famille, de la population et de la santé publique sur le projet de loi adopté par l'Assemblée Nationale rélatif aux établissements privés . . ." (Conseil de la République, procès-verbal de la séance du 6 juin 1950), p. 2, AN F60/1411. A circular from 1946 also estimated that the number of young people at risk fluctuated around 500,000 (Sous-Secrétariat d'Etat à la Jeunesse et aux Sports, Mouvements de Jeunesse et d'Education Populaire, "Enfance Délinquante," 6 August 1946, AN F44/120).

64. René Fau et Charlotte Memin, "Les Echecs en matière de rééducation," *Enfance*, March–April 1949, 130.

65. "Projet de loi rélatif à la protection de l'enfance et de l'adolescence en danger" (Assemblée Nationale, procès-verbal de la séance du 12 June 1952), pp. 2–3, AN F60/1411.

66. Article 8 of "Ordonnance du 2 février 1945 relative à l'enfance délinquante," in *Lois et décrets*.

67. "Prisons et Prisonniers: Le problème de la délinquance juvénile en France," from "vol. 9 (1er trimestre 1951)" of an unnamed publication, p. 97, CAC: 910333, art. 18.

68. *La Délinquance juvénile en France*, Notes et études documentaires, n. 1.423 (19 January 1951), pp. 5, 12, CAC: 910333, art. 3.

69. See Fishman, *The Battle for Children*, 135–40.

70. For the development of the state's relationship to paternal power in the family over the course of the Third Repubic and Vichy, see Childers, *Fathers, Families, and the State in France*.

71. Magistrat Alfred Potier, "L'Enfance délinquante" (Ministère de la Justice, Direction de l'Education Surveillée, 1953), p. 1, CAC: 910333, art. 3.

72. See Pomfret, *Young People and the European City*.

73. Meyer, *The Child and the State*, 11; and Childers, *Fathers, Families, and the State in France*.

74. Schafer, *Children in Moral Danger*, 4.

75. Chazal, *L'Enfance délinquante*, 32, 17.

76. "Presentation au lecteur," *Sauvegarde* 1 (May 1946): 3.

77. "Loi n. 46-1151 du 22 mai 1946 modifiant les lois du 28 mars 1882 et du 11 août 1936," in *Lois et décrets*.

78. Sénateur Marcelle Delabie, "Rapport fait au nom de la Commission de la famille, de la population et de la santé publique sur la proposition de loi complètant l'article 8 de la loi du 1er octobre 1917 sur la répression de l'ivresse publique et sur la police des débits de boissons, en ce qui concerne les mineurs de moins de 16 ans" (Conseil de la République; procèes-verbal de la séance du 20 nobembre 1952), pp. 1–2, AN F60/1264.

79. Jean Cayeux et Taillaud, "Proposition de loi modifier le loi du October 1917" (Assemblée Nationale; procès-verbal de la séance du 9 January 1952), pp. 1–2, AN F60/1264.

80. Georges Malignac, "Délinquance juvénile et alcoolisme," *Rééducation*, January–February 1954, 27.

81. The farming and distilling lobby quashed these measures, however, and in the end Mendès-France's efforts only succeeded in giving his outspoken rival, Pierre Poujade, ample material for vulgar insult (see Giles, *The Locust Years*, 233–34).

82. "La protection de la jeunesse contre les établissements dont la fréquentation est susceptible de nuire à la santé ou à la moralité juvénile," p. 1, CAC: 910258, art. 161.

83. Ministère de la Santé Publique et de la Population, "Communication sur le problèmes d'ordre familial et social poses aux pouvoir publics par l'éducation des adolescents," p. 4, CAC: 910258, art. 161.

84. Simone Marcus-Jeisler, "Réponse . . . ," *Sauvegarde* 9 (March 1947): 12, 14.

85. Jean-Paul Lacroix, "Pourquoi des adolescents deviennent des assassins?" *Elle*, 31 March 1958, 93–94.

86. Gillain, "The Script of Delinquency," 188.

87. François Truffaut, "Qu'est-ce qu'on va faire du gosse?" *Arts*, 3 June 1959, in clipping file for *Les Quatre cents coups*, BiFi.

88. Ibid.

89. Louis Chavet, "Les Quatre Cents Coups," *Le Figaro*, 5 May 1959, in clipping file for *Les Quatre cents coups*, BiFi.

90. Simone Dubreuilh, "Truffaut a fait un coup de maître," *Libération*, 5 May 1959, in clipping file for *Les Quatre cents coups*, BiFi.

91. White, *Genet: A Biography*, xvii.

92. White, *Genet: A Biography*.

93. Sartre, *Saint Genet*; this work was originally published as *Saint Genet: Comédien et Martyr* (Paris: Librairie Gallimard, 1952).

94. Genet, *L'Enfant criminel*, 29, 30–31, 32, 25.

95. For an account and analysis of the public's preoccupation with such crimes during the July Monarchy, see Nilan, "'Crimes inexplicables.'" For an analysis of the pervasive cultural preoccupation with sexual murder in Weimar Germany, see Tatar, *Lustmord*.

96. Jean-Marc Theolleyre, "A la veille du procès des 'J3': II—La Mythomanie au crime," *Le Monde*, 4 May 1951, 8.

97. Jean-Paul Lacroix, "Pourquoi des adolescents deviennent des assassins?" *Elle*, 31 March 1958, 49–50.

98. "Le Meurtrier n'aurait fait qu'exécuter une décision collective," *Le Monde*, 13 January 1949, 5.

99. Jean-Marc Theolleyre, "A la veille du procès des 'J3': I—Un Fait divers hors série," *Le Monde*, 3 May 1951, 6.

100. Jean-Marc Theolleyre, "A la veille du procès des 'J3': II—La Mythomanie au crime," *Le Monde*, 4 May 1951, 8.

101. André Le Gall, "Les Mythes juvéniles et leurs dangers," *Le Monde*, 6–7 May 1951, 7.

102. For more on *Avant le deluge*, see chapter 3 in Weiner, *Enfants Terribles*.

103. "Le Gang des J-3 de Valence," *Le Monde*, 1 February 1950, 7.

104. Gilbert, *A Cycle of Outrage*.

105. Jean-Paul Lacroix, "Pourquoi des adolescents deviennent des assassins?" *Elle*, 31 March 1958, 48, 93.

106. L. S., "Rendez-vous de juillet," *La Laterne*, 20 January 1950, in clipping file for *Rendez-vous de juillet*, BiFi.

107. Georges Hourdin, "Rendez-vous de juillet," *Radio-Cinéma-Télévision*, 30 September 1956, 39–40, in clipping file for *Rendez-vous de juillet*, BiFi.

108. Pol Gaillard, "Rendez-vous de juillet," *Parallèle*, 20 January 1950, in clipping file for *Rendez-vous de juillet*, BiFi.

109. Jones, *Boris Vian Transatlantic*, 140; and Beever and Cooper, *Paris after the Liberation*, 381–82.

110. Jean-Paul Lacroix, "Pourquoi des adolescents deviennent des assassins?" *Elle*, 31 March 1958, 51, 92–93.

111. Michel Capdenac, "Carné: Je n'accuse pas la jeunesse; mais le mal dont elle souffre," *Les Lettres Françaises*, 16 October 1958, in clipping file for *Les Tricheurs*, BiFi.

112. "Qui sont *Les Tricheurs?* Le Film de Marcel Carné ouvre le débat," *L'Express*, special edition, 16 October 1958.

113. "*Les Tricheurs* interdits dans le canton de Vaud," *Le Monde*, 14 March 1959, in clipping file for *Les Tricheurs*, BiFi.

114. "*Les Tricheurs* interdit à Nice," *L'Humanité*, 5 November 1958; and "*Les Tricheurs* ont gain de cause à Nice mais le film sera interdit aux moins de dix-huit ans," *Le Monde*, 6 November 1958, both in clipping file for *Les Tricheurs*, BiFi.

115. "Avec *Les Tricheurs* Marcel Carné déclare la guerre à la jeunesse," *France Catholique*, 7 November 1958, in clipping file for *Les Tricheurs*, BiFi.

116. "Des jeunes qui ne 'Trichent' pas interrogent Marcel Carné," *L'Humanité-Dimanche*, 26 October 1958, in clipping file for *Les Tricheurs*, BiFi.

117. Maurice Coqeullin, "Grand débat public au CCIF: Pour ou contre *Les Tricheurs* de Marcel Carné," *Combat*, 11 December 1958, in clipping file for *Les Tricheurs*, BiFi.

118. Etienne Fuzellier, "*Les Tricheurs*," *Education Nationale*, 8 January 1959, in clipping file for *Les Tricheurs*, BiFi.

119. Michel Capdenac, "Carné: Je n'accuse pas la jeunesse; mais le mal dont elle souffre," *Les Lettres Françaises*, 16 October 1958, in clipping file for *Les Tricheurs*, BiFi.

120. "Des jeunes qui ne 'Trichent' pas interrogent Marcel Carné," *L'Humanité-Dimanche*, 26 October 1958, in clipping file for *Les Tricheurs*, BiFi.

121. A similar mechanism was at play in the nineteenth century, as murderous children were conceptualized as prematurely, preconsciously perverted. They did not conform to the sociocultural definition of childhood, and thus were not *real* children at all, but little monsters, and were denied the sympathy usually accorded to their age (see Nilan, "'Crimes inexplicables,'" 77–88).

122. Luc Mollet, "*Les Tricheurs*: Par le gros bout de la lorgnette," *Radio-Cinéma-Télévision*, 26 October 1958, in clipping file for *Les Tricheurs*, BiFi.

123. "Exposé des motifs du projet d'ordonnance rélative à l'enfance délinquante," 22 January 1945, p. 2, AN F60/1052.

124. Juge Puzin, "Libres propos," *Rééducation*, November 1947, 8.

125. Cocteau, *Diary of a Film*.

CHAPTER 5. SEX AND THE CYNICAL GIRL

1. The film has also been shown in the United States under the title *The Game of Love*.

2. "Vives protestations contre *Le Blé en herbe*," *La Croix*, 19 March 1954, in clipping file for *Le Blé en herbe*, BiFi.

3. "Reponses à Henri Jeanson," *Paris Comoedia*, 19 March 1954, in clipping file for *Le Blé en herbe*, BiFi.

4. Ibid.

5. *L'Humanité*, 22 March 1954. Interestingly, there was no overt political message in the movie to warrant a Communist's defense, but because the film had riled up the forces on the right, the opposition left found an occasion for political posturing. The moral controversy surrounding the film had provided a moment for Cold War political opportunism.

6. Bauche, *Claude Autant-Lara*, 60–61.

7. *"Le Blé en herbe,"* *Le Drapeau Rouge*, 26 March 1954, in clipping file for *Le Blé en herbe*, BiFi.

8. Pierre Laroche, "Un Film pornographique," *Paris Comoedia*, 24 February 1954, in clipping file for *Le Blé en herbe*, BiFi.

9. Callander, *Le Blé en herbe and La Chatte*, 37.

10. "Reponses à Henri Jeanson," *Paris Comoedia*, 19 March 1954, in clipping file for *Le Blé en herbe*, BiFi.

11. See Spengler, *France Faces Depopulation* (orginally published in 1938); and Klaus, "Depopulation and Race Suicide."

12. Bertillon was a physician and chief demographer for the Department of the Seine. At the end of the nineteenth century he founded the Alliance Nationale pour l'Accroissement de la Population Française, and insisted that depopulation was a man's problem (see Offen, "Depopulation, Nationalism, and Feminism in Fin-de-siècle France"). For more on how the French state imagined the role of men in pronatalism, see Childers, *Fathers, Families, and the State in France*.

13. For more on the Vichy regime's politics on abortion, and on women's civil, economic, and political status in France generally during this period, see Offen, "Depopulation, Nationalism, and Feminism"; Pedersen, "Catholicism, Feminism, and the Politics of the Family during the late Third Republic"; Hause and Kenney, *Women's Suffrage and Social Politics in the French Third Republic*; Cova, "French Feminism and Maternity"; Offen, "Body Politics"; and Stewart, *For Health and Beauty*. To follow the themes of pronatalism, motherhood, and abortion into the Fourth Republic, see Duchen, *Women's Rights and Women's Lives in France*.

14. Not all feminists or women's activists agreed on this strategy, however. Many based their claims for women's rights on abstract ideas of justice, liberal republicanism, and egalitarian citizenship.

15. Duchen, *Women's Rights and Women's Lives in France*.

16. Beauvoir, *The Second Sex*, 267, 34.

17. Ibid., 280, 359, 336.

18. See Chapter 4, on delinquency.

19. *La Délinquance juvénile en France*, Notes et études documentaires, n. 1.423 (19 January 1951), p. 4, CAC: 910333, art. 3; and Chazal, *L'Enfance délinquante*, 8.

20. Sous-Secrétariat d'Etat à la Jeunesse et aux Sports, Mouvements de Jeunesse et d'Education Populaire, "Enfance Délinquante," circular of 6 August 1946, AN F₄₄/120.

21. *La Délinquance juvénile en France*, Notes et études documentaires, n. 1.423 (19 January 1951), p. 4, CAC: 910333, art. 3.

22. Chazal, *L'Enfance délinquante*, 8.

23. Simone Marcus-Jeisler, "Réponse . . . ," *Sauvegarde* 9 (March 1947): 11.

24. Docteur Le Moal, "Le Vagabondage féminin: Causes psycho-physiologiques de la prostitution," *Rééducation*, March–April 1954, 16.

25. Ibid., 16, 21, 24, 26.

26. Mossuz-Lavau, *Les Lois de l'amour*, 159; see also Duchen, *Women's Rights and Women's Lives in France*.

27. Berge, *L'Education sexuelle chez l'enfant*.

28. H. Michard, "Rapport sur les règles fondamentales à observer dans la lutte contre la délinquance juvénile," Organisation 1949, p. 45, CAC: 910258, art. 163.

29. Ibid., p. 14.

30. Fishman, *The Battle for Children*, 213–15.

31. See Chapter 4.

32. Jean-Paul Lacroix, "Pourquoi des adolescents deviennent des assassins?" *Elle*, 31 March 1958, 49.

33. "Le Meurtrier n'aurait fait qu'exécuter une décision collective," *Le Monde*, 13 January 1949, 5.

34. Jean-Marc Theolleyre, "A la veille du procès des 'J3'; I—Un fait divers hors série," *Le Monde*, 3 May 1951, 6.

35. "Douze heures de confrontation sans resultat," *Le Monde*, 23–24 January 1949, 5.

36. Crawley, *Bébé*, 52.

37. Valerie Duponchelle, "BB-Vadim: Le Scandale suranné," *Le Figaro*, 11 August 1992, in clipping file for *Et Dieu créa la femme*, BiFi; "Ingénue perverse," *L'Express*, 7 December 1956, in clipping file for *Et Dieu créa la femme*, BiFi; Edgar Morin, "Amour et érotisme dans la culture de masse," *Arguments* 21 (1st Trimester 1961): 52; Crawley, *Bébé*, 44.

38. Roberts, *Bardot*, 25–42.

39. *Elle*, 2 May 1949; *Elle*, 8 May 1950, 14–19, 26–27.

40. Vadim, *Bardot, Deneuve, Fonda*, 14, 50–65; and Roberts, *Bardot*, 66–109.

41. Vadim, *Bardot, Deneuve, Fonda*, 133; and Roberts, *Bardot*, 133.

42. Crawley, *Bébé*, 35.

43. Roger Vadim, "Les Jeunes préparent une surprise," *L'Express*, 5 May 1957, in clipping file for *Et Dieu créa la femme*, BiFi; and Beauvoir, *Brigitte Bardot and the Lolita Syndrome*, 7.

44. Roberts, *Bardot*, 131.

45. Beauvoir, *Brigitte Bardot and the Lolita Syndrome*, 7.

46. "Ingénue perverse," *L'Express*, 7 December 1956, in clipping file for *Et Dieu créa la femme*, BiFi.

47. Maurice Ciantar, "En cas de malheur," *Paris Jour*, 17 September 1958, in clipping file for *Et Dieu créa la femme*, BiFi.

48. François Truffaut, "En cas de malheur," *Arts*, 10 September 1958, in clipping file for *Et Dieu créa la femme*, BiFi.

49. Max Favelli, "En cas de malheur," *Paris-Presse*, 3 September 1958, in clipping file for *Et Dieu créa la femme*, BiFi.

50. André Besseges, "Quand le sordide devient publicitaire, agressif et désespéré," *France Catholique*, October 1958, in clipping file for *Et Dieu créa la femme*, BiFi.

51. Jean d'Yvoire, "En cas de malheur . . . tirons le signal d'alarme," *Radio-Cinéma-Télévision*, 5 October 1958, in clipping file for *Et Dieu créa la femme*, BiFi.

52. For a good analysis of Bardot's films, in addition to biographical information, see French, *Bardot*.

53. Jacques Doniol-Valcroze, "Et Dieu créa la femme . . . ," *France-Observateur*, 13 December 1956, in clipping file for *Et Dieu créa la femme*, BiFi.

54. Beauvoir, *Brigitte Bardot and the Lolita Syndrome*, 16.

55. Vadim, *Bardot, Deneuve, Fonda*, 113.

56. Beauvoir, *Brigitte Bardot and the Lolita Syndrome*, 20.

57. Quoted in Crawley, *Bébé*, 36.

58. Morin, *The Stars*, 29, 30.

59. Beauvoir, *Brigitte Bardot and the Lolita Syndrome*, 10, 12, 13, 18.

60. André Besseges, "Quand le sordid devient publicitaire, agressif et désespéré," *France Catholique*, 4 October 1958, in clipping file for *Et Dieu créa la femme*, BiFi.

61. François Truffaut, "*Et Dieu créa la femme* . . . ," *Arts*, 5 December 1956, in clipping file for *Et Dieu créa la femme*, BiFi.

62. Claude de Givray, "Nouveau traité du Bardot . . . suivi du petit à BB cédaire," *Cahiers du Cinéma*, May 1957, in clipping file for *Et Dieu créa la femme*, BiFi.

63. Joe Hyams, "Brigitte Bardot: 'Je suis la jeune fille française,'" *L'Express*, 10 August 1956, 18.

64. Michel Perez, "Et Dieu créa la femme . . . ," *Cinéma*, no. 57 (January 1957): 107–9.

65. Beauvoir, *Brigitte Bardot and the Lolita Syndrome*, 21.

66. Hourdin, *Le Cas Françoise Sagan*, 47.

67. Pauvert, *Nightbird*, 19–28; Miller, *Françoise Sagan*.

68. Pauvert, *Nightbird*, 35.

69. Ibid., 11; and Miller, *Françoise Sagan*, 5.

70. François Mauriac, Editorial, *Le Figaro*, 6 June 1954.

71. Emile Henriot, "La Vie Littéraire: *Bonjour tristesse* de Françoise Sagan," *Le Monde*, 12 May 1954, 9.

72. Sagan, *Bonjour Tristesse*, 7.

73. Ibid., 31.

74. Pierre Rousseaux, "Françoise Sagan et son premier livre," *Le Figaro Littéraire*, 5 June 1954, 1; Mourgue, *Françoise Sagan*, 126.

75. Miller, *Françoise Sagan*, 69–70.

76. Madeleine Chapsal, "Françoise Sagan vous parle . . . ," *L'Express*, 13 September 1957, 17.

77. Hourdin, *Le Cas Françoise Sagan*, 59.

78. Pierre de Boisdeffre, quoted in Mourgue, *Françoise Sagan*, 6.

79. Madeleine Chapsal, "Dans un mois, dans un an," *L'Express*, 6 September 1957, 23.

80. Madeleine Chapsal, "Françoise Sagan vous parle . . . ," *L'Express*, 13 September 1957, 16.

81. Hourdin, *Le Cas Françoise Sagan*, 7, 43, 61, 63, 65, 100.

82. Mourgue, *Françoise Sagan*, 5, 6, 122, 120, 128.

83. Roberts, *Bardot*, 156–65.

84. Pauvert, *Nightbird*, 41.

85. Ibid., 40.

86. See Chapter 1 for a brief discussion of *mal du siècle* in the context of the postwar futurist discourse.

87. J.-P. Reynaud, "Un Professeur parle du mal du siècle," *L'Express*, 2 August 1957, 16.

88. F. Gay, "Peut-on encore éduquer la jeunesse," *Foi Education*, May 1952, 70.

89. Mireille Baumgartner, "Mal du siècle 1952 et jeunes générations," *Foi Education*, May 1952, 83–84.

90. "La Crise de la jeunesse," *Cahiers Pédagogiques*, 3 December 1957.

91. Hourdin, *Le Cas Françoise Sagan*, 57.

92. Thierry Maulnier, "*Un Certain sourire* est-il un roman rose?" *Le Figaro Littéraire*, 26 May 1956, 7.

93. Nourissier, *Les Chiens à fouetter*.

94. J.-P. Reynaud, "Un Professeur parle du mal du siècle," *L'Express*, 2 August 1957, 16.

95. Docteur Le Moal, "Le Vagabondage féminin: Causes psycho-physiologiques de la prostitution," *Rééducation*, March–April 1954, 20.

96. Robert Jacques, "Voici comment vivent les troglodytes de Saint-Germain-des-Prés," *Samedi-Soir*, 3 May 1947.

97. Ibid.

98. Vian, *Le Manuel de Saint-Germain-des-Prés*. Vian wrote this book in the 1950s specifically as a countermeasure to the half-truths and sensationalism of the *pisse-copie* journalism that circulated about Saint-Germain. He died, however, fifteen years before its publication. *Le Manuel* describes the clubs, the jazz, and the personalities of the late-1940s scene. See also Hanoteau, *L'Age d'or de Saint-Germain-des-Prés*, for a catalog of the literary and artistic scene as well as the infamous nightlife and the emerging celebrities of the Quarter from the 1930s to the 1950s.

99. *Inter*, 26 May 1948.

100. *Dernière Heure*, 24 November 1948.

101. Vian, *Le Manuel de Saint-Germain-des-Prés*, 51.

102. Ibid., 53.

103. François Mauriac, Editorial, *Le Figaro*, 30 May 1949; François Mauriac, Editorial, *Le Figaro*, 6 June 1949; and François Mauriac, "Le Figaro Littéraire interroge la jeunesse intellectuelle," *Le Figaro Littéraire*, 25 June–6 August 1949.

104. See Beauvoir, *Force of Circumstance*, vol. 1, *After the War*, 141–42, 181–87, 230.

105. Robert Jacques, "Voici comment les troglodytes vivent de Saint-Germain-des-Prés," *Samedi-Soir*, 3 May 1947.

106. *La Presse*, 3 January 1949.

107. *Flash*, January 1950.

108. *Samedi-Soir*, 15 January 1949.

109. *La Presse*, 3 January 1949.

110. *Samedi-Soir*, 15 January 1949.

111. Beever and Cooper, *Paris after the Liberation*, 387.

112. See Berge, *L'Education sexuelle chez l'enfant*.

113. Mossuz-Lavau, *Les Lois de l'amour*, 137, 140; on the campaign for legalized contraception, see also Duchen, *Women's Rights and Women's Lives in France*, 173–86.

114. Kanters and Sigaux, *Vingt ans en 1951*; Giroud, *La Nouvelle Vague*.

115. Duquesne and IFOP, *Les 16–24 ans*, 107, 110.

116. Karnow, "France: The Younger Generation," 34.

117. Karnow, *Paris in the Fifties*, 237.

118. As quoted in White, *Genet: A Biography*, 170.

119. Genet, *The Thief's Journal*, 214, 171, 87.

120. Chazal, *L'Enfance délinquante*, 39–44.

121. Initially, in 1942, the age of majority for heterosexual acts was thirteen; it was raised to fifteen in 1945. For a thorough examination of the legal status of homosexuals in modern France, see Gunther, "The Elastic Closet."

122. For more on Leduc, see Courtivron, *Violette Leduc*; for criticism, see Hughes, *Violette Leduc*.

123. See "Les Fruits verts," *L'Express*, 17 April 1954, 14; and Géoris, *Françoise Mallet-Joris*. For more on Mallet-Joris, see Becker, *Françoise Mallet-Joris*.

124. Lignière, *Françoise Sagan et le succès*, 11, 128.

125. See Roberts, *Civilization without Sexes*; and Stewart, *For Health and Beauty*.

126. Duchen, *Women's Rights and Women's Lives in France*, 10, 12–14.

127. Amouroux, *La Grande histoire des Français après l'Occupation*, vol. 9, *Le Reglement de comptes* (Paris: Laffont, 1991), 121, as cited in Duchen, *Women's Rights and Women's Lives in France*, 14.

128. Beauvoir, *Force of Circumstance*, vol. 1, *After the War*, 30.

129. See Smith, *Ladies of the Leisure Class*; and Sohn, *Chrysalides*.

130. Michele Firk, "L'Anachronique jeunesse du cinéma français," *Cinéma*, May 1959, 61.

131. Pierre Voldemar, "Y a-t-il un mal de jeunesse?" *Jeune Europe*, 15 April 1954, 7.

CHAPTER 6. TARZAN UNDER ATTACK

1. Horn, "Comics," 15.

2. See Barker, *A Haunt of Fears*; Wright, *Comic Book Nation*; Rubenstein, *Bad Language, Naked Ladies, and Other Threats to the Nation*; Lent, *Pulp Demons*.

3. Raoul Dubois, "La Presse pour enfants de 1934 à 1953," *Enfance*, November–December 1953, 379.

4. Louis Raillon, "Front common des Educateurs," *Educateurs*, January–February 1946, 2.

5. André Fournel, "Alerte aux parents! Les publications enfantines ne doivent par être une semence de démoralisation pour les générations futures!" *Le Parisien Libéré*, 17 July 1946, 2.

6. Roger Labrusse, "Le Point de vue des parents: La Presse enfantine, problème délicat, problème soluble," *Enfance*, November–December 1953, 456.

7. Emmanuel La Gravière, "L'Enfance, notre première souci," *L'Aube*, 27 October 1948, 4.

8. "L'Application de la loi du 16 juillet 1949 sur les publications destinées à la jeunesse de 1955 à 1957," *Pour la Vie*, 1959, 17, in an unmarked file, CNBDI.

9. "Le Conseil supérieur de la magistrature devant la recrudescence de la criminalité juvénile," *Le Monde*, 1–2 February 1948, 3.

10. Paul Gosset, quoted in the *Journal Officiel de la République Française: Débats parlementaires, Assemblée Nationales* [hereafter cited as *Débats parlementaires*], 21 January 1949, 90.

11. *Débats parlementaires*, 3 July 1949, 4096 (emphasis added).

12. *Débats parlementaires*, 21 January 1949, 97. Solange Lamblin and Jacques Bardoux introduced these terms, respectively, in the desire to create a new, morally upright, staunchly patriotic, and democratically devoted citizenry in response to the specific context of the war and Occupation.

13. For a formal analysis of comic books as media, see McCloud, *Understanding Comics*; and Barker, *Comics*. For a more semiotic approach, see Tilleul, *Pour analyser la bande dessinée*.

14. For a general overview of the development of comic strips, see Couperie and Horn, *A History of the Comic Strip*; Filippini, *Histoire de la bande dessinée en France et en Belgique*; and Groensteen, *Astérix, Barbarella & Cie*. For the place of comics in the history of French juvenile publications more generally, see Forment, *Histoire de la presse des jeunes et des journaux d'enfants*.

15. For an overview of American comics in France, see Maurice C. Horn, "American Comics in France."

16. In 1935 French draftsmen formed a new union to join the two preexisting ones in an effort to defend their positions in the industry and to make protectionist demands on the French government. At the outbreak of the war, there was a project underway to limit the amount of foreign material allowed in French publications, but this legislation remained unrealized after the collapse of the Third Republic. For more on this, see Thierry Crépin, "Défense du Dessin Français: Vingt Ans de protectionisme corporatif," *Dessin Français*, 26–30, in an unmarked file, CNBDI.

17. The Nazis published their own comic magazine for French youth. *Le Téméraire* was intended to indoctrinate young French readers with Nazi ideals and featured comic strips with dark, hook-nosed villains and blond, Aryan heroes. For an analysis of *Le Téméraire*, see Ory, *Le Petit Nazi illustré*. In a similar use of comic and cartoon icons as propaganda, Vichy even produced cartoon reels for the cinema that showed Mickey Mouse dropping bombs on defenseless French villagers (see the documentary *L'Oeil de Vichy*, directed by Claude Chabrol).

18. The Communist press published *Vaillant*; the Catholic press reestablished *Coeurs-Vaillants* (in which "Tintin" appeared, though in 1946 the comic strip graduated to its own publication); and in 1944 Marijac (Jacques Dumas), who would go on to dominate the postwar French comic industry, began the paper *Coq Hardi*, which featured "Les Trois Mousquetaires du Maquis."

19. For an overview of the dominant publications of this period, see Filippini, *Les Années cinquante*.

20. See Crépin, "Le Myth d'un front commun"; also, Ory, "Mickey Go Home!"

21. The bill was the result of a combined effort from the Communist-dominated Union Patriotique des Organisations de Jeunesse (UPOJ) and the Catholic organization Commission d'Etude des Journaux d'Enfants (CEJE).

22. Couperie and Horn, *A History of the Comic Strip*, 93–95.

23. See *Débats parlementaires*, 2 July 1949, 4102–3. Interestingly, despite these attacks, the popular Communist comic book *Vaillant*, which was set in the Resistance, took its style and themes from American comics (see Pidard, "Les Illustrées pour la jeunesse de l'après-guerre," 20).

24. See *Débats parlementaires*, 21 January 1949, 91–92.

25. Paul Winkler, "Réponse aux accusations de député communiste André Pierrard," 25 January 1949, in an unmarked file, CNBDI.

26. A 1947 survey in *Mon Journal* revealed that its readers preferred Captain Marvel Junior and Hopalong Cassidy to the French counterparts ("Résultats du concours," *Mon Journal*, June 1947, 7).

27. "Procés verbal de la sous commission chargée d'examiner les publications, séance du 9 November 1950," CAC: 900208, art. 1.

28. Raoul Dubois, "Les Journaux pour enfants," *La Pensée*, July–August 1951, 75.

29. Bauchard, *La Presse, le film, et la radio pour enfants*, 95.

30. G. Legman, "Psychopathologie des comics" (trans. H. Robillot), *Les Temps Modernes*, May 1949, 916.

31. For more on the French postwar debates about America's role in France, see Kuisel, *Seducing the French*; Ross, *Fast Cars, Clean Bodies*; Pells, *Not Like Us*; Mathy, *French Resistance*.

32. Horn, "American Comics in France," 51, 57–58.

33. Henri Wallon, "Préface," *Enfance*, November–December 1953, 26.

34. Jean Chazal, "Le Point de vue d'un juge des enfants," *Enfance*, November–December 1953, 451–53.

35. "Savez-vous ce qu'il y a dans les journaux d'enfants?" parts 1–5, *Educateurs*, January–February, March–April, May–June, July–August, and September–October, 1947.

36. Louis Pauwels, "Combien d'enfants tuez-vous par semaine?" *Combat*, 30 December 1947, 1.

37. Louis de Philippe, "Que lit-on 'A l'Hombre'?: Tarzan, Zorro, et les Trois Mousquetaires," *Combat*, 23 August 1949, 1–12.

38. "Un garconnet de 10 ans abat son petit camarade avec le pistolet de son pere!: En volant imiter Zorro," *Parisien Libéré*, 17 June 1954.

39. Jean Ballandras, "Le Report Ballandras," 1948, in an unmarked file, CNBDI. The Ballandras Report was subsequently quoted frequently during the Assembly debates.

40. Jules Moch to the messieurs les Préfets, "Publications dangereuse pour la moralité publique," 8 April 1948, CAC: 760173, art. 40.

41. "Les Bons, les moins bons, les mauvais journaux d'enfants sont exposés rue de Châteaudun," *Le Monde*, 20 May 1948, 4.

42. For more on the rivalry between Catholics and Communists concerning policies for youth, see Whitney, "The Politics of Youth."

43. Christophe Chavdia, "La Loi du 16 juillet 1949 sur les publications destinées à la jeunesse: Le Sexe des anges ou l'enfance philosophale," DEA Histoire de la Science Juridique Européene, 1997, pp. 42, 52, in an unmarked file, CNBDI.

44. Commission, "Thèmes généraux inspirant les représentations et recommandations aux éditeurs des journaux pour enfants," 1950, 2, CAC: 910258, art. 159.

45. Bauchard, *La Presse, le film et le radio pour enfants*, 36.

46. Réné Masson, "La Presse enfantine," *Le Populaire*, 16 December 1947, 2.

47. Pihan and Soumille, *La Presse enfantine*, 6.

48. Gershorn Legman, "Psychopathologie des 'comics,'" *Les Temps Modernes*, May 1949, 916–31.

49. L'Abbé Pihan, "Observation sur le projet de représentations et recommandations aux éditeurs," 1 October 1950, CAC: 900208, art. 1.

50. "Notice sur l'application de l'article 14 de la loi du 16 July 1949 sur les publications destinées à la jeunesse (préparées en 1954, ont été révisées en 1958)," pp. 3–4, CAC: 900208, art. 1.

51. For the discourse on sexuality and gender roles in postwar France, see Mossuz-Lavau, *Les Lois l'amour*; Duchen, *Women's Rights and Women's Lives in France*; and Weiner, *Enfants Terribles*.

52. *Débats parlementaires*, 2 July 1949, 4099.

53. Commission de Surveillance et de Contrôle des Publications destinées à l'Enfance et à l'Adolescence, "Séance du 2 March 1950 procès-verbal," pp. 2–3, CAC: 900208, art. 2.

54. For these, the commission established seven principal genres: police/crime (which featured an investigative reporter, detective, or spy); adventure (stories of

voyages and exotic exploration, including science fiction); superhero (a protagonist with magical or superhuman powers); Western (stories set in the American West); historical (often set in the chivalric Middle Ages); war (modern conflicts); and children's (animal characters and popular cartoons) (*Compte Rendu . . . 1950*, 10, 12–15).

55. Ibid., 18–20.

56. Ibid., 22–30.

57. Ibid., 31–34.

58. "Procès-verbal . . . séance du 9 November 1950," p. 8, CAC: 900208, art. 1.

59. "Savez-vous ce qu'il y a dans les journaux d'enfants?" *Educateurs*, September–October 1947, 452.

60. "Adieu à Tarzan," *Tarzan*, 3 May 1952, 3.

61. Editorials attacking *Tarzan* appeared in the following newspapers and periodicals: *Le Monde, Le Figaro, Educateurs, L'education Nationale, Réeducation, Enfance, Les Temps Modernes, Combat*; and in books such as Lanoux, *L'Enfant en proie aux images*; Bauchard, *La Presse, le film, et la radio pour enfants*; and Pihan and Soumille, *La Presse enfantine*.

62. Vigilax, "Le Mythe de Tarzan," *Educateurs*, July–August 1950, 396; Pihan and Soumille, *La Presse enfantine*, 15; "Toujours la press enfantine, encore un exemple!" *La Croisade de la Press*, June 1950, 51; and Lanoux, *L'Enfant en proie aux images*, II-2.

63. See the Tarzan communiqué, "A Bon Entendeur . . . ," 29 April 1950, in an unmarked file, CNBDI; and "Adieu à Tarzan," *Tarzan*, 3 May 1952, 3.

64. Tarzan communiqué, "A Bon Entendeur . . . ," 29 April 1950, in an unmarked file, CNBDI.

65. See, for example, the scathing sarcasm of Vigilax, "Le myth de Tarzan," *Educateurs*, July–August 1950, 395–99.

66. Bauchard, *La Presse, le film, et la radio pour enfants*, 36.

67. Pihan and Soumille, *La Presse enfantine*, 6.

68. "Savez-vous ce qu'il y a dans les journaux enfants?" *Educateurs*, March–April 1947, 451.

69. *Compte Rendu . . . 1950*, 24.

70. Pihan and Soumille, *La presse enfantine*, 35; and "Savez-vous ce qu'il y a dans les journaux d'enfants?" *Educateurs*, March–April 1947, 451.

71. Soumille, "Tarzan, l'homme-singe," *Educateurs*, July–August 1953, 300.

72. Bauchard, *La Presse, le film, et la radio pour enfants*, 34.

73. Pihan and Soumille, *La Presse enfantine*, 3.

74. For more on the perception of Tarzan as a reactionary figure, see Fouilhe, *Jounaux d'enfants, journaux pour rire?* 54–56.

75. Vigilax, "Le Myth de Tarzan," *Educateurs*, July–August 1950, 397.

76. Armand Lanoux, "Si nous capturions Tarzan," *Education Nationale*, April 1950, 3–4.

77. Soumille, "Tarzan, l'homme-singe," *Educateurs*, July–August 1953, 301.

78. See Lanoux, "Si nous capturions Tarzan," *Education Nationale*, April 1950, 3–4; and Vigilax, "Le Myth de Tarzan," *Educateurs*, July–August 1950, 395–99.

79. For an historical overview of this attitude, see Lebovics, "Once and Future Trustees of Western Civilization."

80. Raoul Dubois, "La Loi du 16 July 1949," *Enfance*, November–December 1953, 444–45.

81. "Loi du 29 novembre 1954," in *Lois et décrets*.

82. For such a criticism, see Jacques Perret, "On peut museler la presse enfantine," *La Bataille*, 21 January 1948, 1, 7. See the response of André Marie, the Keeper of the Seals, to this question during Assembly debates (*Débats Parliamentaires*, 21 January 1949, 4096); see also the speech by René Mayer, the next Keeper of the Seals, to the commission, on 2 March 1950 (p. 4), CAC: 900208, art. 2.

83. Jean Chapelle, "Rapport sur le projet de représentations et recommandations aux éditeurs de journaux pour enfants," 13 October 1950, 4, CAC: 900208, art. 1.

84. Jean Chapelle, "A la Commission de Surveillance et de Contrôle," 29 March 1955, CAC: 900208, art. 1.

85. Jean Effel, *Le Figaro Littéraire*, 29 January 1949, 3.

86. Fouilhe, *Journaux d'enfants, journaux pour rire?* 108–29.

87. Pierre Fouilhe, "Le héros et les ombres," *Enfance*, November–December 1953, 395–401.

88. Fouilhe, *Journaux d'enfants, journaux pour rire?* 136–50.

89. See the question-and-answer session recounted in Pierre Fouilhe, "La Presse Enfantine, discussion et intervention de M. Menard," *L'Ecole des parents*, March 1956, 13–23.

90. At the time of Mouchot's initial prosecution, Article 2 did not yet include the term "ethnic prejudices," as amended on 29 November 1954.

91. *Fantax* was mentioned frequently in the Assembly debates and remains a sought-after collectible today.

92. *Big Bill le Casseur* began publication in 1947, and *P'tit Gars* began in 1952.

93. See "Annexe 1: Décisions judiciares relatives aux poursuites intentées contre un éditeur de publications destinées à la jeunesse, pour infraction aux dispositions de l'article 2 de la loi du 16 juillet 1949," in *Compte-rendu . . . 1958*, 39–54.

94. *Compte-rendu . . . 1958*, 45.

95. For an overview of these court proceedings, see the *Compte-rendu des travaux de la Commission de contrôle* for the years 1950, 1954, and 1958; see also Fourie, "Les Effets de la loi de 1949"; and Christophe Chavdia, "La Loi du 16 juillet 1949 sur les publications destinées à la jeunesse: Le Sexe des anges ou l'enfance philosophale" (DEA Histoire de la Science Juridique Européene, 1997), pp. 117–20, in an unmarked file, CNBDI. For a juridical analysis, see Jurisprudence, "Le Climat d'un récit, quel que soit le dénouement de ce dernier peut suffrir à déterminer une condamnation," *La Presse Française*, December 1961, 32–38.

96. Mouchot's company, Les Editions Pierre Mouchot, became La Société d'Editions Rhôdaniennes (SER). Pierre Mouchot died in 1966 and subsequently became a mythic icon for the industry and for comic book aficionados, due to his defiance of censorship and his heroic challenge to the commission's authority.

97. "Un Jugement de la Cour d'Appel de Lyon met en échec la loi contrôle de la presse enfantine," *Votre Enfant*, May 1956, in an unmarked file, CNBDI.

98. Antoine Lestra, "A l'attention des chefs de famille," *La Croix*, 2 April 1956, in an unmarked file, CNBDI.

99. Cour de Cassation, "L'Application de la loi du 16 juillet sur les publications destinées à la jeunesse," *Pour La Vie*, 1959, 8, in an unmarked file, CNBDI.

100. Ibid., 14.

101. Jean Chappelle, "L'Influence de la presse pour enfants est-elle aussi grand qu'on veut bien le laisser croire?" *La Presse Française*, December 1961, 35–36, in an unmarked file, CNBDI. In fact, the commission had authorized a study at the University of Paris, begun in 1956, to examine the effects of violence in comic books on 380 girls and 630 boys. The results, which did indicate some correlation between violent images and violent behavior, were, however, inconclusive and required further study (see appendix 2, in *Compte Rendu . . . 1958*).

102. *Compte Rendu . . . 1954*, 8–9.

103. Ibid., 10, 31.

104. Ibid., 10–11.

105. In 1956 he was given a three-month suspended sentence and fined 50,000 (old) francs. For a complete list of these convictions and a complete title list of publications forbidden for sale to minors, see appendixes 3 and 4, in *Compte Rendu . . . 1958*, 59–113.

106. Mathilde Leriche, "La Presse du coeur pour les petites filles," *Vers l'Education Nouvelle*, April 1954, 3–7.

107. *Compte Rendu . . . 1954*, 23.

108. Ceccaldi, "Note: Disques relevant des articles 2 ou 14 de la loi du 16 juillet 1949," 7 October 1958, CAC: 910258, art. 159.

109. "Décret n. 45-1472 du 3 juillet 1945," CAC: 900208, art. 55.

110. Pivasset, *Essai sur la signification politique du cinéma*, 127–28.

111. Lanoux, *L'Enfant en proie aux images*.

112. Armand Lanoux, "Si nous capturions Tarzan," *Education Nationale*, 27 April 1950, 3–4.

113. Michel Le Bourdelles, "Notes sur le Cinéma et la Délinquance Juvénile," *Rééducation*, July 1948, 25–31.

114. Le Comité de rédaction, *Ciné Jeunes*, 1955, 3, in clipping file for *Le Blé en herbe*, BiFi.

115. "Rapport de Commission d'enquêtes et d'études sur la réforme de la reglementation du contrôle des films cinématographiques," 1961, p. 8, CAC: 760173, art. 36.

116. Charles Dautricourt, "Les Raisons d'un reportage," *Ciné Jeunes*, 1955, p. 2; and Le Comité de rédaction, *Ciné Jeunes*, 1955, p. 1, both in clipping file for *Le Blé en herbe*, BiFi.

117. *Compte Rendu . . . 1950*, 17.

118. *Paris-Presse*, 26 February 1953, in clipping file for *Manina, la fille sans voile*, BiFi.

119. "Loi du 6 août 1955," in *Lois et décrets*. Subsequently, in Nevers, the manager of a movie house was sentenced to pay 10,000 (old) francs in fines and 10,000 (old) francs in damages for displaying film posters, "contrary to decency" ("Jugement du 29 mars 1957," in *Compte Rendu . . . 1958*, 34).

120. Association Nationale du Cinéma pour l'Enfance et la Jeunesse, "Premières Réalisations Pratiques," CAC: 860430, art. 1.

121. Ministre de l'Information, "Contrôle des films cinématographiques," 1952–59, CAC: 760173, art. 40.

122. "Commission d'enquêtes et d'études sur la réforme de la réglementation du contrôle des films cinématographiques," p. 8, CAC: 760173, art. 36.

123. Comité d'Etudes Cinématographiques, "Note sur le projet de réforme de la censure," p. 2, CAC: 760173, art. 36.

124. Union Féminine Civique et Sociale, "Note rélative au cinéma," December 1959, p. 2, CAC: 760173, art. 36.

125. "Décret 61-63 du 18 janvier 1961 concernant l'accés des mineurs aux salles de cinéma," in *Lois et décrets*.

126. There are publishers who have difficulty with the commission from time to time, notably the comic book publisher Elvifrance, which has a Web page dedicated to challenging the commission and the 1949 law (see http://perso.club-internet.fr/poncetd/CENSURE/EF_CENSURE.htm). In 1999, the Centre National de la Bande Déssinée et de l'Image (CNBDI), in Angoulême, even held a conference— "50 Years of Censorship?"—which brought together academics, artists, and publishers to discuss the history, merits, and failings of the 1949 law (see Chavdia, *"On tue à chaque page!"*).

127. This resurgence was not simply about the reemergence of erotic or violent content in comic books, however. There was a greater appreciation in the sixties for the draftsmanship and artistic quality of comics as well. Most influential, perhaps, was the work of Moebius (Jean Giraud), who began to publish his serials in the mid-1960s, emphasizing artistic design and vision over text and plot. Moreover, this coincided with a more general rehabilitation of comics as an artistic and literary medium. Over the course of the sixties, a series of critical studies championed comics as having artistic, sociological, historical, and literary merit. Clubs and salons emerged as critical forums to appreciate and promote comics, while the work of Francis Lacassin, for example, proclaimed comics to be the "ninth art," a term that has had lasting relevance. Jacques Marny placed comics within a long literary tradition, and Gérard Blanchard (among others) placed comics within the historical

trajectory of Western civilization, and French civilization in particular, from the Lascaux caves to the Bayeux tapestry and on. In 1967 the Musée des Arts Decoratifs even sponsored a special exhibit on comics. This rehabilitation solidified the domestic industry and helped to establish today's widespread acknowledgment and appreciation of comics in France (see Lacassin, *Pour un neuvième art*; Marny, *Le Monde étonnant des bandes dessinées*; Blanchard, *Histoire de la bande dessinée*; and the accompanying volume to the museum exhibit, *A History of the Comic Strip*, by Couperie and Horn).

128. Crépin, *"Haro sur le gangster!"*

EPILOGUE

1. *The Young Face of France*, 3, 63.

2. On 1 June 1958 the National Assembly voted to give Charles de Gaulle emergency powers to form a new government and, effectively, voted itself and the Fourth Republic out of power. The growing crisis in Algeria, which the Fourth Republic seemed incapable of resolving, combined with the interminable instability of government coalitions to undermine what remained of confidence in the Fourth Republic's parliamentary system of government. De Gaulle's immediate priority was the creation of a new constitution that increased the power of the presidency and the executive branch over that of the prime minister and the National Assembly. In September 1958 a national referendum provided de Gaulle and his new constitution with the large majority and public mandate he sought. The Fifth Republic was inaugurated. A second referendum, in 1962, established the president's election by direct universal suffrage, thus reinforcing de Gaulle's notion that the president's authority represented and was responsible to the French people rather than to political parties or parliamentary deputies.

3. Ambassade de France, *France and the Rising Generation*. There was also a marketing campaign in the American media that emphasized similar themes for the promotion of tourism in France (see Endy, *Cold War Holidays*, 154–55).

4. Hamon and Rotman, *Génération*, vol. 1, *Les Années du rêve récit*, 43–44.

5. The Institut Français d'Opinion Publique (IFOP) continued to conduct social scientific surveys, polls, and inquests seeking to reveal the attitudes, tastes, behaviors, temperaments, and feelings of the young. One such study was published in 1962, while the next, ironically, was published in the spring of 1968. There were, as well, other publications of the survey/interview format, such as *La Génération du twist et la presse française* (1962), which reprinted excerpts from a myriad of press articles as part of the "History Day by Day" series. Also, the Centre d'Etudes Politiques et Civiques published a study called *La Jeunesse d'aujourd'hui* (1964). In 1965 Natacha and Jean Duché published *Des jeunes filles parlent*, which featured the monologues of twenty-six young women aged fifteen to twenty-four describing their backgrounds, lives, and attitudes towards sex, marriage, and the future.

6. This worry, expressed in the *mal du siècle* and delinquency debates of the 1950s, continued with such works as Emile Copfermann's *La Génération des blousons noirs* (1962) and Antonin Bondat's *La Crise de la jeunesse* (1965), which both predicted ill-fated destinies for France due to its depraved youth. Meanwhile, other works examined youth as constituting a new social body for France; these included Jean Jousselin's *Une Nouvelle jeunesse française* (1966), Gérard Marin's *Les Nouveaux français* (1967), and Jérôme Ferrand's *La Jeunesse* (1968).

7. For a detailed analysis of the political significance of symbols, see Kertzer, *Ritual, Politics, and Power*.

8. Queneau, *Zazie dans le Metro*.

9. Jacques Marny's *Les Adolescents d'aujourd'hui* (1965) sought to decipher, decode, and explain this phenomenon for adult France. For an overview of the 1960s youth culture, see Sohn, *Age tendre et tête de bois*.

10. The introduction of the 45 rpm single, the prevalence of concert touring, and the new radio program gave this youthful and energetic music inroads into France, though it arrived a little later there than in Germany or Britain. Elvis Presley, Johnny Hallyday, and Françoise Hardy became early staples of the ranked singles countdown.

11. *Salut les copains!* organized, publicized, and standardized the French pop youth culture of the early 1960s; see Pascal Ory, *L'Aventure culturelle française 1945–1989*, 156–57. The Filipacchi quote is from Marwick, *The Sixties*, 101–2.

12. Marwick, *The Sixties*, 104–5; see also Sirinelli, *Les Baby-boomers*.

13. See Marwick, *The Sixties*, 105.

14. See Ory, *L'Aventure culturelle française*, 18; Popkin, *A History of Modern France*, 323; and Gilbert Salachas, "Interview d'Alain de Sédouy," *Presse Actualité*, March–April 1973, 12–21. I want to thank Tamara Matheson for providing me with the latter material.

15. Morin, *Commune en France*, 149.

16. See, for example, Pomfret, "'A Muse for the Masses'"; and Pomfret, *Young People and the European City*.

17. One famous example involves François Missoffe, the Minister of Youth and Sports, who came to Nanterre in January 1968 to inaugurate the opening of a swimming pool. He was confronted by Daniel Cohn-Bendit, among others, who demanded to know why Missoffe and his ministry failed to address the issue of sexuality for the young. In response, Missoffe retorted: "With your looks, no wonder you have a problem. But you can always take a dip in the swimming pool to cool off." This response typified the Fifth Republic's attitude toward all matters that the young raised as problems or issues of youth that should be open for debate and discussion (Missoffe is quoted in Brown, *Protest in Paris*, 6; and Mossuz-Lavau, *Les lois de l'amour*, 142–45). There are more examples as well; Michael Seidman traces several, particularly the conflicts over dormitories, in *The Imaginary Revolution*.

18. Michael Seidman makes an argument for seeing 1968 as a culmination of

the activity of the 1960s, or at least as an event of continuity as opposed to one of rupture (see Seidman, *The Imaginary Revolution*).

19. One of the legacies of 1968 was to force open the door to this type of examination; see chapter 3 in Ruosso, *The Vichy Syndrome*.

20. "Europe: Youth Rebels," *L'Express*, 22–28 April 1968.

21. The most prominent of these is the two-volume work by Hamon and Rotman, *Génération*. But a recent counterpart is Sirinelli, *Les Baby-boomers*. Sirinelli takes issue with Hamon and Rotman, claiming that their "generation" was not really at the core of 1968, and that it was the younger, "baby-boomer generation" born between 1945 and 1953 that was at the heart of the struggle. Kristin Ross marvelously critiques this sociologic familial interpretation and the related "confessional narratives" in *May '68 and Its Afterlives*.

22. Though Daniel Cohn-Bendit was known as "Danny the Red," he did not identify himself as a Communist but as an anarchist. Apparently, his nickname had originated from his hair color rather than his political predilections.

23. Viénet, *Enragés and Situationists in the Occupation Movement, France, May 1968*, 77.

24. For an in-depth account of the depoliticized representations and reductive circumscriptions of 1968, see Ross, *May '68 and Its Afterlives*.

25. Aron, *The Elusive Revolution*.

26. See Ross, *May '68 and Its Afterlives*.

27. See, for example, the political polemic of Michel Field and Jean-Marie Brohm, *Jeunesse & révolution*.

Bibliography

ARCHIVAL SOURCES CONSULTED

Archives Nationales, Paris (AN)

F1a: Actes Constitutionnels, Lois, d'Ecrits et Arrêtes, 1940–1952

F2: Reconstruction

F17: Haut-Commissariat à la Jeunesse et aux Sports

F42: Cinéma

F44: Jeunesse et Sports

F60: Dossiers de Procédure Législative

Bibliothèque de l'Histoire de la Ville de Paris (BHVP)

Bibliothèque du Film, Paris (BiFi)

Bibliothèque Nationale de France, Paris (BNF)

Centre des Archives Contemporaine à Fontainebleau, Seine-et-Marne (CAC)

Ministère de la Jeunesse et des Sports

F44bis

790592

860419

860430

860446

900208

900210

Ministère de l'Education Nationale

840754

840756

910258

910333

Ministère du Culture

    840231

Santé et Protection Sociale

    760173

    760177

    760179

    770393

Services du Premier Ministre

    790447

    810076

Centre Nationale de la Bande-Dessinée et de l'Image, Angoulême, France (CNBDI)

Service Historique de l'Armée de Terre à Vincennes (VIN)

    Etat-Major de l'Armée de Terre (1945–1972)

        7T: 1er Bureau: Sections effectifs—Recrutement et législation—Personnels puis (1973); Bureau Effectifs—Personnels puis (1992); Bureau de Planification des Resources Humaines; Bureau des Personnels Civils

        19T: Direction des Personnels Militaire de l'Armée de Terre

        1R: Cabinet du Ministre de la Défense

        2R: Cabinet du Secrétaire d'Etat aux Forces Armées "Terre"

        4Q: Etat-Major de la Défense Nationale (1944–1948)

        9R: Contrôle de l'Armée de la Terre

        16R: Commission Armées-Jeunesse; Commission Permanente de Publication et de Refonte du Bulletin Officiel des Armées

UNESCO Library and Archives, Paris

PERIODICALS: NEWSPAPERS, JOURNALS, REVIEWS, MAGAZINES

Arguments
Art Ménager et Culinaires
Art Ménagers
Arts
L'Aube (Paris)
La Bataille (Lille)
Cahiers du Cinéma
Les Cahiers Français
Cahiers Pédagogiques
Ciné Jeunes
Cinéma
Coeurs Vaillants
Combat (Paris)
Contacts Electriques
Critiques
La Croisade de la Presse
La Croix
Dernière Heure (Algiers)
La Documentation Française Illustré
Le Drapeau Rouge (Paris)
L'Ecole des Parents
Educateurs
Education Nationale
Elle
Enfance
Esprit
L'Express
Fascicules Armée-Jeunesse
Le Figaro (Paris)
Le Figaro Littéraire (Paris)
Flash
Foi Education
Force Ouvrière (Paris)
France Catholique (Paris)
France Illustration
France-Observateur (Paris)
Frivolet
L'Humanité (Paris)
L'Humanité-Dimanche (Paris)

Information Sociales
Inter
Jeune Europe
Journal Officiel
La Laterne
Les Lettres Françaises (Paris)
Libération (Paris)
Marie France
Le Monde (Paris)
Mon Journal
La Nef
Les Nouvelles Littéraires (Paris)
Parallèle
Paris Comoedia
Le Parisien Libéré (Paris)
Paris Jour
Paris-Presse
Pas à Pas
La Pensée
La Pensée et L'Action
Le Peuple
Le Populaire (Paris)
Pour la Vie
La Presse (Paris)
La Presse Française: Jurisprudence
Prospective
Radio-Cinéma-Télévision
Rééducation
Salut les Copains!
Samedi-Soir (Paris)
Sauvegarde
Soulèvement de la Jeunesse (Paris)
Tarzan
Technique, Arts, Sciences
Les Temps Modernes
Time
Travailleuses Familiales
Vers l'Education Nouvelle
Votre Enfant

OTHER SOURCES

Alaimo, Kathleen. "Adolescence in the Popular Milieu in France during the Early Third Republic: Efforts to Define and Shape a Stage of Life." Ph.D. diss., University of Wisconsin, 1988.

Alleg, Henri. *The Question*. New York: G. Braziller, 1958.

Amar, Marianne. *Nés pour courir: Sport, pouvoir et rebellions, 1944–1958*. Grenoble: Presses Universitaire de Grenoble, 1987.

Ambassade de France. *France and the Rising Generation*. New York: Service de Presse et d'Information, 1965.

Andrieu, Claire, Lucette Le Van, and Antoine Prost, eds. *Les Nationalisations de la Libération: De l'utopie au compromis*. Paris: Presses de la Fondation Nationale des Sciences Politiques, 1987.

Ariès, Philippe. *Centuries of Childhood: A Social History of Family Life*. Translated by Robert Baldick. New York: Vintage Books, 1962. Originally published as *L'Enfant et la vie familiale sous l'ancien régime* (Paris: Librairie Plon, 1960).

Armand, Louis, and Michel Drancourt. *Plaidoyer pour l'avenir*. Paris: Calmann-Levy, 1961.

Aron, Raymond. *The Elusive Revolution: Anatomy of a Student Revolt*. Translated by Gordon Clough. New York: Praeger, 1969.

Augustin, Jean-Pierre, and Jacques Ion. *Des loisirs et des jeunes: Cent ans de groupements éducatifs et sportifs*. Paris: Les Editions Ouvrières, 1993.

Austin, Joe, and Micheal Nevin Willard, eds. *Generations of Youth: Youth Cultures and History in Twentieth-Century America*. New York: New York University Press, 1998.

Autant-Lara, Claude. *Le Blé en herbe* [Ripening Seed]. 1953. Film. (VHS available from René Chateau Video, France)

———. *En Cas de malheur* [Love Is My Profession]. 1958. Film. (VHS/DVD available from René Chateau Video, France)

Azéma, Jean-Pierre. *From Munich to the Liberation, 1938–1944*. Translated by Janet Lloyd. New York: Cambridge University Press, 1984.

Azéma, Jean-Pierre, and Olivier Wieviorka. *Vichy, 1940–1944*. Paris: Perrin, 1997.

Babcock, Arthur E. *The New Novel in France: Theory and Practice of the Nouveau Roman*. New York: Twayne Publishers, 1997.

Baecque, Antoine de. "L'Homme nouveau est arrivé: La 'Régéneration' du français en 1789." *Dix-Huitième Siècle* 20 (1988): 193–208.

———. *La Nouvelle Vague: Portrait d'une jeunesse*. Paris: Flammarion, 1998.

———. "La Révolution française et les âges de la vie." In *Age et politique*, edited by Annick Percheron and Réné Rémond. Paris: Economica, 1991.

Bailleau, Francis. *Les Jeunes face à la justice pénale: Analyse critique de l'application de l'ordonnance de 1945*. Paris: Syros, 1996.

Barker, Martin. *Comics: Ideology, Power, and the Critics*. Manchester, U.K.: Manchester University Press, 1989.

———. *A Haunt of Fears: The Strange History of the British Horror Comics Campaign*. London: Pluto, 1984.

Barsamain, Jacques. *L'Age d'or du yéyé: Le Rock, le twist, et le variété française des années 60*. Paris: Ramsay, 1983.

Barthes, Roland. "Les Deux critiques." In *Essais critiques*. Paris: Le Seuil, 1964.

———. "Littérature objective." *Critiques* 10 (July–August 1954): 581–91.

Batigny, Ludivine. "Pierre Mendès-France et les jeunes: Leur soutien est ce que j'ai de plus précieux." *Matériaux pour l'Histoire de Notre Temps* 63–64 (July–December 2001): 148–54.

Bauchard, Philippe. *La Presse, le film, et la radio pour enfants*. Paris: UNESCO, 1952.

Bauche, Freddy. *Claude Autant-Lara*. Paris: Editions L'Age d'Homme, 1982.

Beauvoir, Simone de. *Brigitte Bardot and the Lolita Syndrome*. New York: Reynal, 1959.

———. *Force of Circumstance*. Vol. 1, *After the War, 1944–1952*. Translated by Richard Howard. [1965]. Reprint, New York: Harper Colophon Editions, 1977.

———. *Force of Circumstance*. Vol. 2, *Hard Times, 1952–1962*. Translated by Richard Howard. [1965]. Reprint, St. Paul, MN: Paragon House, 1971.

———. *The Second Sex*. Translated and edited by H. M. Parshley. [1952]. Reprint, New York: Vintage Books, 1989.

Beauvoir, Simon de, and Gisele Halimi, eds. *Djamila Boupacha*. Paris: Gallimard, 1962.

Becker, Jacques. *Rendez-vous de juillet* [July Rendezvous]. 1949. Film. (VHS available from Water Bearer Films; DVD available from Studio Canal, France)

Becker, Jean-Jacques, and Serge Berstein. *Victoire et frustrations, 1914–1929*. Paris: Editions du Seuil, 1990.

Becker, Lucille Frackman. *Françoise Mallet-Joris*. Boston: Twayne Publishers, 1985.

Beever, Antony, and Artemis Cooper. *Paris after the Liberation: 1944–1949*. London: Penguin Books, 1994.

Beneath the Paving Stones: Situationists and the Beach, May 1968: Texts. Collected by Dark Star. London: Dark Star, 2001.

Bénéton, Philippe. "La Génération de 1912–1914: Image, myth et réalité." *Revue Française de Science Politique* 21 (October 1971): 981–1009.

Berge, André. *L'Éducation sexuelle chez l'enfant*. Paris: Presse Universitaires de France, 1952.

Berlanstein, Leonard. "Vagrants, Beggars, and Thieves: Delinquent Boys in Mid-Nineteenth Century Paris." *Journal of Social History* 17 (Summer 1992): 531–52.

Bernège, Paulette. *De la méthode ménagère*. Paris: Dunod, 1928.

Blanchard, Gérard. *Histoire de la bande dessinée: Une Histoire des histories en images de la préhistoire à nos jours*. Paris: L'Inter, 1969.

Bloch, Marc. *Strange Defeat*. Translated by Gerard Hopkins. London: Oxford University Press, 1949.

Bodiguet, Jean-Luc. *Les Anciens élèves de l'ENA*. Paris: Presses de la Fondation Nationale des Sciences Politiques, 1978.

Bollon, Patrice. *Morale du masque: Merveilleux, zazous, dandys, punk, etc.* Paris: Editions du Seuil, 1990.

Boltansky, Luc. *The Making of a Class: Cadres in French Society.* Translated by Arthur Goldhammer. Cambridge: Cambridge University Press, 1987.

Bonamy, Bernadette. "Pour une histoire des Travailleuse Familiales rurales et populaires." *Les Cahiers du GRMF* 3 (1985): 291–310.

———. *La Travailleuse Familiale: Taches et interrogations d'une profession sociale.* Toulouse: Editions Eres, 1986.

Bondat, Antonin. *La Crise de la jeunesse.* Paris: Editions du Cerf, 1965.

Borneque, André-Raymond, ed. *La Presse et l'équilibre moral des jeunes.* Paris: ERF, 1959.

Bourdieu, Pierre. "Youth Is Just a Word." In *Sociology in Question.* Translated by Richard Nice. London: Sage Publications, 1993.

Bourdieu, Pierre, and Jean-Claude Passeron. *The Inheritors: French Students and Their Relation to Culture.* Translated by Richard Nice. Chicago: University of Chicago Press, 1979.

Brake, Mike. *The Sociology of Youth Culture and Youth Subcultures.* London: Routledge and Kegan Paul, 1980.

Bresson, Robert. *Pickpocket.* 1959. Film. (DVD available from Criterion Collection, no. PIC150)

Britton, Celia. *The Nouveau Roman: Fiction, Theory, and Politics.* New York: St. Martin's Press, 1992.

Brown, Bernard E. *Protest in Paris: Anatomy of a Revolt.* New York: General Learning Press, 1974.

Brubaker, Rogers. *Citizenship and Nationhood in France and Germany.* Cambridge, MA: Harvard University Press, 1992.

Burrin, Philippe. *France under the Germans: Collaboration and Compromise.* Translated by Janet Lloyd. New York: New Press, 1996.

Callander, Margaret M. *Le Blé en herbe and La Chatte.* London: Grant and Cutler, 1992.

Campbell, Beth M. "High Fashion and the Reconstruction of Postwar France, 1945–1960." Ph.D. diss., Rutgers University, 1998.

Camus, Albert. *Between Hell and Reason: Essays from the Resistance Newspaper Combat, 1944–1947.* Selected and translated by Alexandre de Gramont. Hanover, NH: Wesleyan University Press, 1991.

Carné, Marcel. *Les Tricheurs* [The Cheaters]. 1958. Film. (DVD available from Studio Canal, France)

Cayatte, André. *Avant le déluge.* Film. 1954. (VHS available from www.Amazon.fr)

Chabrol, Claude. *L'Oeil de Vichy* [The Eye of Vichy]. New York: First Run Features, 1993. (VHS/DVD)

Chabrol, Véronique. "L'Ambition de 'Jeune France'." *Les Cahiers de L'Institut d'Histoire du Temps Present* 8 (June 1988): 105–16.

Champagne, Roland A. "Jean Genet in the Delinquent Colony of Mettray: The Development of an Ethical Rite of Passage." *French Forum* 26, no. 3 (Fall 2001): 72–90.

Charlot, Bernard, and Madeleine Figeat. *Histoire de la formation des ouvriers, 1789–1984.* Paris: Minerve, 1985.

Chauvière, Maurice. *Enfance inadaptée: L'Héritage de Vichy.* Paris: Les Editions Ouvrières, 1980.

Chavdia, Christophe, ed. *On tue à chaque page!: La Loi de 1949 sur les publications destinées à la jeunesse.* Paris: Editions du Temps, 1999.

Chazal, Jean. *L'Enfance délinquante.* Que sais-je?, no. 563. Paris: Presses Universitaires de France, 1958.

Childers, Kristen Stromberg. *Fathers, Families, and the State in France, 1914–1945.* Ithaca, NY: Cornell University Press, 2003.

Clément, René. *Jeux interdits* [Forbidden Games]. 1952. Film. (DVD available from Criterion Collection, no. FOR230)

Closon, Francis-Louis. *Un Homme nouveau: L'Ingenieur-économiste.* Paris: Presses Universitaires de France, 1961.

Cocteau, Jean. *La Belle et la bête* [Beauty and the Beast]. 1946. Film. (DVD available from Criterion Collection, no. BEA130)

———. *Diary of a Film: La Belle et la bête.* Translated by Ronald Duncan. New York: Roy Publishers, 1950.

Cohen, Paul. "Heroes and Dilettantes: The Action Française, Le Sillon, and the Generation of 1905–1914." *French Historical Studies* 15 (Fall 1988): 673–87.

Commission Ministerielle d'Etude. *La Réforme de l'Enseignement: Projet soumis à M. Le Ministre de l'Education Nationale.* Paris: Ministère de l'Education Nationale, 1947.

Compain, Eva. *La Science de la Maison: Cours d'enseignement ménager théorique et pratique.* Paris: Les Editions Foucher, 1946.

Compte Rendu des travaux de la commission de surveillance et de contrôle des publications destinées à l'enfance et à l'adolescence au cours de l'année 1950. Melun: Imprimerie Administrative, 1950.

Compte Rendu des travaux de la commission de surveillance et de contrôle des publications destinées à l'enfance et à l'adolescence au cours de l'année 1954. Melun: Imprimerie Administrative, 1954.

Compte Rendu des travaux de la commission de surveillance et de contrôle des publications destinées à l'enfance et à l'adolescence au cours de l'année 1958. Melun: Imprimerie Administrative, 1958.

The Condition of Women in France, 1945 to the Present: A Documentary Anthology. Selected and edited by Claire Laubier. London: Routledge, 1990.

Copferman, Emile. *La Génération des blousons noirs: Problèmes de la jeunesee française.* Paris: François Maspero, 1962.

Couperie, Pierre, and Maurice C. Horn. *A History of the Comic Strip*. New York: Crown Publishers, 1968.

Courtivron, Isabelle de. *Violette Leduc*. Boston: Twayne Publishers, 1985.

Cova, Anne. "French Feminism and Maternity: Theories and Policies, 1890–1918." In *Maternity and Gender Politics: Women and the Rise of European Welfare States, 1880s-1950s*, edited by Gisela Bock and Pat Thane. London: Routledge, 1991.

Cowans, Jon. "Fear and Loathing in Paris: The Reception of Opinion Polling in France, 1938–1977." *Social Science History* 26, no. 1 (Spring 2002): 71–104.

———. "French Public Opinion and the Founding of the Fourth Republic." *French Historical Studies* 17 (Spring 1991): 62–95.

———. "Visions of the Postwar: The Politics of Memory and Expectation in 1940s France." *History and Memory* 10 (Fall 1998): 68–101.

Crawley, Tony. *Bébé: The Films of Brigitte Bardot*. London: LSP Books, 1975.

Crépin, Thierry. *"Haro sur le gangster!" La Moralisation de la presse enfantine, 1934–1954*. Paris: CNRS, 2001.

———. "Le Myth d'un front commun." In *On tue à chaque page!: La Loi de 1949 sur les publications destinées à la jeunesse*, edited by Christophe Chavdia. Paris: Editions du Temps, 1999.

Crête, Jean, and Pierre Favre, eds. *Générations et politiques*. Paris: Economica, 1989.

Crouzet, Paul. *Bachelières ou jeunes filles?* Paris: Privat-Didier, 1949.

Crozier, Michel. *The World of the Office Worker*. Translated by David Landau. Chicago: University of Chicago Press, 1971.

Crubellier, Maurice. *L'Enfance et la jeunesse dans la société française, 1800–1950*. Paris: A. Colin, 1979.

Danan, Alexis. *Maisons de supplices*. Paris: Denoël et Steele, 1936.

Dank, Milton. *The French against the French: Collaboration and Resistance*. Philadelphia: Lippincott, 1974.

Day, Charles R. *Schools and Work: Technical and Vocational Education in France since the Third Republic*. Montreal: McGill-Queen's University Press, 2001.

Debré, Michel. *Trois républiques pour une France*. Paris: Albin Michel, 1984.

Donzelot, Jacques. *The Policing of Families*. Translated by Robert Hurley. Baltimore: Johns Hopkins University Press, 1979.

Douin, Jean-Luc, ed. *La Nouvelle Vague 25 ans après*. Paris: Cerf, 1983.

Downs, Laura Lee. *Childhood in the Promised Land: Working-Class Movements and the Colonies de Vacances in France, 1880–1960*. Durham, NC: Duke University Press, 2002.

Dreyfus, François G. *Histoire de Vichy*. Paris: Perrin, 1990.

Druon, Maurice. *L'Avenir en désarroi*. Paris: Librarie Plon, 1968.

Duché, Natacha, and Jean Duché. *Des jeunes filles parlent*. Paris: Flammarion, 1965.

Duchen, Claire. "Occupation Housewife: The Domestic Ideal in 1950s France." *French Cultural Studies* 2 (February 1991): 1–12.

————. *Women's Rights and Women's Lives in France, 1944–1968*. London: Routledge, 1994.

Duquesne, Jacques, and the Institut Français d'Opinion Publique (IFOP). *Les 16–24 ans*. Paris: Editions du Centurion, 1963.

Edwards, Nancy Jocelyn. "The Science of Domesticity: Women, Education, and National Identity in Third Republic France, 1880–1914." Ph.D. diss., University of California at Berkeley, 1997.

Endy, Christopher. *Cold War Holidays: American Tourism in France*. Chapel Hill, NC: University of North Carolina Press, 2004.

Etudes Sociales Nord Africaines. *Les Jeunes nord-africains en métropole*. Paris: 1955.

Evans, Martin. *The Memory of Resistance: French Opposition to the Algerian War, 1954–1962*. New York: Berg, 1997.

Farmer, Sarah. *Martyred Village: Commemorating the 1944 Massacre at Oradour-sur-Glane*. Berkeley: University of California Press, 1999.

Ferdinand, Roger. *Ils ont vingt ans*. Paris: M. Céalis, 1948.

————. *Les J3 ou La Nouvelle Ecole*. Paris: Librarie Théatrale, 1944.

Ferrand, Jérôme. *La Jeunesse: Nouveau tiers état*. Paris: Robert Laffont, 1968.

Feuer, Lewis S. *The Conflict of Generations: The Character and Significance of Student Movements*. New York: Basic Books, 1969.

Field, Michel, and Jean-Maris Brohm. *Jeunesse & révolution: Pour une organisation révolutionnaire de la jeunesse*. Paris: Librarie François Maspero, 1975.

Filippini, Henri. *Les Années cinquante*. Grenoble: Editions J. Glénat, 1977.

Fishman, Sarah. "Absent Fathers and Family Breakdown: Delinquency in Vichy France." In *Becoming Delinquent: British and European Youth, 1650–1950*, edited by Pamela Cox and Heather Shore. Burlington, VT: Ashgate, 2002.

————. *The Battle for Children: World War II, Youth Crime, and Juvenile Justice in Twentieth-Century France*. Cambridge, MA: Harvard University Press, 2002.

————. "Juvenile Delinquency as a 'Condition': Social Science Constructions of the Child Criminal, 1936–1946." *Proceedings of the Western Society for French History: Selected Papers of the Annual Meeting*. Boulder: University of Colorado Press, 1997.

————. "Youth in Vichy France: The Juvenile Crime Wave and its Implications." In *France at War: Vichy and the Historians*, edited by Sarah Fishman, Laura Lee Downs, Ioannis Sinanoglou, Leonard V. Smith, and Robert Zaretsky. Oxford: Berg, 2000.

Flanner, Janet. *Paris Journal: 1944–1965*. Edited by William Shawn. New York: Atheneum, 1965.

Flynn, George Q. "Conscription and Equity in Western Democracies, 1940–1975." *Journal of Contemporary History* 33, no. 1 (January 1998): 5–20.

Fondation Charles de Gaulle. *Charles de Gaulle et la jeunesse: Colloque international*. Paris: Plon, 2005.

Footit, Hilary, and John Simmonds. *The Politics of Liberation: France, 1943–1945.* New York: Holmes and Meier, 1988.

Forment, Alain. *Histoire de la presse des jeunes et des journaux d'enfants (1768–1988).* Paris: Editions Eole, 1987.

Fornäs, Johan, and Göran Bolin, eds. *Youth Culture in Late Modernity.* London: Sage, 1995.

Fouilhe, Pierre. *Journaux d'enfants, journaux pour rire?* Paris: Centre d'Activité Pédagogique, 1955.

Fourie, Jean. "Les Effets de la loi de 1949." *Le Collectioneur de Bandes-Dessinées* 57/58 (1988): 16–18.

Fournier, Christiane. *Nos Enfants sont-ils des monstres?* Paris: Fayard, 1959.

Fox, Barbara. "Rejuvenating France: The Creation of a National Youth Culture after the Great War." Ph.D. diss., University of Massachusetts, Amherst, 2002.

French, Sean. *Bardot.* London: Pavilion, 1994.

Friedmann, Georges. *Problèmes humains du machinisme industriel.* Paris: Gallimard, 1946.

Frith, Simon. *Sound Effects: Youth, Leisure, and the Politics of Rock 'n' Roll.* New York: Pantheon, 1981.

Frost, Robert L. "Machine Liberation: Inventing Housewives and Home Appliances in Interwar France." *French Historical Studies* 18, no. 1 (April 1993): 109–30.

Furet, François, and Jacques Ozouf. *Reading and Writing: Literacy in France from Calvin to Jules Ferry.* Cambridge: Cambridge University Press, 1982.

Furlough, Ellen. "Selling the American Way in Interwar France: Prix Uniques and the Salon des Art Ménagers." *Journal of Social History* 26 (Spring 1993): 491–520.

Gabrysiak, Michel. *Cadres qui êtes-vous?* Paris: Robert Laffont, 1968.

Galland, Olivier. *Les Jeunes.* Paris: Editions La Découverte, 1984.

Gandy, Alain. *La Jeunesse et la Résistance: Réseau Orion, 1940–1944.* Paris: Presses de la Cité, 2001.

The Gangrene. Translated by Robert Silvers. New York: Lyle Stuart, [1960].

Garrier, Gilbert. *Histoire sociale et culturelle du vin.* Paris: Bordas, 1995.

La Génération du twist et la presse française. Paris: Editions Galic, 1962.

"Generations." Special Issue, *Daedalus* 107 (Fall 1978).

"Les Générations." Special issue, *Vingtième Siècle* 22 (April–June 1989).

Genet, Jean. *L'Enfant criminel.* Paris: Paul Morihien, 1949.

———. *The Thief's Journal.* Translated by Bernard Frechtman. New York: Grove Press, 1964.

Géoris, Michel. *Françoise Mallet-Joris, essai, suivi de Une inconnue, Françoise Lilar, poetesse de quinze ans, par Frédéric Keisel.* Collections Portraits, no. 7. [Brussels]: Pierre De Méyère, [1964].

Gilbert, James. *A Cycle of Outrage: America's Reaction to the Juvenile Delinquent in the 1950s.* New York: Oxford University Press, 1986.

Giles, Frank. *The Locust Years: The Story of the Fourth French Republic, 1946–1958*. London: Secker and Warburg, 1991.

Gillain, Anne. "The Script of Delinquency: François Truffaut's *Les 400 Coups* (1959)." In *French Film: Texts and Contexts*, edited by Susan Hayward and Ginette Vincendeau. London: Routledge, 1990.

Gillis, John R. *Youth and History: Tradition and Change in European Age Relations, 1770–Present*. New York: Academic Press, 1974.

Giroud, Françoise. "La Fondation de 'L'Express.'" *L'Histoire* 109 (March 1988): 92–94.

———. *I Give You My Word*. Translated by Richard Seaver. Boston: Houghton Mifflin, 1974.

———. *La Nouvelle Vague: Portraits de la jeunesse*. Paris: Gallimard, 1958.

Godard, Jean-Luc. *A Bout de souffle* [Breathless]. Film. 1960. (DVD available from Fox Lorber)

Gordon, Bertram M. *Collaboration in France during the Second World War*. Ithaca, NY: Cornell University Press, 1980.

Gorsuch, Anne E. *Youth in Revolutionary Russia: Enthusiasts, Bohemians, Delinquents*. Bloomington, IN: Indiana University Press, 2000.

Grall, Xavier. *La Génération du djebel*. Paris: Les Editions du Cerf, 1962.

Granet, Marie. *Les Jeunes dans la Résistance: 20 ans en 1940*. Paris: Editions France-Empire, 1985.

Groensteen, Thierry. *Astérix, Barbarella & Cie: Trésors du musée de la bande dessinée d'Angoulême*. Paris: Somogy Editions d'Art, 2000.

Guinot, Jean-Pierre. *Formation professionnelle et travailleurs qualifiés depuis 1789*. Paris: Editions Domat-Montchrestien, 1946.

Gunther, Scott. "The Elastic Closet: Legal Censure and Auto-Censure of Homosexuality in France." Ph.D. diss., New York University, 2001.

Gurrieri, Georgia Gloria. "New Waves: Literature and Cinema in Postwar Paris." Ph.D. diss., University of Iowa, 1992.

Hall, Stuart, and Tony Jefferson, eds. *Resistance through Rituals: Youth Subcultures in Postwar Britain*. London: Hutchinson and Co., 1975.

Halls, W. D. *The Youth of Vichy France*. Oxford: Clarendon, 1981.

Hamon, Hervé, and Patrick Rotman. *Génération*. 2 vols. Paris: Editions du Seuil, 1987.

———. *Les Porteurs de valises: La Résistance française à la guerre d'Algérie*. Paris: Albin Michel, 1979.

Hanoteau, Guillaume. *L'Age d'or de Saint-Germain-des-Prés*. Paris: Editions Denoël, 1965.

Hause, Steven C., and Anne R. Kenney. *Women's Suffrage and Social Politics in the French Third Republic*. Princeton, NJ: Princeton University Press, 1984.

Hebdige, Dick. *Subculture: The Meaning of Style*. London: Routledge, 1979.

Hecht, Gabrielle. *The Radiance of France: Nuclear Power and National Identity after World War II.* Cambridge, MA: MIT Press, 1998.

Heller-Goldenberg, Lucette. "Histoire des Auberges de Jeunesse en France des origins à la Libération (1929–1945)." Thèse doctorat d'Etat, Université de Nice, 1985.

Hellman, John. *The Communitarian Third Way: Alexandre Marc's Ordre Nouveau, 1930–2000.* Montreal: McGill-Queen's University Press, 2002.

———. *The Knight-Monks of Vichy France: Uriage, 1940–1945.* Montreal: McGill-Queen's University Press, 1993.

Histoire de la bande dessinée en France et en Belgique: Des origins à nos jours. Edited by Henri Filippini et al. Grenoble: Editions J. Glénat, 1979.

A History of Young People in the West. Edited by Giovanni Levi and Jean-Claude Schmitt. 2 vols. Vol. 1 translated by Camille Naish; vol. 2 translated by Carol Volk. Cambridge, MA: The Belknap Press of Harvard University Press, 1997.

Hitchcock, William I. *France Restored: Cold War Diplomacy and the Quest of Leadership in Europe, 1944–1954.* Chapel Hill: University of North Carolina Press, 1998.

Hoffmann, Stanley, ed. "The Effects of World War II on French Society and Politics." *French Historical Studies* 2 (Spring 1961): 28–63.

———. "Paradoxes of the French Political Community." In *In Search of France*, edited by Stanley Hoffmann et al. Cambridge, MA: Harvard University Press, 1963.

Holt, Richard. *Sport and Society in Modern France.* Hamden, CT: Archon Books, 1981.

Holveck, Florent. "Jeune Alsace." *Sommaire*, Spring 1995.

Home, Stewart. *The Assault on Culture: Utopian Currents from Lettrisme to Class War.* London: Aporia Press and Underground Books, 1988.

Horn, Maurice C. "American Comics in France: A Cultural Evaluation." In *For Better or Worse: The American Influence in the World*, edited by Allen F. Davis. Westport, CT: Greenwood Press, 1981.

———. "Comics." In *Handbook of French Popular Culture*, edited by Pierre L. Horn. New York: Greenwood Press, 1991.

Horne, Alistair. *A Savage War of Peace: Algeria, 1954–1962.* New York: Viking Press, 1977.

Hourdin, Georges. *Le Cas Françoise Sagan.* Paris: Les Editions du Cerf, 1958.

Hughes, Alex. *Violette Leduc: Mothers, Lovers, and Language.* London: W. S. Maney and Son, 1994.

Isou, Isidore. "Les Manifestes du soulèvement de la jeunesse (1950–1966)." *Documents Lettristes* 8 (August 1983).

———. *La Stratégie du soulèvement de la jeunesse (1949–1968).* Paris: Centre International de Création Kladologique, 1968.

Jackson, Julian. *France: The Dark Years, 1949–1944*. New York: Oxford University Press, 2003.

———. *The Popular Front in France: Defending Democracy, 1934–1938*. Cambridge: Cambridge University Press, 1988.

Jacquier-Bruère [Michel Debré and Emmanuel Monick]. *Refaire la France: L'Effort d'une génération*. Paris: Plon, 1945.

Jaeger, Hans. "Generations in History: Reflections on a Controversial Concept." *History and Theory* 24 (1985): 273–92.

Jauffret, Jean-Charles. *Soldats en Algérie, 1954–1962*. Paris: Editions Autrement, 2000.

Jones, Christopher M. *Boris Vian Transatlantic: Sources, Myths, and Dreams*. New York: Peter Lang, 1998.

Jouhaud, Christian. "La 'Belle Epoque' et le cinéma." *Le Mouvement Social* 139 (April–June 1987): 107–13.

Journal officiel de la République Française: Débats parlementaires, Assemblée Nationales. Paris: Imprimerie des Journaux Officiels, 1946–79.

Journal officiel de la République Française: Lois et décrets. Paris: Imprimerie des Journaux Officiels, 1946–79.

Jousselin, Jean. *Jeunesse, fait social méconnu*. Paris: Stock, 1959.

———. *Une Nouvelle jeunesse française*. Paris: Editions Edouard Privat, 1966.

Judt, Tony. *Past Imperfect: French Intellectuals, 1944–1956*. Berkeley: University of California Press, 1992.

Kanters, Robert, and Gilbert Sigaux. *Vingt ans en 1951: Enquête sur la jeunesse française*. Paris: René Julliard, 1951.

Karnow, Stanley. *Paris in the Fifties*. New York: Times Books, 1997.

Kedward, H. R. *Resistance in Vichy France*. New York: Oxford University Press, 1978.

Kedward, H. R., and Roger Austin, eds. *Vichy France and the Resistance: Ideology and Culture*. Totowa, NJ: Barnes and Noble, 1985.

Kedward, H. R., and Nancy Wood, eds. *The Liberation of France: Image and Event*. Oxford: Berg Publishers, 1995.

Keniston, Kenneth. "Youth: A 'New' Stage of Life." *American Scholar* 39 (Autumn 1970): 631–54.

Kertzer, David I. *Ritual, Politics, and Power*. New Haven, CT: Yale University Press, 1988.

Kessler, Marie-Christine. *La Politique de la haute fonction publique*. Paris: Presses de la Fondation Nationale des Sciences Politiques, 1978.

Kindleberger, Charles. "The Postwar Resurgence of the French Economy." In *France: Change and Tradition*, edited by Stanley Hoffman et al. London: Victor Gallancz, 1963.

Klaus, Alisa. "Depopulation and Race Suicide: Maternalism and Pronatalist Ideologies in France and the United States." In *Mothers of a New World*, edited by Seth Koven and Sonya Michel. New York: Routledge, 1993.

Koreman, Megan. *Expectation of Justice: France, 1944–1946.* Durham, NC: Duke University Press, 1999.

Kriegel, Annie. "Generational Difference: The History of an Idea." *Deadalus* 107 (1978): 23–38.

Kuisel, Richard F. *Capitalism and the State in Modern France: Renovation and Economic Management in the Twentieth Century.* Cambridge: Cambridge University Press, 1981.

———. *Seducing the French: The Dilemma of Americanization.* Berkeley: University of California Press, 1993.

Lacassin, Francis. *Pour un neuvième art: La Bande dessinées.* Paris: Union Générale d'Editions, 1971.

Lacouture, Jean. *Pierre Mendès-France.* Translated by George Holoch. New York: Holmes and Meier, 1984.

Lagrou, Pieter. *The Legacy of Nazi Occupation: Patriotic Memory and National Recovery in Western Europe, 1945–1965.* Cambridge: Cambridge University Press, 2000.

Lanoux, Armand. *L'Enfant en proie aux images.* Paris: Association Nationale du Cinéma pour l'Enfance et la Jeunesse, 1949.

Lapierre, J. W., and Georges Noizet. *Le Civisme des jeunes.* Paris: Ophrys, 1961.

Laroque, Pierre, ed. *La Politique française en France depuis 1945.* Paris: La Documentation Française, 1985.

Le Béguec, Gilles. "Pierre Mendès-France et la technocratie." *Matériaux pour l'Histoire de Notre Temps* 63–64 (July–December 2001): 112–18.

———. "Les Premiers pas de la République des énarques." *Bulletin de l'Institut d'Histoire du Temps Présent* 71 (June 1998): 8–23.

Le Betorf, Hervé. *La Vie parisienne sous l'Occupation.* Paris: Editions France-Empire, 1997.

Lebovics, Herman. *Mona Lisa's Escort: André Malraux and the Reinterpretation of French Culture.* Ithaca, NY: Cornell University Press, 1999.

———. *True France: The Wars over Cultural Identity, 1900–1945.* Ithaca, NY: Cornell University Press, 1992.

Le Breton, Auguste. *Les Hauts murs.* Paris: Presses de la Cité, 1956.

Lebrigand, Yvette. "Les Archives du Salon des Arts Ménagers." *Bulletin de l'Institut d'Histoire du Temps Present* 26 (December 1986): 9–13.

Leduc, Violette. *La Bâtarde.* Translated by Derek Coltman. New York: Riverhead Books, 1965.

Lemalet, Martine, ed. *Lettres d'Algérie, 1954–1962: La Guerre des appelés, la mémoire d'une generation.* Paris: Edition Jean-Claude Lattés, 1992.

Lent, John A., ed. *Pulp Demons: International Dimensions of the Postwar Anti-Comics Campaign.* Teaneck, NJ: Fairleigh Dickinson University Press, 1999.

Lignière, Jean. *Françoise Sagan et le succès*. Paris: Les Editions du Scorpion, 1957.

Loiseau, Jean-Claude. *Les Zazous*. Paris: Le Sagittaire, 1977.

Looseley, David L. *The Politics of Fun: Cultural Policy and Debate in Contemporary France*. Oxford: Berg Publishers, 1995.

Lottman, Herbert R. *The Purge*. New York: William Morrow and Company, 1986.

Louis, Patrick. *Skinheads, Taggers, Zulus & Co*. Paris: La Table Ronde, 1990.

Loyer, Emmanuelle. *Le Théâtre citoyen de Jean Vilar: Une Utopie d'après-guerre*. Paris: Presses Universitaires de France, 1997.

Maier, Charles S. "The Two Postwar Eras and the Conditions for Stability in Twentieth-Century Western Europe." *American Historical Review* 86 (April 1981): 327–52.

Malle, Louis. *Les Amants* [The Lovers]. Film. 1958. (VHS available from New Yorker Video)

———. *Ascenseur pour l'échafaud* [Elevator to the Gallows]. 1957. Film. (DVD available from Criterion Collection, no. CC1627D)

Mallet-Joris, Françoise. *The Illusionist*. Translated by Herma Briffault. New York: Farrar, Strauss, and Young, 1975. Originally published as *Le Rempart des béguines* (Paris: Julliard, 1951).

Mannheim, Karl. "The Problems of Generations." In *From Karl Mannheim*, edited by Kurt H. Wolff. New Brunswick, NJ: Transaction Publishers, 1971.

Marin, Gérard. *Les Nouveaux français*. Paris: Editions Bernard Grasset, 1967.

Marly, Diana de. *Christian Dior*. New York: Holmes and Meier, 1990.

Marny, Jacques. *Les Adolescents d'aujourd'hui: Culture, loisirs, idoles, amours, religion*. Paris: Editions du Centurion, 1965.

———. *Le Monde étonnant des bandes dessinées*. Paris: Editions du Centurion, 1968.

Martin, Michel L. *Warriors to Managers: The French Military Establishment since 1945*. Chapel Hill: University of North Carolina Press, 1981.

Marwick, Arthur. *The Sixties: Cultural Revolution in Britain, France, Italy, and the United States, 1958–1974*. Oxford: Oxford University Press, 1998.

Mathiot, Ginette. *Comment enseigner l'éducation ménagère ou les elements de l'art de former une maitresse de maison*. Paris: Bibliothèque Pédagogique, 1957.

Mathy, Jean-Philippe. *French Resistance: The French-American Culture Wars*. Minneapolis: University of Minnesota Press, 2000.

Mauger, Gérard. *Hippies, loubards, zoulous: Jeunes marginaux de 1968 à aujourd'hui*. Paris: La Documentation Française, 1991.

———. *Les Jeunes en France: État des recherches*. Paris: La Documentation Française, 1994.

McCloud, Scott. *Understanding Comics: The Invisible Art*. Northhampton, MA: Kitchen Sink Press, 1993.

McMillan, James F. *Twentieth-Century France: Politics and Society, 1898–1991*. London: Edward Arnold, 1992.

McRobbie, Angela. *Feminism and Youth Culture: From "Jackie" to "Just Seventeen."* Boston: Unwin Hyman, 1991.

Mendès-France, Pierre. *A Modern French Republic.* Translated by Anne Carter. New York: Hill and Wang, 1963.

Meyer, Philippe. *The Child and the State: The Intervention of the State in Family Life.* Cambridge: Cambridge University Press, 1983.

Miller, James I. "Reconstructing the Nation in the Regions: State Planners, Immigration, and the Crucible of National Modernization in the Moselle, 1947–1962." Ph.D. diss., University of Chicago, 2005.

Miller, Judith Graves. *Françoise Sagan.* Boston: Twayne Publishers, 1988.

Milward, Alan S. *The New Order and the French Economy.* Oxford: Oxford University Press, 1970.

———. *The Reconstruction of Western Europe, 1945–1951.* Berkeley: University of California Press, 1984.

Mioche, Philippe. *Le Plan Monnet: Genèse et elaboration, 1941–1947.* Paris: Publications de la Sorbonne, 1987.

Mitterauer, Michael. *A History of Youth.* Translated by Graeme Dunphy. Oxford: Blackwell Publishers, 1992.

Monaco, James. *The New Wave: Truffaut, Godard, Chabrol, Rohmer, Rivette.* New York: Oxford University Press, 1976.

Moretti, Franco. *The Way of the World: The Bildungsroman in European Culture.* Translated by Albert Sbragia. London: Verso, 2000.

Morin, Edgar. *Commune en France: La Métamorphose de Plodémet.* Paris: Fayard, 1967.

———. *L'Esprit du temps.* Paris: Plon, 1962.

———. *The Stars.* Translated by Richard Howard. New York: Evergreen Press, 1960. Originally published as *Les Stars* (Paris: Editions du Seuil, 1957).

Mossuz-Lavau, Janine. *Les Lois de l'amour: Les Politiques de la sexualité en France de 1950 à nos jours.* Paris: Document Payot, 1991.

Mounier, Emmanuel. "La Jeunesse comme mythe et la jeunesse comme réalité." *Esprit* 1 (December 1944): 143–51.

Mourgue, Gérard. *Françoise Sagan.* Paris: Editions Universitaire, 1958.

Nava, Mica. *Changing Cultures: Feminism, Youth, and Consumerism.* London: Sage, 1992.

Neret, Jean-Alexis. *Les Carrières féminines.* Paris: Editions Lamarre, 1953.

Nicolas, Jean. "Génération 1789." *L'Histoire* 123 (June 1989): 28–34.

Nilan, Cat. "'Crimes inexplicables': Murdered Children and the Discourse of Monstrosity in Romantic-Era France." In *Becoming Delinquent: British and European Youth, 1650–1950,* edited by Pamela Cox and Heather Shore. Burlington, VT: Ashgate, 2002.

Noiriel, Gérard. *Workers in French Society in the 19th and 20th Centuries.* Translated by Helen McPhail. New York: Berg, 1990.

Nora, Pierre. "General Introduction: Between Memory and History." In *Realms of Memory: Rethinking the French Past*, vol. 1, *Conflicts and Divisions*, under the direction of Pierre Nora. Translated by Arthur Goldhammer; English-language edition edited and with a foreword by Lawrence D. Kritzman. New York: Columbia University Press, 1996.

———. "Generation." In *Realms of Memory: Rethinking the French Past*, vol. 1, *Conflicts and Divisions*, under the direction of Pierre Nora. Translated by Arthur Goldhammer; English-language edition edited and with a foreword by Lawrence D. Kritzman. New York: Columbia University Press, 1996

Nord, Philip. "The Legacy of *Jeune France*." Paper delivered at the Society for French Historical Studies, Stanford University, March 2005.

Nourissier, François. *Les Chiens à fouetter*. Paris: René Julliard, 1956.

Novick, Peter. *The Resistance versus Vichy: The Purge of Collaborators in Liberated France*. New York: Columbia University Press, 1968.

Offen, Karen. "Body Politics: Women, Work, and the Politics of Motherhood in France, 1920–1950." In *Maternity and Gender Politics*, edited by Seth Koven and Sonya Michel. New York: Routledge, 1993.

———. "Depopulation, Nationalism, and Feminism in Fin-de-siècle France." *American Historical Review* 89 (June 1984): 648–76.

Ory, Pascal. *L'Aventure culturelle française, 1945–1989*. Paris: Flammarion, 1989.

———. *Les Collaborateurs, 1940–1945*. Paris: Seuil, 1976.

———. "Mickey Go Home! La Désaméricanisation de la bande-dessinée (1945–1950)." In *On tue à chaque page!: La Loi de 1949 sur les publications destinées à la jeunesse*, edited by Christophe Chavdia. Paris: Editions du Temps, 1999.

———. *Le Petit Nazi illustré: Une Pédagogie hitlérienne en culture française, "Le Téméraire" (1943–1944)*. Paris: Editions Albatros, 1979.

Osgerby, Bill. *Youth in Britain since 1945*. Oxford: Blackwell Publishers, 1998.

Oustby, Ian. *Occupation: The Ordeal of France, 1940–1944*. New York: St. Martin's Press, 1998.

Ozouf, Mona. "Regeneration." In *A Critical Dictionary of the French Revolution*, edited by François Furet and Mona Ozouf; translated by Arthur Goldhammer. Cambridge, MA: Harvard University Press, 1989.

Parent, Francis, and Raymond Perrot. *Le Salon de la Jeune Peinture: Une Histoire, 1950–1983*. Montreuil: Jeune Peinture, 1983.

Pauvert, Jean-Jacques, ed. *Nightbird: Conversations with Françoise Sagan*. Translated by David Macey. New York: Clarkson N. Potter, 1980.

Paxton, Robert. *Vichy France: Old Guard and New Order, 1940–1944*. New York: Columbia University Press, 1972.

Pedersen, Susan. "Catholicism, Feminism, and the Politics of the Family during the late Third Republic." In *Mothers of a New World*, edited by Seth Koven and Sonya Michel. New York: Routledge, 1993.

Péguy, Charles. *Notre jeunesse*. Paris: Editions Gallimard, 1910.

Pells, Richard. *Not Like Us: How Europeans Have Loved, Hated, and Transformed American Culture since World War II*. New York: Basic Books, 1997.

Perec, Georges. *Things: A Story of the Sixties*. Translated by David Bellos. London: Harvill, 1990.

Perruchot, Henri. *La France et sa jeunesse*. Paris: Hachette, 1958.

Peyrade, Jean. *Jeunes hommes*. Paris: Spes, 1959.

Picard, Raymond. *Nouvelle critique ou nouvelle imposture*. Paris: J-J Pauvert, 1965.

Pidard, Gilles. "Les Illustrées pour la jeunesse de l'après-guerre (1945–1959)." Université de Paris X. UER d'histoire mémoire de maitrise.

Pihan, Jean, and Gabriel Soumille. *La Presse enfantine: Les Surhommes, les gangsters, les bagarres, les comics et petit commerce*. Paris: Lugdini, 1952.

Pivasset, Jean. *Essai sur la signification politique du cinéma: L'Exemple française, de la libération aux événements de mai 1968*. Paris: Editions Cujas, 1971.

Poiger, Uta G. *Jazz, Rock, and Rebels: Cold War Politics and American Culture in a Divided Germany*. Berkeley: University of California Press, 2000.

Pomfret, David M. "'A Muse for the Masses': Gender, Age, and Nation in France, Fin de Siècle." *American Historical Review* 109 (December 2004): 1439–74.

———. "Representations of Adolescence in the Modern City: Voluntary Provision and Work in Nottingham and Saint-Etienne, 1890–1914." *Journal of Family History* 26, no. 4 (October 2001): 455–79.

———. *Young People and the European City: Age Relations in Nottingham and Saint-Etienne, 1890–1940*. Aldershot, UK: Ashgate, 2004.

Popkin, Jeremy D. *A History of Modern France*. Englewood Cliffs, NJ: Prentice Hall, 1994.

Prost, Antoine. "Jeunesse et société dans la France de l'entre-deux-guerres." *Vingtième Siècle* 13 (January–March 1987): 35–43.

Queaneau, Raymond. *Zazie dans le Metro*. Paris: Librarie Gallimard, 1959.

Realms of Memory: Rethinking the French Past. Under the direction of Pierre Nora; translated by Arthur Goldhammer. English-language edition edited and with a foreword by Lawrence D. Kritzman. 3 vols. New York: Columbia University Press, 1996.

Rearick, Charles. *The French in Love and War: Popular Culture in the Era of the World Wars*. New Haven, CT: Yale University Press, 1997.

Reconstructions et modernisation: La France après les ruines, 1918–1945. Exposition of the National Archives at the Hotel Rohan, January–May 1991, organized under the direction of the Archives of France and the Ministry of Culture, Communication, and Public Works. Paris: Archives Nationales, 1991.

Renouard, Yves. "La Notion de génération en histoire." *Revue Historique* 1 (1953): 1–23.

Resnais, Alain. *Hiroshima, mon amour*. 1959. Film. (DVD available from Criterion Collection, no. HIR050)

Rigby, Brian. "The Reconstruction of Culture: *Peuple et Culture* and the Popular

Education Movement." In *The Culture of Reconstruction: European Literature, Thought, and Film, 1945–1950*, edited by Nicholas Hewitt. New York: St. Martin's Press, 1989.

Rioux, Emmanuelle. "Les zazous: Un Phénomène socio-culturel pendant l'Occupation." Thèse, Université de Paris-X Nanterre, 1987.

Rioux, Jean-Pierre. *The Fourth Republic, 1944–1958*. Translated by Godfrey Rogers. Cambridge: Cambridge University Press, 1987.

———, ed. "Politiques et pratiques culturelles dans la France de Vichy." Special issue, *Les Cahiers de L'Institut d'Histoire du Temps Present* 8 (June 1988).

Roberts, Glenys. *Bardot*. New York: St. Martin's Press, 1984.

Roberts, Mary Louise. *Civilization without Sexes: Reconstructing Gender in Postwar France, 1917–1927*. Chicago: University of Chicago Press, 1994.

Roseman, Mark, ed. *Generations in Conflict: Youth Revolt and Generation Formation in Germany, 1770–1968*. New York: Cambridge University Press, 1995.

Ross, Kristin. *Fast Cars, Clean Bodies: Decolonization and the Reordering of French Culture*. Cambridge, MA: MIT Press, 1995.

———. *May '68 and Its Afterlives*. Chicago: University of Chicago Press, 2002.

Rousselet, Jean. *Jeunesse aujourd'hui*. Paris: Flammarion, 1960.

Rozier, Jacques. *Adieu Philippine*. 1960. (VHS available from Ciné Vidéo, France)

Rozier, Willy. *Manina, la fille sans voiles* [The Girl in the Bikini]. 1952. (DVD available from KVP, France)

Rubinstein, Anne. *Bad Language, Naked Ladies, and Other Threats to the Nation: A Political History of Comic Books in Mexico*. Durham, NC: Duke University Press, 1998.

Ruosso, Henry. *The Vichy Syndrome: History and Memory in France since 1944*. Translated by Arthur Goldhammer. Cambridge, MA: Harvard University Press, 1991.

Sabot, Jean-Yves. *Le Syndicalisme étudiant et la guerre d'algérie: L'Entrée d'une génération en politique et la formation d'une élite*. Paris: Editions L'Harmattan, 1995.

Sagan, Françoise. *Bonjour Tristesse*. Translated by Irene Ash. New York: E. P. Dutton, 1955.

Salachas, Gilbert. "Interview d'Alain de Sédouy." *Presse Actualité* 81–82 (March–April 1973): 12–21.

Sartre, Jean-Paul. *Saint Genet: Actor and Martyr*. Translated by Bernard Frechtman. New York: Pantheon Books, 1963.

Sauvy, Alfred. *La Montée des jeunes*. Paris: Calmann-Lévy, 1959.

Sauvy, Alfred, and Michel Debré. *Des français pour la France*. Paris: Gallimard, 1945.

Schafer, Sylvia. *Children in Moral Danger and the Problem of Government in Third Republic France*. Princeton, NJ: Princeton University Press, 1997.

Schalk, David L. *War and the Ivory Tower: Algeria and Vietnam*. New York: Oxford University Press, 1991.

Schivelbusch, Wolfgang. *The Culture of Defeat: On National Trauma, Mourning, and Recovery*. New York: Metropolitan Books, 2003.

Sciences appliqués: Classe de fin d'études, écoles des filles. Paris: Librarie Hatier, 1947.

Scott, Joan Wallach. *Gender and the Politics of History*. New York: Columbia University Press, 1988.

Seidman, Michael. *The Imaginary Revolution: Parisian Students and Workers in 1968*. New York: Berghahn Books, 2004.

Shennan, Andrew. *Rethinking France: Plans for Renewal, 1940–1946*. Oxford: Clarendon Press, 1989.

Sherman, Daniel J. *The Construction of Memory in Interwar France*. Chicago: University of Chicago Press, 1999.

Sirinelli, Jean-François. *Les Baby-boomers: Une génération, 1945–1969*. Paris: Fayard, 2003.

———. *Générations intellectuelle: Khâgneux et normaliens dans l'entre-deux-guerres*. Paris: Fayaud, 1988.

Smith, Bonnie G. *Ladies of the Leisure Class: The Bourgeoises of Northern France in the Nineteenth Century*. Princeton, NJ: Princeton University Press, 1981.

Sohn, Anne-Marie. *Age tendre et tête de bois: Histoire des jeunes des années 1960*. Paris: Hachette Literature, 2001.

———. *Chrysalides: Femmes dans la vie privée, XIXe–XXe siècles*. Paris: Publications de la Sorbonne, 1996.

Søland, Birgitte. *Becoming Modern: Young Women and the Reconstruction of Womanhood in the 1920s*. Princeton, NJ: Princeton University Press, 2000.

Spengler, Joseph J. *France Faces Depopulation: Postlude Edition*. Durham, NC: Duke University Press, 1979.

Spitzer, Alan B. *The French Generation of 1820*. Princeton, NJ: Princeton University Press, 1987.

———. "The Historical Problem of Generations." *American Historical Review* 78 (December 1973): 1353–85.

Springhall, John. *Youth, Popular Culture, and Moral Panics: Penny Gaffs to Gangsta-Rap, 1830–1996*. New York: St. Martin's Press, 1998.

Stewart, Mary Lynn. *For Health and Beauty: Physical Culture for Frenchwomen, 1880s–1930s*. Baltimore: Johns Hopkins University Press, 2001.

Stock, Phyllis H. "Students versus the University in Pre–World War Paris." *French Historical Studies* 7 (Spring 1971): 93–109.

Sweets, John F. *Choices in Vichy France: The French under Nazi Occupation*. New York: Oxford University Press, 1986.

Tatar, Maria. *Lustmord*. Princeton, NJ: Princeton University Press, 1977.

Tilleul, Jean-Louis. *Pour analyser la bande dessinée: Propositions théoriques et pratiques*. Louvain-la-Neuve: Academia, 1987.

Troyansky, David G. "Generational Discourse in the French Revolution." In *The French Revolution in Culture and Society*, edited by David G. Troyansky, Alfred Dismaru, and Norwood Andrew, Jr. New York: Greenwood Press, 1991.

Truffaut, François. *Jules et Jim* [Jules and Jim]. 1962. Film. (DVD available from Criterion Collection, no. JUL080)

———. *Les Quatre cents coup* [The 400 Blows]. 1959. Film. (DVD available from Criterion Collection, no. CC1586D)

Vadim, Roger. *Bardot, Deneuve, Fonda*. Translated by Melinda Chamber Porter. New York: Simon and Schuster, 1986.

———. *Et Dieu créa la femme* [And God Created Woman]. 1956. Film. (DVD available from Criterion Collection, no. AND110)

Vann, Richard T. "The Youth of *Centuries of Childhood*." *History and Theory* 21, no. 2 (1982): 279–97.

Veneigem, Raoul. *The Revolution of Everyday Life*. Translated by Donald Nicholson-Smith. London: Left Hand Books and Rebel Press, 1983.

Vian, Boris. *I Spit On Your Grave* [*J'irai cracher sur vos tombes*]. 1946. Reprint, New York: Audubon, 1971.

———. *Le Manuel de Saint-Germain-des-Prés*. Paris: Editions du Chêne, 1974.

Vidal-Naquet, Pierre. *Torture: Cancer of Democracy, France and Algeria, 1954–1962*. Translated by Barry Richard. Baltimore: Penguin, [1963].

Viénet, René. *Enragés and Situationists in the Occupation Movement, France, May 1968*. New York: Autonomedia, 1992.

Vieujean, Jean. *Jeunesse aux millions de visages*. Paris: Casterman, 1961.

Voldman, Danièle. *La Reconstruction des villes françaises de 1940 à 1954: Histoire d'une politique*. Paris: L'Harmattan, 1997.

Wakeman, Rosemary. *Modernizing the Provincial City: Toulouse, 1945–1975*. Cambridge, MA: Harvard University Press, 1997.

Weber, Eugen. *Peasants into Frenchmen: The Modernization of Rural France, 1870–1914*. Stanford, CA: Stanford University Press, 1976.

Weiner, Susan. *Enfants Terribles: Youth and Feminity in the Mass Media in France, 1945–1968*. Baltimore: Johns Hopkins University Press, 2001.

———. "Youth." In *French Culture and Society: The Essentials*, edited by Michael Kelly. London: Arnold, 2001.

Werth, Alexander. *The Lost Statesman: The Strange Story of Pierre Mendès-France*. New York: Abelard-Schuman, 1958.

White, Edmund. *Genet: A Biography*. New York: Vintage Books, 1993.

Whitfield, Lee C. "The Rise of Student Political Power and the Fall of French Imperialism in North Africa: Montpellier, 1954–1962." *Proceedings of the Annual Meeting of the Western Society for French History* 18 (1991): 515–23.

Whitney, Susan Brewster. "The Politics of Youth: Communists and Catholics in Interwar France." Ph.D. diss., Rutgers University, 1994.

Williams, Alan. *Republic of Images: A History of French Filmmaking*. Cambridge, MA: Harvard University Press, 1992.

Winter, Jay. "Forms of Kinship and Remembrance in the Aftermath of the Great War." In *War and Remembrance in the Twentieth Century*, edited by Jay Winter and Emmanuel Sivan. London: Cambridge University Press, 1999.

———. *Sites of Memory, Sites of Mourning: The Great War in European Cultural History*. London: Cambridge University Press, 1995.

Wohl, Robert. *The Generation of 1914*. Cambridge, MA: Harvard University Press, 1979.

Wright, Bradford W. *Comic Book Nation: The Transformation of Youth Culture in America*. Baltimore: Johns Hopkins University Press, 2001.

The Young Face of France. Paris: Printed by La Documentation Française for Le Centre de Diffusion Française, 1959.

Index

abortion, 190–91, 220
A Bout de souffle (film; Godard), 31, 167
Adieu Philippine (film; Rozier), 221
adults: and juvenile delinquency, 94, 160–67; organizing and imagining youth, 27–28, 230–31, 276–77; youth as contrast to, 9–11, 37–39
Affamée, L' (Leduc), 224
age categories: as analytic tools, 7–10; association with temporal categories, 38–39, 41; organizing principle of youth identity, 276–77, 278, 281
Aide aux Mères (Assistance to Mothers), 72, 73
Aide des Jeunes à la Reconstruction (AJAR), 64–65; and young delinquents, 159
Aimez-vous Brahms? (Sagan), 209
ajisme. See youth hostels
alcoholism: Mendès-France's attack on, 100, 164; youth and, 163–64, 306n97
Algeria, family workers in, 82
Algerian war, 128–32; protests against, 130–32, 134; support for, 134; young people and, 131, 136
Alleg, Henri, 130
Allegret, Marc, 198
Amants, Les (*The Lovers*) (film; Malle), 221
Amis des Maisons des Jeunes, Les, 105
Amitiés particulières, Les (*Special Friend-ships*) (Peyrefitte), 223
And God Created Woman (film; Vadim). See *Et Dieu créa la femme*
Angers Three, The, 142, 172

Arguments (journal), 49, 197
Ariès, Philippe, 13, 49
Armand, Louis, 41, 85
Army Youth (Armées-Jeunesse) Com-mission, 127–28; and protest against Algerian war, 129
Aron, Raymond, 283
artistic life, incorporation of the young into, 101
Arts (magazine): condemnation of Upris-ing Youth, 47; 1957 analysis of French youth, 42; on young celebrities, 35
Ascenseur pour l'échafaud (film; Malle), 172
Asphyxie, L' (Leduc), 224
Assistance to Mothers, 72, 73
Association des Ecrivains et Artistes Révolutionnaires (AEAR), 104
Association des Maisons de la Culture et des Cercles Culturels (AMC), 104
Association of Film Creators, 186
Astérix (comic book), 265
athleticism. *See* sports
Autant-Lara, Claude: *En cas de malheur*, 200–201. See also *Blé en herbe, Le* (film; Autant-Lara)
Avant le déluge (film), 172
Avenir est à vous, L' (television program), 275

Balcon, Le (*The Balcony*) (Genet), 169
Barbarella (comic book), 265–66
Bardot, Brigitte, 35, 196, 197–206, 212; Beauvoir on, 200, 202, 204–5; as mythic icon, 229; publicity poster for *The Girl in the Bikini*, 264

Ripening Seed (film; Autant-Lara). See *Blé en herbe, Le* (film, Autant-Lara)
Rise of the Young, The (Sauvy), 48–49
Robbe-Grillet, Alain, 28
Rohmer, Eric, 30
Rollin, Louis, 144
Rousseau, Jean-Jacques, 27
Rousso, Henry, 39
Rozier, Jacques, 221

Sagan, Françoise, 35, 41, 196, 206–19; Bardot and, 205; *Bonjour tristesse*, 206–9, 225; criticism of, 214; as mythic icon, 229; opposition to the war in Algeria, 133–34; response to Nouvelle Vague survey, 32; as spokesperson for youth, 209
Saint Genet: Comédien et martyr (Sartre), 169
Saint-Germain-des-Prés, 174–75, 176, 214, 215–19
Saint-Laurent, Yves, 35
Saint-Ogan, Alain, 244
Salon des Arts Ménagers, 79
Salon des Jeunes Peintres, 101
Salut les copains! (radio show), 273–74
Samedi-Soir (newspaper), 215, 218
Sangnier, Marc, 117
Sarrailh, Jean, 146
Sarraute, Nathalie, 28
Sartre, Jean-Paul, 20; and corruption of the young, 217; and existentialism, 215; and Genet, 168; and MJC, 108; *Saint Genet: Comédien et martyr*, 169
Sauvegarde (journal), 147
Sauvy, Alfred, 51; on Nouvelle Vague study, 34; and obligatory national service for girls, 72; *The Rise of the Young*, 40–41, 48–49
Schaeffer, Pierre, 104
Scheld, Vincent, 141, 172
school, deficiencies of, 113
Scouts, 28
Second Sex, The (Beauvoir), 192–93
Seduction of the Innocent (Wertham), 243
Seize millions de jeunes (television series), 275
Sermeus, Jacques, 172
Servan-Schreiber, Jean-Jacques, 97
Service Civique de la Jeunesse, 60, 61, 295*n*23, 296*n*41

Service Familial de Jeunes Filles, Le, 73
service organizations, 295*n*23; and Resistance, 61, 295*n*23; of Vichy, 60
sexual education, 194, 219
sexuality: Bardot and female norms of, 202–3; class and codes of conduct, 227–28; comic books and, 242–44, 267; cynicism and, 205, 209, 218, 230; delinquency and, 193–94; studies of the young on, 220. See also homosexuality
Shaaf, Yvan, 142
Shirmann, Richard, 117
Sigaux, Gilbert, 36, 41
Simon, Claude, 28
Situationists, 47, 283
social leveling, popular education and, 102–3
social workers, *travailleuses familiales* recognized as, 82
Soulèvement de la Jeunesse. See Uprising Youth
Soulèvement de la Jeunesse (newspaper), 45, 47
Spirit of the Time, The (Morin), 49
sports: promotion of, 121; youth hostels and, 120
Stars, The (Morin), 49
state intervention in family affairs: children at risk and, 160; during Third Republic, 162–63
Strange Defeat (Bloch), 21–22
strikes of 1947, 54; and collapse of Tripartism, 66; and government interest in family worker program, 77
strikes of 1968, 283
student radicalism, 132–33
studies of the young, 272; Agathon survey of 1912, 26; Blanzat's report on youth's moral state and civic spirit, 93–94; government report on problems of youth, 94–95; sexuality in, 220; 1960 survey of veterans, 131; survey on effect of World War II on young people, 147–48. See also Kanters, Robert; Nouvelle Vague study (*L'Express*)
suffrage, 136, 191
Suhard, Cardinal, 58
summer vacation camps, 120–21
surveys. See studies of the young
"Syndicat des enfants terribles, Le" (Perret), 47

Lightning Source UK Ltd.
Milton Keynes UK
UKHW010716140521
383642UK00013B/451